EMERGING PERSPECTIVES ON AMINATA SOW FALL

EMERGING PERSPECTIVES ON AMINATA SOW FALL
THE REAL AND THE IMAGINARY IN HER NOVELS

EDITED BY
DR. ADA UZOAMAKA AZODO

Africa World Press, Inc.

P.O. Box 1892
Trenton, NJ 08607

P.O. Box 48
Asmara, ERITREA

Africa World Press, Inc.

P.O. Box 1892
Trenton, NJ 08607

P.O. Box 48
Asmara, ERITREA

Book design: Aliya Books
Cover design: Ashraful Haque
Book cover photo: Ada Uzoamaka Azodo

Library of Congress Cataloging-in-Publication Data

Emerging perspectives on Aminata Sow Fall : the real and the imaginary in her novels / edited by Ada Uzoamaka Azodo.
    p. cm.
Includes bibliographical references and index.
ISBN 1-59221-556-4 (cloth) -- ISBN 1-59221-557-2 (pbk.)
1. Fall, Aminata Sow--Criticism and interpretation. I. Azodo, Ada Uzoamaka, 1947-

PQ3989.2.F177Z64 2007
843'.914--dc22
                   2007021931

CONTENTS

❄ ❄ ❄

❊❊❊

❊❊❊

❊❊❊

ACKNOWLEDGMENTS

❄ ❄ ❄

My sincere gratitude goes to Anne Koehler, reference librarian at Indiana University Northwest, for always tirelessly responding to my call for yet another book or academic journal article through Interlibrary Loan.

I also make special mention of Africa World Press in-house editor, Angela Ajayi, who has worked with me through three books now, ensuring that we produce a camera-ready copy of which we could be proud.

DEDICATION

For
Michael Valentine
and our progeny
Uchendu, Queen-Ije, Chijioke, and Okechukwu

PREFACE

❄ ❄ ❄

This volume of essays on the emerging perspectives on Aminata Sow Fall seeks to anthologize present knowledge about the writer and her creative works and the critical reception of these works. Readers will find in the general Introduction the substance of her original essays and the many interviews she has accorded to scholars all over the world. There is an overview of the writer's background, ideas, literary and critical works, the contributors' essays, and the author's cultural and intellectual affiliations with three not-for-profit and non-governmental institutions: C.I.R.L.A.C. (*Centre International d'Études, de Recherches et de Réactivation sur la Littérature, les Arts et la Culture*), a veritable centre for excellence at Saint-Louis, the old capital of Senegal; C.A.E.C. (*Centre Africain d'Échanges et d'Animations Culturels*), a centre for cultural promotion with a publishing house of its own, Khoudia Press, and B.A.D.L.E. (*Bureau Africain pour la Défense des Libertés de l'Écrivain*), in Dakar, the present capital of Senegal, for the promotion of writers' rights. Yearly, these three organizations attract artists and scholars of all kinds to Senegal. Furthermore, in Book One readers will find six originals essays on the author's social vision, in Book Two an exploration of the imaginary of the author's texts and, in Book Three an English version of a major interview with Aminata Sow Fall executed and translated from the French original by Ada Uzoamaka Azodo specifically for publication in this volume. Three contributors' essays written in French bear a preceding "Editor's Synopsis" in English. The contributors in the order they present are Lucy M. Schwartz,

Kahiudi Claver Mabana, Jeanne-Sarah de Larquier, Mame Selbee Diouf Ndiaye, Marco D. Roman, Léa Kalaora, and Ada Uzoamaka Azodo. I feel confident that this anthology will help the understanding of Aminata Sow Fall as a human being, illuminate her writings and standing in world literatures, and particularly make a significant contribution to the study of African francophone literature world wide.

Ada Uzoamaka Azodo, *Editor*
Indiana University Northwest

INTRODUCTION:
AMINATA SOW FALL, NOVELIST

BACKGROUND, IDEAS, LITERARY WORKS, AND CRITICAL RECEPTION

ADA UZOAMAKA AZODO

❄ ❄ ❄

AMINATA SOW FALL, NOVELIST

This introduction brings all the salient aspects of the author and her works together here in one volume, so scholars after us can spend valuable time exploring the depth of imagination of this illustrious daughter of Africa. Second, this publication has an added objective of working to achieve better notoriety for the author in the English speaking world, so that there would be a larger demand for her books for classroom us there, and a motivation for publishers to translate more of her works in English. It cannot be but for economic considerations that only one of her books, the second novel, *La grève des Bàttu*, is in English translation today. The rest, seven in number, are still waiting to be made accessible to English speakers. Yet these are novels that have mostly been translated in languages that have not as many users as the English language in the world — Russian, Finish, Swedish, Sanskrit, German, Danish, Chinese, Spanish, Swahili, etc. It is just inconceivable that such an important African writer should remain so relatively unknown to the English speaking world for so long.

AMINATA SOW FALL'S BACKGROUND

Aminata Sow Fall was born on April 27, 1941 in Saint-Louis, an island and peninsula in the northern, Sahel region of Senegal, situated between the long and the short arms of the River Senegal. In 2005, over three days, Friday, April 8 through Sunday, April 10, four Senegalese institutions—Société Goethe du Sénégal, the Mayor's Office, the Centre Socioculturel de la Commune d'Arrondissement Pattie d'Oie, and the Fondation Konrad Adenauer— organized a colloquium in Stèle Mermoz, the seat of the Fondation Konrad Adenauer in Dakar, to celebrate Sow Fall's sixty-fourth birthday and also the 25th anniversary of her winning the Prix Littéraire d'Afrique Noire for *La grève des Bàttu* in 1980, which novel had earlier in 1979 been short-listed for the Prix Goncourt, the highest honor that an author could win in France for any literary work.

Saint-Louis, founded in 1659, was the old capital of Senegal until Dakar took over. It is often compared to New Orleans in the United States of America, due to its rich history, and the fact that it has typically French narrow streets, beautiful patios, and balconies made of wood. Even today, renovation efforts attempt to keep these attributes that help to make Saint-Louis a unique corner of the world. Saint-Louis was not a major slave port and depot like the Gorée Island near Dakar mainland. On the contrary, it was a prosperous and the main trading port of Senegal in the 18th and 19th centuries, and the town grew rich as a result. But then followed a neglect, which shows in the enormous number of dilapidated buildings, which sometimes fall over and disposing the inhabitants to great danger of being crushed to death. A tour guide explained to me that the owners had returned to France and, apparently, forgot their real estate property in Senegal. Perhaps, their progeny never knew about the existence of these pieces of property. For the indigenes, efforts at rehabilitation are difficult and sparse, for money is scarce.

Today, Saint-Louis has a reputation of being a cross-road of cultures and ideas, due to the influences of the French and the Arabs, which were soon assimilated and modified, producing a blend of cultures, well-being, and know-how unrivalled anywhere in the world.

The culture, cuisine, and fashions of Saint-Louis are all her own. The whole city of Saint-Louis can be toured in less than two hours *en calèche*, for horse drawn carriages are a tradition there, or for a longer time on foot. A magnificent bridge connects the two sides of the town over the Senegal River.

Aminata Sow Fall grew up in a relatively well-off family, for her father was a treasurer. Her mother was thus privileged to be a house-wife with live-in servants and others that came from time to time from the village to work at their house. Her mother was able to devote her attention to the upbringing of her children. And she had a taste for fine clothing too, and she often looked so properly dressed, like a true *diriyanké*, a sort of upper class woman of mixed breed, African and European. Neighbors always thought she was on the verge of leaving the house to go to somewhere. For Aminata Sow Fall, theirs was a conservative, stable, united, and harmonious family, which allowed her to achieve self-fulfillment. There were books everywhere to read, books her father bought, and other books that her older siblings brought home at the end of the school year as prizes won for studies well done. There were also all the visitors from the village, for the parents were very hospitable and generous. Other young people, friends of the older siblings also came. So, Aminata Sow Fall learned early from people she met everyday. She marveled at the fantastic and marvelous stories the people from the village told about life over there. In her father's house, Aminata Sow Fall woke up everyday to the sight of the splendor of the River Senegal from her window, and beyond that to the magnificence of the still greater expanse of water, the Atlantic Ocean. She used to stand there and gaze at the spectacle and dream, allowing her imagination to wander in spite of herself. That was somewhat the time period the creative artist was in the making without knowing it!

On the island of Saint-Louis, Sow Fall attended the Koranic school for her religious education, and the French school for her secular education. At home, she benefited from informal education, which inculcated dignity in the human being, no matter her or his station in life. For example, she picked up the moral lesson that girls were human beings, no more no less. Just because you are a girl does not mean that you are inferior. Girls can strive as much as boys and can go as far as they are able to with their education. She was also schooled in tolerance for the other, who must not be humiliated, no matter her or his class in the society. She also learned that education was meant to give you a means of livelihood, responsibility, and work for your self-esteem and independence.

After primary school, Sow Fall went further for two years to high school Lycée Faidherde. Then she left for Dakar to continue at the Lycée Van Vollenhoven, now Lycée Lamine Guèye, renamed after the Senegalese Deputy, Mayor of Dakar, and first president of the Association Nationale Sénégalaise, because her older sister, Arame, had just gotten married and had to relocate to Dakar to attend the Université de Dakar, now renamed Université Cheikh Anta Diop. According to Sow Fall, their mother had suggested that she go to keep her sister company. In Dakar, then, Sow Fall completed her secondary school education and sat for the two parts of her baccalaureate, the high school leaving certificate examination. Later, she left for France to train as an interpreter. While in Paris, she also took classes in teaching with a concentration in French language and literature at the Sorbonne. Then in 1963, love came her way, when she met Mr. Samba Sow, a fellow Senegalese, recently graduated in economics, and a popular athlete playing with a basketball team that toured several regions of France. They got married on May 30, 1963. Suddenly, finding her hands too full, Sow Fall dropped the program for her training as interpreter, in order to concentrate only on the academic studies at the Sorbonne.

On her return to Senegal, after a seven-year sojourn in France, Sow Fall became a high school teacher, also teaching sometimes in institutes, such as l'Institut Cesti for the training of journalists in Dakar. Later, she was appointed to the Commission Nationale de Réforme de L'Enseignement du Français, a body charged with adapting the program content of the teaching of French to African realities. While at the institute, Sow Fall and the group was able to produce several textbooks for grammar and literature for the senior classes in those subjects. Still later, when she became director of Centre d'Études des Civilisations, she worked towards the valorization of the Senegalese patrimony. It was also at this time that she began a book length work that would lunch her later as a writer of fiction.

AMINATA SOW FALL'S IDEAS

WRITING

Aminata Sow Fall grew up loving to read and write, but never really dreamed of becoming a writer as such. Then, at the Sorbonne, some days she would scribble some plays, poems, or short stories in the library, which were never really finished. However, on her return to Senegal, she found a world on a fast pace, changed, and dehumanized, thanks to the reign of money, which meant more to the generality of citizens than their own neighbor's welfare. And the writer in Aminata Sow Fall was born; she wanted to talk about what she observed around her as a fellow, but sensitive, citizen. The neglect of human dignity and the love of wealth and money struck her as incompatible with being properly human. The Senegalese society provided ample and ready material for her outcry against this trampling on human dignity. The rest is fiction, imagination, and the writer's intention is to draw attention to the ills of society, in order to galvanize the people themselves to do something about it. Aminata Sow Fall thought that with the era of protests and Negritude under colonialism over, it was time to look inward and talk about African reality and soul.

Thus, the objective of her writing is not, as some critics have thought, to show that what a man can do a woman can do as well. On the other hand, she merely wants to exercise her freedom as a human being, not as a woman, but as a concerned citizen, to put her thoughts down on paper. It is not a competition with men, for there is no indication for that. Sow Fall declares herself contented to be a woman, a citizen of her society. Nonetheless, she is not in favor of men doing their studies with assiduity while women do theirs with levity, contented to patiently wait for a rich and generous man to come, marry them off, and carry them away into dream land. Many women, she notes, are able to write, but just do not do it, because they are not so motivated.

She nonetheless avows that family comes first for her, adding that if she has to choose between her teaching career, writing, and her family, she would drop the first two and take her husband and six children. Fortunately, the case has never arisen, for her husband is very supportive of her writing endeavor. Indeed, it was Samba Sow who showed the manuscript of her first novel, *Le Revenant,* to a neighbor who was a professor at the Université de Dakar then, and this neighbor, having found it suitable for publication, suggested that she submit it to the then Nouvelles Éditions Africaines in Dakar. Samba Sow still constantly gives her the benefit of positive criticism and encouragement. Sow Fall says she fits in writing time wherever possible in the family routine; it could be very early in the morning, before dawn, for a couple of hours, or when she is away on a writing vacation, or simply during the day, when she appears to have some free time.

Aminata Sow Fall finds that the novel genre is the most appropriate for narrating the history of the people in post independent Africa, for it fits in with her desire to talk about the social ills, and affords her the opportunity to use her imagination. That way, through fiction, the author is better able to reach her audience and push it to react to her writing. She is nonetheless against any kind of writing that appears to present Africans in reference to other cultures. The best way to earn universal respect for Africa and its peoples, she says, is to present African epistemologies as they are, and then leave other cultures to make an effort to understand them and communicate with their owners their agreement or disagreement with what they have read and learned about them. This strategy could be at the expense of writing for an African audience on a first level, whereas on a second level it could still confer on the work a universal appeal. She avows that most people in the world yearn for similar things; it is only the local color that is different from culture to culture.

For Sow Fall, all writing is subversive, because they pose questions that need answers. So, it is not possible that she could be a moralist as some critics think, for her role is to raise questions and the readers are to act on the questions raised. For this reason, Sow Fall concedes that characterization is very important for her and the reader needs to investigate characters for authorial messages. However, under the writer's pen, a character once created takes on a life of her or his own as the story unfurls, and is in no manner any more under the control of the writer. Fictional characters are like children, you raise them, she adds, but some day, like healthy birds they must fly away, out of your control. You lose all responsibility for their actions. All you can do is hope that a tiny thread of your teachings remain to link the parent to the child. It is so with creative writing, says Aminata Sow Fall. On the other hand, readers or critics come to the round table, thanks to the writing of an author, each with her or his understanding of the text, for a true *"banquet où tout le monde apporte"* (Aas-Rouxparis, 210). It is amazing to Sow Fall how people from different backgrounds appear to understand one another through books. Cross-cultural understanding is further enhanced by adaptation of books to theatre and film, for even illiterate people can follow what has been said.

As a writing style, Sow Fall still prefers to put things down in ink on paper, before going to word processing on the computer. Sow Fall has made a success of her creative writing, for she is now known world wide. She numbers among the first hundred persons in Senegal impacting society in a very important way. And, this critical anthology entirely devoted to her life and works is a further testimony of her world renown.

AMINATA SOW FALL AND CONTEMPORARY WRITERS

Whereas male Senegalese writers began writing in the 1930s, the women did not begin until the late 1970s. Aminata Sow Fall views the considerable gulf between men's and women's achievements in literary creation as not due to nature or Islam, but rather to the fact that men were first educated in the Western way before women. Women who had some education did not have enough of it to motivate them to write seriously. Second, it also has to do with African traditional perception of a woman who is expected to be effaced, and to stay in the domestic and private space of the home, leaving the public arena for the men. Thereafter, men have written more than women.

However, since the United Nations 1975 declaration of the first decade for women's development in Africa, women have started writing autobiographical and socio-realist works. Aminata Sow Fall's first novel, *Le Revenant* (1976), was the first by a woman in the Senegalese post independent era. Her second novel, *La grève des Bàttu* (1979), was already published for three weeks, while Mariama Bâ's first, *Une si longue lettre*, was still with the publishers in Dakar.

Along with Sembène Ousmane and Bâ, Sow Fall does not shy away from social realism, preferring not to talk about abstractions as does Seyni Mbengue of *Royaume de sable*, and Amadou Ndiaye of the historical novel *Assoka ou les derniers jours de Koumbi*. Cameroonian journalist Muokolo interviewed Sow Fall in the Cameroon and found that so many male Senegalese writers prefer the subject themes that are not present in their society, and it took the arrival of the women on the literary scene for social realist novels to be born in Senegal (54). Aminata Sow Fall believes this is all due to evolutionary changes in the Senegalese novel, which under colonization took the form of protest literature, combating, protesting, and contesting the whole idea of the subjugation of Africans on their own soil, and the denigration of

African traditions and customs by foreign powers. Early writers thus attempted to recover a usable past. After the 1960s and the era of independence, however, the structure of the novel modified to reflect the new issues that the people were facing.

Today, the Senegalese novel focuses on social criticism and psychological exploration of fellow citizens, men and women, with minimal reference to the whites, former French colonialists. For Sow Fall, it is a conscious choice that she has made, as a woman writer and as a concerned citizen who happens to be a woman. It is an individual choice to partake in the responsibility of the integral development of the African, man and woman. Moreover, if Senegalese women writers appear all to be dealing with nearly the same issues about society, such as polygamy, it is because all artists are sensitive people exposed to the same issues in society, which they apprehend in their various ways of perceiving phenomena, depending on their nature and personality. Sow Fall has noted a close similarity between her novel, *La grève des Bàttu* and Mariama Bâ's first novel *Une si longue lettre*. Both treat characters that portray family ceremonies in similar ways, where the eldest daughter urges her mother not to accept and to revolt against their father taking a second wife. However, whereas Bâ makes the central theme of her novel polygyny, for Aminata Sow Fall the general disregard of the value of human beings and human dignity seems to be in focus.

Sow Fall nonetheless thinks that polygyny is an optional marriage arrangement, but still refrains from making any kind of statement for or against it at the national or international level, for that would serve no useful purpose. It is an institution that will pass and disappear with time, given that it was once valid to grow the numbers for agricultural work. Now, more and more women do not want to share their husbands, although this is certainly said with the tongue in the cheek, for some modern women prefer the freedom that a polygamous marriage affords them, and shun monogamy. What is more, since 1971, when the Family Code was enacted in Senegal, which requires a new couple to indicate before nuptials their option for polygamy or monogamy, there are more polygamous households than monogamous ones (Aas-Rouxparis, 209). Aminata Sow Fall believes that women should have a choice in the matter and should be able to reject polygyny if they do not like it. Hence she makes the thrust of her literary work the situation of women in the society generally, their education and economic independence, so that they can make decisions about their lives with their human dignity on their backs. Women should be respected in society, so that they can assume their destiny with self-agency, rather than submit to the humiliating lot and space that society has reserved for them.

Meanwhile, the subject themes of Senegalese literature continue to evolve with younger writers. New themes include violence and death among the youth, conveyed poignantly in short fiction genre. Sow Fall cites journalist Aminata Sophie Dièye's "Destiny System" in the collection *Saison d'amour et de colère*, edited by journalist and writer Boubacar Boris Diop and Hélène Bezençon as worthy of merit, not to mention Aminata Ndiaye's poems in the same collection (Aas-Rouxparis, 212).

Finally, although there are certainly advantages in writing for the cinema and/or turning already written novels into film, yet Sow Fall shies away from all of the above, leaving them to filmmakers, whose calling it is to do such things. It is worthy of mention that Cheikh Oumar Cissoko has made a film version of *La grève des Bàttu* with the title *Bàttu*, and Mossa Sène Absa has also made a film of the same novel entitled *Tableau ferraille*. Sow Fall disagrees with Sène that the heroine Asta Diop in *Douceurs du bercail* and the heroine Gagnesiri of *Tableau ferraille* are the same kind of women. She nonetheless respects the filmmaker's license, vision or perspective of a work of art (Aas-Rouxparis, 211).

Sow Fall hopes that people in politics and creative writers would work hand in hand for the edification of society. Politicians should not harass artists in their mission of indicating the ills of society that need to be redressed, nor should writers become motivated by corruption to talk about things that are nonexistent. Otherwise, leaders should pay attention to writers and do their best to redress wrongs for the people's benefit. If this is done, there would cease to be the phenomenon of literatures of exile in the diaspora, which seems to be growing in number, rather than diminishing. Nobody would gain from the death of African literature, and people in leadership should desist from proscribing certain authors and their texts and/or forbidding their publication at all.

ORAL TRADITION AND WRITING

Some critics see a parallel between Aminata Sow Fall, a modern woman and an African writer, and her traditional counterparts whose art and performance were oral. Both Sow Fall and the oral artist are engaged in story telling, stories that convey moral ideas for education and retransmission of culture to the people. Therefore, tales, be they novels or oral histories, have the function of entertainment and education of society. Even filmmakers are also engaged in the education of the people and their re-acculturation. It is in this way that artists tackle the problems of illiteracy, which is still a wide-spread phenomenon in Africa. Some 70% of the people still cannot read or write, and this is at the root of abject poverty, and the slow economy of publishing, for publishers do not have enough of the readers' market to support their business. That means that writers are not encouraged to produce, and even those who could write, but have not yet started, are not motivated to begin.

Indeed, for Aminata Sow Fall, there is no opposition between orality and literacy, only a complimentary association. Orality can help literacy to reach those readers who are not able to read, just because they have not learned to read. Republishing works in oral forms can help to reduce difference. For example, there will be no real rupture between a Francophone writer and her non Francophone reading public, since a potential reader can have someone else tell him or her what is in the book in a language they can perhaps not read, but can understand.

The multimedia, perhaps most importantly television, is a factor that helps writing. When a writer appears on television, people easily recognize that artist, whether they can read her or his books or not. They begin to ask questions, even possibly asking friends, neighbors or relatives to tell them in simple words of their common language what the writer has said in the books.

BOOK PUBLISHING

The future of book publishing, for reasons that are not difficult to see, also preoccupies Aminata Sow Fall. It is a bleak future, for competition on the world scene is killing African publishing houses, and the writers are the first to feel the pinch. State governments, avows Sow Fall, should accord subventions to publishers, in order to help them survive. On the other hand, governments should also demand that publishers perform. Publishers need a lot of imagination and commercial astuteness and aggressiveness to break down the barriers that must be crossed before books can sell. There is a lot of potential in Africa in spite of problems, which are not, however, impossible to surmount (Kiba 1993).

The recent balkanization of the multinational Nouvelles Éditions Africaines (NEA) in Dakar, Lomé, and Ivory Coast, into privately funded and separate institutions, spells the enormity of the problem affecting publishers and publishing houses, and by extension, African writers. Hachette reportedly bought over the Ivory Coast branch, with a possibility of merger with Nathan publishers. Even the one in Dakar, now renamed, Nouvelles Éditions Africaines du Sénégal has changed management (Aas-Rouxparis, 212). All these changes go to show that financial and management problems plague African publishing houses and publishers.

At the presidency of the Association of Senegalese writers, Aminata Sow Fall had endeavored, with the cooperation of her colleagues, to speak up about the value of books as daily companions for education, leisure, culture, and knowledge. They founded a Journée du Livre to bring books to the attention of Senegalese citizens (ICA).

WRITTEN AFRICAN LITERATURE AND VERNACULAR LANGUAGES

Aminata Sow Fall has disclosed to at least one of her interviewers that she would write in Wolof, if the material conditions for such a venture would present themselves. For now, she continues to write in French, which she had spent a great part of her school days at all levels studying.

She concedes that the use of African proverbs and other witticisms inside the French text help to Africanize the language. Such a resultant text is no longer in the French of Europe, but French confectioned in Africa to respond to the needs of the society and its people. The use of the proverbs in the text, she explains, serves to inject the Wolof world in a text of French expression, Wolof spoken by some 90% of Senegalese people. Wolof words in French texts, therefore, are not there as exotic objects, to bastardize the French language. Rather, they hold something that is just not there or possible to express fully in French. There are just such aspects of culture that cannot be recaptured as translation progresses from the original language to the translated version, essentially because many aspects of the history, anthology, and culture that words carry along with them are lost in translation. It mirrors a rare opportunity for an African country to have a homogeneous language. An African writer feels nonetheless frustrated at not being able to fully transmit her sensibilities in the foreign language as succinctly as possible. It is at such occasions that the writer interjects vernacular words, and leaves them there, not to adulterate the language of expression, but rather to throw her voice into the discourse (Lebou).

The ideal, says Sow Fall, is to write in the language of the people, in order to reach them the best. But, with the absence of a real literary public in Wolof, it is difficult yet to write entirely in an African language without losing the majority of your audience. What is more, are African publishers really ready to publish in vernacular languages?

For the moment, all that writers can do, adds Sow Fall, is use the language of expression that history has given them; it is not their fault. All the same, the writer should Africanize as often as possible for the sake of the 30% who can read the published books.

Moreover, it is important to note that literate or not, there is always communication between the literate and the illiterate. Those who can read help out those who cannot, by either reading to them or telling them what is in the books.

THE POLITICAL FUNCTIONS OF WRITTEN AFRICAN LITERATURE

Aminata Sow Fall's artistic strategy is not to teach society what it must do about the social ills it faces, but to point out the problems she sees, and then allow the people to do something about them and about themselves. For that reason, she cherishes her freedom from any kind of ideology. In order to reflect on issues, interpret them, and express herself without inhibition, she shuns ideological leanings or party adherence and loyalty, which could prove limiting and confining. She does not see herself as a Marxist, although some critics have tended to read Marxism in her second work, *La grève des Bàttu*. African writers must write in such a way that other cultures of the world can understand Africa through their writings, just as Africans understand Europeans and other peoples through their writings.

The African writer must first write with Africa in mind and for Africans. She must explore issues and trends in Africa that trouble the social and political landscapes—power, money, and gender, abuse of the disadvantaged, by the elite and other advantaged persons, like the rich.

POLITICS AND POWER

Aminata Sow Fall cannot conceive a situation reserved exclusively for men, which women cannot enter. For that reason, she is unabashed in her castigation of new African leaders in the post independence era. She disapproves of so-called Fathers of the nation, their ministers and other personnel, due to their self-serving bent, often at the expense of the people who put them in power. She believes that women reserve the right to engage in politics, go into management of public affairs, and observe the goings-on in their society. It is from this belief that Sow Fall in her novels has never really dwelt on the possibility of a barrier between men and women. On the contrary, human dignity is her primary focus anywhere it seems to be trampled upon, well beyond politics at the national and international levels. It is the cynicism of the masses, she holds, which helps to make dictators in Africa and elsewhere in the world, allowing a small pocket of privileged people in high places to manipulate the rest of the populace.

Aminata Sow Fall makes a political statement about certain African governments throwing out citizens of other African nations. Zaire, and before that Ghana, which threw out Nigerians during that nation's civil war, 1966-1970, are cases in point. Nigeria staged a reprisal after the war. A lot of human distress, suffering, and bad blood are engendered by such happenings, states Sow Fall, adding that all sons and daughters of Africa should be free to go wherever they like on African soil without hindrance. African leaders expulsing other Africans from their political space only go to reconfirm to other nations in the West that Africans should be treated inhumanely; it reconfirms the negative and disrespectful image Europeans have of Africans. It empowers others to be racist towards Africans, allowing European leaders to be deplorable in their dealings with Africans on the questions of immigration and emigration. Sow Fall sees the novel genre as an appropriate mode for her dreams, her wonder, and her imagination, and forum for venting her anger (Kiba 1993). Is it possible to engage in politics without getting dirty? Is politics synonymous with Manichaeism? For Sow Fall, it is inconceivable that some women would support their husbands' bid for dirty power for their own selfish ends (ICA 24).

FEMINISM

Aminata Sow Fall categorically declares that she is not a feminist, if that means following a certain kind of ideology that stipulates what womanhood is all about or should be. She nonetheless works for the causes of women who are often oppressed in African societies and the rest of the world. She affirms her femininity, and works for the promotion of human dignity for women and men. She sees herself first and foremost as a human being, a citizen of her country, just like any other Senegalese.

She lauds true friendship between women, and often mentions her own particular and long term friendship with her bosom friend, Madame Marième Diouri, whom she could always be caught telling her most intimate secrets. It is to Madame Diouri that she dedicated her book *L'EX-pere de la nation*. True friendship, she demonstrates, can even go across borders nationally and internationally, between the North and the South, as demonstrated with the pair Anne-Asta in *Douceurs du bercail*. True friendship, she adds, can exist in the world of human beings, and expansively, touching everyone in the whole community of the friends.

Indeed, women do have many problems in society, not the least of which is polygyny. It debases womanhood, setting women in competition with one another, while the men stand aside and watch the war of words and physical fights. Certain feminist or female associations, like the Mouvement de la Libération Féminine (MLF) and others, have attempted in their own ways to resolve the myriad problems that Senegalese women face. But, Sow Fall believes that there should be an indigenous feminism that is not modeled after the European examples, essentially because of the cultural differences between the two world blocks. The European radical and militant feminism struggles in an adversarial opposition against men, but this does not work in Africa. Sow Fall is not surprised, because one cannot legislate against cultural practices easily. Polygyny, for example, is endemic in the culture and any law against it would not work. So, why even try? The only thing a sensitive artist can do is lobby for respect and dignity for women, who must get education to fortify them, open their eyes, and with awareness and confidence negotiate for their preferences.

Right now, many African women still appear blind to who they are individually. They doubt their strengths as women and as human beings. They lack the ability to redirect their thinking faculty to new ways of seeing themselves and life in general. It is with re-education that the African woman will be able to demand her human rights, and her proper place in society as a citizen. Then she will be able to take charge of her life without having to submit to anyone for a piece of mussel in her mouth, and a bottle of drink for her throat (Hammond, 94). Aminata Sow Fall urges women to complain, when, and if, their wishes as citizens of their country and community are not met. Women should feel fulfilled and satisfied about who they are as women (Kiba 1979). One could go as far as to say that God did not make a mistake when they were created as women.

HUMANISM

Aminata Sow Fall is concerned about the human dignity of all, men and women, more than feminism. On the occasion of the Jubilee Celebration of the UNESCO Universal Declaration of Human Rights, Aminata Sow Fall did not hesitate to draw attention to the inherent inalienable rights of all members of the human family, not to mention their rights to equal treatment, which are the basis for justice, freedom, and peace in the world. It is by honoring women's rights that the conditions of life for men and women all over the world can be improved. Any contravention of the universal principles of human rights, asserts Sow Fall, shows how farther away human beings are from realizing their set goals and objectives, and marks the insults and prejudices that are the lot of certain sections of the world: «*Certaines blessures perdurent et parfois s'aggravent, comme autant d'insultes à la conscience humaine. Les notions d'égalité, de fraternité et le sens du partage, n'ont pas profité tout le monde*» (Réunion de Paris, «Les droits de l'homme à l'aube du XXIe Siècle.» *Maison de l'UNESCO*, 7 et 8 décembre, 1998). Because we are a human family, as the UNESCO declaration asserts, in the foregoing statement Sow Fall throws in her voice for the physical, moral, material, and spiritual integrity of all members of the human race and their obligation to see to the eradication of poverty, and the provision of decent living space, and healthcare for all. Sow Fall also decries the present ill-effects of globalization, in spite of its advantages in the fields of knowledge and information. Globalization privileges the Haves in its economic system, and the Have-nots are left with pittance and lack of wellbeing. Both in the North and in the South, globalization causes unemployment, and allows only the barest mini-

15

mum for subsistence. Hence education for the masses is the key for combating the negative effects of globalization, which has apparently come to stay, unfortunately. Women can only gain from sound education, which alone will ensure their economic and financial independence and freedom to take charge of their persons, welfare, and wellbeing. Culture, adds Sow Fall, allows human beings to go beyond merely consuming and acquiring wealth to dreaming of human nobility. As a writer, Sow Fall says that she strives with every book she writes to conquer her right to dream, despite the uphill task of finding publishers, who would only insist on the profitability of the author before accepting her writing; most often they embrace only the works of those writers that are likely to make money for them.

It is for these reasons that Aminata Sow Fall makes effort to embrace a part of the human family wealth in her country, Senegal, to plead the cause of the less privileged as part of the fold, with their own inherent nobility that has nothing to do with their station in life on the social ladder. In her writing, Sow Fall attempts to give back to the underprivileged people their human dignity, integrity, and inalienable right to be respected, without regard to their age, sex, gender, origin, race, or religion. The disadvantaged poor are also all over the world where human beings are suffering degradation, oppression, discrimination, and subjugation, not only in Senegal. Sow Fall rejoices at the universal attempts, albeit infrequent and half-hearted, at solidarity to fight abuses of all sorts, due to misuse of power.

In the year 2000, the *Newsmagazine* recognized Sow Fall for her activities in the cultural production domain, for giving nobility and grace to the human race. Sow Fall is convinced that literature, art, and culture, generally speaking, are very important in the formation of individuals and societies. Her achievements in C.A.E.C. (Centre d'Animation et d'Échanges Culturels) in Dakar, since 1989, holds annually a *Café Littéraire* to this end.

THE AMINATA SOW FALL CULTURAL AND INTELLECTUAL CENTERS

Aminata Sow Fall has founded three cultural centers with the purpose of promoting culture for the nobility of the human race. C.A.E.C. (Centre Africain d'Échanges et d'Animations Culturels), founded in 1989, is housed in the HLM Fass Paillotte in Dakar, Senegal. It comprises a publishing company, Khoudia Press, and a book store.

Its mission is to regroup authors of Wolof, Pulaar, and other ethnic origins from Senegal for literary activities. Every year, *Le Café Littéraire* brings together all those interested in transforming their dreams into reality, through working for the ennobling of the human race beyond the satisfaction of the basic instincts and needs of food, shelter, and clothing for survival. Furthermore, C.A.E.C. works towards the promotion of reading and publishing in Senegal, in particular, and in general, Africa and the world.

C.I.R.L.AC. (Centre International d'Études, de Recherche et de Réactivation sur la Littérature, les Arts et la Culture), also founded in 1989 extends the aims and objectives of C.A.E.C. It is an idealistic institution, which holds that social development goes hand in hand with cultural development in human affairs. C.I.R.L.A.C. has an Institut d'Études et de Découvertes, which meets for six weeks, in May/June, yearly, in Saint-Louis, for the study of aspects of the region, and for exchanges, relaxation, and conviviality. Scholars and students attend from all over the world. When completed — for a functional centre already exists where all the activities presently take place — C.I.R.L.A.C. would have a grand lecture hall, a theatre, a guest house, and a library.

B.A.D.L.E. (Bureau Africain pour la Défense des Libertés de l'Écrivain) is an integral part of C.A.E.C. in promoting culture and nobility of spirit among attendees, particularly writers, who should go away and help in the task of changing the world by working for cooperation between government leaders and writers in the edification of the human being and society.

It is, indeed, an arduous task that Aminata Sow Fall has set herself. But, she is elated to know that she has religion behind her, hence she speaks with a lot of spirituality and philosophy. She is a staunch and practicing Moslem, who, going by her pronouncements and writings would like to spread her vision, namely, that human beings working hard together can uplift mankind. She does not hesitate to add that in that vision Islam is no different from Buddhism, Christianity, Zen, African religions, and any other world religions. Their sole concern appears to be to honor the human being that God created in his own image.

RELIGION, SPIRITUALITY, AND PHILOSOPHY

Il n'y a aucun mal à jouer à son aise du jardin légitimement acquis.

[There is nothing wrong in playing with ease in a garden legitimately acquired].

The above is a verse from the Qur'an, which Sow Fall has turned into a personal guiding philosophy. Her work is anchored on this philosophy of the mastery of self, resistance, and transcendence of one's own capabilities. As she has said in interviews, this verse is the driving force of her being, her activities, and her view of things. It is a philosophy of hard work, and total self-dependence. It gives an individual her or his true dimensions of a being for whom everything is possible. Sow Fall believes that human beings are second only to God in their *grandeur* and nobility.

Furthermore, the mystique of effort is one of the cardinal values that any people can cultivate for their own progress, she believes. In this light, the past must be understood, not as a static thing, but as something dynamic. Progress should be a process that continues to reexamine and enrich the past, not discard it. That would mean modernity with a vision for the future, and hope in the ability of the human being to take charge of the human condition. The past can be bad only when it is fixed in a static form, with no opportunity for change. Nonetheless, what is kept and what is discarded of the past, must be carefully thought through, carefully selected, before a binding decision is made. Even then, as soon as mistakes come to light, they must be rectified. The human being is worth all of that effort.

In dealing with human issues, it is important to maintain a sense of humor, for human beings can get over more than a few problems that way. When we look at things squarely, in order to understand them in their essence, then it becomes possible for us to humanize them with a pinch of humor. Human beings should not be hurt in their dignity; it is the worst that anyone can do to a fellow human being. That is tantamount to terrible and negative violence that can fracture human society in the end. On the contrary, positive violence can be engendered with the kind of strength only seen in woman and the river; both woman and river are creatures endowed with prodigious power, hidden, however, in their innermost parts.

If only women could discover their enormous strength that passes all human understanding, which strength could help in the transformation of society, then humanity would gain from their women. Men are aware of this power, this ability of women, and are sometimes afraid of it. Therein lies the significance of patriarchy, namely, to encapsulate the power of women, so that men can control them. Men resort to all kinds of subterfuges to counteract women's power. However, women are not even aware of their power to move things and move the world, due to social repression. It is therein that lurks human tragedy in the present, and motivation for change in human society for progress in the future.

AMINATA SOW FALL'S LITERARY WORKS

In this section, we explore the contents of Aminata Sow Fall's novels according to herself, beginning with the first, *Le Revenant* up till the eighth and last so far in 2007, *Festins de la détresse*.

LE REVENANT

According to the author, this novel, *Le Revenant* (1976) arose out of her passion to communicate with her people her disappointment at finding, after a seven-year sojourn in France, that human relations had taken second place to materialism and love of money in Senegal. One day, she picks up her pen and a piece of paper and begins to write the fictional story of a man, Bakar, who refuses to acknowledge the power that money can confer on the individual. The story of Bakar narrates Wolof belief in the supernatural world that surrounds the living. Sow Fall is influenced a lot by her French studies both in Senegal and in France, values very much that education, and is very specially struck by the story of the difficult love of Tristan and Iseult as told by Barbey d'Aurevelly, due to the presence of the supernatural and magic in there, which elements also exist in African oral tradition, tales, stories, and legends.

LA GRÈVE DES BÀTTU

This second novel (1979), short-listed for the Prix Goncourt, the highest French literary Prize in 1979, won the Prix de l'Afrique

Littéraire Noire. The subject of criticism is the beggars, who are really part of the ontological landscape and the topography of Senegalese Muslim world. Traditionally, they are the talibés, students of the Qur'an, obliged to learn humility, grace, and communication skills by begging for their food at appointed times of the day. Some of them are from well-off families that have no problem taking care of them. Still, they are obliged to beg by tradition. In modern Senegal, however, things have changed, and this pillar of Islam, part of the five cardinal pillars, has been abused by people who are not really poor, but who want to exploit people by begging. They are lazy folks that take advantage of their religion to get through life easily without working hard. That is the point that Kéba Dabo makes in the novel, with which Sow Fall somewhat agrees. The real poor, she says, are too dignified to beg; it is only the fakes that wantonly bare themselves and their infirmity to the public. However, this characterization of a whole group with one stroke of the arm leaves out those in the cracks who are really needy. Sow Fall is against neglecting those who are really in need of help. Sow Fall believes that beggars, for whatever reason that they beg, are victims of society. Their integrity, needs, and aspirations should be shared by all, so that they are not pushed to resort to begging as a means of livelihood. It is such things as rural exodus towards the city, and the demands of modern living, which cause so many social problems, constraining a section of humanity to live by begging in their own country.

L'APPEL DES ARÈNES

Aminata Sow Fall's third novel (1982) treats the uprooting of a young Senegalese lad from his ancestral roots by been-to parents too eager to display assimilationist tendencies that make their young person become alienated from his African roots. Such parents as Diattou and Ndiogou, protagonists of *L'Appel des arènes*, raise children who are on the margin of society, and therefore grow up as social misfits. The child-protagonist of the novel, Nalla, does not regain his equilibrium until he reconnects with his relatives, friends, and culture in general, thanks to his tutor, Mr. Niang, who starts a chain reaction that saves him.

L'Ex-père de la nation

L'Ex-père de la nation is Aminata Sow Fall's fourth novel, published in 1987. It is also her first political novel, as such. In this novel, Madiama, the former Father of the nation recounts in the first person narrative voice a confession of his presidency, its ups and downs, and his eventual removal by a coup d'état. Aminata Sow Fall sets out to explore how people in leadership inadvertently fail, due to a conspiracy of the sycophants all around them to keep from them the truth of the situation of the nation, so that they, the sycophants, could continue to satisfy their selfish desires.

Le Jujubier du patriarche

The subject of this 1993 fifth novel is the Senegalese caste system. Whereas, at the beginning of times, there is an interdependency of the nobles and the Plebeians, things change in modern times with the society restructured around the money economy. Because of Sow Fall's belief that human beings are the sum total of their moral qualities, she sees the urgency in addressing this cultural aspect of a people, which tends to divide the people into Haves and Have-nots. In this novel, it is a question of integration, regeneration, and restoration of the moral and material interests of society, and of human dignity. Focusing on the traditional past, where the caste system was all important, the author analyzes the relationships of those in the caste and the nobles over them from historical and sociological perspectives, but does not forget that mentality has a lot to do with reality, needs, aspirations, and so on.

Douceurs du bercail

The subject theme of *Douceurs du bercail* (1998) arises from the author's work in the Ministry of Culture and her observation that the youth of Senegal think that it is all over for their country and that the only way to make a head way in their life is to go abroad to France. It is then that she suggests to the Minister of Culture that something needs to be done to keep the young people at home happy until they have at least their Master's degree, if they are not able to get a scholarship to go to France.

In this novel, therefore, Sow Fall treats the contemporary problems of a society in mutation in relation to itself and other places. The author denounces the failures or abuse of a society in crisis, like laziness of workers, mainly bureaucrats, difficulty of living, and customs surrounding certain festivities and traditions.

On the other hand, Sow Fall valorizes all those aspects of society that tend to honor nobility of heart, work, solidarity, courage, epic, and cult of the earth, things that promote human dignity, such as wisdom and spirituality. They are everlasting and fundamental values, for they are the center where human values reside. That explains why Sow Fall's writings are able to cross barriers of race, government, class, religion, and so on, to reach people in all the continents of the world. Hence, Sow Fall believes that human beings must not despair of the Mother Earth, nourishing and nurturing at all times. Happiness is possible here, if we know how and where to look for it. Human beings may not be ideal, but they are carriers of ideals, and so merit to be respected in their integrity. That is just what Aminata Sow Fall means when she says that the most important human value is dignity. The old and the past must be respected and must evolve in time, in order to remain valuable to human beings in the present and the future.

Just as with the ideal couple, it is important to give and to receive, to foster love and human understanding. It is important to learn to love with intelligence and humility, not passion and pride. Sow Fall states:

> Les combats et les tempêtes font partie du charme de la vie du couple. C'est quand on finit par régler tous les problèmes d'aspérité que chacun finit par savoir que l'autre existe. C'est quand on accepte qu'on doit exister ensemble que chacun garde son intégrité. On finit par avoir un seul regard et une seule direction parce que l'intelligence et l'amour se rejoignent (Aas-Rouxparis, 205).

> [Fights and tempests are all part of life as a couple. It is only when differences are settled that each one gets to know the other better. It is when one lives and lets the other live that each one has her or his integrity. Then they can begin to look in one direction with love and intelligence; *Azodo's translation*].

Therefore, Sow Fall explores the earth on two planes: the level of the African continent, and the level of the Earth as that planet that supports human life. Human beings must do all that is possible to tend the earth with care, love and understanding, so that it will continue to nurture human life.

Un grain de vie et d'espérance

The original idea behind this cook book (2002), states Sow Fall, is a French lady journalist's solicitation. Paradoxically, when Sow Fall sat down to write, as she confesses, she discovered that the content was always in her and her culture waiting to be harnessed. The idea of the novel is to explore Senegalese ways of cooking and eating as part of a much larger work that explores the art of eating and cooking all over the world among different peoples. Sow Fall decides to structure her book along the lines of 33 questions and answers, followed by a sample recipe from a Senegalese Parisian-based chef, Margo Harley. The author explores the cultural bases of cooking and eating the Senegalese way, and how the idea goes beyond merely filling the stomach to becoming a statement about how a people live, about their culture.

Festins de la détresse

Aminata Sow Fall says simply of her eighth novel (2005) that like its predecessors it explores the fact that some people like to live off of the suffering of others. It is the inaugural novel of a new series entitled "Terres d'écritures," and co-published by nine francophone houses, seven of which are African. Among these publishing houses are Aminata Sow Fall's own Librairie Khoudia, and Lausanne Éditions d'en bas publishing house. Their philosophy is to tailor the cost of production of the work to the purchasing power of each individual country, in order to encourage reading in the South closer to what it is in the North. This explains the notion of "livre équitable," which figures on the book cover, an imitation of the commercial cliché "commerce équitable," meaning balance of trade in world global economic system.

Critical Reception of Aminata Sow Fall's Writings

As novelist, Aminata Sow Fall is important, because her works are multidisciplinary; they can be used in the Humanities and Social Sciences, in the disciplines of Religion, and Philosophy, International Studies and History, French and Francophone Studies, African and Africana Studies, Sociology, and Women's Studies, among so many others.

Another reason Aminata Sow Fall is a very important African writer is that of all the female Senegalese novelists she is the one that most embodies "original and diversified female talent: (Pffaf, 339). Third, with her 1976 publication of her first novel, *Le Revenant*, Aminata Sow Fall was truly the first Senegalese female writer. More than any of her contemporaries, she deals with general social problems without undue reference to feminine preoccupations. Fourth, Sow Fall's *oeuvre* does not have a hint of autobiography so dear to first time African writers, especially women in African literature. On the other hand, notes I.T.K. Egonu, Sow Fall's objective as a writer is to act as the conscience and soul of her society. Quoting an article in a Dakar newspaper, *Le Soleil* of January 17, 1984, page 9, Egonu states:

> The writer is the best defender and protector of the cultural identity of the society. The writer has social responsibilities. There are moral and social problems because of confusing foreign influences. The writer should help to identify and define the ideals which should govern our actions in the face of the assaults by those foreign influences. Literature must, therefore, become a part of our national preoccupations. Literature is as important as bread and oxygen (68-69).

Fifth, for Aminata Sow Fall, literature must have social and political functions, but should not be moralizing or didactic, for she does not believe in the notion of art for art's sake. Sixth, she shuns extreme religion when it seems to interfere with people's responsibility to take their life into their own hands, through making an effort and working hard. She condemns excessive religious zeal that would make people first run to the marabouts for divination, before they reflect lucidly on their problems, in order to find solutions to them.

In this study, all the essays are new, and have never been published anywhere else before. They are all retained for publication here to highlight emerging perspectives on Aminata Sow Fall. The differences in approaches and perspectives from one contributor to another demonstrate the varied and widening knowledge on Aminata Sow Fall, and illuminate her novels.

Throughout this volume, readers will see the duality of vision so characteristic of Aminata Sow Fall, going from the real to the imaginary. The thrust of the volume is to highlight the social vision of the author, but also her profound imagination about traditional Africa with all its beliefs, customs, philosophy, and spirituality. Critics' acknowledgment of Sow Fall's social vision has given rise to the bulk of social-realistic studies on the author and her works. But, the imaginary side has not received consistent and sustained treatment yet, although acknowledged. This volume intends to fill that gap by doing a sustained study of her novels from the angle of the imaginary. The imaginary, a method of investigation that is anthropological, valorizes the contributions to human knowledge of the less quantifiable and less concrete aspects of human life, such as dreams, visions, legends, epics, the supernatural in general, and so on and so forth.

BOOK 1: THE REAL IN THE NOVELS OF AMINATA SOW FALL

This section on Aminata Sow Fall's social-realist vision begins with an article by Lucy M. Schwartz, who has spent the bulk of her profession as a university teacher of French and Francophone female fiction and contemporary French culture, and focusing especially on George Sand. Schwartz recently published a translation of George Sand's *Le Secrétaire intime* (1834) as *The Private Secretary*, "a story of a princess, the absolute ruler of a kingdom whose life explores issues of leadership by women, male jealousy, and problems faced by women who want both political power and committed relationships," as the book's back cover synopsis states. Schwartz's background in social criticism has enabled her contribution to this volume. Her essay, "Re-valuing Traditional Patrimony," dwells on the social conflicts in contemporary Senegal, between tradition and modernity. Beginning this volume with this chapter helps to frame the anthology, given that the symbols it highlights across the author's novels will be more fully explored with greater ease when the imaginary aspects of the novels are treated. The reader is privileged to revisit the social-realist aspects of the author's *oeuvre*, and thereafter is poised to explore more profoundly the African soul. Schwartz shows what African culture brings to the roundtable of world cultures, what is ennobling about human nature, and the reconstruction of human dignity, through a look at tradition and its role in elevating the human being to a further height.

The next contributor is Kahiudi Claver Mabana, with "Aminata

Sow Fall et la cause feminine," a feminist reading of *Douceurs du bercail*. But, more importantly, his objective is to push for the rethinking of the notion of leadership, with the hope that Africans can learn from a woman, Asta, the protagonist of the novel, a woman of great dignity and ability to change the face of Africa and the world with love. Mabana, with a background in philosophy and theology, has transferred his knowledge base into French and Francophone literature where he researches African mythical worlds. His scholarship has given rise to two books: *L'univers mythique de Tchicaya à travers son oeuvre en prose* (1998), and *Des Transpositions francophones du mythe de Chaka* (2002).

The third essay is Jeanne-Sarah de Larquier's «La Stratégie du projet humaniste: Une question de dignité.» De Larquier brings to this volume a background in French and Francophone literatures and cultures, with a focus on African Sub-Saharan and French women authors, and especially in regard to humanism. She has earlier published an article in *The French Review*, "Pour un humaniste du compromis dans *Un chant écarlate* de Mariama Bâ (2004), and written another, "Ama Ata Aidoo's Our Sister Killjoy: (He) Art-to-Heart for a humanistic Squint" (2005), among many others. Her present reading of *Douceurs du bercail* goes beyond feminism to unravel Sow Fall's "humanistic aura." She views the novel as the author's "ode to human dignity." This study also prolongs the ideal of Fanon and Senghor on humanism and universal brotherhood and sisterhood.

Mame Selbee Diouf Ndiaye's chapter, "When the Subaltern Speaks: A New Historiography," takes a completely different approach from the last two contributors. Ndiaye's studies and teaching in race, gender, and identity in African women's writing motivated her exploration of Aminata Sow Fall's contributions to gender studies, through the exploration of the author's socio-historical vision in her creative writing. Ndiaye's doctoral dissertation on "Intersections of Race and Gender in three Black Women's Texts" [Toni Morrison, Aminata Sow Fall, and Zoë Wicomb], from the University of Kansas, locates her theoretical contribution in the postcolonial tradition, and presents a deconstructive reading of the neocolonial Africa that addresses the relationship between the subaltern (Gramsci) and hegemonic power. In this new historiography, the voice of the subaltern is opposed to any kind of dialogue or discourse on Africa that is elitist. The subaltern rewrites the imperialist's project of domination in Africa and all over the world, imposing a reconstruction of the colonial narrative, in order to undermine a hegemonic historiography of Africa.

The contribution from Marco D. Roman, "Building Community through the Exchange Ritual," is again a postcolonial reading of Senegalese society and the conflict created by modernity marked by individualism, and tradition marked by communalism. Roman problematizes the true meaning of *zakat*, alms giving, as one of the five cardinal pillars of Islam, when the needy (the beggars) are in a position of submission and the givers (the rich) pose like neocolonialist dominators. Employing sociologist and social theorist Pierre Bourdieu's thoughts on the theory and practice of ritual exchange, he disapproves of the violence inherent in the gift exchange in which the *richer* gives to the *poorer*. Roman posits Islam as a means *sine qua non* of moderating the inherent violence, for Islam makes it possible for the giver, who is ordinarily the dominator, to become the dominated, and the receiver, to become empowered in his neediness. This is precisely what happens in *La grève des Bàttu*, when Minister Mour Ndiaye reverts to the position of the dominated and the beggars to the position of kings. Roman has published an article "Reclaiming the Self through Silence" (2000) in *Crossing the Bridge: Comparative Essays on Medieval European and Heian Japanese Women Writers*, and another essay, "A Modern Exemplum of the Immigrant Experience: Sembène Ousmane's 'La Noire de....,'" in a co-authored volume entitled *European Culture in a Changing World: between Nationalism and Globalism* (2002)

Léa Kalaora contributes her essay, "Engagement et nature du réalisme chez Aminata Sow Fall," from a background in geography and anthropology, and a master's thesis on, "Être ancré et moderne: réalisme et engagement chez Aminata Sow Fall," which is a theoretical exploration of Sow Fall's social commitment and her representation of an imagined Africa different from French realism and portrayals of Africa in earlier critical studies. More specifically, Kalaora uses her recent interview with Sow Fall, and almost all of her novels to recall the influences of the realism of African oral literature on the novels of Aminata Sow Fall. It is a social realism that remains inseparable from the author's social and literary commitment, and riveted on the local and a return to it, given that it is possible to be at once traditional and modern. Kalaora has earlier published an article, "Centres commerciaux et flux urbains, étude de cas: Century City en Afrique du Sud" in "Paquebots Urbains," in *Flux Cahiers scientifiques internationaux Réseaux et Territoires* (2002).

BOOK 2: THE IMAGINARY IN THE NOVELS OF AMINATA SOW FALL

This second section of the volume explores "The Imaginary in the Novels of Aminata Sow Fall" in which Ada Uzoamaka Azodo explores the author's long search for the African soul. Evidently, unlike many authors of the imaginary, Sow Fall is aware of this aspect of her novels, given her hints to it both in the works and in her interviews with scholars. It is nonetheless possible that certain elements of the imaginary in her work elude her as a creative artist. Critics and thinkers unearth these hidden aspects of the creative work, through the exploration of clues by the writer's unconscious and the symbols and images planted everywhere. Explained is the notion that creativity and criticism are intertwined, working together for the edification of humanity. Criticism is not secondary to creativity, but rather is one and the same with it, for the creative writer needs the critic to make her work understood by the literary public. This study then is an effort to co-author the writer's texts. It deals with the difficult subject of linking the literary work with the African mind or thought. The invisible world of dreams, visions, and the supernatural are in privileged positions, just as are legends, folktales, songs, and dances, etc. The fantastic and mysterious often push the writer to lapse into word play, outlandish allegories, symbols, flashbacks, even to intervene in the run of the story. These are all aspects of oral literature that Sow Fall employs for entertainment and educational purposes, often turning inwards for inspiration.

Furthermore, this study intends to save Sow Fall's works from the monomania of socio-historical study so common to critics, which invariably links the writer's works to her social milieu. I nonetheless avow my selfish pride and pleasure in attempting an oblique study of the texts from the angle of the imaginary, for I believe it helps to explore the deeper meaning of a difficult text of a difficult author, by concentrating on the symbolic details of the work. My background in the theory of the imaginary gave rise to a doctoral thesis, later published in 1993 as *L'imaginaire dans les romans de Camara Laye*. S. Ade Ojo recommends it for its rigorous analytical approach to Guinean Laye's novels, and which opens up the so-called impenetrable mystical thoughts of the author to the non-initiated. [1] Raymond O. Elaho also cited the work as eschewing the usual monotonous banalities often heard about Laye's work, but rather concentrating on an audacious and original interpretation, the kind usually seen with writers of

French *nouveaux romans.* [2] Then, M. A. Johnson sees the analysis and interpretation of Laye's texts through the angle of the imaginary as a good point of reference for all critics who would like to embark on experimental new criticism.[3]

Indeed, this work opens our eyes to the limiting nature of socio-criticism as a method of analyzing and interpreting literature, and to the invaluable benefits of the imaginary, which privileges knowledge from myths, legends, epics, dreams, and visions, and other less quantifiable aspects of life. With the emergence of myths come the emanations of the unconscious even in texts that are ordinarily seen as predominantly committed, and profoundly and socially realistic. However, this study will aim at a convergence of the knowledge gained from socio-realistic and imaginary studies of Aminata Sow Fall's literary work.

Lastly, because I treat each novel individually in this second section of the volume, each study is self-contained, but can also become part of the whole. The word "Saga," appended to each title, means a work of lofty, epic-stature adventure or experience in prose form. As a strategy, it gives the chapters uniformity on a first level of reading. A further underlying unity of this study is a certain internal progression through the ordeal of ritual initiation from *Chaos, Symbolic Death, Rebirth,* and through *Return.* The neophyte, having proved her- or himself worthy to receive new knowledge, learns some lessons that are passed on through mysterious language, symbols and images. Talking about the ritual of initiation, readers will find where they do occur consistently in this study, the following four cardinal stages of initiation:

√ *Chaos* - isolation of the neophyte, separation from her or his community, what Gilbert Durand calls in *Les Structures anthropologiques de l'imaginaire* (1984), "*régime schizomorphe.*"

√ *Symbolic Death* - stay in, or journey to, the beyond, or reintegration with Mother Earth, a sort of *regressus ad uterum,* what Gilbert Durand also calls, "*régime mystique.*"

√ *Renaissance* – rebirth of the neophyte at the end of the period of reclusion, marked by a public outing, and the adoption of a new name, what Gilbert Durand has called, "*régime synthétique.*"

√ *Return* - the neophyte returns to her or his community and people. For all initiations that succeed, there is a lesson learned, and a return to the community to impart the new knowledge gained.

The lesson is often the knowledge of the collectivity's culture in which the candidate was born. The knowledge is metaphysical knowledge, knowledge of the people's cosmogony, the group's understanding of ontological issues, such as the mystery of birth, origins of death, origins of the earth's dual [or should it now be multiple!] sexes, what happens to human beings after death, etc. There are also social and practical knowledge, like the ability by the individual to be an adult and do things like one in the community.

There are three degrees or levels of initiation, as Roger Chemain has detailed in his 1986 illustrous work, *L'Imaginaire dans le roman africain d'expression française.*

√   *The first degree* is accessible to age-group adolescents, for puberty rites, or such like. It is the lowest, the simplest, and the most common type of initiation, involving ritual immolation, or circumcision, of boys and girls, so that they could be socialized as young adults into their community.

√   *The second degree* requires a more rigorous selection of the neophytes. It is for heroic initiations, or initiations into dance societies. The neophyte can be rapt with "furor." Hence, the ordeal is meant to teach him the lessons of discipline.

√   *The third degree* and last type of initiation and also the most serious, is accessible only to very rare individuals, like priests, sorcerers, and shamans. The neophyte is led directly to confrontation with the sacred, the supernatural, and the divine even in physical life (Chemain, 247-249).

Obviously, many of the studies in this section fall into the first degree of initiation category, although other kinds of initiation with no proper structure as indicated above take place throughout the lives of the individuals, whether they are in secular or secret societies. One of the initiations is purely heroic. Now, because the hero battles with supernatural forces in the middle of the river as he prepares for his future role as leader and reconciler of two warring, but interrelated, factions, it is somewhat shamanic as well.

BOOK 3: INTERVIEW WITH AMINATA SOW FALL

This interview was executed essentially for publication in this volume, and covers all the eight novels of the author to date. Three questions were framed to cover salient aspects of the imaginary in each novel. Only in one instance, *Un grain de vie et d'espérance*, is there a deviancy, for the previous answer takes care of the question that follows. The sum total of the questions and the author's answers give a fair idea of the author's, and by extension, Wolof and/or African world, views on such questions as life, death and the hereafter, fate and destiny, ethics and work, the Earth and the human condition, culture and tradition, history and legends, growing up and idols, money and happiness, myths and epics, and so on and so forth.

GENERAL CONCLUSION

This introduction has presented the background, ideas, literary works, and the critical reception of Aminata Sow Fall's writing, including the chapters in this volume. Second, the structure of this volume includes its division into three cardinal parts or books, which can also be read as autonomous units. We hope that our readers will enjoy reading this volume and that it will serve university teachers and their students in the classroom, as well as contribute to a better knowledge and understanding of Aminata Sow Fall and her literary works.

NOTES

All citations are on the back cover of the book, *L'imaginaire dans les romans de Camara Laye*:

1. This is S. Ade Ojo's assessment of the book.

2. Raymond Elaho's view of the book.

3. This refers to M. A Johnson's impression of the book.

WORKS CITED

Aas-Rouxparis, Nicole. "'Écrire, c'est un banquet où tout le monde apporte': Entrevue avec Aminata Sow Fall." *Women in French Studies* (WIF) Vol. 8, 2000: 203-213.

AMINA. "Une Interview d'Aminata Sow Fall." See also this web site: www.arts.uwa.edu.au/AFLIT/AMINASow Fall82.html

Azodo, Ada Uzoamaka. *"The Dilemma of a Ghost*: Literature and Power of Myth." In: Ada Uzoamaka and Gay Wilentz. Eds. *Emerging Perspectives on Ama Ata Aidoo.* Trenton, N.J.: Africa World Press, 1999. 213-240.

_____. *L'imaginaire dans les romans de Camara Laye* (Studies in African and African American Culture Series, vol. 4. James L. Hill. General Editor). New York: Peter Lang Publisher, 1993.

Bacaly, Mathieu. "Les Cours Sainte Marie de Hann ouvrent la salle Aminata Sow FALL: Les Maristes immortalisent l'auteur de *La grève des Bàttu*."(publié le 23 novembre 2005; http:fr.allfrica.com/ stories/printable/200511230380.html. ACTUALITÉ par Wal Fadjri de Dakar, 23 novembre 2005.

Cazenave, Odile. "Gender, Age, and Reeducation: A Changing Emphasis in Recent African Novels in French, as Exemplified in *L'Appel des arènes* by Aminata Sow Fall." *Africa Today* Vol. 38, no. 3, 1991: 54-62.

Chemain, Roger. *L'imaginaire dans le roman africain.* Paris : L'Harmattan, 1986.

Crosta, Suzanne. «Les Structures spatiales dans *L'Appel des arènes* d'Aminata Sow Fall.» *Revue Francophone de Louisiane.* Spring, Vol. 111, no. 1, 1988.

De Larquier, Jeanne-Sarah. «Pour un humanisme du compromis dans *Un chant écarlate* de Mariama Bâ.» *The French Review*, May 2004.

_____. "Ama Ata Aidoo's *Our Sister Killjoy*: (He)art-to-Heart for a Humanistic Squint." *SORAC, Journal of African Studies*, 2005.

Durand, Gilbert. *Les Structures anthropologiques de l'imaginaire.* Paris: Bordas, 1984.

Egonu. I.T.K. "Aminata Sow Fall: A New Generation Female Writer From Senegal." *Neophilologus.* Vol. 75, January, 1991: 66-75.

Gaasch, James. "Aminata Sow Fall: Entretiens avec James Gaasch." *Éditions Xamal*, Dakar, Senegal, 2000. www.arts.uwa.edu.au/ AFLIT/int_gaasch2.html

H, Edwidge. "Entretiens avec Aminata Sow Fall: *Festins de la détresse*." *Africultures.* Le 26 septembre, 2005. www.africultures.com.

Hammond, Thomas N. "Entretien avec Aminata Sow Fall." *Présence Francophone*, Vol. 22, 1981: 191-195.

Hawkins, Peter. "An Interview with Senegalese Novelist Aminata Sow Fall. *French Studies Bulletin*. Spring 1987: 19-21.

Institut Culturel Africain. "Unknown Writer: An Interview with Mrs. Aminata Sow Fall." *ICA Information: Bulletin de l'Institut Culturel Africain*. No. 18, 1988: 23-24.

Kalaora, Léonora. «Centres commerciaux et flux urbains, étude de cas: Century City en Afrique du Sud.» In : «Paquebots Urbains.» *Flux Cahiers scientifiques internationaux Réseaux et Territoires* 2002, no. 50: 63-67.

Kiba, Simon. Interview de Aminata Sow Fall. "Le 5ème livre d'Aminata Sow Fall, *Le Jujubier du patriarche*.» Paris: *Les Interviews d'AMINA*, no. 276, 1993.

_____. Une Interview d'Aminata Sow Fall. « Aminata Sow Fall: Son second roman est présélectionné pour le Goncourt.» *Les Interviews d'AMINA*. No. 83, 1979: 16-17. www.arts.uwa.edu.au/ AFLIT/ AMINASow Fall79.html

L'Alliance Franco-Sénégalaise de Ziguinchor, vendredi 11 et 12 novembre. "Lire en fête." "Rencontre avec Aminata Sow Fall— Du *revenant* à *Festins de la détresse*: itinéraire d'une femme écrivain." Conference-débat animé par l'auteur, samedi 12 novembre, 2005.

Lebon, Cécile. «L'écriture, une parcelle de rencontre: Entretiens avec Aminata Sow Fall.» *Notre Librairie*. Vol. 136, January-April, 1999: 65-68.

Mabana, Kahiudi Claver. *L'Univers mythique de Tchicaya à travers son œuvre en prose*. Bern: Peter Lang Publisher, 1998.

_____. *Des Transpositions francophones du mythe de Chaka*. Bern: Peter Lang Publisher, 2002.

Montmollin, Michel de. « Plongé en Afrique noire. Aminata Sow Fall: *Festins de la détresse*.» Édition d'En bas, Lausanne, 2005.

Moukoko, Gobina. «Entretiens avec Aminata Sow Fall.» *Le Cameroun Littéraire*. Vol. 1, 1983: 53-56.

Ndiaye, Baye Ousmane. «Aminata Sow Fall, Lauréate du meilleur livre de gastronomie: La gourmandise des Lettres.» *Le quotidien,* Sénégal, 2004.

Pfaff, Françoise. «Aminata Sow Fall: l'écriture au féminin.» *Notre Librairie.* Vol. 81, 1985: 135-138.

Roman, Marco D. "Reclaiming the Self through Silence" In: *Crossing the Bridge: Comparative Essays on Medieval European and Heian Japanese Women Writers,* 2000.

Roman, Marco D and Alexis Downs. "A Modern Exemplum of the Immigrant Experience: Sembene Ousmane's *'La Noire de....'*" In: *European Culture in a Changing World: Between Nationalism and Globalism,"* 2002.

Schneeberger, Jane-Lise. "Entretiens avec Aminata Sow Fall: La Tradition n'est jamais figée." *Un seul monde NP3,* septembre 2005: 30-32.

Schwartz, Lucy M. *Le Secrétaire intime: A Critical Edition.* Paris: Les Éditions de l'Aurore, 1991.

_____. *The Private Secretary* (translation into English of Romantic novelist George Sand's *Le Secrétaire intime* (1834)). New York: Peter Lang Publisher, 2004.

Sentoo. "La literature doit comporter "une porte d'entrée" pour tout le monde," par Aminata Sow Fall, 15 novembre 2005. www.sonatelmultimedia.sn/sentoo/fr/culture/suite

_____. "Je n'ai jamais eu d'ambitions littéraires," par Aminata Sow Fall, 16 novembre, 2005. www.sonatelmultimedia.sn/sentoo/fr/culture/suite

Sow Fall, Aminata. « Les droits sociaux et culturels sont-ils bien partagés?» Réunion de Paris, Maison de l'UNESCO, 7 et 8 décembre, 1998.

www.unesco.org/opi2/reuniondeparis/index.htm

_____. *Festins de la détresse.* Lausanne: Editions d'En bas, 2005. [Coll. Terre d'écritures].

Xalimac A. "*Festins de la détresse* de Aminata Sow Fall: un cri de Coeur pour le retour de l'humanisme." 23 July, 2005. www.xalima.com/aufeminin/modules.php?name=News&file=article&sid=42

BOOK ONE

THE REAL IN THE NOVELS OF AMINATA SOW FALL

THE REAL IN THE NOVELS OF AMINATA SOW FALL

❄ ❄ ❄

Introduction

On a des problèmes sociaux et il fallait donc en parler.
Et je pense que le roman est encore le meilleur moyen
d'expression pour rendre compte de ces problèmes.
Et c'est pourquoi j'ai choisi le roman.

[We have social problems and so it was necessary to talk about them.
And I believe that the novel is still the best medium of expression
For taking account of these problems.
And that is why I have chosen the novel; *Azodo's translation*].

— Aminata Sow Fall. "Entretien avec Aminata Sow Fall," by
Thomas N. Hammond. *Présence Francophone*

The 1940s saw the birth of the African novel out of the upheaval of European colonization of Africa, followed by attempts by African writers to understand the workings of colonization, to protest it, and criticize the new African leaders that took over from the colonialists. They were also the years of the birth of social realism as an important literary and artistic term in African literature, according to Emmanuel Ngara. After the 1960s, the new African leaders became worse than the former colonialist dispossessors, and so the new African novel traces the changes brought about by modernity in conflict with traditions, and later bears witness to the complexities, contradictions, and instabilities of the postmodernist era. It was a modern adaptation of African storytelling tradition.

The early African writers whose creative writings in one form or another mirror the social reality of the times include men like Amos Tutuola, Camara Laye, Chinua Achebe, Ngugi wa Thiong'o (then James Ngugi), and later female writers, especially after the 1975 dedication of the first decade of the celebration of women's rights, writers such as Flora Nwapa, Grace Ogot, Ama Ata Aidoo, Mariama Bâ, Aminata Sow Fall, and others.

Clearly, realism has "a thousand faces," to borrow Joseph Campbell's famous phrase, being equivocal and varying from one au-thor to the other. Whereas Achebe's *Things Fall Apart* uses a historical tradition to protest the "falling apart," the break up, of African com-munal cohesion, peace, and harmony with the coming of the Europe-ans, not to mention the subsequent denigration of the black person cast as inferior in the world, Amos Tutuola employs the folktale tradi-tion to do the same thing, even as Camara Laye uses ritual and oral tradition to recover a more usable African past, which had been erased by the dominant white power. When the women began to write in the late second half of the 70s, they affirmed a feminist ideology to combat traditional and modern forms of patriarchy, which they saw to be as oppressive and subjugating as colonization. It was in this way that social realism became a way or a method of literary creation for many an African writer.

Aminata Sow Fall's unique intervention in literary creation has not just brought another female writer into creative writing after her male predecessors; it has also turned realism into an equivocal term. Realism in African literature is not any longer just an observation of the happenings — peoples, things, and practices, and everyday occur-rences — it is also about heroism, and the not-so-everyday activities, because legends, epics, and many other forms of heroic dimensions abound side by side with mundane happenings in Aminata Sow Fall's novels. Life is not just about human comedy, but also about the ances-tors and the gods' intervention in human affairs to dictate morality, ideals, and values, side by side with social reality, the bad, the good, the sordid, and the ugly. Clearly, in Sow Fall's fiction, the gods are not absent, for the novels marry the spiritual with the material. Her texts

38

are largely accounts of social reality in which individuals and groups are fashioned after the times, their values defined, and meaning made of their lives.

Thus, the novel, according to Sow Fall, is a literary form that studies society scientifically, with the aim and technique of observing, but also analyzing and producing social understanding, and revealing the workings and movements of society after the 1960s, when most African new states gained political independence from the former colonial powers with the "Suns of Independence" [Kourouma].

Sow Fall hopes that social comprehension of reality would lead to a democratic vision of the government of the people, by the people, for the people, and ultimately to change. Very gladly, she cites a few African authors whose work do not merely show the traditional spaces reserved for women as oppressive, for they at the same time show the same traditional women standing up for women's human rights. A good example is Doguicimi in Paul Hazoumé's novel of that title, who even in her subaltern position confronts the king, reproaching him publicly on his style of governance. Sow Fall also cites La Grande Royale in Cheikh Hamidou Kane's *L'aventure ambigue*, who makes the singular decision of sending children to the French school to learn "to conquer without being in the right," and inviting the womenfolk — a thing never heard of — to attend a political rally.[1] Sow Fall approves of this woman's actions, on the grounds that her mission incarnates the image of the traditional woman as nurturer and also invests her with a political role. We see an author whose commitment as a writer resides in her passion to guide the destiny of her people and nation; it condones modernity and tradition at the same time.

Aminata Sow Fall belongs to no particular literary school, since the very notion of realism is anti-school, as she affirms. Following any kind of ideology runs counter to the notion of speaking frankly. Moreover, it completely, sincerely, and exactly expresses limitations, conventions, and individualizations in the social milieu and the times. Sow Fall's writing is a form of writing that calls for deep commitment on the part of the artist, who must be part and parcel of her people's harrowing historical and cultural experiences. Sow Fall is a writer of her own, who is not a feminist *per se*, although she defends women's rights. Rather, her vision is that of literature working for the good of all in the society.

If Aminata Sow Fall appears to "dislike" most of her protagonists, since they all invariably fail, it is not just due to their indecision, stupidity, foulness, and fetidness, but also because the artist loathes the social reality they represent — from the elite, the modern society after independence, and back to the elite, new leaders in power, who greedily keep everything to themselves, denying the populace of essential services. As far as feminism goes, Sow Fall disapproves of women protagonists who do not demonstrate measure in their action. She cites Mariama Bâ's Ramatoulaye who refuses to leave despite Modou Fall's ill-treatment of her. She also cites Ramatoulaye's daughter, Daba, and Rabi of *La grève des Bàttu*, two women who are representatives of the new generation, who are not in the least interested in being nurturing like traditional women, for they do not see their liberty as equally important as the traditional roles given to them.

What nature does Sow Fall's writing take, then? She appears to respond by stating:

C'est qu'ici le modernisme n'exclut pas la mesure, et les femmes à la plume l'ont perçue. Libération oui, mais par des moyens dignes et conformes à l'esprit de mesure et de pudeur qui ne sont pas incompatibles avec le droit à la liberté. [2]

[Modernity here does not exclude measure, and women writers have taken note of that. Liberation, yes, but with worthy means that conform to the spirit of measure and modesty, both of which are not incompatible with the right to freedom; *Azodo's translation.*]

Sow Fall writes social satire, and she pokes fun at the modern times when compared with the traditional era. She goes so far as to posit a return to African traditions and all its usable aspects as a worthy alternative and/or a necessary counter to the present. There might be a certain paradox lurking in the foregoing statement, until one observes that the realism/tradition duality inherent in Aminata Sow Fall's writing is equally open to criticism, for Sow Fall is at once a realist and a traditionalist.

Social realism, according to Sow Fall, is a trampoline for getting at traditionalism, which includes the valorization of myths, legends, oral traditions, and rituals as important aspects of the past. Sow Fall's expressive language, although French, has an underlying Wolof diction and style, transforming the writing into a valuable work of art that promotes a social comprehension of reality. It is knowledge the reader could use for action in the local and global societies. At the UNESCO celebration, where she protests the inequality in social and cultural rights between the North and the South, Sow Fall states that the artist works towards conserving her right to dream, so that she can maintain culture in the face of the new assaults by material accumulation and technological advancement. [3]

The contributors and their chapters bear witness to the artist's keen eye in observing, analyzing, and interpreting reality to the reader: the role of tradition, and the need to revalue the African patrimony; .a new brand of feminism as a concern, because women do not often realize the power they have to be a catalyst for the reformation of the world; gender relations, power, and dominance in human affairs; search for human dignity amidst the chaos of the present; the tradition of the exchange ritual as a means of community building, and the artist's commitment in regard to her social vision.

NOTES

1. Aminata Sow Fall. «Du pilon à la machine à écrire.» *Notre Librairie*, 1983: 73-77.

2. Aminata Sow Fall. «Le Droits sociaux et culturels sont-ils bien partagés?» http://www.unesco.org/opi2/reuniondeparis/fall.htm

3. Aminata Sow Fall. «Du pilon à la machine à écrire.» *Notre Librairie*, 1983: 73-77

WORKS CITED

Hammond, Thomas N. "Entretien avec Aminata Sow Fall." In: *Présence Francophone* No. 22: 192.

Aminata Sow Fall. « Du pilon à la machine à écrire. » *Notre Librairie*, 1983.

_____. "Le Droits sociaux et culturels sont-ils bien partagés ? » http://www.unesco.org/opi2/reuniondeparis/fall.htm

RE-VALUING
TRADITIONAL PATRIMONY

LUCY M. SCHWARTZ

❊ ❊ ❊

The novels of Aminata Sow Fall are filled with social conflict. In her article entitled "Cultural Conflict in the Novels of Two African Writers, Mariama Bâ and Aminata Sow Fall," Susan Stringer outlines the major fault areas. She cites the conflict between the community and the individual, the country and the city, and most important, what she calls the "violent confrontation between the traditional African belief in continuity through living the same life as one's ancestors and the Western idea of 'progress.'"[1] It is important to note that these conflicts mirror one another. Valuing the community over the individual is a traditional African belief, which was developed in the village (country) and is often lost in the city because of Western influence there. This conflict is present in various degrees in all the novels of Sow Fall. The conflict is so vital that Stringer in her book *The Senegalese Novel by Women: through Their Own Eyes* calls it "the basic theme of Senegalese women's writing."[2]

Yet while the struggle between traditional African ways and Western ideas exists at the center of many novels by African women,

Lucy M. Schwartz, Ph.D., is a professor of French and Francophone literatures and contemporary French culture studies, and chairperson of the Department of Modern Languages, Buffalo State University, Buffalo, New York.

and some by African men as well,[3] it is not resolved in the same way by any two writers. In fact, in some Francophone African novels, it is not resolved at all.[4] For Aminata Sow Fall African tradition is the anchor which will help steady the country in the midst of these cultural storms. In 1985, Sow Fall directed a program at the Center for Study of Civilizations which, according to her, was charged with the mission of re-valuing traditional patrimony.[5] Thus, in addition to her writing, she worked in other ways to restore the value which the traditional way of life had lost.

In her first novel *Le Revenant* (1976) the Animist traditions of the village seem at first to be absent or non-existent. In their place traditional Islamic ceremonies of baptism and death are shown to be, in the city, corrupted by Western ideas of consumerism and individualism. At the beginning, it is easy to believe that the reader is in a Senegalese village. It is a typical Sunday morning — women are gossiping while walking to market; young girls are sitting in the courtyards of their houses washing dishes and scrubbing pots; father has gone to the mosque. Yet we are in a suburb of Dakar, and our protagonist Bakar quickly boards a crowded bus where he is pushed around by women whose faces are bleached by "*xeessa*l," a cosmetic which becomes a symbol in this novel. This whitening of their faces (but not their hands or arms) is the first indicator of the Western influences, which have distorted traditional values.

Bakar is surrounded by people who care about him and who cherish traditional values — his mother Ngoné, the young Nabou, his mother's ward, his friend Sada whose home every Sunday becomes a club for men playing the card game "*belote.*" Although Sada's wife Maïmouna uses "*xeessal*" on her face, she, like Bakar`s mother, clings to the traditional woman's role in society. She hates being invaded by twenty of Sada's friends every weekend, but brings it up rarely and smiles:

> Car le châtiment le plus terrible pour une épouse est d'être cataloguée "siiskat." L'égoïsme ne se pardonne pas, mais il est encore plus grave chez la femme qui doit être mère, épouse, et soeur de tout le monde (17).[6]

> [For the most terrible punishment for a wife is to be seen as a «siiskat.» Selfishness is unpardonable, more so in a woman who ought to be everyone's mother, wife, and sister].

If she fails to give in to her husband she would become an egotist, when as a woman she is supposed to be everyone's mother, wife, or sister. This clearly shows that communal values still have great importance here far from the village where the husband and wife have an individual house in a wealthy suburb. Maïmouna is torn between the traditional values that she was brought up believing in and the temptation of the Western life she has discovered in Dakar. In relation to gender roles, Sow Fall is aware that tradition is not always good. Kind men become "brutes" at the card table and, pushed by other men, decide to "tell off" or "repudiate" their wives, just as women like Bakar's mother cannot understand their sons, because tradition forbids their asking what is really wrong.

The story of Bakar's family is an example of the evolution of the society. The members of this family leave their village to go to the city where they are very poor and have a two-room hut for six people. There is not enough room to store all the cooking and eating supplies in the one room. There is a communal kitchen, but no one uses it any more. Each family prefers to make its own meals in front of its door. Thus, the village ways begin immediately to disappear as communal activities become the domain of individual families. Bakar's father is a carpenter, but he has little work and cannot support the family. His mother gets up at 4 a.m. to buy fish from the fishermen as they come in and resell it at the market for little profit. So, Bakar quits school at the age of fifteen, to work to try to get his family out of poverty. They would not have been rich if they had stayed in the village, but they would have been able to grow food and they would not have been surrounded by people of greater means, conspicuously consuming all of the products of Western life which can be bought.

Finally, the way out of poverty appears to be the beauty of Yama, Bakar's older sister. Because of her beauty, she is able to marry a rich man who does not care about her origins. Yama gives the impression that she does not care about money by spurning the money he gives when she dances at a traditional ceremony called a "taneber." Yet she becomes enamored of the power she exercises with her beauty. She had always been fond of yielding power in the family. However, things are much more difficult for Bakar who falls in love with Mame Aïssa Guèye, a girl from a good family. Her father believes in tradition and wants her to marry a person who comes from the same caste. Yama understands this and sees the power of money to overcome obstacles, as Aminata states hereunder:

Elle connaissait les rapports entre deux conceptions, deux attitudes, deux manières de résoudre les problèmes. Avec le bouleversement des structures sociales, une puissance nouvelle avait été créée et faisait concurrence à celle qui, jusque-là, s'était considérée comme seule digne d'égard. Les uns, se retranchant derrière la naissance, le passé glorieux et le rôle historique des ancêtres, regardaient avec un certain mépris ceux qui ne devaient leur notoriété qu'à l'argent (34-35).

[She understood the connection between the two conceptions, the two attitudes, and the two ways of dealing with the problems. With the demolition of social structures, a new power had been created, which competed with the one that was there before, and this one that had thought itself the only one worthy of consideration. These latter, hiding behind the birth, the glorious past and historic role of the ancestors, looked down on those others whose notoriety was based solely on money].

Yama understands that Mame's father is completely swayed by tradition and the traditional caste system; thus, she gives Bakar money and tells him to pay his regards to Mame's mother. Finally, the power of money prevails; Bakar is able to wed the woman he loves.

Unfortunately, instead of living happily every after, he decides to give his wife everything she has ever wanted, even when he does not have the money to pay for it. Sada warns him against this line of action:

Justement, les femmes il faut les freiner, mon vieux! Ne pas les habituer aux folles dépenses. Faire ce qu'on peut et leur faire comprendre que c'est ce que l'on peut. Avec elles, c'est un cercle vicieux, infernal, dès qu'on accepte leurs caprices dans ce domaine, on s'enlise jusqu'au bout, et Dieu sait où l'on peut se retrouver (37).

[Of course, women need to be controlled. They must not be allowed to form the habit of spending uncontrollably. One can only do what one can by them, and make them understand that is all one can do. It is a vicious, infernal, cycle with women. As soon as one begins to indulge their whims in spending, one gets bogged down, stuck to the end, and only God knows how one will end up].

Here Sow Fall is attacking the material desires of women who gain their social status from money. Bakar finds at his daughter's baptism that Islamic ritual is replaced by a competition between the women to see who can give the most gifts (41). The gifts no longer have any relationship to the needs of the baby who could not possibly wear the two hundred *"pagnes"* (skirts) she is given or bathe in the six bathtubs. Sow Fall calls this constant battle of the gifts *"matraquage"* (pummeling).

Bakar, whose family has never been tarnished by any misdeed, finds himself in prison for embezzling from his employer, the postal service. Then he finds out who his real friends are. Salla, his mother, and his sister Bigué and her husband Yoro, his lawyer, come to visit him often; and Nabou brings him his dinner every evening. But Yama never comes and Mame's father is quick to blame his wife and "the women" for Bakar's fall. He says so to his wife:

> ...tu as compté sur l'argent et maintenant tu nous fais récolter le déshonneur. Vous les femmes, vous êtes des démons, des démons trop sensibles à l'argent, aux folies, à la renommée. Eh bien, maintenant, débrouille-toi (55).

> [...you put your trust in money and now you make us reap dishonor. You, women, you are demons, demons too much after money, extravagance, and fame. Well, now, you have to get yourself out of the mess].

His wife is hurt by this reproach and decides to turn Mame against her husband whom she continues to love. Before Bakar gets out of prison, Mame asks for a divorce and becomes the third wife of a wealthy man.

In prison Bakar discovers traditional music which has an unexplainable power over him:

> ...des notes de khalams et de coras qui pinçaient toute sa sensibilité en tirant, comme au plus profond de son être les fibres les plus inaccessibles; et cela se traduisait par un instant de bonheur indescriptible, de béatitude même, pendant lequel Bakar se sentait littéralement hors de lui-même (52).

> [... notes from the khalam and the cora, which struck at his entire sensibility, by pulling, as it were, at the most inaccessible fibres of the innermost part of his being, and this translated into a moment of indescribable happiness, of beatitude even, during which Bakar felt literally outside of himself].

This music is played by traditional instruments, which Bakar is not used to hearing. It calls him out of himself in an almost Proustian way, helping him to visualize God, paradise, and eternal happiness. In contrast to this beautiful music, the other radio program he hears in prison is the obituary announcements, the *"bulletin nécrologique."* This is a list of the people who have died, prominently featuring their important friends. Sometimes so many friends and relatives are listed that the name of the dead person is left out or forgotten. Bakar sees this as another symptom of the hypocrisy of people who use the death of a loved one for their own social promotion.

He does not find anywhere else on earth the kind of happiness that the traditional instruments brought him. After he has been dismissed by Yama, who is afraid he will take away from the prestige of her "salon," and cursed by his father after he comes home drunk, he decides to take revenge on Yama and this hypocritical society using the tools that have become the symbols he hates—*"xeessal"* and the *"bulletin nécrologique."*

Bakar goes to his childhood neighborhood, Colobane, which has decayed so much that it now houses bars and brothels. Yet he finds freedom there:

> Colobane défiait la morale, les principes, les traditions ...Et à la longue il se sentit fasciné, envoûté même, par le débordement apparent de bonheur dont faisait preuve tout ce monde qui ne semblait s'encombrer de soucis d'aucune sorte (77).

> [Colobane defied morality, principles, traditions... And, in the long run, he felt fascinated, even bewitched, by the apparent happy outbursts of all these people who seemed completely free of any sort of cares].

Bakar is unable to judge whether this is true happiness or only the appearance of happiness; yet he is enthralled by these people who do not worry about what others think or how much money one has. In a sense Bakar has returned to the village where everyone shares a similar income, but in the village the moral traditions are still present.

In Colobane, Bakar meets a kind woman, Hélène Ndiaye, who has recently come from a village. She cares for him without regard for his income or status, but she cannot marry him because he cannot support her, and she has promised to return to the village to marry. Clearly, tradition is important for Hélène, who helps him get his revenge on Yama and the hypocritical society. Hélène leaves his clothes on the beach when no one is there. Then Bakar is declared drowned.

Bakar bleaches his skin with *"xeessal,"* hears the *"bulletin nécrologique,"* which features Yama, and attends his own funeral where no one recognizes him. The author tells us that the women turn his funeral into a fiesta and a competition of who can give the most money (120).

A final symbol of the hypocrisy of this funeral where no one cares about the dead is seen in a woman wiping the plates with her dirty robe, as indicated below:

> Dans la cour, près des marmites, la femme, qui tout à l'heure se mouchait avec le pan de son boubou, essuyait une assiette plate avec ce même pan. Et bientôt, on mangera dans ces assiettes qu'on aura lavées puis resalie avec des boubous, des pagnes poussiéreux, des mouchoirs de tête gras. Elles ont la manie d'essuyer… (121-122)."

> [In the yard, close to the cooking pots, the woman who was just blowing her nose with the fold of her pagne was wiping a shallow plate with the same pagne. And soon, people will eat out of the same plates, which will have been washed and again dirtied with the boubous, dusty pagnes, and greasy scarves. They have this mania of always wiping things…].

The plate, which appears clean, but actually is dirty, because the woman just blew her nose into her pagne and then proceeded to wipe it with her dirty clothes, becomes a symbol of the whole ceremony. As the unknown speaker explains, he no longer eats at ceremonies since he went to the toilet once and saw the conditions under which things were kept.

Bakar, who with the *"xeessal"* looks like the ghost of the title of the work, waits until the funeral is over then knocks at the door. When the shocked family finally opens the door, he explains that God has sent him to get his *"sarax,"* the money which has been contributed in his name. According to Sow Fall, the family does not see that Bakar has played a trick on them, and actually believes he is a ghost, for in a culture that believes in the supernatural, every phenomenon that presents as a miracle is calmly accepted as such, without question:

> Ils perdirent toute faculté de raisonnement au point que personne ne songea que Bakar leur avait joué un tour. Car celui-ci ressemblait bien à un spectre avec son caftan trop ample, son corps squelettique et son teint affreusement pâle. Dans un monde où l'on croit aux miracles, tout phénomène qui se présente comme un miracle est tranquillement accepté (124).

> [They lost all their faculty of reasoning to the point that no one thought
> that Bakar had played them a trick, for he looked very much like a
> ghost, what with his ample boubou, emaciated form, and extremely
> pale complexion. In a world which believes in miracles, every phe-
> nomenon that presents as a miracle is calmly accepted as such].

Because of the animist tradition according to which the ancestors are
always around the living, and Bakar's thin appearance, the trick succeeds, becoming a miracle. While this so-called miracle does not in
any way solve Bakar's problems, it does accomplish his revenge.

At the end of *Le Revenant* the reader concludes that the traditional ways of life of the ancestors are perverted in contemporary
Sénégal by the power of money and that women are instrumental in
this process. This is especially disheartening, because women as
Françoise Pfaff points out, are traditional story tellers[7] and, with the
griots (oral historians and ritual storytellers), are guardians of the traditions.

In Sow Fall's next novel *La grève des Bàttu* (1979), it is a different
tradition under attack. The novel focuses on the Islamic duty to give
to the poor. The *Bàttu* are the poor, the unfortunate, the crippled and
maimed — in short, the beggars who make giving alms possible. Bàttu
literally means «basin», the half of a hollowed-out gourd which the
beggars extend to people when asking for aid. In a classic struggle
between the old African ways of doing things and the «new» European ways, the city government wants to throw out the beggars for
making tourists uncomfortable. This, of course, is a direct attack on
one of the five pillars of Islam, *zakat* or alms giving, which means both
«purification» and «growth». This principle comes into conflict with
the need of the unnamed city (probably Dakar) to attract tourists and
thus to develop jobs for the population. The tourists and the jobs are
based on a European model of life, which may not be appropriate for
Africa, while the presence of the beggars and the duty to give alms
seem to be positioned as traditional values.

The main character of the novel, Mour Ndiaye, is devoured by
ambition. A government agent charged with public safety, he dreams
of becoming vice president of the country. In addition to being ambitious, he also has a firm, perhaps superstitious, belief in divination,
and regularly consults *marabouts*. The French word, *marabout*, taken
from the Arabic, means an Islamic hermit or holy man, often credited
with supernatural powers. Mour goes to seek one of these, Kifi Boukoul,

when he is being seriously considered for the vice presidency of his country. At this critical time in his life, the reassurances of Seringue Birama, a local marabout, do not seem adequate. So, Mour goes to a far away village of sheep herders known for the «*infallible science*» of its marabouts. Mour finds a man known for kilometers in each direction as «*the man whom nothing resists.*» People say that Kifi talks to the *djinns*, spirits lower than the angels who can take the forms of humans or of animals and influence human beings for good or evil.

No one has ever seen Kifi's face, which he hides behind a long Arab scarf called in French a *chèche*. All anyone can see are his small red eyes which Sow Fall describes as «*having a glance which cuts like a steel blade*» (75)[8]. Mour hires Kifi and brings him to the house of his first wife, Lolli, who is the keeper of all «*maraboutic secrets*» (76). Kifi closes himself up for seven days and seven nights in Lolli's house, seeing no one and eating only the couscous in warm water left at his door. After this retreat Kifi gives Mour the results of his divination. He promises him that he will become vice president, if he sacrifices a bull, all of one color, preferably fawn. He must also slaughter it at his own house and divide it into seventy-seven parts and distribute it to the people who carry the *bàttu*. In addition, Kifi emphasizes that this offering must be given in all sections of town, but only to the truly needy who would die without this food.

The irony of the tale appears here, because Mour cannot fulfill these conditions, and has only himself to blame. It is he who has chased the beggars from the town, so that now they are all in one suburb where everyone who wants to offer them alms must go. He goes to the beggars and (ironically) begs them to go back to their old places in the city only for a day (so he can give them his sacrifice), and gives them money for the service. They promise to go, but do not, thus ending his hopes of the vice presidency.

Mour's dependence on marabouts and his belief in them is in sharp contrast to the independent personality of Kéba Dabo, Mour's lieutenant, who refuses to help him bring the beggars back. Kéba is passionate about the beggars and takes a personal interest in their eradication. He believes that poverty is not an excuse for begging, which destroys self respect and dignity. He feels very strongly about this, because he was very poor as a child, and his mother taught him to respect himself and never beg for alms. For him the *Bàttu* are the false poor who steal from the truly, dignified, and respectable poor. When Mour asks Kéba to call the beggars back, Mour explains that from childhood he has learned to get rid of his *"fears, his worries, his night-mares"* with things that you give to beggars, like three sugar cubes, a candle, and a piece of cloth (98).

Kéba is incapable of understanding Mour's superstition, because he has never given anything to the poor and never chased his fears this way. He has always been a faithful assistant to Mour, devoted to doing his very best work, but Kéba Dabo is strictly honest and sees that Mour wants the beggars back as a personal favor, not because it is best for the country. Kéba refuses to betray his civic duty in this way, even though he realizes that he may lose his job. Kéba, the up-right civil servant, puts Mour's superstition and egotism into relief as Mour realizes that his hopes of the vice presidency are lost forever when Kéba will not help him. Here Kéba fails to defend the African tradition of the *Bàttu*. He behaves like a realist, or a Europeanized bureaucrat. Paradoxically, Kéba's refusal to help Mour actually pun-ishes Mour for his attack on the *Bàttu*.

Mour returns, exhausted and hungry, to the home of Sine, his second wife. He realizes that it has been weeks since he has thought of anything besides Kifi Bokoul, the vice presidency, and the beggars. The three are spinning in his head, and he can no longer see the «*unseizable image of Kifi.*» Seringue Birama has completely disappeared from his universe. His wife Sine turns on the television and «the voice of the speaker, in a solemn tone, which makes the same impression on him as if *"he were hearing and seeing God"* (130; my italics), announces that another man has been chosen vice president. This passage is a parody of the many divination revelations, which Mour has received in this text. It forms the final irony here as the television becomes the seer and God himself clearly tells Mour that his sacrifice has been re-jected and he will not fulfill his ambition. The message is clear that he is wrong to chase away the beggars and selfish to wish to be vice presi-dent. Clearing away all the diviners and marabouts, Sow Fall suggests that God is on the side of the poor and needy, and His graces cannot be obtained by a rich sacrifice, but rather by upright conduct. The end of the novel can be interpreted as a defeat of superstitions and the triumph of Islam and African customs and traditions. On a deeper level, the reader is convinced that the *Bàttu* as an African tradition have won since they have survived, persisted, as African traditions tend to do; and they continue to live happily in a small colony where every devout Moslem must come to give them alms.

L'Appel des arènes (1982) features a woman who has intention-

ally rejected African traditions for Western ways. Diattou, after studying midwifery in Europe, comes back to Sénégal with her husband
Ndiogou who has studied veterinary medicine. They do not intend to
ignore totally their past, but rather to move on, distancing themselves
from the past: "*prendre [leurs] distances par rapport au passé*" (100). [9]
Ndiogou does this, because he wants to forget the caste system that
makes him superior to others, whereas Diattou, full of personal ambition, wants to create a new caste system where she, the modern one, is
superior to everyone else. Diattou follows her credo of individualism,
cutting off relationships with her family, insulting all her neighbors
who decide she is a "*mangeuse d'âme*," a witch who eats souls; she
even throws out Monsieur Niang, her son's tutor, and also throws out
the family *griot* who has come to the city to be sure her son knows
about his heritage. When she insults the *griot* by telling him he only
comes for the money, he replies that she is an unworthy daughter of
her mother, lamenting that the baobab tree has given birth to a brush
of thorns: "*Tu n'es pas la digne fille de ta mère. Le baobab a engendré une
épine.*" (108). The symbolism of the baobab tree, which has born a
thorn, rather than a fruit, is central to African traditions and is also
the center of the thematic structure of this work as indicated below.

   L'Appel des arènes goes farther than Sow Fall's two previous novels. It shows the despair and alienation of people who have lost their
traditions, but it also points to a solution, suggested by the paradise
Bakar finds in the traditional music. Diattou's son, Nalla, feels a great
need for tradition in the shape of "dreams" (108), myths, poetry, and
rituals. He is terribly disappointed that he is circumcised in a hospital
and does not have the traditional coming of age ceremony in the men's
hut. Diattou and Ndiogou might have made him a European, and
kept him from knowing about his heritage, if they had taken him to
Europe with them, but they left him for four years in a village with
Diattou's mother, Mame Fari, who told him stories and created a life
for him that he remembers as a lost paradise, a simple life of happiness
without wealth.

   This paradise is recreated when Nalla meets the star wrestler,
André, who tells him stories about his native Saalum. André introduces him to Malaw and the world of traditional wrestling, which
brings to the city the lost traditions of traditional music ("*tam-tams*")
and songs that draw from the epic poetry of the myths told by the
griots. Malaw leaves his village and goes to the city to fulfill the dying
request of his father to save the people lost in the city, by building an
arena that calls to them and reminds them of their traditions. He does

this in memory of his sister, Anta Lô, who, seduced in the city, kills her child, and later dies in police custody inexplicably. Malaw also recreates the village in his house, which is not a single family dwelling but a compound where many people of different families live together. His father says that people will come to the arena because they cannot resist the call of the earth (128).

The earth is the place where they are rooted. Nalla's teacher Monsieur Niang knows this and is closely tied to his former village. Niang is worried about Nalla, all alone in his nuclear family and about his parents, alienated and cut off from their roots. He thinks it is very positive that Nalla wants to return to his grandmother, symbol of the earth and the link with the earth, and says: *"La grand'mère c'est encore la terre...Le lien avec la terre."* [*The grandmother is still the earth... the link with the earth*]. Malaw introduces this theme more completely as Nalla goes with him every week to make an offering at the foot of the baobab tree. He explains to Nalla that he has made an offering to his ancestors and that the baobab is a "symbol of life" (69) whose roots go deeply into the "nourishing" earth to connect with the ancestors buried there. These roots are also the community that nourishes and supports each member, especially children. However, for Diattou, the roots have become a gigantic octopus that imprisons her, limiting her freedom (122). She has forgotten all the community did for her when she was young. She has even forgotten that they helped her to go to Europe.

Diattou and Ndiogou see wrestling as old fashioned and barbarous. They do not understand that it interests their son because of his respect for bravery, dignity, and courage.

Finally, thanks to a physical contact when Nalla cries, Ndiogou remembers the fun he used to have playing with his son and the stories he loved when he was a boy. He realizes that Nalla needs a community to support him. Thus, the story has a partially happy ending as Ndiogou is reconciled with his son, wrestling, and tradition. However, Diattou still remains lost.

Le Jujubier du patriarche (1993)[10] explores the idea that tradition is not fixed; it can be modified to fit modern situations. Here Aminata Sow Fall takes on the caste system which is one of the least positive elements of African traditions.

The family of Naarou has been tied to Yelli's family by friendship and tradition for 700 years; therefore when Yelli marries his cousin Tacko, Naarou's mother Penda, Yelli's adopted sister, gives the six-year old Naarou to them to help in their house work. But Penda and

Naarou are descendants of Warèle and Biti, slaves to Yelli and Tacko's ancestors; and Penda's mother Sadaga married Tacko's father causing Tacko's mother Kantôme to die of a broken heart. Naarou calls Tacko "Mother," but Tacko nourishes resentment of her in her heart. When Yelli has lost all his income, due to bad investments, Naarou prospers because of the good sense of her husband Amsata, and Bouri, Tacko's daughter, is abandoned by her husband, Tacko can contain herself no longer and insults Naarou by calling her a slave and forbidding her and Bouri from ever coming to her house again. Penda tries to heal this painful breach in the family. However it is Yelli, aided by the *griot* Naani, who finds a solution.

The novel opens with a pilgrimage to Babyselli, the village where their ancestors lived. Then a flashback shows how the pilgrimage came about. Yelli and Naarou organized it when they heard from Naani that the jujube stump on the tomb of Yellimané the ancestor had begun to sprout for the first time in generations.

Of course, this tree, like the baobab in *L'Appel des arènes*, is a symbol of tradition. The tradition of the ancestors had been dying, and the tree whose roots reached to the ancestor's grave seemed to die several generations ago when greedy people took the fruit and leaves for their own use, as a fetish to safeguard their personal health and income. The community was destroyed by this selfishness and individualism. The new sprouts give the community one last chance, which Naarou and Yelli seize by planning a pilgrimage.

Another symbol of the tradition is the dry canal, the old source of the Natangué River where the epic story of the ancestors took place. It guards the mystery and permanence of the dreams, and has been dry for a long time but the crystals in its bed return the echo of the epic song which tells the adventures of the ancestors.[11] Thus it is the song which keeps the tradition alive in the epic song when the river has gone and the jujube stump looked dead:

> Il a tari depuis bien longtemps, mais il a eu le temps de se cristalliser pour mieux rendre l'écho du chant épique qui conte les aventures extraordinaires de leurs glorieux ancêtres (9).

> [It has been dried up a long time now, but has had the time to crystallize in order to better render the echo of the epic song that relates the extraordinary adventures of their glorious ancestors].

Naarou has always loved the epic song, even when she was a child.

At the age of thirteen she had memorized and could recite more than 1,000 lines of it. She has a mystical relationship to the epic song (67):

> Les longueurs par lesquelles le chant se désigne trouveront une nouvelle fonction: celle de prolonger le temps d'émerveillement et l'immense bonheur de se sentir des liens concrets avec des personnages qui, jusque là, lui paraissaient réels mais si désincarnés (30).

> [The long lines of the epic song will take on a new function, that of prolonging the period of wonder and the immense happiness of feeling some substantial links with persons who, up till then, appeared to him at once real and so disembodied].

> Le chant: un amour, une passion qui ne la quittera jamais et dont la flamme–non dévastatrice heureusement – brillera peut-être au-dessus de sa tombe quand elle rejoindra Dioumana dans le lit du fleuve Natangué (69).

> [The song: a love, a passion that will never leave her and whose flame – non devastating, fortunately – will shine perhaps above her tomb when she joins Dioumana in the bed of the River Natangué].

Her joy on hearing and singing the song reminds us of Bakar's joy upon hearing the traditional music, and Nalla's enchantment when he hears the tam-tams. She is carried into another world and feels the links that tie her to the ancestors like the roots of the jujube tree. It is because of her great love for this song that she is so upset when unworthy *griots* change the song by adding new people so that they can get money from them. This is an example of the corruption of tradition by Western values as in *Le Revenant* and *La grève des Bàttu*.

When Naarou is insulted by Tacko, she tells Penda that she is going to "claim her part of the epic" (69). She means that she will make it clear that her ancestors, the slaves, were the real heroines of the story. In the epic Warèle hid a copper ball for her granddaughter Biti to find when she was old enough and told her to give it to Yellimané when he was going through the circumcision ritual. Biti does this and is killed, but with the copper ball Yellimané is able to rescue his mother Dioumana who has slept in her ancestor Tarou the whale for twenty years. The slaves have an absolutely essential role in the story. Naarou intends to claim them when she sings at Yelli's father Macodou's funeral, but instead she insults Tacko by mentioning Sadaga without knowing the story.

So, Yelli realizes that nothing can heal the family except the pilgrimage. He puts an advertisement in the paper announcing that all descendants of Almamy Sarebibi (Yellimané's father) invite the whole community "regardless of sex, ethnicity, or religion" (92) to join them in a pilgrimage to Babyselli to honor the Almamy's memory. There is another encouraging sign (and symbol) — it has rained and the "dry" canal is full of water.

Naani tells one part of the epic story during the pilgrimage, Tacko begins to believe in finding good health in the future and reconciles with Naarou. The following year they continue the pilgrimage, but Bouri and Naani have died. Naarou asks permission of Naani's son to recite a part of the song-poem in memory of Bouri. According to Anne V. Adams,[12] Naarou gives contemporary relevance to the tradition and the "cultural misrepresentation of it by the upper-caste branches of the clan" (93). In other words, her version shows the importance of women and slaves in the narrative. In this work, Sow Fall tries a new narrative structure that weaves African oral tradition around the Western-style text. Sow Fall revives the power of tradition and rewrites it, making it meaningful to contemporary audiences.

Douceurs du bercail (1998) continues Sow Fall's exploration of the new uses for tradition and the new ways of integrating tradition into modern life. This is the only one of her novels to take place partially in Europe. In it she and her heroine Asta hope to reverse the flow of people from Africa to Europe and the flow from the country to the city. By demonstrating to her readers the "sweetness of home" (literally the sheepfold) she hopes to keep them from assuming they must go to Europe for an education or a job. But she does not stop at showing how wonderful home is; she vividly dramatizes all the degrading and unjust things that can happen to Africans in Europe.

Asta, who has a Western education, a good job, and all the required paperwork to represent her country at an economic summit in France, is so harassed by customs and passport authorities at the airport that she finally tries to keep her dignity by attacking the official who tries to search her vagina for illicit drugs. As a result, she finds herself held *incommunicado* for five days in a prison in the basement of the airport where the immigrants who are going to be expelled wait to be put on a charter plane.

Asta spends her time listening to the other detainees who have all sorts of horror stories. They tell her about people who were legal and had all the proper paperwork treated unjustly, and also about clandestine immigrants who are sent back. She hears a chorus of griev-ances and becomes friends with several of the people. The stories are not only about people unfairly treated in France; but also of the people unfairly treated in Sénégal, where people are deprived of medical care, if they do not have money to bribe the officials, and who can lose scholarships to prestigious schools for the same reason. They realize, like Bakar, that too much money goes into celebrations in Sénégal; money that could go into development.

Asta realizes that the French authorities know just what they are doing and had arranged the conditions of detention to be the most uncomfortable possible, while still feeding them, to discourage the immigrants from trying again. They are disoriented by the bright light that glows twenty-four hours a day. Many of them have no place to sit; and the guards try to keep them from sleeping. Asta sees how indignity and humiliation provoke violence when there is a riot; the police turn off the lights and two women are raped. Yet in the midst of this upsetting situation many of the immigrants remember their tra-ditions and talk about the earth. Asta says:

> Quand je sortirai d'ici, je serai plus à l'aise pour dire à mes frères, soeurs, parents et amis, que l'eldorado n'est pas au bout de l'exode mais dans les entrailles de notre terre (87).

> [When I leave this place, I shall feel more comfortable to say to my brothers, sisters, parents and friends, that Eldorado is not to be found at the end of the exodus but in the belly of the earth].

> Malgré tout je continuerai à prêcher: aimons notre terre; nous l'arroserons de notre sueur et la creuserons de toutes nos forces, avec courage. La lumière de notre espérance nous guidera, nous récolterons et bâtirons (88). [13]

> [Despite everything, I will continue my sermon: let us love our planet earth; we shall water it with our sweat and cultivate it with all our strength, and with all our courage. The light of our hope will guide us, and we shall harvest and we shall build].

Eldorado is not to be found in exile but in Africa in the land, she says. This recalls the thematic structure of *L'Appel des arènes* and *Le Jujubier du patriarche*. The tradition is like the earth, it does not yield fruits willingly. Much work and courage are necessary to cultivate it. The metaphors here are agricultural. Hope, however, is essential.

In the misery of this confinement there is still hope. Dianor, who is an actor and a poet, becomes the *griot* of the group, singing and telling stories. Quite familiar with the Western literary heritage, Dianor compares their endless wait for a plane to Samuel Beckett play, *Waiting for Godot*. This and his blues song cause general hilarity, dancing, and singing. The disparate immigrants have become a community in their celebration (50).

Out of this tragic situation Asta creates a new community. Taking with her Dianor, the griot; Sega, the intellectual; Yakham, the young man who was cheated out of his chance to attend school; and others, she buys some land in the country in Sénégal and starts a commune. They follow tradition carefully. First of all, they bring their elders with them. Mame Fanta, Asta's mother and Yakham's mother help and advise them. Then they pay courtesy calls on all twelve chiefs of the village and pour milk and honey into the river as an offering to the river goddess. Then Fanta tells the chiefs that hereafter they are in solidarity one with another, *"désormais unis par les liens sacrés du voisinage"* (204); her daughter will pay close attention to it. They are now tied into the tradition even though they were not born there. These ties hold the community together like the roots of a tree in their common reliance on the earth.

The neighbors are, of course, skeptical about these people from the city whom they call "those from the houses of cement." But within a few months they recognize how much they love the earth even though they know little about it. Thus the neighbors believe they will succeed.

The commune is named Naatangué which means "happiness, abundance, and peace." But this happiness is not readily apparent. At the end of the first year they are discouraged, because the promised loan to divert some of the river for irrigation does not materialize. But they find another way, discovering *guewê*, a plant which is used in perfumes. It turns out to be abundant and of good quality; so they sell it to get their commune started. They eventually grow crops, make cloth out of cotton, dye it, and make pottery. All their products are sold under the brand name *"Douceurs du bercail"* which explains another meaning of the title. Now the "fold" is their home in the country as well as Africa to which they have returned.

At the end of nine years they have a traditional harvest celebration to which all the neighbors come. Other people come as well. Didier, the husband of Asta's French friend Anne, comes to the celebration which is dedicated to her (Anne's) memory where Dianor sings the story of the woman in the river as he had promised to her.

The celebration is dedicated to Anne because she was one of the first to see and believe in Naatangué. She had believed when her daughter died that she would see her no more, but now that Anne is dead, the villagers do remember her and her spirit which, like the African ancestors, stays in that place.

Dianor has been blinded by a snake, but he can see the future even better now that he is blind. He has become a visionary while still weaving baskets with his wife to help the commune.

In *Douceurs du bercail* all the traditional themes of Sow Fall's previous books are gathered together. In *Le Revenant* and *La grève des Bàttu* she exposes some of the problems caused by the absence and neglect of the traditions. In *L'Appel des arènes* she suggests a possible solution. In *Le Jujubier du patriarche* she works this solution out in more detail, showing how to correct inequalities in class and gender caused by the tradition. In *Douceurs du bercail* she creates an ideal community, suggesting how modern people can go back from the city to the land and find happiness and prosperity.

NOTES

*   Translations in English are the author's.

1.   Published in *SAGE: A Scholarly Journal on Black Women*, Student Supplement 1988, 36-37.

2.   New York: Peter Lang, 1996, 144.

3.   The first work which comes to mind is Cheikh Hamidou Kane's *Ambiguous Adventure* originally published in Paris by Juilliard in 1961. It was translated into English by Katherine Woods and published in New York by Collier Books in 1969. Several works of Sembène Ousmane also fit this description as do most Francophone African novels written under colonialism.

4.   Again L'Aventure *ambiguë* comes to mind.

5.   Françoise Pfaff, "Aminata Sow Fall: l'écriture au féminin," *Notre librairie* 81 (1985): 135.

6.   All quotations from *Le Revenant* are from the 1976 edition by Nouvelles Editions Africaines, and the page numbers are indicated in parentheses in the body of this article.

7. "Enchantment and Magic in Two Novels by Aminata Sow Fall," *College Language Association Journal* 31.3 (March 1988): 339.

8. All quotations from *La grève des Bàttu* are translated by myself and taken from the 1979 edition by Nouvelles Editions Africaines (Dakar, Abidjan, and Lomé). Page numbers are indicated in the body of this article in parentheses.

9. References to and quotations from *L'Appel des arènes* are from the 1982 edition by Nouvelles Editions Africaines, and the page numbers are indicated in parentheses in the body of this article.

10. Published by Editions Khoudia in Dakar. *L'Ex-père de la Nation* (Paris: L'Harmattan, 1987) is not included in this discussion as it has fewer allusions to traditions than the other works. All references to *Le Jujubier du patriarche* are to this edition.

11. This idea is analyzed in great detail by Florence Martin in her article "Echos et graines de voix dans *Le Jujubier du patriarche* d'Aminata Sow Fall," *French Review* 74.2 (December 2000): 296-307.

12. "Revis(it)ing Ritual: The Challenge to the Virility of Tradition in Works by Efua Sutherland and Other African Writers," *Matatu* 21-22 (2000): 85-94.

13. Quotations and references are from Nouvelles Editions Ivoiriennes edition and included in the text in parentheses. See also the interview with Sow Fall about this novel, Nicole Aas-Rouxparis, "Ecrire, c'est un banquet où tout le monde apporte: Entrevue avec Aminata Sow Fall," *Women in French Studies* 8 (2000): 203-213.

WORKS CITED

Aas-Rouxparis. "Ecrire, c'est un banquet où tout le monde apporte: Entrevue avec Aminata Sow Fall," *Women in French Studies* 8 (2000): 203-13.

Adams Anne V. "Revis(it)ing Ritual: The Challenge to the Virility of Tradition in Works by Efua Sutherland and Other African Writers," *Matatu* 21-22 (2000): 85-94.

Blair, Dorothy S. *Senegalese Literature: A Critical History.* Boston: Twayne, 1984.

Boni-Sirera, Jacqueline, "Littérature et société: Etude critique de *La grève des Bàttu* d'Aminata Sow Fall," *Revue de littérature et d'esthétique Négro-Africaine* 5 (1984): 59-89.

Case, Frederick Ivor. "Le Discours Islamique dans les Romans d'Aminata Sow Fall." *Commentaries on a Creative Encounter.* eds. Keith E. Baird and Jean-François Gounard. Albany: New York African-American Institute, 1988.

Cazenave, Odile. "Gender, Age, and Reeducation: A Changing Emphasis in Recent Novels in French, as exemplified in *L'Appel des arènes* by Aminata Sow Fall." *Africa Today* 38.3 (1991): 54-62.

Crosta, Suzanne. "Les Structures spatiales dans *L'Appel des arènes* d'Aminata Sow Fall." *Revue Francophone de Louisiane* 3.1 (1988): 58-65.

Kane, Cheikh Hamidou. *Ambiguous Adventure.* Paris: Julliard, 1961.

Gadjigo, Samba. "La Comédie humaine sénégalaise: Interview accordée par la romancière sénégalaise Aminata Sow Fall le 14 janvier 1987." *Komparatistische Hefte* 15-16 (1987): 219-24.

Mokwenye, Cyril. "Aminata Sow Fall as Social Critic: An Interpretation of *Le Revenant* and *La grève des Bàttu*." *Neohelicon* 19.2 (1992): 211-21.

Niang, Sada. "Modes de Contextualisation dans *Une si Longue Lettre* et *L'Appel des arènes*." *Literary Griot* 4.1-2 (1992): 111-25.

Obinaju, Nwabueze Joe. "Human Rights Echoes in Aminata Sow Fall's *The Beggars' Strike*." *Neohelicon* 22.1 (1995): 295-310.

Okafor, Nididi R. "Aminata Sow Fall: Cas du *Revenant*." *Neohelicon* 18.1 (1991): 89-97.

Okeke-Ezigbo, Emeka. "Begging the Beggars: Restoration of the Dignity of Man in *The Beggars' Strike*." *Neohelicon* 19. 1 (1992): 307-22.

Perraudin, Pascale. "Littérature africaine francophone: (en) marge(s) du discours ou la différence par le jeu dans *Le Jujubier du Patriarche* d'Aminata Sow Fall." *MIFLC Review* 4 (October 1994): 10-18.

Pfaff, Françoise. "Aminata Sow Fall: l'écriture au féminin." *Notre Librairie* 81 (1985): 135-38.

_____. "Enchantment and Magic in Two Novels by Aminata Sow

Fall." *College Language Association Journal.* 31.3 (March 1988): 339-59.

Schiavone, Cristina. "A Propos de *Le Jujubier du Patriarche*: Entretien avec Aminata Sow Fall." *Francophonia* 14.27 (1994): 87-95.

Sow Fall, Aminata. *L'Appel des arènes.* Dakar: Nouvelles Editions Africaines, 1982.

_____. *Douceurs du bercail.* Abidjan: Nouvelles Editions Ivoriennes, 1998.

_____. *L'Ex-père de la nation.* Paris: L'Harmattan, 1987.

_____. *Un grain de vie et d' espérance.* Paris: Françoise Truffaut, 2002.

_____. "L'Oeuvre littéraire d'Aminata Sow Fall." *Notre Librairie* 118 (July-Sept. 1994): 25-28.

_____. "Social Vision in Aminata Sow Fall's Literary Work." *World Literature Today* 63.3 (Summer 1989): 411-15.

Guèye, Médoune. "La Question du féminisme chez Mariama Bâ et Aminata Sow Fall." *French Review* 72.2 (December 1998): 308-19.

Hammond, Thomas N. "Entretien avec Aminata Sow Fall." *Présence Francophone* 22 (1981): 191-95.

Herzberger-Fofana, Pierrette. "L'Islam dans les romans féminins sénégalais." *Frankophone Literaturen Ausserhalb Europas.* Ed. János Riesz. Frankfort: Peter Lang, 1987.

Jaccard, A.C. "Les Visages de l'Islam chez Mariama Bâ et Aminata Sow Fall." *Nouvelles du Sud* 6 (1986-87): 171-82.

Lemotieu, Martin. "Interférence de la religion musulmane sur les structures actuelles de la société Négro-Africaine: L'exemple de *La grève des Bàttu* d'Aminata Sow Fall." *Nouvelles du Sud* 6 (1986-87): 49-60.

Martin, Florence. "Echos et grains de voix dans *le Jujubier du patriarche* d'Aminata Sow Fall." *French Review* 74.2 (December 2000): 296-307.

Miller, Mary Kay. "Aminata Sow Fall's *L'Ex-père de la nation*: Subversive Subtexts and the Return of the Maternal." In: *Postcolonial*

Subjects: Francophone Women Writers. Eds. Mary Jean Green, Karen Gould, et al. Minneapolis: University of Minnesota Press, 1996.

_____. *La grève des Bàttu.* Dakar: Nouvelles Éditions Africaines, 1979.

_____. *Le Jujubier du patriarche.* Dakar: Editions Khoudia, 1993.

_____. "Pratiques langagiers dans la littérature négro-africaine." *Ethiopiques* 3. Nos.1-2 (1985): 61-66.

_____. *Le Revenant.* Dakar: Nouvelles Éditions Africaines, 1976.

Stinger, Susan. "Cultural Conflict in the Novels of Two African Writers, Mariama Bâ and Aminata Sow Fall." *SAGE: A Scholarly Journal on Black Women* Supplement (1988): 36-41.

_____. *The Senegalese Novel by Women: Through Their Own Eyes.* New York: Peter Lang, 1996.

Thomas, Dominic. *Postcolonial African Writers: A Bio-bibliographical Critical Source Book.* eds. Pushpa Naidu Parekh and Siga Fatima Jagne. Westport, CT: Greenwood P, 1998.

Wills, Dorothy Davis. "Economic Violence in Postcolonial Senegal: Noisy Silence in the Novels of Mariama Bâ and Aminata Sow Fall." *Violence, Silence, and Anger: Women's Writing as Transgression.* ed. Deirdre Lashgari. Charlottesville: UP of Virginia, 1995.

Wylie, Hal. "The Political Science of Sembène and Fall: Senghor Revisited." *Carrefour de Cultures: Mélanges offerts à Jacqueline Leiner.* ed. Régis Antoine. Tübingen: Gunter Narr Verlag, 1993.

AMINATA SOW FALL ET LA CAUSE FÉMININE

Kahiudi Claver Mabana

❄ ❄ ❄

EDITOR'S SYNOPSIS

This chapter acknowledges Aminata Sow Fall as a serious woman writer who knows that her word carries a lot of weight locally and internationally, hence her speech is always measured and well thought out. Feminism for her is much more fundamental than merely carrying a poster and promoting an ideology. On the contrary, Aminata Sow Fall's persona, Asta Diop, her principal heroine in *Douceurs du bercail*, is a model for African women, who must learn to discover their God-given ability to do and dare. Africans in general should love Africa, they should love living in Africa, and not alienate themselves by fleeing to Europe to be happy. African women must capitalize on their qualities and help in the rebuilding of Africa's prestige at home and abroad. Friendship between women, across the bar-

---

Kahiudi Claver Mabana, Ph.D., is a lecturer in French and African Literature at the University of West Indies, Cave Hill Campus, Barbados, and has a background in philosophy and theology.

65

riers of race and culture, when necessary, is crucial for the transformation and survival of women.

❀ ❀ ❀

Au colloque "Présence des cultures africaines" organisé par l'Unesco-Suisse à Fribourg du 19 au 23 octobre 1988, j'avais posé à Mme Aminata Sow Fall la question de savoir comment elle se sentait dans sa peau de romancière. Elle m'avait répondu à peu près en ces termes: "C'est comme un défi d'être femme africaine, mère de famille, fonctionnaire et écrivain. Les gens vous regardent avec des yeux bizarres. Quoi qu'il en soit, nous les femmes avons un message que les hommes ne peuvent pas transmettre à notre place." Ce dialogue retentit encore en moi comme s'il datait d'hier. Depuis, chaque fois que je lis un livre d'une Africaine, j'y recherche volontiers la spécificité féminine.

Depuis une vingtaine d'années, l'œuvre d'Aminata Sow Fall est au centre d'un nombre croissant d'études critiques. Elle a été souvent récupérée, en des termes contradictoires, par le mouvement féministe tantôt l'accusant de ne pas ménager la femme, tantôt l'encensant comme une voix particulière et originale. Loin de céder à une vague féministe quelconque, il convient de partir strictement des textes sans au préalable y projeter des préjugés ni des tendances idéologiques, avec pour seul but de dégager objectivement l'intention littéraire de cette fresque narrative. Comme dirait Florence Martin: "Chantre des laissés pour compte, elle donne la parole à ceux à qui l'on ne prête pas l'oreille; des *bàttu* (mendiants tendant sébile); un enfant fasciné par la tradition de la lutte; un employé des postes devenu voleur et emprisonné; un dictateur déchu derrière les barreaux. ..." (Martin 2001: 296) Le roman *Douceurs du bercail* évolue autour d'une intellectuelle africaine arrêtée et refoulée à la frontière française alors qu'elle se rendait à une conférence internationale. De tous les romans publiés à ce jour par Sow Fall, *Le Jujubier du patriarche* et *Douceurs du bercail* sont les seuls dont les protagonistes sont des femmes: Asta et Penda sont présentées dans des contextes qui, souvent, sollicitent la sympathie du lecteur.

Notre propos concerne essentiellement le personnage féminin de *Douceurs du bercail*. "Il s'agit de reconstituer la syntaxe des comportements humains mis en œuvre par le récit, de retracer le trajet des "choix" auxquels, en chaque point de l'histoire, tel personnage, est fatalement soumis..." (Barthes 1977: 27) La protagoniste féminine est méticuleusement construite, somptueusement enrichie de vertus héroïques, et dynamisée par une force intérieure.

1. Une intrigue sur fond de malentendus

"L'avion a atterri sous une pluie battante. Asta répond à peine aux souhaits de l'hôtesse de l'air et emprunte le couloir" (4). L'incipit lui-même est révélateur. La fin du voyage est brouillée par une intempérie. Prélude sans aucun doute des péripéties que va connaître la protagoniste Asta Diop comme si la nature annonçait une tournure violente des événements. La fin du vol VA 18 du 11 février 199... ouvre de nombreux pans de possibilités narratives. C'est cet inattendu qui focalise l'intérêt du récit et rend particulier le serein voyage effectué par Asta Diop.

La Sénégalaise se sent victime d'un concours de circonstances malheureuses. Contrôlée suspicieusement par des agents de police sans scrupule alors que tous ses documents sont en ordre, agressée dans l'intimité de son corps, Asta est obligée d'étrangler la maladroite douanière. Cependant, la nouvelle sera reprise à la une de la presse: "Immigration: un drame évité de justesse à Roissy" Anne Lemaire, son amie française, qui est allée l'attendre n'en croit pas ses oreilles ni ses yeux. Dès que la nouvelle s'est confirmée, Anne et son mari Didier vont solliciter l'appui de l'Ambassade du Sénégal. Réponse mitigée sinon négative des diplomates qui ne se sentent pas du tout concernés. Dans le "dépôt" ou "l'escale" où elle est escortée et jetée menottes aux mains, Asta fait la connaissance de Codé, Sega, Yakham, Dianor et Balou. Au hasard des conversations, chacun expose ses expériences. Les discussions qui au départ n'ont pour but que de casser la monotonie du temps débouchent sur des affinités de vues et d'émotions. Un incident provoqué par une agression de Sega par le mari d'une dame qu'il a insultée, se termine par une bagarre et une coupure d'électricité. Dans ce laps de temps des fillettes et des femmes sont violées. Une fois de plus, la presse se fait l'écho de l'expulsion de deux cents quatre vingt-sept "immigrés clandestins" parmi lesquels figure Asta. Sept mois plus tard, Anne rend visite à Asta à Dakar. Cette dernière, licenciée de son travail, est désormais consultante en développement et vient d'acquérir un terrain à exploiter sur les bords du fleuve Sénégal. C'est le début de l'exploitation de *Naatangué*, une ferme agricole montée avec l'apport de Dianor, Yakham, Laaba, Paapi, Fanta, et Daba Sangharé.

L'histoire évolue suivant deux lignes croisées et selon deux plans temporels. Un pan se passe à Paris, un autre à l'aéroport. Axée autour d'Asta et d'Anne, la narration fait de va-et-vient entre le passé et le présent depuis leur première rencontre à la maternité où elles furent internées pour les soins de leurs enfants nées prématurées Maram et Désirée. Si les premiers chapitres alternent entre le "dépôt" et Paris, les trois derniers chapitres se passent entièrement au Sénégal. Il y a donc: 1. L'arrestation d'Asta à la frontière française; 2. Les recherches d'Anne Lemaire; 3. Asta, menottée, est escortée au "dépôt"; 4. Anne sollicite l'intervention de l'ambassade sénégalaise; 5. Réflexion d'Asta sur la vie, la terre; 6. Présentation de Yakham; 7. Expulsion de 287 immigrés clandestins; 8. Evocation de la première rencontre entre Anne et Asta; 9. Séjour d'Anne chez Asta au Sénégal; 10. Visite du terrain du futur *Naatangué*; 11. Exploitation du site agricole. En dépit de cette simple linéarité événementielle, ce roman à thèse est construit sur de longs retours en arrière qui, toujours, justifient, expliquent l'épisode suivant. Comme l'enchaînement des épisodes laisse peu d'espaces à la conjecture, il serait erroné de prendre la romancière au mot. *Douceurs du bercail* ou l'amour de sa terre natale, c'est le titre d'une partition musicale créée par l'artiste Dianor alors qu'il a perdu l'usage de ses yeux à la suite d'une morsure d'un serpent à lunette.

2. LE TRIOMPHE DU "FÉMININ"

Dans l'ensemble, *Douceurs du bercail* présente la femme sous les traits luisants de la réussite, de la résistance, de la mesure et de la vertu. A considérer la protagoniste et son adjuvante principale, on est frappé par leur relation très intime avec leur mère. Dans les cas, la mère sert de guide. L'amitié qui lie Asta Diop et Anne Lemaire, basée sur un commun amour de l'Afrique, a une histoire beaucoup plus profonde que ne laisse transparaître la structure de surface du roman. Les arrière-fonds culturels et historiques étant différents, il sera intéressant de considérer les points de convergence et d'écart entre ces personnages. Aussi, s'agit-il davantage d'un triomphe du féminin qui dépasse les frontières géographiques, culturelles et raciales.

2:1. ASTA DIOP, LA PROTAGONISTE

Sociologue communicatrice de son état, Asta est une femme

divorcée, mère de trois enfants: Maram, Sira et Paapi. Les deux filles étudient à Paris sous la protection d'Anne Lemaire tandis que Paapi, le plus jeune, fourbit encore ses armes au pays. Asta se montre très attachée à son fils dont elle ne voudrait pas se séparer de si tôt.

Elle était mariée à Diouldé, un footballeur professionnel qui lui en a fait voir de toutes les couleurs en la trompant, en l'humiliant, en la frappant comme une bête de somme. Vedette consacrée du grand monde, Diouldé n'hésitait pas à l'humilier en public jusqu'à dévoiler des secrets d'ordre intime. En toute discrétion et consciente de l'intégrité de sa famille, Asta cherchait à sauver les apparences jusqu'au jour où, réagissant à une remarque de son amie, elle dévoile la cause de sa maigreur et de son dépérissement: "Salaud, tu veux me tuer. J'en ai marre, tu es un monstre" (167) Cette révolte éloquente d'un être élevé dans la stricte observance des règles du mariage symbolise le moment réel où Asta a décidé la séparation dont la requête de divorce ne sera que la formalité légale.

Intelligente, mûre et dotée d'un sens très développé de l'observation, Asta a des convictions fermes qu'elle tient pour sacrées, fruit d'une éducation traditionnelle bien intériorisée. "Aimons notre terre", dit-elle (53). L'expérience du "dépôt" est décisive pour son avenir. Pourquoi aller ailleurs, émigrer, alors que l'on peut bien vivre dans son pays natal ? Pourquoi mendier sa nourriture chez le voisin alors qu'il suffit de cultiver la terre, sa propre terre, pour s'alimenter ? Elle n'ignore pas qu'un tel discours sonne faux aux yeux de ses contemporains préoccupés des solutions faciles, des gains fabuleux susceptibles d'enrichir en un tour de main. Elle cultive par contre "la mystique de l'effort" (76). Elle croit en des valeurs comme l'amour ou la fidélité, négligées par ce siècle de violence où l'homme est plus proche de l'animalité.

Asta réfléchit longuement sur la vie, le monde, les relations humaines, les valeurs issues de la tradition. Ses méditations l'amènent à des prises de position claires sur certaines questions qui touchent à la situation humaine comme la fracture sociale, la pauvreté, l'injustice, l'éducation scolaire et familiale, l'analphabétisme. Ses points de vue sur l'Afrique et son avenir reposent sur des arguments solidement construits dans son esprit. Intellectuelle érudite, elle sait expliquer avec des mots très simples des réalités parfois mal comprises ou mal acceptées par d'autres; c'est le cas des concepts de *téranga* et de *teey* (156-158).

Elle voue une dévotion particulière à sa mère Fanta dont les opinions se révèlent souvent justes à la fin. Cette dernière lui a enseigné à être digne, pragmatique, et réaliste en lui répétant à temps et à contre-temps: "Tant que va la vie, tout peut arriver" (86). Cet adage lui a permis de prendre certaines surprises avec philosophie, d'éviter les déceptions les plus cuisantes, de gérer les incongruités de la vie, de ne pas désarmer devant les malheurs, les échecs. Ce qui lui a forgé un caractère de fer, de fermeté et de rigueur. L'expérience de "l'escale" l'a amenée à une résolution sans équivoque qui correspond parfaitement à la personnalité de la sociologue sénégalaise: "Quand je sortirai d'ici, je serai plus à l'aise pour dire à mes frères, sœurs, parents et amis que l'eldorado n'est pas au bout de l'exode mais les entrailles de notre terre. Chanson éculée, bien sûr. Refrain connu depuis l'aube des temps, maintes fois entendu dans ma jeunesse" (87).

La détermination qu'Asta Diop affiche transcende les simples slogans. Il s'agit pour elle de passer des mots aux choses, des idées aux actions. Un défi à relever. Elle en fait un point d'honneur. Changer sa terre en pays de cocagne pourquoi pas? Ce n'est ni la nouveauté ni l'originalité du propos qui l'intéressent mais sa pertinence, sa vérité, vu que la pensée selon laquelle "l'eldorado n'est pas au bout de l'exode mais les entrailles de notre terre" est intemporelle, éternellement vraie. Le fait que plus personne n'y croie n'implique nullement sa fausseté. Femme idéaliste au premier abord certes, mais elle réussit à fonder intellectuellement ses motivations profondes. Ce qui est fascinant chez cette érudite, c'est son sens de la contrepartie et du pragmatisme. Dans un souci d'objectivité et d'honnêteté critique, elle s'applique à confronter ses idées avec la sagesse populaire ou ancestrale. Ainsi, elle recourt non pas aux arguments de ses professeurs d'université, mais aux simples mots du griot Mapenda: "Le monde sera toujours (...). Ce sont les êtres, les surfaces et les décors qui changent avec le temps" (87). N'est-ce pas là une philosophie profonde de la vie ? N'est-ce pas là une pensée qui rappelle la théorie aristotélicienne des substances et des accidents, de l'être et du devenir ? Les notions d'acte et de puissance chez Aristote constituent l'essentiel du devenir, amènent à une vision réaliste et sélective du monde.

Plus concrètement, Asta a une claire vision de son devenir. Face à la bouillante radio cancan de Dakar, face à toutes les éventuelles insultes et ignobles insinuations provoquées par sa mésaventure parisienne, elle démontre une forte conscience de sa force intérieure, elle ne s'inquiète que pour ses proches—Anne, ses enfants, ses parents, Labba—qui éprouveront de la honte et du mal à la voir vilipendée par les "gens":

Ils vont souffrir... Le journal, la radio, la rumeur. Pour moi, c'est consommé. A présent, c'est leur peine qui me fait surtout mal... Moi, je m'en sortirai; jusqu'ici toute ma vie a été un combat... Enfin... pas toute ma vie... mais depuis ce jour où, après avoir tant rêvé d'amour et de bonheur, j'ai rencontré Diouldé... Trop beau... Trop beau, trop fragile" (86).

Ce passage présente d'Asta une personnalité optimiste à outrance, bien que la réalité lui rappelle quelquefois les illusions dont elle se nourrit. Une personnalité orientée vers le mieux, le meilleur. Une personnalité que rien ne décourage ni ne détourne de son idéal. Bref une femme forte, consciente de ses moyens, et qui sait exactement ce qu'elle veut et où elle va.

Son analyse de la société actuelle repose sur la notion de mesure. Dans certaines valeurs comme la légendaire solidarité africaine, le *teranga*, elle sait lucidement discerner les bonnes intentions des abus de la démonstration ou de l'indiscrétion. Il existe des communautés villageoises où "personne n'y quémande, personne ne demande l'aumône... (...) Dans ces villages-là chacun travaille, même les handicapés qui n'ont pas perdu l'usage de leurs bras (...) chacun sait qu'on doit les aider. On attend la nuit profonde. (...) Et la vie continue sans gloire pour les uns et sans honte pour les autres" (155).

Dans la conception de la sociologue Asta, l'autre Afrique tant rêvée et ignorée des consommateurs de médias occidentaux pose ses fondements sur de solides principes de dignité, de solidarité et de respect. Sans forcément partager les théories marxistes, elle constate avec une certaine amertume que les Occidentaux, dans leur condescendance, ont réussi à faire croire que "nous ne sommes capables de rien." Logique qui légitime les droits du dominateur ou du colonisateur sur le dominé ou le colonisé! Le rôle du sociologue ne consiste-t-il pas d'abord à observer le phénomène social en termes objectifs avant d'esquisser des pistes de solutions? Selon Asta Diop l'Afrique, forte de son expérience séculaire, porte en elle-même les piliers de son développement social et économique. Ce qui l'amène à critiquer l'éducation que Diouldé et elle-même ont donnée à Maram et Sira restées en France, loin de leurs racines africaines, ignorantes de la langue sénégalaise, trop libres à ses yeux vis-à-vis des valeurs traditionnelles africaines. Elle ignore complètement la *terre* africaine.

Le culte de la terre culmine avec la réalisation du projet de *Naatangué*. C'est un rêve qu'elle a couvé pendant longtemps, comme elle l'annonce à son amie: "Anne, tu n'es même pas capable de deviner ! Depuis six mois je te dis que je cherche un terrain à la campagne pour en faire un jardin. C'était un rêve, une obsession. Eh bien, ma chère, j'ai mon terrain" (187). Cette satisfaction d'un désir longtemps porté en elle la comble de joie, comme si elle prenait sa vengeance sur toutes les forces qui s'opposent à sa liberté de mouvement et de créativité. Une terre à transformer en un jardin grandiose et salutaire, c'est l'amorce du développement tant espéré. Il est donc temps de concrétiser le dit par des réalisations concrètes, de passer à l'action.

2:2. ANNE LEMAIRE, L'ADJUVANTE

Née de François et Lise Lebeau, Anne éprouve un vrai sentiment d'amitié pour Asta. Elles se sont rencontrées pour la première fois dans un hôpital où elles avaient été retenues pour les soins de leurs fillettes prématurées. Comme par hasard, elles occupaient des lits voisins. La conversation a tout de suite pris l'allure de retrouvailles car Anne avait vécu trois années au Sénégal, précisément à Saint-Louis où elle a étudié à l'Institution Mère Anne-Marie. En effet, avec sa famille continuellement mutée d'un pays à l'autre elle a sillonné presque toutes les colonies françaises d'Afrique. Pendant que son père oeuvrait comme fonctionnaire colonial, sa mère publiait des articles sur les cultures africaines. La relation entre Anne et Asta s'était renforcée au fil des jours bien qu'Anne ait quitté l'hôpital au bout de quatre jours, Désirée la fille d'Anne étant décédée. Asta l'avait consolée et réconfortée autant qu'elle le pouvait. Anne est revenue voir la petite Maram, chargée de cadeaux. "Une belle page venait de s'ouvrir pour une longue amitié. Une amitié vraie qui ignore les barrières – toutes les barrières – et vole au-dessus des calculs intéressés, de petites et grandes mesquineries, des mensonges et des faux – semblants" (165-166).

Depuis, Anne a été de tous les combats de la vie de son amie. Elle l'a soutenue dans toutes les tournures inattendues qu'a prises sa vie. Témoin sympathique du divorce de Dioudé et d'Asta, elle a moralement et psychologiquement soutenu cette dernière. Les procédures légales une fois terminées, elle l'a aidée à traverser la période "vide" qui s'en est suivie et à refaire sa vie dans un délai raisonnable. Au retour d'Asta au Sénégal, elle s'est occupée à encadrer la scolarité des enfants Maram et Sira à Paris. Bref, elle est devenue pour Asta le soutien, la sœur, la confidente, la consolatrice, l'amie de toutes les épreuves. Chaque fois qu'Asta revenait en France, c'est elle qui s'occupait des démarches nécessaires pour l'obtention des visas: certificats d'hébergement, lettres d'invitation. Elle a également rassemblé les papiers pour le dernier voyage d'Asta et se trouvait à l'aéroport pour l'attendre.

Ne l'ayant pas vue, elle a entrepris toutes les démarches nécessaires pour la retrouver, toquant aux portes de la société aérienne, téléphonant à Dakar au bureau d'Asta d'abord, ensuite à son ami Labba. Très émue de savoir son amie en difficultés, elle éprouve de la peine à imaginer Asta au fameux "dépôt," subissant la plus vilaine des humiliations. Elle ne comprend pas qu'une femme aussi distinguée, digne et courtoise qu'Asta venue en mission soit traînée dans la boue, la honte, parmi la bande des clandestins détestés en France, prêts à être expulsés. Volontairement, elle refuse de croire à l'évidence de son arrestation. Elle repart pour l'aéroport, mais la police de frontière ne la laisse pas contacter Asta. Lorsque la nouvelle de la détention de cette dernière à la frontière française se confirme, elle va avec Didier solliciter l'intervention officielle de l'ambassade du Sénégal. Peine perdue ! L'ambassade décline ses responsabilités. Enragée et déçue devant cette fuite en avant, elle s'emporte: "A quoi sert votre ambassade alors, si vous ne pouvez même pas protéger vos ressortissants ! C'est votre rôle de leur porter assistance non !" (77) Primesautière, battante, déterminée, elle retrouve l'énergie de ses années d'études pendant lesquelles elle marchait avec les camarades pour des causes sociales, exhibant des pancartes sur lesquelles étaient écrites leurs revendications. L'arrestation de son amie est un camouflet pour elle, elle se bat jusqu'au bout de ses forces. Signe manifeste de la profondeur de son amitié pour Asta.

Caractère passionné, Anne Lemaire croit en certaines valeurs humaines. Comme Asta, elle est idéaliste, mais une idéaliste doublée de féministe. Le combat de la femme est au centre de ses pensées, car sa dignité n'a pas de prix. "Si j'avais les moyens, j'aurais créé un centre d'entraînement pour apprendre aux femmes non seulement à se défendre mais à marquer leur tortionnaire d'une balafre sur le front afin que tout le monde le reconnaisse" (138). Face à la violence dont les femmes sont victimes, non seulement tous les moyens de défense sont bons, les moyens de défense doivent être également violents, dissuasifs et fermes. Une version agressive d'un féminisme qui ne se contente pas de revendiquer des droits, mais de défendre physiquement "le corps," au besoin par la force. Il faudrait cependant que cette défense soit seulement préventive sinon au titre de représailles. Même idéaliste, Anne demeure pragmatique.

Ses convictions reposent sur des principes que partage également Asta. "Anne y croit. L'amour, la raison et le respect sauveront l'humanité de ses cauchemars" (148). Aux grands idéaux des politiques elle oppose l'amour, la raison et le respect, principes humains par excellence. Ces vertus constituent à ses yeux la clé pour la lutte contre la fracture sociale, la pauvreté... pour le développement. Et le développement passe par des actions concrètes. Aussi, n'hésitera-t-elle pas à soutenir Asta dans la réalisation de son rêve en lui fournissant des essences: "Ils avaient aussi planté les espèces qu'Anne avait envoyées en grande quantité, pas au hasard, mais selon les renseignements puisés dans des encyclopédies (...)" (216). Dans le contexte des relations qui unissent ces deux amies, une telle contribution comporte sans aucun doute des connotations émotionnelles et symboliques très fortes.

Dans cette amitié entre Anne et Asta règne une solide foi mutuelle: "Asta elle-même, en chair et en os; entière, ni brisée, ni fichue, ni foutue [...] Son rêve [...] je suis sûre qu'elle le réalisera" (189). Ou plus loin, lorsqu'elle formule ses adieux: "Je reviendrai pour ton amitié, ton courage, ta dignité [...]" (199). Admiration mutuelle et respect caractérisent cette amitié qui ouvre, toujours, des chemins d'espoir, de retrouvailles. Car au-delà de cette relation, il y a deux femmes: une Française et une Sénégalaise.

2.3. LES MÈRES: LISE LEBEAU, MAME FANTA ET DABA SANGHARÉ

L'adage "Telle mère, telle fille" ne s'appliquerait qu'aux deux premières. Sans pousser la ressemblance jusqu'au bout, il paraît utile de circonscrire l'importante contribution des mères dans *Douceurs du bercail*. Bien que Daba Sangharé soit liée à son fils Yakham, ce personnage apporte un éclairage supplémentaire à cette section.

Lise Lebeau, la mère d'Anne, est une femme érudite qui utilise son séjour africain pour se cultiver, faire des recherches sur les peuples et les cultures d'Afrique. Les nombreux déplacements de sa famille à travers les colonies françaises l'ont suffisamment outillée pour écrire des articles pertinents sur l'Afrique. Un titre du genre "Saint-Louis ville de beauté et de *téranga*" publié dans un grand journal est assez révélateur de son talent et de ses intentions. Elle cherche à briser les barrières d'incompréhension entre les peuples. Elle a appris à sa fille à voir autrement le monde, à concevoir autrement les choses. Elle lui a communiqué la passion des Africains et de leurs cultures. Outre le savoir et la curiosité, elle lui a légué une bibliothèque dans laquelle Anne trouvera les espèces qui seront plantées à *Naatangué*.

Mame Fanta, bien que son rôle soit discret, est un personnage important dans la vie de sa fille. Ayant développé avec elle une relation de sincère intimité, elle l'a éduquée dans les lois sacrées de la tradition. Réaliste et dotée d'un jugement équilibré, elle la met en garde contre son footballeur de fiancé: "Avec le baccalauréat en poche, tu vas épouser un footballeur ! Ce garçon pas plus haut que trois calebasses superposées [...] Asta, la vie n'est pas un rêve ! [...] Le mariage, c'est du sérieux" (174). Quoique non lettrée, elle est fière de l'avantage de sa maturité sur la jeunesse: "Vous les jeunes, vous croyez que nous sommes dépassés [...] Nous savons regarder la vie mieux que vous" (175). Elle participe à tous les combats de sa fille. Sa présence à *Naatangué* est très efficace: non seulement elle négocie les relations de bon voisinage avec les douze chefs de village de la région en offrant les symboles exigés par la coutume, elle invoque également la bienveillance de la "grande dame invisible du fleuve" sur *Naatangué*. Car c'est elle, et non pas Asta l'intellectuelle, qui connaît les règles de ces négociations et les prières incantatoires utiles. Selon toute apparence, Asta n'y a pas été initiée. En outre, elle maîtrise la technique de la teinture et de la vannerie.

Daba Sangharé, la mère de Yakham est un personnage fascinant. Mère de famille, travailleuse, battante, forte, elle a pleine confiance en son fils Yakham. Résolue à ne jamais céder à la résignation ni au découragement, elle affiche sa détermination sans ambages: "(...) tant qu'il y aura du muscle dans mes bras et de la force dans mes mains, je roulerai mon couscous et nous vivrons sans rien devoir à quiconque" (114). Fière, esprit travailleur qui refuse la facilité, la femme de Gora Cissé est naturellement courageuse, intrépide, elle se montre également imperturbable devant l'adversité. Elle insuffle un caractère de battant à Yakham, lui inculque le sens de la persévérance et du sacrifice: "*Un enfant qui pleure ne sera pas un homme*" (112) ou plus loin: "*arme-toi de ton jom et de ton fayda*" (dignité et force de caractère; 113). Lorsqu'elle perd sa main droite et qu'elle est presque condamnée, elle défend à son fils Yakham de ne jamais céder à la fatalité. Lorsque son fils, après avoir échoué en médecine, manifeste le désir de se rendre en Europe, elle n'hésite pas, quoique cela lui brise le cœur, à se séparer de ses trois précieux bijoux pour les frais du visa et à s'endetter pour l'achat du

ticket: "[...] les biens, mon Dieu, c'est pour sauver l'honneur" (121).
Ce qui démontre un détachement vis-à-vis des biens matériels, et surtout
un sens poussé de l'honneur.

2.4. Autres personnages féminins: Codé, Faballa, la vieille femme de Bakhna

Douceurs du bercail présente d'autres portraits de la femme en
fonction des circonstances. On peut aisément distinguer: la policière
française, Codé la femme qui s'accommode des revers de l'immigration,
les secrétaires indifférentes de la bureaucratie sénégalaise, Caline et
Faballa les filles mères aux mœurs douteuses, Wouri la femme
extrovertie de la société sénégalaise, ainsi que la vieille femme de
Bakhna.

La douanière française spécialement chargée du contrôle des
femmes est celle par qui le malheur d'Asta est arrivé. De tortionnaire à
la main gantée, elle est en l'espace de quelques instants devenue la
célèbre victime agressée dans l'exercice de ses fonctions et
unanimement défendue par la presse, la radio et l'opinion. La femme
agent de police a été étranglée par Asta parce qu'elle a osé fouiller son
corps de façon indécente: "Asta réalise qu'une main insolente bifurque
et cherche à forcer un passage fermé. Asta serre les jambes. La main
insiste; elle a de la vigueur et, sûrement, de l'expérience. Asta ne veut
pas être vaincue. Elle sursaute. "Jamais!" se dit-elle. Une rage bestiale
la saisit" (27). Plutôt que de relever l'abus, les médias racistes et
xénophobes insisteront aveuglément sur la violence de l'Africaine, sans
se préoccuper des raisons qui ont poussé celle-ci à commettre ce
"crime." La tortionnaire étant devenue la victime, Asta est arrêtée,
séquestrée et mise au "dépôt" avant d'être ignominieusement expulsée
vers son Sénégal natal sans être entendue d'aucune instance judiciaire.

La grosse Sénégalaise Codé donne l'air d'être une habituée des
cales de la police des frontières. Optant de survivre à tout prix à ces
traitements inhumains imposés aux candidats à l'immigration, Codé
s'adapte aisément à sa nouvelle situation. A Asta dépitée qui refuse de
manger, elle manifeste sa méprise pour la police française de frontière:
"Ces gens sans cœur ne méritent pas que tu te prives de l'essentiel. Tu
n'as pas faim, peut-être, ton corps en a besoin [...]" (44). A son avis,
toutes les souffrances et humiliations qu'endurent les étrangers sont
dues aux "caprices de Blancs qui maintenant nous chassent comme
des malpropres alors qu'ils déambulent chez nous à leur aise" (45). En

d'autres mots, les Blancs ne respectent pas les Noirs et ne leur rendent pas la réciprocité de l'accueil qu'ils reçoivent en Afrique. Elle dénonce par ces paroles l'injustice, l'inégalité de traitement et le manque de respect institutionnalisés vis-à-vis des Africains.

Que ce soit au bureau où travaille Asta, que ce soit à l'ambassade à Paris, les secrétaires de la bureaucratie sénégalaise représentent "le laxisme et la paresse considérés par elle [Asta] comme des maladies mortelles du continent" (59). C'est à peine que le problème du voyage d'Asta est pris au sérieux par la prétendue secrétaire du Patron, davantage préoccupée à commander sa bouteille de coca et des cacahuètes. Celle de l'ambassade n'est pas mieux. L'incompétence, l'indifférence et l'inefficacité dont font montre toutes ces dames élégantes et modernes, sont ahurissantes, déboussolantes.

Caline et Faballa représentent la catégorie des filles-mères réputées aux mœurs douteuses. La "fofolle" Française de dix-huit ans a eu une aventure rocambolesque: "éméchée au sortir d'une boîte de nuit, elle avait laissé faire une bande de jeunes gens, sur le banc d'un jardin public et avait ainsi 'ramassé' une grossesse; elle avait voulu la garder pour voir comment c'était d'être maman, puisque elle-même n'avait jamais connu sa mère qui l'avait abandonnée sur le parvis d'une église" (157). La légèreté de l'expression donne, de toute évidence, la mesure de l'irresponsabilité de sa locutrice alcoolique et clocharde. Quant à Faballa, elle est la sœur de Yakham, fille de Saba Dangharé. Le bilan de sa débauche est parlant, ainsi que s'en exclame Daba: "Trois enfants *sans père* n'est pas une double calamité. Le pire est qu'elle s'en fout [...] c'est à croire qu'elle a perdu la tête" (109). Mère sans ressources, elle vit aux crochets de ses parents, dans la concession familiale. En plus de la femme aux petites vertus, Faballa incarne un esprit rebelle, une chipie insouciante, insolente qui déteste viscéralement son frère Yakham, le préféré de la famille.

Au Sénégal de la fête où tout se célèbre, Wouri la sœur de Dianor représente la femme extrovertie de la société urbaine. "Plus il y a la misère, plus on festoie" (92) [...] "mais des fois on organise deux baptêmes ou trois pour le même bébé [...] On fête même l'échec des gosses à l'examen" (93). Ne pouvant supporter que le fils de la voisine pauvre ait réussi alors que le sien soigné aux dernières griffes de la mode vestimentaire a échoué, "Wouri a tout simplement organisé un festin monstre pour permettre à l'heureux fiston de dire au revoir à ses camarades et copines. Et le clou de tout cela [...]: une attestation d'inscription dans une célèbre université polonaise [...]" (94).

Impressionniste à outrance, Wouri est de la race des femmes que le prestige, le goût du luxe et l'argent enivrent. Comportement typique du tiers-monde où le paraître compte plus que l'être.

La vieille femme Dondé Amari est en quelque sorte l'ange salvateur de *Naatangué*. Pendant que les démarches pour l'obtention du crédit s'enlisaient et qu'un certain désespoir se pointait sur les visages des pensionnaires de la ferme, la vieille a été surprise en train d'arracher des arbustes de la concession. A son cou pendait un collier en *guewê*. Les *guewê* sont des boules qui se ramassent au bord des fleuves et dont on prépare de "décoctions aux vertus aphrodisiaques" insolentes. Méprisant Yakham, elle se comporte en maîtresse du terrain car elle en connaît les secrets. Personnage sorti d'un autre temps et surgi de nulle part, cette vieille en haillons pourrait être assimilée à la déesse du fleuve. C'est le berger Doro qui l'apprivoise grâce à un chant merveilleux, un hymne qui la ramène à des sentiments plus conciliants. Daba ayant confirmé la valeur de cette découverte, *Naatangué* va désormais exploiter cette manne tombée du ciel tant prisée par les femmes des villes.

2.5. Les hommes: Didier, Yakham, Dianor, Doro, Paapi

Le mari d'Anne est un homme aux grandes qualités. Didier Lemaire soutient entièrement sa femme dans son entreprise de sauver l'honneur d'Asta. Partageant beaucoup d'idées de sa femme concernant les Africains, il est proche de sa femme, l'assiste de ses conseils et avis, discute de tous les détails de ce que celle-ci entend entreprendre. L'entente et la cordialité sont parfaites entre les deux époux.

Yakham dont le nom signifie savant était voué à réussir dans la vie. Elève brillant, il vit sa bourse d'études pour la France détournée par les agents du gouvernement au profit d'un autre moins méritant. Une année de cours en médecine suffit pour brûler ses ambitions intellectuelles. Prenant conscience de sa responsabilité familiale, il a décidé d'émigrer en Europe pour travailler. Daba Sangharé a donné ses trois bijoux d'héritage et s'est endettée pour couvrir les frais du visa et du voyage. Malheureusement, les choses ne se sont pas déroulées de façon heureuse en dépit de quelques colis qu'il leur a expédiés. C'est au "dépôt" qu'il s'est joint au groupe formé d'Asta, Codé, Sega et Dianor.

Dianor, instituteur devenu par la force des choses musicien, est l'amuseur du groupe. Artiste talentueux, il compose des chansons sur la vie quand l'inspiration lui vient à la rescousse. Poète et animateur original, il contribuera énormément à l'érection de *Naatangué*. On lui doit notamment la trouvaille du titre du roman: *Douceurs du bercail*. Personnage droit et fidèle, il est un travailleur bien élevé, critique et lucide.

Doro incarne le registre pastoral dans le roman. Berger de son état, il s'est aventuré en ville où, faute d'instruction, il n'a pu travailler que comme veilleur de nuit dans une propriété privée. Mis en prison à la suite d'un cambriolage dans la maison dont il avait la charge, il s'est résolu de revenir à Bakhna pour jouir d'une vie calme et paisible. Ce retour au bercail illustre une des conséquences directes de l'exode rural qui, pendant des années, a vidé les villages de leur population active. Un problème contre lequel Asta lutte avec acharnement. Homme du pays, berger élevé dans cet univers pittoresque, Doro connaît les vallons et les secrets du fleuve; il maîtrise les us et coutumes du terroir. Au projet de *Naatangué*, il sert de boîte de résonance des indigènes de la région.

Le petit Paapi, le "fils à maman," ne joue qu'un rôle secondaire. Il est évoqué dans tous les propos d'Asta et Anne; il est membre à part entière du projet *Naatangué*. Contrairement à ses sœurs Maram et Sira, il vit et étudie au Sénégal; et par-dessus tout l'enfant adoré de sa mère est initié aux traditions indigènes.

Le récit de *Douceurs du bercail* fait briller la personnalité d'Asta au contact de tous les autres personnages. Ce n'est pas seulement Anne qui lui voue une profonde admiration, mais tous ceux qui l'ont approchée au "dépôt." Femme de vertu et d'honneur, elle inspire une maturité puisée aussi bien dans son éducation scolaire que de son acquis familial. Le retour à la terre inaugure un nouvel espoir, un tournant décisif dans sa vie. Asta, qui avait juré à Anne qu'elle ne se marierait plus jamais, va finalement renouer avec le bonheur conjugal en épousant Balou lorsque le florissant *Naatangué* devient pleinement rentable.

3. UN HYMNE PASTORAL À LA TERRE-MÈRE

Douceurs du bercail, c'est l'histoire d'une amitié entre deux femmes et leurs familles. Les couples Anne-Didier et Asta-Dioulé partagent assurément une complicité qui sera brisée avec le divorce des deux Africains. Mais c'est plutôt Anne et Asta qui sont les plus concernées dans cette relation qui transcende les différences raciales, culturelles et toutes sortes de préjugés vis-à-vis de l'Autre. Une amitié qui traverse bien des épreuves. De quoi contredire un adage masculinisant qui prétend que "les femmes ne construisent jamais seules un village" et le pessimisme antiféministe qu'il véhicule.

Récit d'une coopération, récit d'une coopérative. De Paris à Bakhna, du "dépôt" à *Naatangué*, c'est le parcours d'une fidélité sans failles, la concrétisation finale d'une coopération de plusieurs mains. Un champ est défriché pour la culture des plantes dont les racines s'ancreront dans le sein de la terre où l'accueil de l'étranger et la solidarité entre les gens constituent des valeurs plutôt que des mots vides. Ce jardin rappelle par bien des points l'optimisme et la tolérance que présente Voltaire dans *Candide*. Non seulement que Candide demeure pareillement fidèle à sa Cunégonde en toutes circonstances, mais surtout qu'ils acquièrent un domaine pour y cultiver des denrées alimentaires: "Cela est bien dit," répondit Candide, "mais il faut cultiver notre jardin" (Voltaire 2002: 189). La phrase finale du conte philosophique de Voltaire est réellement vécue à *Naatangué*.

La différence avec Candide est que l'initiative de ce jardin revient à Asta, une femme mûre, non aventurière, mais éclairée par le seul espoir d'une vie meilleure fondée sur une entière confiance en la terre. *Naatangué* accomplit le rêve libérateur et stimulant d'une femme décidée à jouir des merveilles de sa terre natale. A travers chaque coup de houe dans la terre, à travers chaque bourgeon qui germe du sol, s'écrit en lettres de sueur un hymne poétique à la terre mère. Un jardin, c'est le lieu mystique de la création végétale où l'homme collabore étroitement au dessein divin de renouveler continuellement le monde. *Naatangué* incarne la mystique symbolique de la femme en tant que protectrice et conservatrice de la race humaine. Le jardin, du fait qu'il relève de la créativité de l'homme, refait un lien archétypal brisé depuis des temps immémoriaux. Teinture, vannerie, poterie, élevage, cueillette du *guewê*, maraîchage, cultures de rente, tissage, etc., forment la gamme des activités pratiquées à *Naatangué*.

Comme dans le roman pastoral, le bonheur ici consiste dans la contemplation du décor champêtre et dans l'utilisation responsable des ressources de la nature. La culture des espèces minutieusement triées par Anne revêt le sens symbolique d'une intime proximité, d'une renaissance qui dépasse les contingences spatio-temporelles. Anne

Lemaire, même morte, demeure de façon permanente présente à *Naatangué*. Car on ne le dira jamais assez: "La terre ne ment pas" (214).

CONCLUSION

Le roman *Douceurs du bercail* pourrait se prêter à plusieurs interprétations. Alors que les féministes y verraient le triomphe unilatéral de la femme combattante, les linguistes un terrain pour une fructueuse investigation sur les fonctions argumentatives des expressions proverbiales ou sentencieuses, l'approche adoptée dans cette étude s'est davantage attachée à la constitution du personnage féminin que présente Aminata Sow Fall. A travers Asta, Anne et les autres personnages féminins moins lumineux, c'est l'image même de la femme qui est livrée, mise en confrontation avec différentes situations. Le dénouement du roman laisse croire que la vision de Sow Fall sur la femme est nettement positive, ouverte sur un avenir meilleur malgré les déconvenues inhérentes à toute entreprise humaine.

Il n'a pas été nécessaire d'exploiter la métaphore de la femme et du fleuve, le mythe de la sirène communément appelée *Mamiwata ou Mamiwater*. Il n'a pas également été question de l'attachement d'Asta à la pratique sorcière, qui n'entrave nullement sa lucidité intellectuelle ni religieuse. L'étude s'est limitée à recoudre les liens souterrains à la mère et à la terre. Le retour à la terre constitue, à plusieurs égards, un refondement symbolique de la renaissance féminine.

Dans ce roman, Aminata Sow Fall touche à différents problèmes actuels que connaît le continent africain – émigration, exil, corruption, pauvreté, fracture sociale, mendicité, éducation, mégestion, sous-développement – à partir du regard et de l'engagement d'Asta, une femme sociologue exemplaire qui livre son expérience de la vie. A l'émigration humiliante vers l'Europe Asta préfère les douceurs du bercail, l'amour du pays et de la terre. A l'aliénation mentale elle oppose une identité autarcique cependant ouverte envers l'Autre: "Aimons notre terre." Une interrogation fondamentale sur le leadership de l'Afrique s'impose. Serait-il insensé de penser que les femmes pourraient réussir là où leurs collègues masculins ont lamentablement échoué?

ŒUVRES CITÉES

Aminata Sow Fall. *La grève des Bàttu*. Dakar: Nouvelles Editions Africaines, 1979.

_____. *L'Appel des arènes*. Dakar: Nouvelles Editions Africaines, 1982.

_____. *Douceurs du bercail*. Abidjan: Nouvelles Editions Ivoiriennes, 1998.

Ajala, John D. "Aminata Sow Fall as a Spokeswoman for the Under-privileged." *CLA Journal*, XXXIV, No. 2 (1990): 137-152.

Barthes Roland. "Analyse structurale des récits. *Poétique du récit*. Paris: Seuil, 1977.

Beguin, M et J. Goldzink. Eds. *Voltaire, Candide ou l'optimisme*. Paris: Larousse, 2002.

Cazenave, Odile. "Gender, Age, and Reeducation: A Changing Emphasis in Recent African Novels in French, as Exemplified in *L'Appel des arènes* by Aminata Sow Fall." *Africa Today*. 38.3 (1991): 54-62.

Egonu, I.T.K. "Aminata Sow Fall: A New Generation Female Writer from Senegal." *Neophilologus* 75 (1991): 66-75.

Guèye, Médoune. "La Question du féminisme chez Mariama Bâ et Aminata Sow Fall – L'examen de la typologie du personnage féminine chez Mariama Bâ et Aminata Sow Fall." *The French Review* 72. 2 (1998): 308.

Martin, Florence. "Echos et grains de voix dans *Le Jujubier du patriarche* d'Aminata Sow Fall." *The French Review* 74.2 (2000): 296.

Ormerod, Beverly et Jean-Marie Volet. "Aminata Sow Fall." *Romancières africaines d'expression française*: le Sud du Sahara. Paris: L'Harmattan, 1994: 133-136.

Stringer, Susan. "Cultural Conflict in the Novels of Two African Writers, Mariama Bâ and Aminata Sow Fall." *Sage. Supplement* (1988): 36-41.

LES CLÉS DU PROJET HUMANISTE

UNE QUESTION DE DIGNITÉ

JEANNE-SARAH DE LARQUIER

❄ ❄ ❄

"Il faudra bien, pourtant, briser les murailles de la culture-prison, il faudra bien, un jour, retourner en Afrique." [It will be necessary, so to speak, to break the culture-prison walls, and someday, it will become important to make a return to Africa] (Sartre, XVII… *Editor's translation*).

EDITOR'S SYNOPSIS

This study on Aminata Sow Fall's sixth novel, *Douceurs du bercail* explores the author's idea of humanism, which recalls Frantz Fanon and L. S. Senghor's ideas about the impertinence of the yearning of young people for the cultural prison of the West. An educated Senegalese woman, Asta Diop, goes to France as a *bona fide* delegate to an international conference on the World Economic Order. Her travel papers are all in order, but that does not save her from immigration woes once she lands at a Parisian airport. A brawl en-

Jeanne-Sarah de Larquier, Ph.D., is currently an assistant professor of French and Francophone literatures and cultures at Central Michigan University, Michigan, and has recently accepted a similar position for Fall 2007 at Pacific University, Oregon.

sues when she hits out at the customs female warden who attempts to shove her gloved hands into her vagina to search for some hidden contreband goods. Asta is handcuffed, led away by the border police, and confined in what appears to be a cave in the bowel of the earth, where illegal immigrants from Third World countries await deportation by charter flights to their countries. The critic's view, which coincides with the authorial intention, is that Africans are treated with disrespect in Europe, because they have not learned to respect themselves. Racism, they must learn, often hides behind the cloak of nationalism. Indeed, as Etienne Balibar notes : "The discourses of race and nation are never far apart, if only in form of disavowal: thus the presence of 'immigrants' on French soil is referred to as the cause of an 'anti-French racism.' The oscillation of the vocabulary itself suggests then that, at least in already constituted national states, the organization of nationalism into individual and political movements inevitably has racism underlying it" (1991: 37-67). Africans must stop fooling themselves and must turn back to Africa, discover her beauty and wealth through hard work, and so earn respect from other cultures. Aminata Sow Fall's humanistic project, then, is to valorize Africa and open the eyes of the youth to the folly of thinking that the grass is greener everywhere else but in Africa. Jeanne-Sarah de Larquier employs the arguments of some founding fathers of Negritude, such as Léopold Sédar Senghor and Frantz Fanon, to foster the pertinence of Sow Fallian ideas, and finishes with a recall of Jean-Paul Sartre's vision of interracial friendship and need for transcendence, which are also evident *in Douceurs du bercail*.

❀ ❀ ❀

Tout comme Montaigne thématisait ses *Essais* autour de certaines critiques sociales, avec "Des Cannibales" ou "De l'Institution des enfants," l'œuvre littéraire d'Aminata Sow Fall s'articule autour des problèmes sociaux du Sénégal: l'aliénation par l'argent dans *Le Revenant*, la mendicité et l'hypocrisie dans *La grève des Bàttu*, l'éducation et l'héritage culturel dans *L'Appel des arènes*, la corruption des sphères du pouvoir dans *L'Ex-père de la nation* ou encore le système des castes dans *Le Jujubier du patriarche*. Plus que simple observatrice, Sow Fall a expliqué que les écrivains sub-sahariens avaient le devoir de dénoncer les errances de la société et ne pouvaient encore se targuer de défendre l'art pour l'art.[1] Bien qu'elle ait à maintes reprises défini et revendiqué son rôle comme celui d'une citoyenne, et non pas spécialement d'une féministe, cela n'a pas empêché nombre de critiques de chercher les caractéristiques féministes de son œuvre tout en les opposant à celles plus évidentes de Mariama Bâ. [2] Cependant, avec son sixième roman, *Douceurs du bercail*, il semble qu'analyser le féminisme ou l'antiféminisme d'Aminata Sow Fall soit bien réducteur et que son œuvre s'attache à chanter un humanisme plus fédérateur. Ce roman qui commence avec le cauchemar que vivent les immigrés refoulés à la douane ou reconduits à la frontière n'est-il pas une ode à la dignité humaine, et un cri d'alarme pour la jeunesse du continent noir que l'Occident éblouit? Sow Fall ne signe-t-elle pas ici un formidable projet humaniste voué à redonner aux siens foi en la terre africaine? Bien que le peu de commentaires consacrés à ce sixième roman nous oblige tout d'abord à une étude textuelle, explorer les idées des pères fondateurs de la Négritude explicitera le roman sowfallien. En plus d'illustrer le complexe d'infériorité noir identifié dans *Peau noire, masques blancs*, en dénonçant la jeunesse africaine aveuglément fascinée par la France, l'auteur semble vouloir rappeler à ces nouvelles générations la pertinence actuelle de certains idéaux passés: l'analyse et le rejet de la culture-prison projetée par l'Occident, la fierté en la spécificité de la culture noire chantée par Senghor, mais aussi le besoin de transcendance et d'amitié entre les races signalé par Sartre. Ces critiques tendent tous à annoncer le retour en Afrique prôné par Sow Fall.

Si dans ce roman comme dans les précédents, Sow Fall se fait critique sociale, c'est qu'elle a à cœur de défendre des valeurs trop souvent oubliées, aussi confie-t-elle dans une entrevue avec Nicole Aas-Rouxparis que "La valeur principale, c'est la dignité humaine. Il faut que chaque être soit reconnu dans son intégrité et qu'il soit respecté dans ce qu'il représente. C'est cela que j'appelle la dignité. Je ne dis pas que l'être humain est lui-même l'idéal, mais il est porteur d'idéal" (204). Or, si l'on accepte que Sow Fall défende dans cet opus la dignité, mot dont on trouve plus d'une douzaine d'occurrence dans l'ouvrage, on n'est dès lors pas surpris que l'auteur ait choisi de mettre en exergue des personnages que l'on dépouille de cette qualité. [3] La première moitié du roman décrit ainsi le calvaire d'Asta Diop, une Sénégalaise présentée comme une femme instruite et respectable. Détentrice d'une licence de sociologie et d'un diplôme de journalisme, cette dernière se rend en France pour participer à une conférence sur l'Ordre Economique Mondial. Bien que ses papiers soient en règle, l'étrangère se trouve injustement appréhendée par la Police aux

Frontières avant d'être menée menottes aux poignets au "dépôt" de transit pour tous les reconduits à la frontière en attente de leur charter. Ce lieu, témoin de toutes les exactions, symbolise le processus de déshumanisation auquel de nombreux émigrants sont soumis tandis que leurs espérances se brisent contre l'idéologie suprématiste de l'Occident.

L'écriture de Sow Fall ne manque pas d'étoffer cette déshumanisation au moyen de métaphores animales et de descriptions imagées. En effet, le premier chapitre annonce pas à pas la descente vers le non droit et la progression vers l'horreur. L'arrivée d'Asta à l'aéroport et les formalités d'immigration et de douane dont elle doit s'acquitter sont décrites comme autant de violences à l'encontre de la personne. Ici, c'est Asta qui joue le rôle de focalisateur principal, ce qui ajoute à l'injustice ressentie par le harcèlement que subit une femme exténuée. Le roman débute en soulignant la douleur et la fatigue d'Asta après un vol long et pénible: "L'avion a atterri. (. . .) Malgré ses bras lourdement chargés et ses pieds qui lui font terriblement mal (. . .) elle presse le pas, (. . .). Elle est fatiguée et elle a sommeil" (5). Juste avant le passage à la douane on lit encore "elle marche péniblement, (. . .) elle boitille" (8). Alors que les contrôles — vécus comme un affront à sa personne — se succèdent, on observe un phénomène de déshumanisation très sensible grâce à la métaphore filée d'un animal traqué. La douanière est comparée à "une bête qui piétine sa proie pour mieux l'humilier" (26). Asta est amenée dans "une cage" dans laquelle la fouille au corps qu'on lui impose est assimilée à un viol: "Asta réalise qu'une main insolente bifurque et cherche à forcer un passage fermé. [Elle] resserre les jambes. La main insiste" (27). Spontanément Asta tente de réagir, c'est ainsi qu'"[u]ne rage bestiale la saisit" (27) et que ses mains, comme les "crocs d'un automate, se ferment brusquement sur le cou de [la douanière]" (27). Dans ce lieu d'humiliation, la déshumanisation de la victime automate est accentuée par celle des bourreaux: le douanier est assimilé à une bête, et la douanière n'est qu'une "silhouette" caractérisée uniquement par ses membres: "des mains gantées," "un ongle," "[d]es doigts" (27).

Le refus d'Asta de se laisser soumettre par les attouchements de la douanière, et la violence de sa riposte la conduisent droit au dépôt où elle attend un charter avec les immigrés supposés clandestins. Sow Fall souligne: "L'endroit s'appelle officiellement 'le dépôt'" (39). Or, par définition, un dépôt est un lieu où l'on entrepose des *choses*, des marchandises; ce qui implique que les immigrés ne sont aux yeux des ex-colonisateurs encore que des objets. Yakham, l'un des futurs reconduits, n'hésite pas à faire ironiquement le lien entre son sort et celui de ses ancêtres: "ils avaient mieux: la cale des négriers" (47). Force nous est de constater que le non-respect de ceux que la France a longtemps traités comme des esclaves et des êtres intellectuellement sous-développés se perpétue aux frontières de l'Hexagone. L'auteur contemporain et compatriote de Sow Fall, Ken Bugul, dans son article critique "De la porte du sans retour à la porte du non retour," écrit à l'occasion du cent cinquantième anniversaire de l'abolition de l'esclavage et paru la même année que *Douceurs du bercail*, annonçait déjà ce scandale comme l'une des conséquences directes de l'exploitation historique de l'Afrique par l'Europe:

> Qu'on commence par laisser en paix tous les descendants des victimes qui vivent chez eux [les Occidentaux], qu'ils leur donnent des papiers, des opportunités, des droits comme les autres. Que les tracasseries humiliantes pour l'obtention de visas cessent. Qu'il y ait une libre circulation des biens et des personnes dans le respect et la dignité (30-31).

Le récit de Sow Fall ne fait que renforcer cette vision de l'insupportable choc Nord/Sud qui oppresse encore les Africains.

Face à ce regrettable constat d'hostilité, la grandeur d'âme d'Asta fait contraste. En effet, les valises d'Asta sont chargées d'autant de marques d'hospitalité et de bonté sub-sahariennes; Asta avait bien l'intention de faire plaisir à son amie en apportant un sac "plein à craquer de crevettes séchées, de *bissap*, de *quinquéliba* et d'autres produits sénégalais dont Anne raffole" (8). Hélas, cette initiative se heurte à l'incompréhension du douanier qui ne sait guère apprécier les "jolis poissons gris à fines écailles" (25) enfermés dans le carton d'Asta. Il vaut la peine d'évoquer ici l'ouvrage suivant d'Aminata Sow Fall, *Un grain de vie et d'espérance*, dans lequel elle explique la valeur culturelle et philosophique des plats traditionnels de son pays: "La nourriture est perçue comme un don de Dieu grâce auquel l'espèce vit, se fortifie et se perpétue dans la dignité" (21). Plus loin, dans la section des recettes, le riz au poisson, le *Cebou Dieune*, y est d'ailleurs présenté comme le plat national sénégalais (*Un grain de vie* 134). En apportant avec elle ces mets symboles de générosité, que même l'ambassadeur, apprendra-t-on plus tard, se faisait livrer, Asta ne fait que répondre à la logique culturelle de son peuple qui veut que l'on comble ses hôtes à tout prix. Il n'est pas surprenant par la suite qu'Asta refuse de s'alimenter lorsqu'on amène une pitance de survie aux voyageurs séquestrés. Cette grève de la faim s'explique par l'atteinte à sa dignité, et là encore le septième livre de Sow Fall fait lumière sur ce point: "La dignité est bafouée lorsque l'acte de manger s'accomplit dans les conditions insoutenables que nous offrent les médias dans des zones où la guerre, la pauvreté et la bêtise humaine sévissent et blessent l'humain en plein cœur" (*Un grain de vie* 22). Asta représente alors l'alternative à tout système tyrannique, elle est celle qui n'accepte pas le compromis, fière de sa nation et de ses valeurs. De par sa droiture, le personnage d'Asta fait indéniablement le procès du dépôt où elle se trouve emprisonnée et souligne l'aberration de ce lieu et de ces règles.

Sow Fall, qui a étudié les Lettres Modernes à la Sorbonne avant même de se familiariser avec la littérature africaine, ne peut ignorer le parallèle entre ce lieu et la littérature de l'Absurde qui florissait durant les dernières années de la colonisation, et dont elle se sert ici comme moyen stratégique pour renforcer sa dénonciation des conditions de vie. [4] Ainsi, le dépôt est caractérisé comme un espace introuvable qui échappe à toute cohérence directionnelle puisque Anne Lemaire, l'amie française d'Asta, avait parcouru un véritable labyrinthe pour tenter de trouver cette geôle, en vain: "Cela s'était traduit par un marathon épouvantable entre terminaux, sous-sols, couloirs en spirale et retour au point de départ" (67). Le dépôt y est encore représenté comme un espace intemporel où les captifs ont perdu la notion du temps: "Le jour... ou la nuit? Rien ne permet de le savoir. Il n'y a plus de cycle, plus de jour, plus de nuit. [. . .] Les lignes du temps, brisés. Autant dire le chaos" (83). Dans cet enfer égaré qui semble défier le temps, un personnage quasi-fantôme, introduit comme un certain "quelqu'un," ébauche un pastiche de la fameuse pièce de théâtre, *En Attendant Godot*, écrite par Samuel Beckett, l'un des maîtres de l'absurde:

En attendant Godot, dodo, dodo
A l'escale Godot, que c'est bon dodo
En attendant Godot, dodo, dodo
C'est bon c'est beau c'est nice dodo
On peut bien penser au pays, dodo
Avec l'espoir qui fout le camp, dodo
Et les petites nanas qui racolent, racolent, dodo
Et les *paa* qui rasent les murs qui s'effritent dodo. (50)

Cet appel à l'intertextualité affine subtilement l'ambiance insoutenable parmi les voyageurs traqués. Avec cette appartée beckettienne Sow

Fall incite le lecteur à se remémorer ces autres textes du canon littéraire qui ont cerné le caractère interminable et oppressant de l'attente, nommément *Huis-Clos* de Jean-Paul Sartre, *Le Désert des Tartares* de Dino Bizzato, *Le Procès* de Franz Kafka, ou encore du côté de la littérature africaine: *Le Vieux nègre et la médaille* de Ferdinand Oyono, *La Carte d'identité* de Jean-Marie Adiaffi et parmi tant d'autres, *Tu t'appelleras Tanga* de Calixthe Beyala. Notons que la principale caractéristique tangible du dépôt réside dans son éclairage aveuglant abject: "l'insolente lumière blanche des projecteurs" (40), "la lumière blanche qui semblait la [Asta] traquer" (44), "l'omniprésence de cette lumière blanche qui frappe" (83), les "faisceaux impitoyables des projecteurs" (84), "la terrible inquisition des projecteurs" (85). Outre la brutalité de l'éclairage, l'invraisemblance du lieu et la perte de la notion du temps déshumanisent et angoissent les innocents. La récurrence de la question "quand" (43, 50, 51, 52, 84, 107) dramatise l'attente et rajoute à l'insupportable. Les faits, comble de l'inhumain, comportent une certaine réminiscence de la Shoah: tous ces personnages éreintés, traqués sont en attente d'un "convoi" (107), "dans une inconfortable promiscuité" (107), alors qu'on leur vaporise "un gaz parfumé" (107). Ces conditions de détentions atteignent leur paroxysme avec le viol de deux des détenues, alors que les lumières s'étaient enfin éteintes pour calmer les esprits échauffés par une bagarre.

Ce drame et cette révélation des horreurs que le vieux continent inflige à tous ceux qu'il identifie comme des ennemis ou des indésirables est plus que jamais d'actualité. En même temps qu'elle s'enorgueillit toujours d'avoir été le berceau des droits de l'homme, la France ferme de plus en plus ses frontières à ceux qu'elle a un jour appelés à sa reconstruction. L'actualité du début du XXIe siècle en France, avec la montée de l'extrême droite aux élections présidentielles et le durcissement des lois sur l'immigration sous la politique sécuritaire de Nicolas Sarkozy a plus que jamais marqué la volonté de distance de la France vis-à-vis du Tiers-Monde. Un article du *Monde* daté du 29 mars 2003 illustre parfaitement le décalage dénoncé par Sow Fall entre le discours officiel des démocraties et les conditions honteuses de son application. Afin d'enrayer les accusations de brutalité lors des expulsions, la Police aux Frontières avait filmé ses interventions, et ce sont ces vidéos que l'article décrit, retenant davantage le tragique de la situation que le manque de brutalités. Le directeur adjoint de la Police aux Frontières aurait déclaré aux immigrés: "La loi de la République dit que quelqu'un qui est arrivé en situation irrégulière en France doit être reconduit dans son pays de départ. Si vous acceptez, il n'y aura pas de problème. Sinon on sera obligés d'utiliser la force. On ne le souhaite pas car on veut vous reconduire dignement." Néanmoins, le journaliste poursuit en décrivant la réalité des fouilles et des humiliations: "'Le jean, c'est pareil, vous l'enlevez'; s'énerve une voix" (Zappi, *Le Monde* 20). La Déclaration Universelle des Droits de l'Homme, modèle pour toutes les démocraties, interdit pourtant la torture et la détention arbitraire: "Article 5: Nul ne sera soumis à la torture, ni à des peines ou traitements cruels, inhumains ou dégradants. (. . .). Article 9: Nul ne peut être arbitrairement arrêté, détenu ni exilé" (Déclaration Universelle des Droits de l'Homme).

En dépit de ces textes, les conditions de vie des futurs expulsés persistent et ces dernières ne sont pas sans rappeler les techniques de soumission découvertes récemment dans les prisons aux mains des Américains: l'interdiction de se coucher que prononcent les gardiens, accentuée par la lumière permanente, équivaut à une forme de torture par privation de sommeil: "C'est pas un dortoir, attendez l'avion ou lorsque vous serez chez vous!" (*Douceurs* 40). De même, la complète ignorance dans laquelle sont laissés les détenus quant à la date de leur libération/expulsion prend une nouvelle dimension quand on songe aux conditions de détention des prisonniers de Guantanamo, retenus sans connaître la date d'un éventuel procès ou d'une possible libération. L'humiliation préalable et l'impunité dans laquelle les deux viols sont commis noircissent encore le tableau de ces zones de non droit qui discréditent les puissances occidentales. La présence d'Asta, dont la narratrice omnisciente rappelle qu'elle était en règle, démontre avec théâtralité les failles de ce système qui prive la personne de sa dignité. La pertinence de ce tableau se vérifie avec les événements récents qui ont ajouté au choc Nord/Sud un nouveau clivage Occident/Orient et imposé à des foules grandissantes le traitement suspicieux et humiliant décrit par Sow Fall. C'est en dénonçant ces moments où l'Homme est piétiné que l'auteur dépasse le romanesque et touche à la réalité contemporaine, mettant en lumière le besoin de revenir plus que jamais à des valeurs universelles de respect et de dignité.

Après la description des faits, Sow Fall crée un espace de réflexion dialectique sur l'immigration en France et l'avenir de l'Afrique. On perçoit notamment à plusieurs reprises ce qui doit être lu comme le discours officiel de la France, qui se présente comme un pays en crise ne pouvant plus absorber le flot des immigrés—"la fracture sociale... l'avenir bouché des générations actuelles... la peste des temps modernes qu'est la pauvreté..." (148) — alors même qu'il définit l'Afrique comme un continent perdu: "Des maladies, des catastrophes, de la pauvreté..." (185) où les jeunes n'ont d'avenir que s'ils parviennent à rejoindre l'Occident. Ce point de vue officiel, manichéen et biaisé, participe des stéréotypes et du complexe de supériorité des Blancs. Les écrits de la presse trahissent particulièrement ce rapport de force. Tel est l'intérêt pour notre lecture des articles de journaux que Sow Fall inscrit dans son texte et dont voici un exemple: "Immigration: un drame évité de justesse. Une Sénégalaise du nom de Asta Diobe [sic] a failli étrangler une douanière au cours d'un simple contrôle de routine à l'aéroport. Les jours de la victime ne sont plus en danger. L'intéressée est actuellement entre les mains de la police des frontières" (53). L'écriture journalistique apparaît alors lapidaire et hautement euphémistique. Le "simple contrôle de routine" élude le quasi-viol de la fouille au corps humiliante que doivent subir les voyageurs suspects du simple fait de leur nationalité. La "victime" était en fait le bourreau du réel "drame" qui s'est joué ce jour, à savoir le bafouement de la dignité humaine. On dénie même à Asta son identité en écorchant son nom, Diop, en Diobe. La suprématie Occidentale institutionnalise de cette façon la phobie des immigrés et la partialité des médias, responsables en grande partie du conditionnement mental qui identifie les Noirs à de potentiels clandestins violents et désespérés.

Face au discours manipulateur des ex-colonisateurs, l'histoire de *Douceurs du bercail* atteste qu'il rôde dans le discours officiel des représentations racistes qui perpétuent l'incapacité de l'Africain à croire en lui-même. Fanon avait synthétisé ce drame des ex-colonies en une phrase: "S[i le Noir] se sent à ce point submergé par le désir d'être blanc, c'est qu'il vit dans une société qui rend possible son complexe d'infériorité, dans une société qui tire sa consistance du maintien de ce complexe, dans une société qui affirme la supériorité d'une race" (80). Or Sow Fall a bien compris la nécessité d'enrayer l'hémorragie d'une jeunesse sub-saharienne qui ne jure que par les lumières du Nord et son roman se fait le révélateur de cette réalité sociologique en permettant de nombreux glissements de texte entre le discours officiel et le discours de certains Africains. Par moments l'énonciateur devient flou, et l'on oublie qui parle: la propagande ou les personnages? L'exemple le plus flagrant est sans doute l'évocation de la rumeur qui enfle au Sénégal après l'annonce à la radio de l'arrestation d'Asta: "ce qui est sûr, c'est que les Blancs ne font rien pour rien; s'ils ont coincé quelqu'un que son pays a envoyé en mission, c'est qu'il y a quelque chose. Ils connaissent les règles de la diplomatie! [. . .] En tout cas cette femme là n'honore pas son pays..." (65-66). Les Noirs sont donc présentés comme ayant une foi aveugle en la justice blanche. Et pourquoi ne l'auraient-ils pas? L'Europe s'est construit une vitrine de textes et de déclarations pour glorifier la droiture de sa justice. Sow Fall a même étendu sa critique sociale au volet économique du racisme dans le passage proleptique où Asta discute dans l'avion avec des reconduits à la frontière. Ils lui expliquent pourquoi ils étaient venus en France, sûrs que le Sénégal n'avait rien à leur offrir: "Rien, ça veut dire: rien pour vivre à l'aise... quoi; acheter les belles choses qu'y a là-bas à foison... quoi. Les habits, la nourriture..." (10). Le capitalisme a su exporter sa propagande implacable. Sow Fall développe par la suite les observations de Fanon en les appliquant à l'économie locale du Sénégal. Le commerçant de *Naatangué*, le jardin idéal d'Asta, rappelle cyniquement que les populations ne reconnaissent de valeur qu'aux produits exotiques en reniant la richesse de leurs propres cultures: "Il savait à quel point, dans le pays, on sous-estime les produits locaux, raffolant de tout ce qui vient de l'extérieur, dénotant ainsi—c'est terrible!—un esprit d'incapacité, de résignation et de négation de soi-même" (*Douceurs* 215). L'histoire contée par Sow Fall confirme que le drame du monde noir n'a pas diminué malgré les cinq décennies écoulées depuis l'ouvrage de Fanon.

Toutefois, par le biais d'une polyphonie narrative, Sow Fall crée un espace de réflexion dialectique sur l'immigration en France et l'avenir de l'Afrique, où les réponses d'Asta et d'Anne vont apparaître merveilleusement lumineuses. Il faut donc s'interroger sur la fonction de cette polyphonie et de ces enchevêtrements de discours. Ne cachent-ils qu'une évaluation diagnostique de la situation ou pourrait-on y voir également une valeur maïeutique qui inciterait à une réflexion personnelle de chaque lecteur, obligé de se situer sur l'échelle des discours possibles. La réaction d'une future rapatriée qui approuve la destruction par les autorités d'un foyer pour immigrés demande analyse: "'Ils ont eu raison! Ils ont eu raison de ra-a-aser le Quartier de la Gare. C'était devenu de la merde! Insupportable pour tous, pour nous aussi [. . .]. Reconnaissez qu'y a des manières de nous faire du tort à nous tous! (. . .). Les racistes, c'est des choses comme le Quartier de la Gare qui leur donnent force et ..." (130). A priori, on ne sait que penser de ces mots prononcés par une femme qui est extérieure au groupe formé autour d'Asta, qui n'a pas de crédibilité établie, et à qui Sow Fall semble couper la parole par le biais de points de suspension. Toutefois, il faut lire ce passage comme un exemple supplémentaire du racisme intériorisé par les Noirs. Il faut également se questionner sur la portée de cet argument, sur un appel à l'intégration et à la discrétion des populations récemment immigrées. Les faits sociologiques donnent raison à cette femme, puisque le Front National enregistre toujours en France ses meilleurs scores dans les quartiers défavorisés où la proportion d'immigrés est la plus forte. Les extrêmes appellent les extrêmes. C'est ainsi à un débat ouvert que cet entremêlement des discours racistes appelle, alors que l'auteur amorce une nouvelle piste de réflexion avec la réponse virulente de Séga: "Est-ce un crime d'aller vers là où pointe l'espoir quand tout semble foutu chez nous? N'avons-nous pas le droit d'exister!... Est-ce un destin de se voir chassé, traqué, écrasé comme nous le sommes à présent!" (130). Les dialogues entre les futurs expulsés qui déroulent leurs histoires et se livrent à la critique sociale rappellent encore une fois le huis clos de Sartre où, comme au dépôt, l'enfermement intemporel prêtait aux leçons de philosophies.

De par cette abondance de dialogues, le roman de Sow Fall dépasse la dimension romanesque et propose un questionnement humaniste maïeutique semblable à ceux des philosophes antiques. En superposant les points de vue officiels, racistes ou modérés, l'auteur invite le lecteur à s'interroger quant à la question de l'immigration en Europe et au retard de développement du Sénégal. Le constat de Ken Bugul, selon laquelle les liens de causalité entre la pauvreté de l'Afrique et la richesse de l'Occident sont hypocritement passés sous silence, est en permanence sous-jacent aux enjeux de ce nouvel humanisme:

> Il faut dire et expliquer aux nouvelles générations que si les Occidentaux sont bien aujourd'hui c'était en partie grâce à la traite des Noirs, si certains se targuent d'être la première puissance du monde c'était en partie grâce à la traite des Noirs, que si l'Afrique est aujourd'hui si pauvre c'est en partie à cause de la traite des Noirs et de la colonisation. (1988: 29)

Asta et Anne, les deux focalisatrices internes, seront alors détentrices du message de retour aux valeurs nobles et génératrices de l'appel au respect et à la dignité. En effet, ce sont bien elles qui se montrent les plus mesurées et les plus généreuses en prônant l'amitié entre les deux blocs Nord/Sud. Par exemple, on assiste à un dialogue entre Anne et Asta sur la nécessité de l'Afrique à trouver en elle-même les moyens de son développement.[5] Au-delà du dialogue, Asta tente de répondre à cette nécessité par ses actes, en mettant en pratique l'idée forte que Sow Fall a confiée dans un entretien avec Cécile Lebon: "*Douceurs du bercail* — le titre le dit — s'articule autour du symbole de la terre. Je veux montrer qu'il ne faut jamais désespérer de la terre, de l'Afrique. Le bonheur est possible en Afrique si l'on recherche la dignité humaine plutôt que l'économique" (68). Or cette réponse par l'action et la terre, ainsi que la réussite de cette entreprise symbolisée par la moisson abondante et festive de *Naatangué*, interpelle par sa proximité avec la conclusion de Fanon dans son analyse du complexe Noir. Après avoir disséqué le discours dominant, noté son influence néfaste sur les Africains, et révélé les rouages racistes des anciens esclavagistes, les ex-colonies n'ont-elles pas le devoir de se construire une existence positive, loin de leur reflet dans les vitrines des anciennes métropoles? Fanon lançait ce cri de rupture: "Il y a de cela longtemps, le Noir a admis la supériorité indiscutable du Blanc, et tous ses efforts tendent à réaliser une existence blanche. N'ai-je donc pas sur cette terre autre chose à faire qu'à venger les Noirs du XVIIe siècle?" (1952 : 85). C'est précisément ce qu'Asta se propose de faire. Refusant d'entrer dans le manichéisme de la France qui l'a rejetée, cette dernière met en pratique son idéal humaniste. Après la négativité et le racisme inhérents à nombre de personnages, Asta et Anne se détachent comme les symboles de la philosophie de Sow Fall, grâce à leur chaleur et à leur ouverture.

La structure du roman elle-même soutient cet humanisme. En effet, la division en chapitres permet d'alterner les points de vue d'Asta et ceux d'Anne. On peut voir dans cet équilibre et cette amitié l'une des valeurs principales de ce projet fédérateur. Les deux protagonistes sont construites en miroir. Elles se répondent l'une à l'autre. Asta est souvent décrite au travers des dires ou pensées d'Anne et inversement. Chacune est garante de la droiture de l'autre. Toutes deux ont un prénom de quatre lettres commençant par la lettre a. Asta, Sénégalaise qui vit un temps en France et Anne, Française qui a passé son adolescence en Afrique, se rencontrent à la maternité parce qu'elles ont fait au même moment un même pari optimiste: celui de donner la vie. Leurs vies privées se répondent étrangement. Anne a perdu son bébé et son frère mais s'épanouit dans un couple idéal, alors qu'Asta a eu trois enfants mais a divorcé d'un mari violent. A la fin du roman, Anne est morte mais son héritage continue à travers son mari. Asta crée un jardin et en dédie à Anne la première moisson. Ce sont des femmes respectables, mais qui passent toutes deux pour folles au moment où elles refusent l'indigne. Toutes deux se révoltent: Asta face à l'humiliation de la douanière et Anne face au refus de l'Ambassade d'aider Asta. Clairement, l'asymétrie disparaît quand on entend leur même amour et leur même foi en l'Afrique.

Immanquablement, c'est dans le discours généreux des deux protagonistes principales que l'on devine celui de Sow Fall. Ni Asta ni Anne ne souffre du manichéisme délirant dénoncé par Fanon.[6] L'une blanche, l'autre noire, l'une en France, l'autre au Sénégal, toutes deux se battent pour une idée universelle de justice. On assiste chez Anne à des critiques envers son pays et le capitalisme sauvage qui aliène les populations, et on entend chez Asta des critiques à l'encontre de ses compatriotes qui, trop souvent, font preuve de laxisme et de paresse. Elles ne sont pas sous l'emprise du discours officiel qui figerait chacune d'elles sur des positions irréconciliables. De plus, chacune se montre néanmoins capable d'apprécier les qualités de sa patrie, comme Anne qui va à la manifestation organisée contre le rapatriement d'Asta et de ses compagnons d'infortune: "'Dieu merci... Mon pays c'est encore cela... Un peuple des grandes causes nobles pour l'honneur de l'Humanité...'" (150). Asta, elle aussi, scelle le salut de l'Afrique dans ses valeurs traditionnelles: "Quand je sortirai d'ici, je serai plus à l'aise pour dire à mes frères, sœurs, parents et amis, que l'eldorado n'est pas au bout de l'exode mais dans les entrailles de notre terre" (87). En évitant le racisme anti-Blanc, et en présentant par Anne une facette digne de l'Europe qui résiste, Sow Fall réussit à avancer vers ce moment de synthèse dont parle Sartre dans son "Orphée noir," préface à l'*Anthologie de la nouvelle poésie nègre et Malgache* de Senghor:

En fait, la Négritude apparaît comme le temps faible d'une progression dialectique: l'affirmation théorique et pratique de la suprématie du blanc est la thèse; la position de la Négritude comme valeur antithétique est le moment de la négativité. Mais ce moment négatif n'a pas de suffisance par lui-même et les noirs qui en usent le savent fort bien; ils savent qu'il vise à préparer la synthèse ou réalisation de l'humain dans une société sans races. (XLI)

L'amitié de ces deux femmes porte l'espoir d'une nouvelle génération de citoyennes. On peut y voir un parallèle avec le père de Yakham (le compagnon d'Asta au dépôt) qui avait connu pendant la guerre une amitié fraternelle et fusionnelle avec un Blanc. La génération d'Asta, qui a grandi avec la décolonisation et sa Négritude, et qui a bénéficié de possibilités d'études en France, va enfin pouvoir générer un humanisme nouveau à vocation universaliste, et transcender les politiques partisanes post-colonialistes. Le lien entre les deux femmes est la clef de voûte de ce roman: au-delà de la dimension politique qui appelle les Africains à croire en eux-mêmes et à participer au développement de leur pays par la terre et l'effort, se greffe la dimension individuelle qui prône l'amitié entre les peuples et ce sans distinction de race.

De même que Sow Fall refuse de céder au racisme anti-Blanc en chantant les espérances de l'Afrique, elle refuse encore de céder aux stéréotypes dans sa caractérisation des personnages. Sa représentation du Noir évite non seulement l'écueil des clichés occidentaux, mais donne aussi aux personnages une complexité originale et inattendue. En ce sens, Sow Fall accompagne encore la pensée de Fanon "On comprend, après tout ce qui vient d'être dit, que la première réaction du Noir soit de dire non à ceux qui tentent de le définir" (*Peau noire* 29). En refusant le manichéisme et en présentant toujours ses personnages en deux temps, l'archétype puis son antithèse, Sow Fall met l'accent sur le besoin de donner une chance à la personne sans faire le jeu des propagandes hégémoniques.

Dans la galerie des portraits qu'elle dresse, l'auteur déjoue ainsi les stéréotypes et les attentes d'un lecteur potentiellement victime du discours officiel. Presque tous les personnages s'offrent au lecteur sous plusieurs angles. Le personnage principal, Asta, est présenté dès le début comme une femme forte qui refuse l'injustice et se révolte sans crainte face aux représentants de l'aliénation: "Tous ces traitements humiliants parce que vous voyez en chacun de nous un futur immigré! Non Messieurs, vous vous trompez. Moi j'habite chez moi, j'y suis bien et je compte..." (16). Mais on apprend beaucoup plus tard qu'Asta a été une femme battue par un mari tyrannique. Après la vision d'une Asta fière, diplômée, défenseuse de la dignité, ce fait nouveau invite à une réflexion moins binaire de la réalité et à une relecture de tous les archétypes. Il en va de même pour les personnages secondaires, avec Yakham qui se présente comme l'immigré clandestin typique. Il travaillait aux Halles à charger des quartiers de viande, ce qui offre l'image d'un pauvre immigré analphabète. Mais on apprend bientôt que Yakham était un surdoué promis à de brillantes études s'il n'avait été la victime de la corruption qui lui a volé sa bourse d'étude. Quant à la mère d'Asta, que l'on pourrait imaginer attachée aux valeurs traditionnelles, elle se révèle en fait être très moderne puisqu'elle conseille à sa fille de s'assurer une indépendance financière avant de se marier. Enfin, le footballeur Dioulé, l'ex-mari d'Asta est un Dieu des Stades et un héros pour la jeunesse, ce qui ne l'empêche pas de se montrer un homme violent et cruel. La complexité des personnages rend tout manichéisme obsolète. Au lieu de brasser des clichés, Sow Fall crédite ses personnages d'une profondeur psychologique et sociologique qui défie le caractère raciste de l'inconscient collectif.

La déconstruction que Sow Fall fait du déterminisme anti-Noir, dont le discours occidental est empreint, ne se limite toutefois pas aux personnages. Elle s'étend à un projet de développement de l'Afrique, symbolisé par le jardin idéal qu'Asta exploite avec brio dans les derniers chapitres. Alors que la majorité du roman décrit le calvaire des immigrés reconduits en Afrique, entrecoupé de digressions narrant la vie des personnages et dévoilant des pans de la vie africaine, on assiste brutalement à une rupture avec toute misère humaine. Dans les 35 dernières pages, Sow Fall résume neuf ans de la vie d'Asta, alors que la première moitié du roman n'en racontait qu'une semaine. Avec ce temps qui s'accélère, Sow Fall relate la réussite d'Asta dans ce qu'elle appelle son rêve: la création par Asta et ses compagnons du dépôt d'un jardin fertile sur une terre jugée sans valeur par les autorités Sénégalaises.[7] Cette épiphanie digne de *Candide* est d'autant plus forte et positive que la majorité du roman dénonçait la déshumanisation des individus. Ce jardin est-il un nouvel Eden africain? Une abbaye de Thélème où chacun travaille de sa propre volonté? Asta avait déjà exprimé son utopie: "aimons notre terre, nous l'arroserons de notre sueur et la creuserons de toutes nos forces, avec courage. (. . .) Nous ne serons plus des voyageurs sans bagages. Nos mains calleuses en rencontreront d'autres en de chaudes poignées de respect et de dignité partagée..." (88). Or elle y parvient avec ce jardin qui symbolise tout l'espoir que suscite le continent de Senghor. Le titre même du roman porte cet optimisme: il souligne à quel point le terroir est une valeur positive. Dans ce nouvel espace, chacun est à sa place, tout est richesse: on y plante et on y moissonne, on y fait des poteries et des teintures. Le "guewê" (21) qui apporte la prospérité à cette terre est d'ailleurs une culture typiquement africaine puisque "les gens du village connaissaient l'existence de cette plante depuis des millénaires" (214-215), ce qui répond au pessimisme selon lequel les produits locaux sont sans valeur. Les villages alentour participent et bénéficient des fruits de ces efforts collectifs. Asta, qui avait juré ne plus se marier, épouse même Babou, un autre prisonnier des douanes. On peut voir dans cette réalisation économique et cette organisation sociale le meilleur de l'Afrique, décrit par Senghor dans son article "Negritude: A Humanism of the Twentieth Century":

Ethnologists have often praised the unity, the balance, and the harmony of African civilization, of black society, which was based both on the community and the person, and in which, because it was founded on dialogue and reciprocity, the group had priority over the individual without crushing him, but allowing him to blossom as a person. I would like to emphasize at this point how much these characteristics of negritude enable it to find its place in contemporary humanism, thereby permitting black Africa to make its contribution to the "civilization of the universal" which is so necessary in our divided but interdependent world of the second half of the twentieth century. (50)

Tous les personnages à qui l'on a bloqué le passage, loin de retourner se donner en pâture à la France qui les a éconduits, finissent heureux à *Naatangué*. Le jardin représente le vrai message d'espoir de Sow Fall, une sorte de legs dans la lignée de Martin Luther King Jr., une utopie où les qualités de chacun et de chaque terre seraient exploitées à leur juste mesure, dans le respect et la dignité. Ce jardin illustre le proverbe wolof énoncé par la narratrice: "*Nit nit ay garabam*," et explicité en note: "Littéralement: l'homme (au sens général) est le remède de l'homme: il n'y a de salut que dans l'Humain" (117). Il souligne donc la nécessité selon l'auteur de croire en la terre, et en ses valeurs épanouissantes.

Avec ce roman donc, Sow Fall transcende les notions réductrices de féminisme ou d'antiféminisme en se présentant comme un écrivain profondément humaniste. Elle traite de la question des Africains qui rêvent d'Occident avec une subtilité qui dénote d'une critique sociale très fine. Si l'épiphanie montre bien à quel point le roman s'oriente vers ses compatriotes, les enjoint à aimer leur pays et à se donner les moyens de le développer, la dénonciation du sort des immigrés en France invite aussi à une réflexion plus poussée sur l'ambivalence des anciens colonisateurs. On pourrait enfin se plaire à tisser le lien entre ce roman et le deuxième d'Aminata Sow Fall, *La grève des Bàttu*, de loin le plus lu. Si, dans l'un, Sow Fall traitait des conséquences inattendues qu'aurait une grève des mendiants au Sénégal, en montrant l'hypocrisie des gouvernements africains face à leur devoir d'aumône prescrit par l'Islam, dans *Douceurs du bercail*, l'auteur dénonce l'hypocrisie du gouvernement français face aux immigrés dont il est pourtant fort dépendant et sans lesquels le complexe de supériorité de la France s'écroulerait bien vite.[8] De même que les nantis musulmans sénégalais ont besoin des mendiants pour pouvoir vivre selon les principes de leur religion, les nantis européens ont besoin des immigrés, clandestins ou pas, pour pouvoir nourrir leur industrie prospère. Yakham explique que les clandestins doivent se limiter aux secteurs suivants: "bâtiment, enlèvement d'ordures, manutention dans les marchés hebdomadaires ou dans les halles" (*Douceurs du bercail* 100). Que se passerait-il pour la France si toute la main d'œuvre immigrée faisait la grève et décidait de rentrer au pays? Que serait Paris sans propreté, sans marchés ou sans chantiers? On comprend que Sow Fall passe outre la petitesse des mesquineries gouvernementales pour rappeler à ses lecteurs qu'en eux, qu'en elle, qu'en chacun subsistent l'espoir et la trace de valeurs dignes d'être célébrées. Toutefois, en recentrant son roman sur l'amitié entre les deux héroïnes principales, Sow Fall a marqué sa distance avec le panafricanisme. Anne et Asta rappellent qu'au-delà d'une regrettable institutionnalisation du racisme par les gouvernements, les individus sont malgré tout capables des amitiés les plus belles et des réalisations les plus optimistes. Ainsi il n'est pas surprenant que son dernier livre, *Un grain de vie et d'espérance*, mette en pratique cette volonté d'amitié internationale, puisque Sow Fall y partage avec ses lecteurs occidentaux la chaleur, la générosité, le rythme et l'amour de la cuisine sénégalaise.

NOTES

1. Aminata Sow Fall a confié dans un entretien avec Françoise Pfaff qu'elle considère l'art pour l'art comme un luxe déplacé: "Nous avons tellement de problèmes que je pense que l'art pour l'art n'est pas un luxe que nous pouvons nous offrir" (Pfaff 136).

2. L'un des romans le plus lu et étudié de la littérature francophone sub-saharienne, *Une si longue lettre* de Mariama Bâ, a fortement nourri et encouragé les lectures féministes de la littérature africaine. Si Mariama Bâ se méfiait du terme féministe auquel elle préférait les substantifs et adjectifs "sœur" et "féminin," celle-ci était néanmoins fortement préoccupée par la condition féminine, elle était d'ailleurs membre de plusieurs associations féminines, dont celle des "Sœurs Optimistes" qu'elle avait fondée. Aminata Sow Fall, quant à elle, a exprimé une distance beaucoup plus nette face au féminisme: "Je ne pense pas que le féminisme colle à nos réalités, j'entends le féminisme à l'occidentale. Je sais très bien que les femmes n'ont pas toujours le beau rôle mais ce n'est pas, à

mon avis, quelque chose d'institutionnalisé" (Gadjigo 221). Ainsi les personnages de ses livres sont majoritairement des hommes et il aura fallu attendre ce sixième roman, *Douceurs du bercail*, pour que Sow Fall mette en scène un personnage principal femme.

3.   Le mot "dignité" fait mine de leitmotiv dans ce roman; il est présent aux pages 17, 45, 61, 88, 120, 123, 134, 150, 154, 168, 199, 209, 217.

4.   Le mot "absurde" est prononcé par Anne à plusieurs reprises (62, 65).

5.   La deuxième moitié du dialogue se lit ainsi, à commencer par la question posée par Anne:

> Et vous vous laissez faire! Pourquoi ne réagissez-vous pas?
>
> Ce n'est pas si simple que cela... Le problème est dans notre mental. Vous nous avez appris à croire que nous ne sommes capables de rien. Même pas de fabriquer une aiguille... Quand nous croirons que nous pouvons, les choses changeront.
>
> Il est temps d'y croire, avant qu'il ne soit trop tard!
>
> Rires de part et d'autre, puis:
>
> C'est juste. Il est temps de croire... que nous devons inventer au lieu de consommer, consommer seulement et oublier... (159)

6.   Fanon définit "manichéisme délirant" en se servant de la définition qui suit: "Bien-Mal, Beau-Laid, Blanc-Noir, tels sont les couples caractéristiques du phénomène que, reprenant une expression de Dide et Guiraux, nous appellerons 'manichéisme délirant'" (Fanon, *Peau noire* 48).

7.   Le mot "rêve" apparaît aux pages 187, 189, 200, 209, 217.

8.   Dans *La grève des Bàttu*, le deuxième roman d'Aminata Sow Fall, les mendiants, tout comme les immigrés dans *Douceurs du bercail*, sont d'abord présentés comme des indésirables: "ces mendiants, ces talibés, ces lépreux, ces diminués physiques, ces loques, con-stituent des encombrements humains. Il faut débarrasser la Ville de ces hommes—ombres d'hommes plutôt, déchets humains" (Sow Fall 1979: 5). Mais un jour ces êtres non désirables se révoltent et les hauts responsables de l'Etat découvrent alors l'interdépendance qui régit leur rapport avec les mendiants. Le

lecteur fera le parallèle entre cette interdépendance et celle qui régit les rapports entre le gouvernement français et ses ressortissants étrangers, surtout à l'heure de la mondialisation nécessitant l'ouverture des frontières (n'oublions pas qu'Asta se rendait justement à une conférence sur l'Ordre Economique Mondial).

ŒUVRES CITÉES

Aas-Rouxparis, Nicole. "'Ecrire, c'est un banquet où tout le monde apporte': Entrevue avec Aminata Sow Fall." *Women in French Studies* 8 (2000): 203-13.

Balibar, Etienne. « Racism and Nationalism. » *Race, Nation, Class: Ambiguous Identities*, 1991: 37-67.

Bugul, Ken. "De la porte du sans retour à la porte du non retour." *Africultures* (11 oct. 1998): 25-32.

Fanon, Frantz. *Peau noire, masques blancs*. Paris: Seuil, 1952.

Gadjigo, Samba. "La Comédie Humaine Sénégalaise: Interview accordée par la romancière Sénégalaise Aminata Sow Fall le 14 janvier 1987." *Komparatistische Hefte* 15-16 (1987): 219-24.

Lebon, Cécile. "L'écriture, une parcelle de rencontre: Entretien avec Aminata Sow Fall." *Notre Librairie: Revue des littératures du Sud* 136 (1999): 65-8.

OHCHR.org. 1996-2004. The Office of the United Nations High Commissioner for Human Rights. 15 juillet 2004. http://www.unhchr.ch/udhr/lang/frn.htm

Pfaff, Françoise. "Aminata Sow Fall, l'écriture au Féminin." *Notre Librairie: Revue des littératures du Sud* 81 (1985): 135-8.

Sartre, Jean-Paul. "Orphée noir." *Anthologie de la nouvelle poésie nègre et Malgache*. Ed. L.S. Senghor. Paris: PU de France 1948. ix-xliv.

Senghor, Léopold Sédar. "Negritude: A Humanism of the Twentieth Century." *I Am Because We Are: Readings in Black Philosophy*. Eds. Fred Hord and Jonathan Scott Lee. Amherst: U of Massachusetts P, 1995. 45-54.

Sow Fall, Aminata. *La grève des Bàttu, ou les déchets humains*. Dakar: NEA, 1979.

_____. *Douceurs du bercail*. Abidjan: Nouvelles Editions Ivoiriennes, 1998.

Stringer, Susan. *The Senegalese Novel by Women: Through Their Own Eyes*. New York: Peter Lang, 1996.

Zappi, Sylvia. "Charters: La police produit une vidéo pour réfuter les accusations de violence." *Le Monde* (29 mars 2003): 20.

WHEN THE SUBALTERN SPEAKS

A NEW HISTORIOGRAPHY

MAME SELBÉE DIOUF NDIAYE

❄ ❄ ❄

A postcolonial reading of *Douceurs du bercail* could emphasize the profound effects of colonization on the writing of history. Postcolonial discourse has allowed the colonized margins to articulate a deconstructive reading of their relationship with hegemonic powers, by presenting a new historiography of the imperialist project. This focus on history in postcolonial discourse is the predilection of the Subaltern Studies group whose project, according to Gayatri Spivak, is "to rethink Indian colonial historiography from the perspective of the discontinuous chain of peasant insurgencies during the colonial occupation"[1] (Spivak 78). Because the subaltern occupies a complex subject position, this new historiography is founded in a dialogic and interlocutory narrative. In fact, the subaltern has to respond to prevailing dominant discourses. On the one hand, he reacts to a colonial narrative that constructs a racial discourse, which places the colonizer in a hegemonic position. On the other hand, he writes back to a defensive nationalist narrative, which perpetuates colonial boundaries. This

---

Mame Selbée Diouf Ndiaye, Ph.D., is a lecturer at Suffolk University, Dakar Campus, Senegal, and teaches race and gender studies.

deconstructive project of the subaltern narrative is the object of my reading of Aminata Sow Fall's *Douceurs du bercail*.

Douceurs du bercail confirms Aminata Sow Fall in the postcolonial tradition. This novel asserts the writer's concern with presenting the voice of the subaltern. In fact, the novel produces a narrative that undermines the tendency of major discourses on Modern Africa to develop an élite culture. This narrative is told through multiple voices that enunciate the complex subjectivity of the modern African. The complexity of this subject position is reinforced by a colonial and neocolonial history that complicates the political, economic and socio-cultural situation of Modern Africa. The subaltern discourse is therefore constructed in a context of discourse hegemony imposed by this history of domination. It is a discourse that appropriates, disrupts, and reconstructs the colonial narrative to undermine a hegemonic historiography of Africa.

As a Western production, colonial discourse frames the history of the relationship between colonizers and the colonized. It is founded on exclusive binaries that confine the colonized in a negative mythical portrayal. According to *Key Concepts in Post-colonial Studies*, colonial discourse:

> ... hinges on notions of race that begin to emerge at the very advent of European imperialism. Through such distinctions it comes to represent the colonized, whatever the nature of their social and cultural histories, as 'primitive' and the colonizer as 'civilized'. Colonial discourse tends to exclude, of course, statements about the exploitation of the resources of the colonized, the political status accruing to colonizing powers, the importance to domestic politics of the development of an empire, all of which may be compelling reasons for maintaining colonial ties. Rather it conceals these benefits in statements about the inferiority of the colonized, the primitive nature of other races [. . .] [2] (Ashcroft, Griffiths, and Tiffin 42-43).

Colonial discourse therefore deprives the colonized of any historical identity prior to colonial time. The colonized is depersonalized through a mythical portrayal that negatively describes him as lazy and incapable of any kind of production. This exclusive portrayal is meant to conceal the economic and political motivations of the colonial enterprise. On the one hand, the colonizer is interested in the continent because it offers a receptacle of natural resources. On the other hand, extending his empire would enhance the political position of the colonizer in his country. Albert Memmi's analysis of the Western discourse on colonialism also emphasizes the subjectivity of this discourse's assumptions. In his chapter about the portrayal of the colonized, he inquires:

> Besides having to define a point of reference, a norm, varying from one people to another, can one accuse an entire people of laziness? It can be suspected of individuals, even many of them as a single group. [...] What is suspect is that the accusation is not directed solely at the farm laborer or slum resident, but also at the professor, engineer or physician who does the same number of hours of work as his colonizer colleagues [...]. By his accusation the colonizer establishes the colonized as being lazy. He decides that laziness is constitutional in the very nature of the colonized [...] [3] (Memmi 80-81).

Albert Memmi refers here to the subjectivity of the colonizer's accusations. Along with the subaltern narrative, he is troubled with the rules of exclusion of colonial discourse and its essentialist racial discourse that conceals the real history of colonialism. Because colonizers want to translate their presence in the colonies as a civilizing mission, colonized people are deprived of any pre-existing culture and they are mythically portrayed in Western discourse as *"simultaneously inferior and wicked, lazy and backward"* [4] (Memmi 83). This selected and distorted history is the major target of the subaltern narrative, which engages in reconstructing the history of Africa and the West.

Nevertheless, it is important for the subaltern to shy away from the defensive position prevailing in nationalist counter discourse. In his response to this negative portrayal, the colonized has produced a defensive counter discourse, which, according to Frantz Fanon, reproduces colonial binaries and racial constructs. It is a nationalist discourse rooted in the exaltation of pre-colonial values. In his essay "On National Culture," Frantz Fanon explains that:

> The native intellectual who decides to give battle to colonial lies fights on the field of the whole continent. The past is given back its value. Culture extracted from the past to be displayed in all its splendor, is not necessarily that of his own country. [...] The efforts of the native to rehabilitate himself and escape from the claws of colonialism are logically inscribed from the same point of view as that of colonialism [5] (Fanon 211 – 12).

The native intellectual who exhibits pre-colonial value is an elitist hero, who uses his assimilation of Western thought to fight back. Unlike the subaltern, this hero is part of the ruling class and he aims at speaking for the nation. He constructs an anti-colonial discourse that is qualified as a reproduction of colonial authority. As Frantz Fanon further states, this intellectual who draws his strength in leadership is engaged in actions "which are less and less attached to the every-present reality of the people" [6] (Fanon 233). This description summarizes the reality of the neocolonial condition that sees the native ruling class claiming to represent a people who does not identify with its authoritarian policies.

Douceurs du bercail is about the life changing experience of Asta Diop, a divorced, middle-aged female worker with three children. She lives in Dakar with her teenage son, Paapi, while her two daughters pursue their studies in France. As the novel opens, Asta is sent by the Senegalese government to a conference on the Global Economic Order, taking place in France. While going through customs in Paris, she is aggressively questioned on the destination and purpose of her trip. Despite the fact that she has legal papers, she undergoes verbal and physical humiliation as customs go through their routine control. After trying hard to tolerate those humiliating moments, Asta explodes when forced to undress for screening. She physically assaults the agent who put her hands between her thighs looking for hidden fraudulent material. As a result, she is arrested and confined in a small cell with illegal immigrants at the airport where she has to wait for the first available charter aircraft to be flown back to Senegal. As Asta endures the disgrace of unsafe and unhealthy conditions of detention, she infiltrates the world of the so-called illegal immigrants. While listening to their stories, she undergoes a life changing experience. Back in Senegal, she refuses to sink into the despair of pessimism after losing her job. Taking her destiny into her hands, she sets up an agricultural project and experiences a decade of hopes and frustrations before she successfully overcomes the obstacles.

Asta Diop is the opposite of the elitist hero in the nationalist novel. The character embodies a subaltern class, defined by Gramsci [7] as a class that has less access to the means by which it may control its own representation and, as a result, has less access to cultural and social institutions (Ashcroft, Griffith and Tiffin 216). The subaltern hero does not claim to represent the people. He disowns the cultural weapon used by nationalists to address crucial issues of the modern West African State.

Douceurs du bercail therefore addresses crucial issues of the

postcolonial discourse. It is a narrative that personifies the consciousness of the subaltern: a consciousness that disrupts the racial construction of colonial discourse and the elitism of the nationalist novel. In
the novel, the characters of Asta and her French friend Anne reveal
the use of a parallel structure to engage a dynamic of disruption and a
reconstruction of hegemonic discourse. Crucial issues of a Western
writing of history are addressed through Anne's narrative.

Anne is a woman whom Asta met at the hospital when both were
having their first child. At that time, Asta was living in France with
her husband. Anne had lived in Africa for some years as her father
was serving in the colonial administration. She happily shared her
stories with Asta and they developed a special bond. Unfortunately,
Anne lost her baby who was born premature and left the hospital in
tears. The moments they shared, however, survived and they became
best friends.

The character of Anne symbolizes Western historiography. The
narrative from her point of view exposes the tendency of the West to
justify the condition of African modern state through cultural defects,
a position rooted in the racial construction of colonial discourse. While
she was discussing with Asta, she mentioned her mother's (Lise) interest in Africa. Lise's life in different parts of West Africa where her
husband has been posted as colonial administrator has strongly influenced her. She developed an interest in the people's culture. Her contact with the natives was basically determined by her Western eye, a
gaze filled with exoticism and colonial prejudice. Talking about her
mother's articles on her experience in West Africa, Anne explains:

> Dans un de ses tous derniers articles avant sa mort, elle se demandait
> si la solidarité africaine ne risquait pas d'engendrer un comportement
> de parasitisme et une mentalité de dépendance, au détriment de la
> créativité et de l'effort soutenu [...] [8] (Fall 154).

> [In one of the last articles she wrote before she passed, she was won-
> dering whether African solidarity was not bound to create a parasitic
> behavior and a dependency mindset that would preclude creativity
> and effort [...] (*my translation*).

Using cultural argument to justify the poor economic condition of
modern African states exemplifies the problematic homogeneity assumed in Western discourse. It is a discourse that looks at Africans as
one racial group; it uses cultural bias to construct the idea of shared

value, in order to create that illusion of homogeneity. When Lise refers to a universal human value (solidarity), she seems to imply that it is the source of a permanent state of dependence to which African countries are reduced, with their total reliance on Western funding and aid. It is an oversimplified reading rooted in the exclusiveness of colonial thought. This major characteristic of colonial discourse is a construction that would not recognize the issue of the exploitation of major resources of the colonized.

Asta offers a deconstructive reply that implies disruption and rewriting of the history of the relationship of the West with its former colony. According to her, to be considered are the real motivations and implications of the colonial experience. Responding to Anne's assumption about the necessity for Africans to stop counting on the West for means of development, Asta says:

> C'est vrai que personne ne pourra nous offrir les moyens de notre développement. C'est même irréaliste de le penser, mais tant que vous autres ne cesserez toujours de nous asservir économiquement sans en avoir l'air, et de nous enfermer dans un cycle infernal en donnant un de la main droite en grande pompe, et en reprenant cent de la main gauche en toute discrétion [. . .] [9] (Fall 159).

> [It is true that no one can provide us with the means of our development. It is even unrealistic to think so. However, as long as we are not economically strangulated in dubious ways, as long as we are not confined in this infernal circle in which we are ostensibly offered one thing with the right hand and unobtrusively deprived of a hundred things with the left hand [. . .] (*my translation*).

Through this assertion, Asta pinpoints the exclusiveness of the colonial narrative. Once again, it is a narrative that ignores the economic and political motivation of the European imperialist adventure. Asta disrupts this narrative with a satirical description of the neocolonial condition in modern African states. She embodies a subaltern discourse, which attacks the cultural argument that founded the mythical portrait of the colonized mentioned by Albert Memmi earlier. Her message is clear: we cannot hide behind cultural argument to justify the exploitation of a people and its resources. The conditions of the neocolonial modern African state have to be read through a power structure that is rooted in a capitalist thought. This subaltern reading is not only illustrated in Asta's reference to the 'Debt' in neocolonial Africa, it is also exemplified in the story of Yakham, the typical young immigrant.

Like Asta, the character of Yakham embodies another subaltern narrative in the novel. Through this character, the novel addresses crucial issues raised by postcolonial discourse such as the assumed homogeneity imposed by imperialist thought, and the racial construction of colonial discourse. Yakham is a young man that Asta meets while in detention in France. The character of Yakham embodies migration waves, which concerns a young African population attracted by 'ideal' conditions in the West. Like many disillusioned young Africans, Yakham is seeking in the West the opportunity denied to him in his own country to earn a living. A brilliant young student in high school, he successfully applies for a scholarship that would take him to France to continue his studies at the university. Unfortunately, he is stripped of his scholarship by a corrupt administration that uses a false pretext to assign the scholarship to another student from the right family, an upper class student. Desperate and disappointed, he relies on his mother's meager resources (she sells peanuts to cover his sons school fees) to pursue his studies at the University of Dakar. Like many students of his age, he fails to pass the first year and is dismissed by the University. His mother decides to sell her jewelry to allow him to pay a dealer who provides him with irregular paper to go to France. He therefore uses a false identity and passes the airport control. In France, he manages to get a job, which allows him to send money to his family in Senegal on a regular basis. Unfortunate circumstances on a routine control take him to the airport's police station where he is incarcerated with other illegal immigrants waiting for the next available charter flight to be sent back to his country.

We are far from the nationalist hero who goes to France, successfully passes his examinations and returns to the motherland with the White man's knowledge and skill. Here we have a subaltern, struggling to survive the tough conditions of a neocolonial world. Yakham's narrative embodies the subaltern's consciousness that constructs a subtle and objective critique of the reality of the complex postcolonial world. When discussing the unfortunate condition of the African with his detained inmates, Yakham refuses to adopt a victimizing position founded on racism. When Sega (one of the inmates) sees race as the source of oppression against Africans, Yakham responds:

La dame vient de dire que les blancs nous chassent. Je ne crois pas que ce soit un problème de peau, essentiellement […] Je dis que le délit de faciès existe mais qu'il est lié à d'autres considérations. Ce n'est pas pour justifier le rejet dont nous sommes victimes de la part des bornés [. . .] [10] (Fall 45).

[The lady just said that White people are kicking us out. I do not think it is fundamentally a question of color … I am saying that racial profiling is a reality, but we should consider other factors. I am not trying to justify our expulsion by narrow-minded people [. . .] (*my translation*).

Yakham admits the existence of racial profiling, but the source of the degrading conditions of Africans has to be sought for in the complex history of the colonial past and its aftermath. Furthermore, he explains:

On perçoit la réalité d'aujourd'hui à travers des gens misérables que l'on voit à la télévision à longueur d'année se débattre dans des catastrophes inimaginables: faim, pauvreté, exterminations interethniques, etc. Et le FMI en plus. Et personne ne nous respecte parce que nous incarnons la misère et que, eux, ils disent qu'il y a la crise chez eux. Nous, génération FMI, nous n'avons plus rien: pas de boulot, pas à manger, rien pour nous soigner, pas d'avenir … Alors, ils ont peur qu'on les contamine. "Vous vouliez l'indépendance, vous l'avez eue, restez chez vous avec votre famine et vos maladies." C'est ça que je voulais dire [. . .] [11] (Fall 48).

[Today's reality is depicted by television, which broadcasts images of wretched people caught in inconceivable disasters: hunger, poverty, genocides, etc. IMF reinforces these images. And we do not deserve any respect because we personify distress while they say they have a crisis at home. We, the IMF generation, do not have anything left; no jobs, no food, no health care, no future [. . .]. Therefore, they fear contamination. "You requested Independence now you have it, therefore stay in your countries and keep your hunger and diseases." That's what I meant (*my translation*)].

According to Yakham the poor treatment immigrants are subjected to in the West does not only result from racial prejudice. It is also the result of the negative depiction of the African through television broadcasts. This biased production subsequently creates in the psyche of the West repulsion for a people accused of failing to achieve development. Immigrants are subsequently viewed as parasites. They have botched their independence and are comfortable in their position of dependence. This description echoes the mythical portrayal of the colonized in colonial discourse. Yakham's narrative therefore displays a fault-less deconstruction of this colonial discourse. The questions implied in the monologue cited above are: How can a people, whose resources have been and continue to be exploited, pretend to achieve development? How is development possible, if economic policies are drawn and imposed on Africans?

The answer for Yakham is not to indulge in a victimized position, but to acknowledge the complex implications of imperialist thought and find a way to undermine the uncomfortable position of the subaltern in a context of global economy. Unlike other illegal immigrants who desperately manage to re-experience exile after being rejected by the West, Yakham as well as Asta believe in effort and struggle. They totally invest themselves in enriching their own land. Their engagement in agriculture in their home country carries a clear message here: value should not be retrieved from the material aspect of life or from the benefit you acquire from a comfortable social position. Value is embedded in the efforts made to achieve goals; it is grounded in the struggle for self-determination and development. Therefore, I agree with Frantz Fanon's definition of national consciousness and locate the consciousness of the subaltern in the fight that the people wage to face the hardships imposed by a complex neocolonial condition.

NOTES

1. Spivak, Gayatri C. "Can the Subaltern Speak?" In: *Postcolonial Discourse and Post-colonial Theory: A Reader*. New York: Columbia University Press, 1994.

2. Ashcroft, Bill. Gareth Griffith and Helen Tiffin. In: *Key Concepts in Post-Colonial Studies*. London and New York: Routledge, 1998.

3. Memmi, Albert. *The Colonizer and the Colonized*. New York: The Orion Press, 1965.

4. Ibid.

5. Fanon, Frantz. "On National Culture." In: *The Wretched of the Earth*. Trans. Françoise Maspero. New York: Grove Press, 1965.

6. Ibid.

7. In *Key Concepts to Post-Colonial Studies*, the authors trace the origins of the term subaltern back to A. Gramsci's *Selections from the*

Prison Notebooks, edited and translated by Quintin Hoare and Geoffrey Nowell Smith, London: Lawrence & Wishart, 1971.

8. Fall, Aminata Sow. *Douceurs du bercail*. Abidjan: Nouvelles Editions Ivoiriennes, 1998.

9. Ibid.

10. Ibid.

11. Ibid.

WORKS CITED

Ashcroft, Bill. Gareth Griffith and Helen Tiffin. *Key Concepts in Post-Colonial Studies*. London and New York: Routledge, 1998.

Fanon, Frantz. "On National Culture." *The Wretched of the Earth*. Trans. Françoise Maspero. New York: Grove Press, 1965.

Hoare, Quintin and Geoffrey Nowell Smith. Eds. and Trans. *Selections from the Prison Notebooks*. London: Lawrence & Wishart, 1971.

Memmi, Albert. *The Colonizer and the Colonized*. New York: The Orion Press, 1965.

Sow Fall, Aminata. *Douceurs du bercail*. Abidjan: Nouvelles Editions Ivoiriennes, 1998.

Spivak, Gayatri C. "Can the Subaltern Speak?" In: *Postcolonial Discourse and Post-colonial Theory: A Reader*. New York: Columbia University Press, 1994.

Thomas, Brook. *The New Historicism and Other Old Fashioned Topics*. Princeton: Princeton University Press, 1991.

BUILDING COMMUNITY THROUGH THE EXCHANGE RITUAL

MARCO D. ROMAN

❄ ❄ ❄

D uring one of the most critical moments in *La grève des Bàttu*, Mour Ndiaye, the Director of the Department of Public Health and Hygiene, demands that Kéba Dabo, his assistant, help him return the beggars to their quarters after they have spent an enormous amount of energy to clear them from Dakar's center. Because Ndiaye seeks the post of Vice-President, he has consulted a marabout who has charged him with fulfilling the Islamic ritual of *zakat* or almsgiving with the understanding that he will receive divine favors for his charity. In Ndiaye's explanation of his illogical request to his assistant, he states:

> Imagine-toi un peu ce que serait l'angoisse de cet homme à qui l'on a appris depuis la plus tendre enfance à décharger ses peurs, ses appréhensions, ses cauchemars, ses craintes dans trois morceaux de sucre, une bougie, une pièce de tissu, toutes sortes de choses enfin,

Marco D. Roman, Ph.D., is associate professor of French and chairperson of the Department of Modern Languages at the Mount Saint Mary's University, Emmitsburg, Maryland.

qu'il donne aux mendiants! Peut-on du jour au lendemain balancer ses croyances? (129).

[Consider for a moment what might be the anguish of this man who has been taught from early childhood to offload his fears, apprehensions, nightmares, and concerns onto three cubes of sugar, a candle, a piece of cloth, and all sorts of other things that he gives to beggars! Might not his beliefs be destroyed from one day to the next?]

Ndiaye's observation of the dichotomy between his own modern life experiences as a functionary in an urban center and his traditional Muslim upbringing in the village raises important questions about the spirit of the Islamic practice of *zakat* itself in a modern context as well as the role that this ritual of exchange has in negotiating social order in postcolonial Senegalese society.

Not surprisingly, then, the diverse critical approaches to Sow Fall's satirical novel have all paid varying degrees of attention to the very practice of *zakat* in their readings. From Peter Hawkins's exploration of the Marxist intertext to Nicki Hitchcott's inquiry into the gendered voice in Sow Fall's narrative, among others, each take stock of what Mbye B. Cham has termed the "the divergence between practice and principle" in the traditional Islamic ritual of *zakat* (170). Although these studies often turn to other concerns in their readings, they beg the question: what exactly does *zakat*, with its beggars in a posture of submission and its givers reminiscent of neocolonialist domination, offer to a post independent African society like Senegal? In seeking a response, the reader's task is complicated by Sow Fall's two literary tendencies, which she has expressed as her motives for writing. They are a particular desire to explore the social and the racial inequalities facing post independence African nations as both Thomas Hammond and Peter Hawkins report in separate interviews with the author (Hammond 192; Hawkins 419), and an equally distinctive tendency to write from a Muslim perspective as Cham has noted (168). Given these literary inclinations, how then should readers regard Sow Fall's portrayal of *zakat* in *La grève des Bàttu*?

In treating this question, scholars have often weighed more heavily in favor of the "modern" reading of *zakat* as a form of begging which invites abuse and regularly results in submission. This is especially surprising, given the abundant studies that have underscored the centrality assigned to ritual in African life as Irène Assiba d'Almeida has argued. Nonetheless, one such study that favors a strictly postcolonial interpretation of the novella entitled "L'espace du don" concludes that

> L'habitude de faire de l'aumône entraîne le peuple à la paresse et à l'hypocrisie, au lieu de l'inviter au travail. Le donner, conçu comme un acte de charité, avilit autant la personne qui offre que celle qui reçoit; il doit pour cela, se dépouiller de toute mystification et se présenter comme un simple échange (non comme un moyen de pression ou de mise en valeur de soi) (Trinh T. Minh-ha 1981: 78-89).

> [The habit of almsgiving leads to laziness and hypocrisy among the citizenry, instead of inspiring them to work. The act of giving, conceived as a charitable act, soils the giver as much as the receiver. Thus the act of giving should be stripped of all mystification and presented as a simple exchange (not for exerting pressure on someone nor for conferring worth on oneself)].

In fact, Trinh T. Minh-ha's observation above on the "violence" of exchange echoes the same conclusions spelled out in the work of such anthropologists as Marcel Mauss, Brotislaw Malinowski, and Claude Lévi-Strauss. While Trinh T. Minh-ha's call for the solution to the ritualized domination in gift exchange falls well within the theoretical schema of postcolonial readings and Sow Fall's own program as a socially conscious writer, it only addresses the social justice half of Sow Fall's narrative project while dispensing with the author's additional concern for exploring the place of Islam in everyday matters of social life (Cham 163).

In order to reconnect these divergent strands of the social and the religious function of the gift, or the practice and the theory of exchange in *La grève des Bàttu*, stated in another way, this essay will draw on the work of Pierre Bourdieu, a noted sociologist and social theorist who has especially focused on the interplay between practice and theory in ritual. His thinking is appropriate for this study; he has based his research of the "practice" of ritual on earlier work that he conducted in the field of ritualized exchange. While Bourdieu continues the line of research begun by Mauss, Malinowski, and Lévi-Strauss with regards to the violence of gift exchange as Maurice Godelier has detailed in *The Enigma of the Gift*, Bourdieu's own particular contribution to exchange theory centers on his observation of the strategic elements in the practice and how one might include strategy in readings of ritual, such as exchange. Bourdieu, therefore, deems the question not to be one of escape from violence, but one that considers how the violence is moderated and what social system serves as an arbiter that aids in the shaping of the violence (Bourdieu 125). Fittingly, this study assigns that role to Islam, a religious institution whose organizing principle calls for adherents to conform to a posture of "submission" emphasized in the institution's very name and ritualized in its gestures. Thus, this essay looks at the circulation of gifts in Sow Fall's novel conceding, before hand, that varying degrees of domination and submission do indeed shape the nature of this and other ritual exchanges. Nonetheless, this study, in its detailed examination of the "grammar of this system of communication," to borrow from John Gould's study, *Myth, Ritual Memory, and Exchange*, will turn to Bourdieu's theories concerning the exchange, in order to reexamine the transformative nature of the circulation of goods in reality and theory, and to consider how, despite postures of submission, the practice of these exchanges leads to a social alchemy that serves to bind and transform the community.

As noted above, what theories, like Trinh T. Minh-ha's, lack, when seen in a different manner, is the recognition of the importance of the practice element in the interpretation of ritual acts. Practice reinserts the context and reintroduces the spontaneous. Bourdieu notes that the practice element corrects the notion that ritual portrays a simple mechanical behavior that is devoid of "consciousness" (80). In an exchange, such as *zakat*, the practice element allows the giver or the performer to be converted into the dominated. Sow Fall demonstrates this aspect in her novella by having the beggars become the ones who call the shots. The beggars hold Mour Ndiaye's fate in the balance. Reinserting the "practice" into the reading of the *zakat* and almsgiving rituals reintroduces a complexity and a deeper appreciation of the ritual as it functions in West African social life.

To move toward a reappreciation of the practice element in the reading of the ritual of *zakat*, the narrator draws the reader's attention to the mechanical nature of almsgiving, thus highlighting the very element that Bourdieu finds to be lacking in a truer interpretation of ritual. The narrator stresses the mechanical element of the ritualized act of giving, through her use of the adverb "encore" in the novel's first sentence: "Ce matin encore le journal en a parlé..." (11), which insists on the automatic, repetitive, and reflexive nature of the begging ritual. Additionally, she highlights the criticized element of the "mechanical," by overlaying the more obvious social criticism of the ritual, which is the perpetuation of a posture of domination that dehumanizes and objectifies. In a very real way, the beggars become machines into which coins are deposited, in order to pass through them on the street corners. Thus, the narrator states:

> Aux carrefours, c'est à souhaiter que les feux ne soient jamais rouges! Mais une fois que l'on a franchi l'obstacle du feu on doit vaincre une nouvelle barrière pour se rendre à l'hôpital, forcer un barrage pour pouvoir aller travailler dans son bureau, se débattre afin de sortir de la banque,…enfin payer une rançon pour pénétrer dans la maison de Dieu (11).

> [At intersections, you wish traffic lights would never turn red. But once the traffic light obstacle is overcome, you have to cross the next barrier in order to get to the hospital, literally force a dam to be able to get to work in your office, fight to get out of the bank,… and lastly pay a ransom to enter the house of God;].

Thus, the accumulation of the barriers of *"encombrements humains"* (11) points to the dehumanization and the *"automatic behaviours"* that are regularly criticized in readings of ritual and particularly in almsgiving as the final words of the above quote illustrate.

Having exposed the mechanical nature of the almsgiving ritual, the narrator relates an anecdote that shocks the natural order and demonstrates that readings of ritual as practice must go beyond the mechanical. Sow Fall shows this, by having the objectified (a blind beggar) speak back to an insult that is hurled at him with the added comment *"à la stupéfaction de tous,"* in order to stress the unexpected (12). What is more, the incident occurs as Kéba Dabo enters a store on a Friday—a symbolic time that recalls the Muslim ritual of community-building through prayer, much like the ritual of *zakat.* This is no coincidence, since Muslim scholars like Ahmed Ali have noted the Koran's regular connection between the pillars of *salat* and *zakat* throughout the sacred text (290). Yet, it is the altercation between the young man and the blind beggar that echoes above all the roots of Bourdieu's study in which he reminds readers that rituals of exchange either material or verbal derive from practice, which takes into account an opponent's posture (80). Thus, the expected posture of submission by a beggar, predictable in a "theoretical" reading of *zakat,* becomes inverted where the dominated assumes the position of the dominating.

The beggar's unanticipated response follows a rhythm, which is carefully narrated in a simple sequence and within a specific context as mentioned earlier. *"Un aveugle a blessé un jeune homme avec sa canne, juste au moment où le jeune homme sortait du magasin alors que le mendiant tâtait le lieu pour y pénétrer. Le jeune homme a insulté le mendiant; celui-ci a riposté"* (12). [A blind man hurt a young man with his cane, just at the time the young man was leaving a store and the blind man was trying to enter the store picking his way with his cane. The young man insulted the beggar, and the latter returned the insult]. This incident and the manner in which it is related serve to draw attention to the element of time in interpreting ritualized exchange. In reading practices of rituals, such as exchange, Bourdieu centralizes the element of "time/rhythm/tempo," which he defines as a ritualized action's directionality (81). Without time, theoretical readings of ritual forget that there is a trajectory in the performance. And, the choice of the movement of the performer of the ritual is determined by urgency (Bourdieu 82). Not taking stock in the element of tempo and the temporal stance of a ritual (context), a performer or interpreter of a ritual, such as *zakat*, loses a sense of the urgent, which Bourdieu equates with the strategic. Without an account of time in a practice, interpreters of a ritual presume that the ritualized act will always follow to a logical conclusion. In fact, interpreters in this vein often remove the ritual from its context and the rhythm from the act. Hence, the beggar's behavior turns on the context in which he finds himself and results in an inversion of the expected where the dominated takes a voice and directs the exchange. On a very small scale, then, this scene exhibits the unpredictable or "urgent" element, which Bourdieu says can account for the variable outcome in rituals of exchange.

The misunderstanding of the contextual and hence the practical element is portrayed in Kéba Dabo's blanket attitude toward almsgiving. In the same passage above, Kéba Dabo embodies a "misreader" of the *zakat* ritual — much like those postcolonial literary critics who have tended to overlook the "practical" in their readings of almsgiving in the novel. Like those readers of *La grève des Bàttu*, who have focused only on the theoretical/postcolonial readings of *zakat*, Dabo objects to this ritual practice because of its capacity to turn a receiver into a being without dignity. Hence, the narrator states: *"il était choqué de voir des êtres humains – si pauvres fussent-ils – porter atteinte à leur dignité en quémandant d'une manière si honteuse et effrontée"* (13). [He was shocked to see human beings — poor as they may be — lower their dignity in a manner so shameful and flagrant by begging]. In reading the ritual outside of time in a theoretical environment, Dabo forgets the context and the temporality/urgency that informs the ritual and that fills the act with its meaning. The narrator again makes this evident by adding to the above lines: *"Il [Dabo] oubliait la faim et la misère qui poussaient certains d'entre eux à mendier pour rappeler aux nantis qu'eux aussi ils existent"* (13). [He [Dabo] was forgetting the hunger and the misery that pushed certain among them to beg in order to remind the endowed that they also exist]. In this additional comment, the narrator reminds the practitioners of the ritual that givers receive benefit from the gift of begging as well as the receiver.

Sow Fall does not only reserve her criticism for those who oppose the ritual, she also illustrates this automatic behavior in the willing practitioners of *zakat*, like Sagar Diouf, Kéba Dabo's secretary. Although Sagar appears to favor almsgiving, her comments suggest that her manner of giving does not occur in the true spirit of Islam. She comments: *"Que veux-tu que j'éprouve? Si j'ai de quoi leur donner, je le leur donne, sinon je continue mon chemin. C'est tout. Et puis, la religion recommande bien que l'on assiste les pauvres; comment vivraient-ils autrement?"* (34). [What do you want me to feel? If I have something to give them, I do otherwise I continue on my way. That's it. And then, Islam recommends that we give to the poor, for how else could they live?]. Sagar follows the letter of the law as her further remarks illustrate: *"A qui les gens donneraient-ils la charité, car il faut bien qu'on la donne, cette charité, qui est un précepte de la religion?"* (35). [To who would people give charity, since one must give this charity that is a precept of Islam?] Her unexamined beliefs about giving being a religious precept that binds giver and given are later emphasized when she reiterates the dilemma between tradition and modernity in African society, which Mour Ndiaye had brought out in his objection to Dabo. In this late scene in the novel, Sagar criticizes Dabo's tenacity in his opinion toward begging, which has truly made him the last and lone opposition to the ritual practice among the main characters. However, Sagar's words only reveal her resigned practice of *zakat* when she states: *"Voilà. Kéba, tu ne peux pas vivre en dehors de ton temps ni de ta société. Il faut bien suivre le même rythme et ce n'est pas pour rien qu'on dit que dans une société, lorsque les gens dansent d'un pied, il faut danser d'un pied..."* (131). [There, Keba, you cannot live outside your time and society. You must follow the same rhythm and it is not for nothing that they say that in a society where people dance on one foot, one must also dance on one foot...] Here, particularly, Sagar demonstrates that her practice of *zakat* favors stability, being part of one's environment, without understanding the strategic quality of ritual.

From the opening scenes, which put into question almsgiving in the urban center, the narrator transports the reader to the village of Keur Gallo where Serigne Birama, Mour Ndiaye's marabout, lives. Besides setting up the frequently cited theme of urban versus village and modern versus traditional, which again ties into the initial dilemma of Mour Ndiaye cited in the introduction to this study, the scene exemplifies an ideal model of the "practice" of ritual exchange. In the urban center, almsgiving takes place between individuals. Following the more traditional Koranic, yet Senegalese, model of *zakat*, this scene describes the exchange practice of alms. In this practice, tithes are given to an institutional representative of Islam who in turn distributes them to the poor. He may also keep them in store for the community's future use, as Donald B. O'Brien describes in *Mourides of Senegal: The Political and Economic Organization of an Islamic Brotherhood* (1971: 91-92). In response to this gift, the receiver bestows blessings on the giver. What strikes the reader is the stark contrast in the giver's response to the receiver. The gratitude of the giver for the opportunity to give is illustrated in Mour Ndiaye's praise for this relationship, which he expresses as follows: "*Ma situation présente, je la dois à Serigne Birama. Cet homme formidable. Je n'étais rien, rien de tout quand je l'ai connu. Je lui dois tout, je ne pourrai jamais le payer en retour*" (18). [I owe my present situation to this formidable man, Serigne Birama. I was nothing, nothing at all, when I got to know him. I owe him everything, and will never be able to pay him back] Ndiaye's use of superlative in relation to the exchange act indeed portrays the Islamic ideal for the almsgiving ritual as a social act that expresses obligation and gain.

What is more, the narrator underscores the reciprocal nature of the "gift-giving" obligation by retelling the event of Ndiaye and Serigne Birama's first encounter, which reminds practitioners that the exchange of life-giving essentials is at the root of the ritual practice. In a dramatic, yet genuine act of charity, Ndiaye offers Serigne Birama a drink of water in a setting that stresses the desolation of the city, much like the thirsty traveler in the wilderness of the desert. The location of the exchange ritual, "*au pied d'un manguier*," (19) [at the foot of a mango tree], symbolizes the life-giving nature of this exchange and recalls the frequent use of the image of the garden of paradise and its fruits in the Koran (Sura II. 25). The narrator adds to the image of this sacred space by designating its location within walls — separate from the chaos of the outside world. The description of the vessel in which the gift of water is offered also characterizes the simplicity and sincerity of the ritual exchange. This reads: *"Rien de beau dans cette boîte à tomate rouillée à l'extérieur, convertie en pot à eau et dont le rebord présentait une dentelure irrégulière"* (19). Like the beggar's bowl (bàttu), it says above, which may take a simple form, the old rusty tomato can becomes the bearer of life and transforms itself into an important instrument that creates social ties. Sow Fall calls attention to this aspect in the final sentence of the exchange: *"Depuis ce jour, une vingtaine d'années se sont écoulées. Jamais Mour n'a eu à douter de Serigne Birama Sidibé"* (21). [Since that day, twenty years or so ago, Mour has never doubted Serigne Birama Sidibé's power]. This comment shows that Mour Ndiaye (the giver) comprehends the benefit that he too receives from the act of giving. Hence, this symbolic gesture produces the effect, which the Islamic ritual of *zakat* strives to generate, and which may be termed a "social alchemy."

Sow Fall recognizes the difficulty of arriving at a true understanding of practice, because practice in ritual, by its very nature, must remain an action and hence tacit in its self explanation. Bourdieu writes of the self-reflective practitioner of ritual: "And there is every reason to think that as soon as he reflects on his practice, adopting a quasi-theoretical posture, the agent loses any chance of expressing the truth of his practice, and especially the truth of the practical relation to the practice" (91). This explains perhaps the difference between Kéba Dabo's and Mour Ndiaye's varying difficulties with mendacity. Although Dabo's stance on begging appears to fit the postcolonial objective of moving toward a socially just society, according to Western standards, a reading of Mour Ndiaye's practice more fully accounts for the complex network of signifying meanings that the ritual of *zakat* holds in West African, and in this instance, Senegalese, social interrelations. Consequently, Sow Fall portrays the destructive quality of self-reflection in ritual, through the character of Kéba Dabo who incessantly comments on the mechanical nature of the ritual and its potential for abuse. His remarks are limited to the theoretical consequences. Thus, Dabo's reflection throughout the text conveys his true loss of faith in the ritual.

On the other hand, Mour Ndiaye's reflection on the ritual's actual practical nature as a participant manifests a continued belief in the potentiality of the ritual to produce positive effects despite his official position. Hence Ndiaye's conflicted feelings about *zakat*, as quoted earlier in this study, point to his continued belief in the efficaciousness of the almsgiving ritual even when he believes he has left the practice behind. Serigne Birama reminds him of this in their visit in chapter three when he states: "*Te battre contre les mendiants, toi qui donnes si volontiers?*" (38). [Fighting the beggars, you who give so willingly?]. In the same vein, references to Ndiaye's relation to almsgiving throughout the novel insist on actions and postures as a practitioner, that is to say, on the potentialities that he believes that the exchange ritual produces. Accordingly, Ndiaye never really theorizes about the begging problem. Ironically, Ndiaye's primary action appears to turn on his perpetual act of giving alms both to Serigne Birama and Kifi Bokoul, and his interest in fulfilling the recommendation to distribute sacrificial meat to the poor. In Ndiaye's own words: "*Cette charité...Je l'offrirai selon les normes...Quoiqu'il m'en coûte...Le poste de vice-président, je l'aurai, il faut que je l'aie...*" (124). [This charity... I will offer it according to the norm... No matter what it costs me... the office of the vice-president, I will have it, I must have it..."]. These words illustrate the very nature of the practice of the ritual as defined by Bourdieu, because it "*brings the same symbol into different relationships...*" (87). In this way, it explains Ndiaye's justification of taking Kifi Bokoul on as a second marabout despite the fact that it jeopardizes his relationship to Serigne Birama. "*Mais aussi, c'est humain que je mette toutes les chances de mon côté...Serigne Birama est incontestablement un homme de science, mais les marabouts ont des voies différentes pour atteindre les pays des mystères, et on dit que ce Kifi Bokoul ne se trompe jamais...*" (119). [It is also human that I should put all luck on my side... Serigne Birama is incontestably a man of science, but the marabouts all have their different means of attaining the world of mysteries, and they say that Kifi Bokoul never makes a mistake]. Thus, Ndiaye's visit to another marabout, which seems only to speak of his arriviste mentality, may in fact point to the substitutionality of symbol in ritual when read using Bourdieu's reappreciation of practice. Moreover, Ndiaye's all-encompassing obsession emphasizes once again this aspect of "practice" in the fact that he continues to give faithfully even if it is in the hopes of political advancement. Almsgiving survives as a privileged ritual in Ndiaye's Islam.

Having established a reading for the exchange ritual that accounts for the "practice" as well as recognized the social problems derived from a theoretical reading of the ritual, we now move to Sow Fall's portrayal of the beggars and their point of view in the following chapters, but particularly in the second. Here, the beggars too recognize the mechanical nature of the act. Sow Fall even names almsgiving as a rite through the mouth of Salla Niang, thus attesting to the author's particular interest in the question of the practice of ritual. Salla Niang states that in all pockets of their society the first gesture by all classes on people is to give: "*Dans quel quartier de la Ville le premier geste matinal n'est-il pas de donner la charité? Même dans les quartiers de toubabs; les toubabs noirs et aussi les toubabs blancs accomplissent ce rite*" (24). [Is there any district of the city in which the first morning gesture is not to give charity? Even in the white district, the black and white elite accomplish the same rite]. Additionally, Sow Fall demonstrates the role of context in the reading of the ritual, because she fleshes out the individual and particularized backgrounds of a variety of beggars—Salla Niang, Papa Gorgui Diop, Nguirane Sarr, and Madiabel—which demonstrates the unpredictable reasons for begging. Each of these figures possesses a story that contextualizes their practice of begging or ritualized receiving, which breaks with the notion that receivers have set traits that make them beggars. As with the three perspectives provided by the administrators or "givers"—Dabo, Ndiaye, and Sagar— the abuse and sincerity of the practice of *zakat* varies with the beggars, which reinforces the notion that ritual exchange need not necessarily produce a mechanical response.

Like the earlier unexpected response of the figure of the dominated, the blind beggar in the first chapter, the second chapter and those that follow portray attitudes toward begging that turn the image of the socially dominated on end. Salla Niang, in particular, appears to have made a career out of the practice of the ritual. In addition, she suggests the protest of the strike, through Nguirane Sarr's prompting in the fifth chapter that operates as the means to reestablish the beggars' domination in this particular instance of the exchange ritual. In many ways, she plays the counter part to Kéba Dabo. She becomes impassioned by the cause, because of human dignity. Seeing Nguirane Sarr beaten for his begging in a later chapter, the narrator tells us that Salla Niang "*souffre du mal de cet homme qu'elle considère comme son propre frère...*" [bears the pain of this man whom she considers as her own brother..."]. Then, Niang adds: "*Voilà ce qu'ils ont fait d'un homme qui malgré sa pauvreté, devrait mériter le respect.*"(47). And, like Dabo, Niang too loses sight of the meaning of *zakat* and becomes obsessed with making the other pay. After the negotiation with Ndiaye, Niang states: "*Ne bougez pas d'ici; que personne ne bouge jamais d'ici! Demain, à cause de nous, il mordra la poussière*" (148). [Do not move from here; let no one ever move from here. Tomorrow, because of us, they will bite dust]. In the fashion of Dabo's exiling of the beggars to the outskirts of the city, Niang's plan to strike and refuse all alms fixes in time what should be the negotiable cycle of giving. Thus, like her administrative counterpart, Niang arrests the essential quality of the give-and-take ritual, which is its potentiality to negotiate new social positions and relations.

Among the beggars, the one who struggles the most with the outside world's reactions toward the ritual is Nguirane Sarr. For this reason, Sarr appears to play the counterpart of Ndiaye who practices the ritual, but is forced to contradict his practices. At first glance, Sarr's co-organizing role in conceiving the strike suggests that he responds with the idea of striking, because of a more theoretical criticism of the ritual. Nonetheless, a closer examination of his actions and words reveals that his motives to strike and thereby the stopping of almsgiving do not derive from a theoretical refusal of *zakat* like those of Niang. Rather, his manner illustrates an essential belief in the integrity of the practice and his desire to continue the act. As the narrator states, Sarr found dignity in the ritual and expresses surprise in the sudden public change in behavior. "*Pourtant, il croyait qu'il avait gagné leur estime et même leur amitié. Il n'avait jamais été inquiété. Pourquoi lui en veulent-ils, lui qui se contente de rester à 'son' feu, de ne jamais aller à l'assaut des voitures...*" (43). [Yet he thought he had gained their esteem and friendship. He had never been worried. Why are they against him, he that is contented to say at "his" light, never going to besiege cars...?]. Sarr's criticism remains on the level of their attack of the act. Again, like that of his administrative counterpart Ndiaye, this does not prevent him from understanding the strategy of the gift exchange. The following lines are crucial to this reading. After describing Sarr's dapper appearance and proud posture, the narrator states that his chosen place for the fattest harvest is the front of the presidential palace: "*Son point stratégique est le rond-point de la Présidence, pour recevoir la pièce lourde de voeux qui symbolise le dernier acte de charité avant l'audience avec le président de la République*" (25). [His strategic position is at the roundabout of the presidential palace so as to receive the coin loaded with wishes, symbolizing the last act of charity before the audience with the president of the Republic]. Not only does Sow Fall lavish attention on his physical appearance like Ndiaye, but she highlights Sarr's participation in *zakat*. Like Ndiaye who incites Dabo to extreme action, Sarr's call to strike is carried out to the letter by Niang. Sarr's call for a rather harsh reaction is driven by exterior forces that cause his anti-governmental behavior, much like Ndiaye's rash action to sweep the streets of all beggars results from the external pressure of the governmental decree and not from a personal conviction.

While these opposing portraits of both the beggars and the administrative officials have drawn our attention to the fact that participants of ritual encompass wide ranges of perspective, which result in unpredictable outcomes, we have seen that they have also demonstrated a behavior that has indicated the rhythmic nature of ritual. As the initial study of the blind beggar in the first chapter reveals, an unexpected response may convert one who is subjugated into the dominant. Thus, "tempo" supplies the complexity and unpredictability of ritualized acts of exchange. It is this rhythm that exposes the strategic nature of the gift-exchange rite. It also reveals the element of potentiality that a ritual act embodies in its practice. While this is most evident in the very premise of Sow Fall's novel, centered on the stoppage of gift-exchange in the symbol of a strike, there are other structural and stylistic elements in the narrative that speak to this indispensable aspect of ritualized practice.

On the stylistic level, tempo appears through the frequent use of ellipses and their implied silences. Not only do these silences portray the give-and-take of speech acts, but they signify the "urgency," which Bourdieu names as a property of practice in ritual (82). Just one brief, but noteworthy, verbal exchange will illustrate Sow Fall's recurrent use of this stylistic technique. In this particular scene near the end of the novel, Ndiaye attempts to convince Kéba that he must help him return the beggars to their proper places in the city:

> Ecoute, Kéba...Il peut toujours nous arriver de prendre des mesures qui, après, se retournent contre nous sans que cette éventualité ait frôlé notre esprit auparavant...Ce problème des mendiants, on n'y avait pas assez réfléchi, peut-être aurait-il mieux valu chercher une autre manière de le résoudre, une manière qui permît de ne pas couper totalement les ponts entre eux et nous... (128-29; ellipses in the original).

> [Listen, Keba. It is always possible that we take measures, which at the end turn badly for us, without our having seen the prospects of it coming at the on start. This problem of beggars, we had not sufficiently reflected on it. It might have been better to find another solution to it, a solution that would not have required burning the bridge between them and us totally...].

First, all the ellipses in this passage are in the original. In fact, there are four additional ellipses on these two pages alone—a stylistic technique repeated throughout the text. Second, Sow Fall's use of these ellipses for expressing the potentialities or strategic positionings that highlight practice in the rite of exchange and its possibility are indicated in this passage by the filler words "écoute" and later in the same paragraph "rassure-toi" and "vois-tu," which are commonly employed to describe a posture of negotiation. Finally, the tense choices, such as the subjunctive "ait frôlé," imperfect subjunctive "permît," and past conditional "aurait-il mieux valu," reinforce the negotiative nature of the rites of exchange in this and other passages in the text; and, once again demonstrate that such acts possess the ability to turn seemingly mechanical rites into strategic responses.

Turning to the structure of the novel, the element of tempo emerges in the alternating point and counterpoint chosen by Sow Fall for the narrative layout, which juxtaposes a scene of administrators interacting in one chapter with a scene of beggars assembled and discussing their strategy in a following chapter. This structure, which highlights negotiation, even appears within certain chapters such as chapter nine. In this chapter, for example, the interchange between Kifi Bokoul and Ndiaye, which focuses on the question of the identity of the beggars *"Qu'est-ce que c'est, les porteurs de bàttu?"* and the act of begging, contrast with Nigurane Sarr's and Niang's principle point of debate that centers on the complaint about givers who never ask the question why some people beg in the first place: *"...pourquoi nous mendions"* (107). In fact, examining the narrative structure of the novel, Mwamba Cabakulu and Boubakar Camara remark these very characteristics in their study of the role of time in *La grève des Bàttu*. Concerning the structure, they conclude that the narrative is linear, although the linearity is also broken with numerous analeptic devices and some prolepses: *"Il s'agit d'un récit linéaire mais qui ne se borne pas à présenter au lecteur une temporalité uniquement liée à la succession des événements qui forment l'intrigue. On note de nombreuses analepses et quelques prolepses utilisées afin de briser la linéarité du récit"* (59). [The narrative is linear, but is not limited to presenting to the reader a time uniquely tied to the sequence of the events of the plot. There are numerous analeptics and some prolepses employed to break the linearity of the narrative]. While Cabakulu and Camara hit upon the fundamental aspects of Sow Fall's narrative technique, they do not attach it to strategy or the central theme of exchange, which exemplifies the practice of this ritual and the discourse negotiation. Just as the blind beggar's harsh response interrupts the mechanical and reminds the reader of ritual functions in relation to time, so too do the novel's elements of style and its structure remind one of the role of tempo in creating the potentiality that informs a reader of the ritual's practice.

One of the last aspects in Bourdieu's study of ritual practice is the role that metaphor plays in elaborating the logic of practice of a ritual. Because ritual is opposed to objectification, it necessarily demonstrates a preference for the metaphorical (Bourdieu 1990: 87-90). The second chapter is especially rich in metaphor and word play dealing with the ritual exchange in this novel. In this sense, two disconnected objects with slightly overlapping characteristics can function in ritual practice to convey the practical logic of a ritual. And, as Bourdieu reminds us, these associations remain loosely connected just as a practice of ritual may embody irregularities that do not seem to obey logic (86). Sow Fall particularly highlights this aspect of the practical element of almsgiving in the symbol of the begging bowl. The simple "bàttu" of the mass of beggars present in the courtyard of Salla Niang for the weekly "tontine" stands out against the "van" or winnowing basket of Salla Niang (24). These seemingly contrasting metaphors for the ritual of almsgiving suggest both poverty and wealth (read hunger and feast), and call forth the "irregularities and even incoherences," which are inscribed in the practice of rituals, such as almsgiving (Bourdieu 86). Moreover, the variety of metaphors used in the novel for the ritualized gift-giving allows for the changeable nature of human fortune, and epitomize the truer unmechanical character of the rite of exchange. Sow Fall, then, further illustrates this point by linking the metaphors of the "van" and the "bàttu" to the "marmites" and the "casseroles" that Madiabel repaired as a *"baay jagal,"* repair man, and blacksmith in his village. In his position as blacksmith, the pots symbolize his wealth and his ability to feed his family. However, when his fortune changes and he loses his business as repairer of cooking pots, he reverts to begging: *"il se convertit au boroom bàttu, sans bàttu, mais main tendue"* (27). [he converts to a dreg of society, without gourd, but with hand held out (for begging)]. This association, which expands the network of the metaphor of the begging bowl to include the contradictory images of wealth and poverty, feast and hunger, in its association with the pots repaired by the village blacksmith, also implies the ability of the gift-giving ritual to lead to the unexpected. Thus, the metaphor of the begging bowl and other symbols associated with it function to denote the complexity of the practice of the exchange ritual where paradoxically opposing terms like giver and receiver intersect.

As the above example illustrates, the metaphor of the *bàttu* and its associations express a reality about the practice of almsgiving that encompasses and describes action that theory alone cannot do. Because of the special role assigned to metaphor in ritual, Bourdieu especially endows the writer with the ability to arrive at *"the principle of the mythopoetic act"* in contrast to the theoretician of ritual who seeks the purely cognitive and logical associations of rites (94). Having exposed the exchange ritual in both theory and practice, then, Sow Fall demonstrates an understanding of her role as writer of ritual, which parallels that of Bourdieu's. Her treatment of the contradictory terms of *zakat*, indeed comprise, as Bourdieu states: a "reconstructing of the socially constituted system of inseparably cognitive ...structures that organizes perception of the world and action in the world in accordance with the objective structures of a given state of the social world" (94).

In view of this mythopoetic insight, Sow Fall thus appears to observe an underlying value in the practice of the ritual of almsgiving that extends to other spheres of social interaction in Senegal. To this end, Sow Fall creates associative links between the practice of *zakat* and secondary themes such as polygamy and marriage which theoretical readings may leave aside. In other words, the metaphor of exchange and its seeming contradictions become woven into the scenes that deal with Lolli and Ndiaye's marriage, Raabi's modern view of women, and Ndiaye's approach to politics. Thus, the initial practical logic of the religious rite of almsgiving serves as a fundamentally socially structuring metaphor for those other ritualized events in Senegalese society named above. In addition, the rite illustrates that the simple religious ritual reverberates throughout Senegalese social relations where negotiations and social "alchemy" regularly take place.

While the critics of *La grève des Bàttu* have tended to put aside the consideration of the "practice" of *zakat* for the quite justifiable reasons of examining Sow Fall's program of social justice, they have turned a blind eye to the author's other prevailing stance, which is her profound commitment as a writer to the depiction, perpetuation, and incorporation of the Islamic faith and its practices into the fabric of a modern Senegalese society. This essay has presented, therefore, a reading of the Islamic ritual that explores the meaning of its "practice," in order to rehabilitate that aspect with the hope of coming to a fuller appreciation of Sow Fall's dexterity as a modern Islamic writer in the West African tradition. Thus, Bourdieu's theory assists the reader in incorporating the practice of the ritual postures and actions into a reading of *La grève des Bàttu* in a way that more fully develops the reader's understanding of both the "reason" and the "raison d'être," as Bourdieu states, of this powerful and continually socially transforming practice (97).

*Translations in English are the author's.

WORKS CITED

Ali, Ahmed. Introduction and Notes. *The Qur'an: A Contemporary Translation by Ahmed Ali*. New York: Quality Paperback Book Club, 1992. 1-6.

Bourdieu, Pierre. *The Logic of Practice*. Trans. Richard Nice. Stanford: Stanford UP, 1990.

Cabakulu, Mwamba and Boubakar Camara. *Comprendre et faire comprendre* La grève des Bàttu *d'Aminata Sow Fall*. Paris: L'Harmattan, 2002.

Cham, Mbye B. "Islam in Senegalese Literature and Film." *Faces of Islam in African Literature*. Ed. Kenneth W. Harrow. Portsmouth, NH: Heinemann, 1991: 163-186.

D'Almeida, Irène Assiba. *Francophone African Women Writers: Destroying the Emptiness of Silence*. Gainesville: U P of Florida, 1994.

Godelier, Maurice. *The Enigma of the Gift*. Trans. Nora Scott. Chicago: U of Chicago P, 1999.

Gould, John. *Myth, Ritual Memory, and Exchange: Essays in Greek Literature and Culture*. Oxford: Oxford UP, 2001.

Hammond, Thomas. "Entretien avec Aminata Sow Fall." *Présence francophone*. 22 (1981): 191-195.

Hawkins, Peter. "An Interview with Aminata Sow Fall." *African Affairs*. 87 (1988): 419-430.

_____. "Marxist Intertext, Islamic Reinscription? Common Themes in the Novels of Sembène Ousmane and Aminata Sow Fall."

African Francophone Writing: A Critical Introduction. Ed. Laïla Ibnlfassi and Nicki Hitchcott. Oxford: Berg, 1996: 163-169.

Hitchcott, Nicki. *Women Writers in Francophone Africa.* Oxford: Berg, 2000.

O'Brien, Donal B. *Mourides of Senegal: The Political and Economic Organization of an Islamic Brotherhood.* Oxford: Clarendon P, 1971.

Sow Fall, Aminata. *La grève des Bàttu.* Paris: Le Serpent à Plumes, 2001.

Trinh T. Minh-ha. "Aminata Sow Fall et l'espace du don." *Présence Africaine: Revue Culturelle du Monde Noir.* 120 (1981): 70-81.

ENGAGEMENT ET NATURE DU RÉALISME CHEZ AMINATA SOW FALL

Léa Kalaora

❄ ❄ ❄

Editor's Synopsis

This theoretical chapter uses almost all the novels of Aminata Sow Fall and the contributor's recent interview with the author in Senegal to explore the link between social realism and the writer's commitment. It would appear that commitment goes hand in hand with realism, a mode of writing that is doubly important for women: as a means of presenting the female condition in Africa and the black racial identity. Kalaora demonstrates that Aminata Sow Fall's artistic commitment is focused on her environment and her relationship with it, not her own identity. Her realism is focused on aspects of oral lit-

Léa Kalaora, M.A., is a doctoral student in ethnology and ethnocriticism in the Department of Anthropology, Université de Montréal, Québec, Canada.

erature and daily activities in her milieu. This strategy of focusing on the local shows that it is possible to be at once traditional and modern.

❀ ❀ ❀

Nous souhaitons montrer, dans cette étude, comment le réalisme des romans de Sow Fall opère, à plusieurs niveaux, un retour[1] vers ce que nous pourrions nommer d'une manière générique le local.[2]

Les spécialistes de l'Afrique semblent attendre de tout écrivain africain qu'il s'engage. Ce défi est double pour les femmes puisque, selon ces mêmes chercheurs, « *les Africaines mènent un double combat : pour l'identité de l'homme noir et pour la libération de la femme* » (Kuoh-Maukoury 1983 : 26). Sow Fall répond à ces deux objectifs par le mode réaliste et non par l'engagement politique. Elle se situe ainsi dans la lignée de Mongo Beti et des romanciers anti-coloniaux de par son engagement au moyen du réalisme, mais s'en écarte de par son refus du politique. Libérée d'un engagement politique destiné à l'Occident et surtout à la France, elle se centre sur sa ville, son milieu et s'engage par « l'exemple, » comme nous allons le voir. En effet, les engagements de Sow Fall se situent dans la proximité qu'elle a avec son milieu et non dans l'affirmation de son identité. Nous verrons, par là-même, comment ses engagements sont proches de ceux de la tradition orale puisque selon Kane, « le réalisme dans la tradition orale est inséparable de l'engagement » car « il est en rapport avec les liens qui soudent l'écrivain ou l'artiste à son groupe » (Kane 1982 : 86).

Ainsi, après avoir vu comment Sow Fall s'engage par le moyen du réalisme, nous verrons comment ce mode opère lui-même un retour vers le local dans le sens où sa forme et fonction empruntent beaucoup à celles des récits oraux.

ENGAGEMENT ET RÉALISME CHEZ SOW FALL: « L'ART DE NE PAS »

Si Sow Fall se tourne strictement vers le réalisme comme forme d'engagement, c'est parce qu'elle s'interdit de lier littérature et politique. En effet, à la différence de ses prédécesseurs, les romanciers anti-coloniaux et les écrivains de la négritude, Sow Fall choisit une position a-politique, non revendicative, non combative affichée. On peut penser que cette position s'explique seulement par le contexte dans la mesure où le combat politique n'aurait plus lieu d'être une fois le Sénégal libéré. Ses prédécesseurs s'engageaient politiquement, par l'écriture et par le mode réaliste, afin d'obtenir une reconnaissance culturelle et politique du monde noir. Si cet engagement est aujourd'hui obsolète, de nombreux romanciers restent tout de même dans une perspective de revendication : critique de l'Occident, critique des pays africains indépendants, dénonciation de l'abus de pouvoir des nouveaux dirigeants, engagement féministe, etc. (Kourouma, Bâ, Ken Bugul, etc.). Sow Fall refuse quant à elle tout engagement explicite qu'il soit politique ou féministe.

Malgré ce refus, elle a publié un roman à caractère fortement politique : *L'Ex-père de la nation*. Ce roman raconte les mémoires d'un ancien chef d'État qui est présenté comme victime : victime de sa femme, de l'opinion, des grandes puissances, des contraintes. Cependant, elle affirme qu'il faut faire de ce roman une lecture plus humaine que politique (Sow Fall 2004).[3] Il est vrai qu'elle dénonce moins le président-dictateur que l'hypocrisie des gens.

De manière presque idéologique, elle s'interdit de lier politique et littérature, de faire de la littérature un acte politique, et cela pour plusieurs raisons. D'une part elle n'a pas la « fibre politique», d'autre part c'est une question de liberté :

> La politique est tout à fait incompatible avec les arts, n'importe quelle politique, politique de pouvoir ou politique d'opposition parce que ça demande d'obéir les yeux fermés (la solidarité du parti...). Moi je veux ma liberté de pensée, ma liberté d'action. (...) Je n'ai pas eu besoin de chercher l'onction de Senghor par exemple. Si on cherche l'onction pour s'imposer en littérature, la littérature ne marche pas (Sow Fall 2004)

De même, elle ne pose pas son identité féminine en termes de combat[4]. Elle a été ainsi fortement critiquée pour ne pas s'être déclarée féministe. Mais si elle ne se déclare pas féministe, cela ne semble pas pour autant signifier qu'elle ne se comporte pas en féministe. En effet, ses discours mettent en avant la force, les vertus des femmes (Sow Fall 2004; Guèye 2000; Pfaff 2000 etc.). Ses romans mettent en scène des personnages de femmes fortes mais non revendicatives, qui ne sont pas en lutte, à la différence des principaux protagonistes de *Une si longue lettre* (Bâ 1979) ou de *Le Baobab fou* (Bugul 1982).

Nous pourrions dire que son féminisme procède par l'exemple : elle présente des personnages de femmes exemplaires, de femmes libérées (Raabi dans *La grève des Bàttu*, Naarou dans *Le Jujubier du patriarche*, Asta Diop dans *Douceurs du bercail*), de femmes fortes positives ou négatives (Salla dans *La grève des Battu*, Yama dans *Le Revenant* qui « *est forte dans le sens du mal, elle met son génie au service de l'inhumain mais elle est forte sans état d'âme* » (Sow Fall 2004).[5] Si elle n'est pas uniquement élogieuse envers les femmes, c'est par souci de réalisme (Sow Fall 2004). Ces figures représentent ce que sera, devrait être (ou ne pas être) la femme moderne africaine. Sow Fall propose de tels modèles afin d'éduquer les femmes (Sow Fall 2004).

Le féminisme de Sow Fall se différencie donc du féminisme occidental qui fonctionne par la revendication, par la lutte. Il peut être vu comme une manière locale, sénégalaise, d'être féministe dans la mesure où, dans la « tradition » orale, on n'affirme pas ce qu'on est, on ne fait que le présenter. Fidèle à ce type d'engagement, elle privilégie l'implicite et procède par l'exemple ou le contre-exemple.

De même, son engagement social fonctionne par l'exemple. Sow Fall semble être fortement engagée socialement; elle se soucie de la dignité humaine. Elle écrit des romans de critique sociale. Elle s'élève contre des pratiques : la polygamie, la mendicité (*La grève des Bàttu*), la superstition (*La grève des Bàttu*), l'hypocrisie (*Le Revenant*) qu'elle replace dans leur contexte social et urbain. En révélant ainsi la situation sociale aux lecteurs, en représentant les problèmes sociaux, elle souhaite arriver à réformer les mœurs. Dans sa critique, elle n'est ni revendicatrice, ni révolutionnaire; elle ne fait que mettre en scène certains problèmes sociaux. Elle reste très locale dans la mesure où elle décrit et critique la vie quotidienne, surtout urbaine du Sénégal. Ses romans sont ainsi très anecdotiques.

Sow Fall refuse donc de se situer (2004). Ce refus demeure ironiquement une prise de position. Ainsi, comme dirait Sow Dieye:[6] «Sow Fall n'est jamais autant femme pour ne pas dire féministe que quand elle affirme ne pas l'être». Elle pratique un « art de ne pas » bien illustré dans un des romans de Melville, *Bartelby* (1976) où l'auteur met en scène un personnage, le greffier, qui systématiquement répond, « j'aimerais mieux pas » chaque fois qu'on lui demande de faire quelque chose. Comme le dit Jeudy dans la présentation du livre de Abèles (2005), « l'art de ne pas, » « plutôt qu'une stratégie de l'évitement, » est « une manière d'éprouver la puissance, » mais surtout une sagésse qui selon l'adage des stoïciens transforme le hasard en destin, « *proche de l'attitude zen qui assume … le hasard des évènements,* » une « *ironie objective,* » qui permet de résister « *à la tyrannie des modèles d'existence* » (121-122).

Nous avons trouvé que « l'art de ne pas » pourrait qualifier l'attitude de Sow Fall dans son désir de présenter la complexité de la société africaine en assumant la violence des contradictions qui lui sont inhérentes.

LE RÉALISME DE SOW FALL : RETOUR VERS DIFFÉRENTES ORALITÉS

Le mode nécessaire pour cet « art de ne pas », cet engagement par « l'exemple » est, comme nous l'avons vu, le réalisme. Il convient donc maintenant de s'attarder plus longuement sur la spécificité du réalisme de Sow Fall.

RÉALISME ET OCCIDENT

Ses prédécesseurs utilisaient également le mode réaliste pour réhabiliter la « négritude, » souligner son originalité et authenticité dans le contexte culturel. C'est d'ailleurs bien par le réalisme que Senghor défendra le roman de Laye Camara (1973), *L'Enfant noir*, accusé de n'être pas assez anti-colonialiste. Nous voici ramenés à Camara.

Lui reprocher de n'avoir pas fait le procès du colonialisme, c'est lui reprocher de n'avoir pas fait un roman à thèse, ce qui est le contraire du romanesque, c'est lui reprocher d'être resté fidèle à sa race, à sa mission d'écrivain. Mais, à la réflexion, on découvrira qu'en ne faisant pas le procès du colonialisme, il l'a fait de la façon la plus efficace. Car peindre le monde négro-africain sous les couleurs de l'enfance, c'était la façon la plus suggestive de condamner le monde capitaliste de l'occident européen (Senghor 1954: 157, cité dans Kane 1982: 90). Le réalisme doit donc servir ici à réhabiliter l'identité noire et à dénoncer le colonialisme après la seconde guerre mondiale. Ce réalisme doit condamner le monde occidental et toucher un public occidental.

Si Sow Fall se situe, par l'emploi du réalisme, en continuité par rapport à ses prédécesseurs, elle s'en distingue cependant par la distance qu'elle met avec le monde occidental et par le public visé.

Tout d'abord, l'objectif premier de son réalisme n'est pas de critiquer le monde occidental. Elle réprouve les mœurs des Sénégalais, ce qu'ils font de ce que l'Occident leur a amené plus que l'Occident lui-même. Par exemple, la mère de Nalla est fortement critiquée pour avoir été aliénée par l'Occident, et pour être devenue trop occidentale (*L'Appel des arènes*). Ce n'est pas l'Occident qu'elle dénonce mais l'adaptation que les Sénégalais en font. Elle ignore presque dans ses romans le monde occidental. Dans *Douceurs du bercail*, les trois-quarts du roman se passent dans un « dépôt » en France où le personnage principal attend d'être renvoyé au Sénégal, mais même là l'occident, à travers la France, n'est critiqué que de manière implicite. Elle-même dit à propos de ce roman :

> Beaucoup de gens pensent que je parle des problèmes actuels des charters, non, non (...) ce n'est pas ça, je peux le prouver (...) ce sont les problèmes d'immigration parce que (...) déjà dans les années 80 je remarquais qu'une mentalité était en train de s'incruster, on pensait qu'il fallait partir coûte que coûte pour pouvoir réaliser quelque chose (...) ces jeunes pensent que rien ici ne peut se faire, il faut peut-être les sensibiliser au fait qu'ils doivent apprendre à créer la richesse chez eux avant d'aller ailleurs (...) voyager est un fait normal (...) mais il faut aller et découvrir dans la dignité (...) on peut créer les conditions de la richesse chez soi et si après on va rencontrer d'autres peuples, ce sera dans le respect mutuel au lieu d'aller s'exposer à des humiliations comme celle d'Asta dans *Douceurs du bercail* (Sow Fall 2004).

De même, elle n'écrit pas explicitement pour les Occidentaux. Cela se distingue par le fait qu'elle s'abstient d'expliciter ce qu'elle met en scène. Lorsqu'elle évoque des coutumes, elle les nomme mais ne les décrit pas avec minutie. Ainsi, à la différence du réalisme des romans de l'époque coloniale,[7] elle ne fournit pas d'ethnotexte.[8] Elle est d'ailleurs intransigeante sur le sujet.

Ainsi, lorsqu'elle présenta aux Nouvelles Éditions Africaines (NEA) *Le Revenant*, son premier roman, elle reçut la réponse suivante: « *si on publie ça, ça ne va pas marcher, les Occidentaux ne vont pas comprendre et ce sont les Occidentaux qui peuvent acheter les livres qui nous permettent de nous en sortir.* » (Sow Fall 2004) Les NEA voulaient donc que Sow Fall reprenne le manuscrit pour en changer « ce qui est trop local » (Sow Fall 2004). Mais elle refusa et le premier tirage de *Le Revenant* (3000 exemplaires) s'est épuisé rapidement. *La grève des Battu* a reçu de la part des NEA la même critique: «*Mettre un nom wolof dans le titre, les mendiants,[9] les Occidentaux ne vont rien comprendre. Or ce sont les Occidentaux dont ils parlaient qui m'ont propulsée sur la scène internationale*» (Sow Fall 2004).

Ne se souciant pas des Occidentaux, ni dans les thèmes de ses romans, ni dans le public visé, Sow Fall peut, à la manière des griots, raconter et mettre en scène presque de manière orale la vie quotidienne des Sénégalais (oralité du quotidien). De même, ne cherchant pas à imiter le mieux possible le réalisme français, elle va au contraire puiser dans le réalisme de la littérature orale.

ORALITÉ DU QUOTIDIEN

Sow Fall écrit comme on parle, elle est ainsi proche de l'oralité selon les mots de Dieng dans le sens «oralité comme mode d'être au quotidien» (Dieng 2004). [10] D'ailleurs, selon Dieng, les femmes africaines représentent en général plus le «vécu au quotidien» dans leurs romans tandis que les hommes s'occupent plus de questions politiques. On trouve ainsi dans les romans de Sow Fall des « *situations caractéristiques du parler dans la société sénégalaise.*» « *Les interactions verbales permettent de saisir comment l'oralité au quotidien, la parole régit à travers des cadres, le fonctionnement social*» (Dieng 2004).

Cette «oralité» (qu'il faut distinguer de l'oralité au sens «littérature» orale) n'est pas présente avec la même intensité dans tous ses romans. En effet, on perçoit, selon Trinh T. Minh-ha, dans *La grève des Bàttu* un « désir net de se dégager des conventions du roman traditionnel, » une « recherche d'un degré parlé de l'écriture » (Minh-ha 1982 : 780). *Le Revenant*, son premier roman, est par exemple écrit au passé simple à la différence de *La grève des Bàttu* qui est principalement écrit au présent. Le style oral se remarque également dans l'emploi dans *La grève des Bàttu* de nombreux adjectifs démonstratifs : « cette Raabi », « ce Mour » (Minh-ha 1982). Ces adjectifs démonstratifs interpellent le lecteur, l'invitent presque à participer. On retrouve ici une des techniques narratives du conte.

Elle est également proche de l'oralité du quotidien par l'emploi de mots wolofs, de proverbes ou d'un français sénégalisé. En effet, les personnages de Sow Fall, dès *Le Revenant*, parlent un « *français sénégalisé d'où les répétitions délibérées de phrases clichées, le jeu des stéréotypes dans les dialogues et l'intervention fréquente du wolof pour exprimer des réalités étrangères à la langue empruntée* » (Minh-ha 1982: 780). Cet emploi de mots wolofs montre un souci de réalisme. Les expressions wolofs sont toujours traduites ou doublées d'équivalents en français dans *Le Revenant*. Mais, dans *La grève des Battu,* sont mis en glossaire seuls les mots ou phrases dont l'explication semble être indispensable à la compréhension du récit (Minh-ha 1982). Le reste constitue « *la part intraduisible de l'expérience sénégalaise. Tout se passe comme si le souci de se faire entendre d'un public étranger ne constituait plus une préoccupation essentielle* » (Minh-ha 1982: 782). On retrouve ici le fait que Sow Fall ne vise pas en premier lieu un public occidental.

Ce réalisme de l'oralité du quotidien est donc bien la conséquence d'un retour vers le quotidien des Sénégalais et vers un public local. Ce quotidien est plus précisément urbain, dakarois. En effet, la plupart de ses romans (*Le Revenant, La grève des Bàttu, L'Appel des arènes, Le Jujubier du patriarche*) se situent à Dakar. Les lieux sont d'ailleurs identiques à ceux de la réalité (La Gueule Tapée ...). Elle est donc réaliste dans ses lieux. Dans ce sens aussi, Sow Fall s'adresse à un public dakarois.

Il est important de préciser qu'un roman peut toucher plusieurs communautés non exclusives l'une de l'autre. Ces diverses communautés se distinguent par leur échelle. Ainsi, par exemple, un roman qui se passe à Dakar, où les lieux sont nommés et réels touchera la communauté urbaine de Dakar qui sera sensible aux détails du roman; l'aspect religieux d'un roman (marabouts ...) parlera aux musulmans du Sénégal; la majorité des Africains de l'ouest se reconnaîtront, quant à eux, dans l'aspect magique et le recours au mythe; les occidentaux pourront s'identifier à d'autres aspects. Et chacun, même s'il ne comprend pas toutes les références apprendra sur les Wolofs, Dakar et le Sénégal. Il y a donc un emboîtement des divers niveaux de compréhension et d'identification d'un roman.

Ce retour vers le local, s'effectue aussi dans le sens d'un retour vers la littérature orale dans la mesure où le réalisme de Sow Fall ne se calque pas sur celui occidental mais emprunte beaucoup au réalisme des récits oraux.

ORALITÉ DE LA « LITTÉRATURE ORALE »: AUX FRONTIÈRES DES RÉCITS ORAUX ET DU ROMANESQUE OCCIDENTAL.

Plus que sur le contenu du réalisme des romans de Sow Fall, nous allons maintenant nous attarder sur sa nature. En effet, si la fiction africaine est un objet privilégié qui nous permet de mieux appréhender les enjeux de l'Afrique contemporaine, il est important, comme nous le rappelle Minh-ha (1982), de s'intéresser également aux écrivains africains pour savoir ce qu'ils peuvent nous apprendre sur le genre romanesque et ses modes.[11] Nous pensons donc que « *le réalisme du roman ne réside pas dans le genre de vie qu'il représente, mais dans la manière dont il le fait* » (Watt 1982[12] : 14).

On compare souvent le réalisme de Sow Fall à celui de Balzac ou de Zola dans la mesure où Sow Fall proposerait, à travers ses romans, une vaste « comédie humaine.» Comme pour ces auteurs, son devoir est de « mentir vrai » dit-elle en reprenant les mots d'Aragon : «*l'auteur de fiction, il ment mais il doit mentir vrai (…) c'est ça l'art, c'est là qu'intervient l'art du romancier, de celui qui fait de la fiction, il doit en même temps mentir mais il doit faire vrai, de telle sorte que tout soit du domaine du possible*» (Sow Fall 2004).[13] Cependant Sow Fall n'a tout de même pas autant le souci de la vérité que les naturalistes français, du moins elle l'a autrement : il est présent plus dans le souci de recréer l'oralité du quotidien que dans la description méthodologique des faits, personnages ou lieux. De même, toujours à la différence des naturalistes, mais tout comme le réalisme de la tradition orale, le réalisme des romans de Sow Fall, «*ne commande pas le rejet des autres procédés de symbolisation. Il n'est jamais conçu comme un moyen pour réfréner la spiritualité*» (Kane 1982: 86). Le réalisme de Sow Fall paraît ainsi avoir un double héritage : il hérite du réalisme français et du réalisme de la littérature orale. Avant d'analyser cela dans le détail, un bref rappel historique me semble nécessaire.

« TRAVELS OF A GENRE »

Le genre romanesque dit moderne (qui correspond à ce que nous appelons communément roman) est apparu au 18eme siècle, dans le contexte de la modernité, en Europe. Il est l'expression d'une société «moderne.» Ce genre s'est trouvé impliqué au 18ème et 19ème siècle, à l'heure de la colonisation et de l'impérialisme, dans des conflits extra-nationaux. En effet, le colonialisme, sous le couvert d'une mission civilisatrice, a voulu apporter une culture avancée et rationnelle. Le genre romanesque fut ainsi «exporté.» A cette époque, le mode utilisé par les romanciers européens était surtout le réalisme (Balzac, Zola …). C'est dans ce contexte que le roman est apparu à la fin du 19ème siècle en Afrique. Le colonialisme n'a pas marqué de façon indélébile toutes les pages des romans africains, cependant il a marqué le mode de production de la littérature.

Il est alors intéressant d'analyser, à l'instar de Layoun (1990) dans le magnifique ouvrage *Travels of a Genre*, les transformations du genre romanesque dans ses nouveaux lieux. En effet, selon Layoun (1990) le roman n'est pas un genre fixe, monolithique mais un genre qui émerge dans des circonstances socioculturelles et littéraires spécifiques et qui se développe en fonction de ce contexte. En d'autres termes, dans le cas de l'Afrique, cela signifie qu'il faut étudier comment le roman « moderne » européen s'est adapté au paysage local, aux formes littéraires (surtout orales : conte, épopée...) existantes. Si certains critiques supposent soit que les Africains ont pris pour modèle le roman français, notamment Balzac et Zola (critique eurocentriste (Chevrier 1974)), soit au contraire que le modèle français constitue une aliénation dont il faut se sortir en faisant appel au folklore, à la contestation, en valorisant les cultures noires (critique afrocentriste), nous considérons, avec Kane (1982), Koné (1996), Okpewho (1992), Ndiaye (2001) et Semujanga (2001), le roman africain contemporain comme un mélange entre récits oraux et romans européens, mixtes dont les proportions varient selon les auteurs.

Les deux orientations critiques afrocentristes et eurocentristes, situent le débat autour de l'africanité des textes et véhiculent des points de vue idéologiques. Le premier nie tout caractère spécifique à la littérature écrite africaine, le second revendique au contraire l'africanité de tels textes en mettant en avant leur originalité. La troisième position déplace ce débat vers le problème du genre romanesque, de l'écriture. Ne cherchant pas une origine unique à la littérature d'Afrique, cette perspective s'intéresse « *au processus plus dynamique de l'écriture littéraire* » (Semujanga 2001: 140) et analyse souvent le contexte historique dans lequel le roman africain se développe. Évidemment, cette dernière position montre une certaine originalité de la littérature d'Afrique (l'emprunt à la littérature orale) mais elle ne place pas cette particularité dans un débat idéologique. Nous adopterons cette approche.

Ainsi, à propos des relations entre le roman africain et le réalisme propre au roman moderne européen, nous verrons comment Sow Fall, à la fois, renouvelle et reproduit le genre romanesque européen tout en y intégrant certains aspects des récits oraux eux-mêmes transformés. Sow Fall résume d'ailleurs très bien cela: « *je suis tout à fait consciente que mes romans sont des romans, mais ce sont des romans qui portent un héritage de la tradition, des contes, des histoires, des légendes* » (Hawkins 1987). Il s'agit donc de faire une analyse transgénérique[14] des textes de Sow Fall, d'y étudier «*les relations entre le roman africain et le genre romanesque d'une part, et le roman et les autres genres de productions culturelles....*» (Semujanga 2001 : 147).

Les éléments présentés dans ce qui suit ne seront pas réellement approfondis, nous nous contenterons d'ouvrir des pistes. Notre objectif se limite à faire sentir aux lecteurs les multiples origines du réalisme des romans de Sow Fall, de lui faire sentir la présence à la fois des récits oraux et d'une esthétique romanesque occidentale.

QUI EST MODERNE ?

La question du genre est une question délicate car elle nous ramène au problème de la modernité.[15] En effet, la plupart des auteurs lorsqu'ils parlent du roman européen sous-entendent «roman moderne » par opposition aux récits, romans du moyen âge et de la période classique. La modernité de ces romans est basée sur la définition occidentale de la modernité. Or, il est clair que, dans le cas de Sow Fall, le roman africain ne répond pas exactement aux qualificatifs qui en font un roman moderne au sens européen. Et pourtant il n'en est pas moins moderne.[16] Comment résoudre ce paradoxe? La réponse en est donnée par Semujanga lorsqu'il nous dit que « *l'inscription des références aux éléments esthétiques de l'oralité et leur mise en narration romanesque ainsi que l'adaptation des démarches esthétiques contemporaines constituent des éléments de l'émergence de la modernité africaine* » (2001: 154).

A travers les différents exemples qui vont suivre, nous verrons à chaque fois comment Sow Fall prend des éléments des récits oraux, dits « traditionnels,» qu'elle intègre et adapte parfaitement au roman dit « moderne » et vice et versa. Ainsi, dans l'écriture de Sow Fall « modernité » et « tradition » cessent de se penser en opposition.

LE RÉALISME REVISITÉ

Tout d'abord, il est important de préciser qu'Aminata Sow Fall ne refuse pas l'héritage français. De toute manière, pourrait-elle y échapper? Elle a fait ses études en France et a enseigné la littérature française; quand on lui demande quels livres l'ont marquée, elle cite les romans de Barbey d'Aurevelly, *Tristan et Iseult* (c'est à partir de la lecture de ce livre qu'elle s'est aperçue que l'occident n'était pas simplement rationnel), ainsi que quelques auteurs étrangers comme Steinbeck (Sow Fall 2004). Sa vision de l'écrivain est très romantique : l'auteur qui l'a le plus touchée est Baudelaire (Sow Fall 2004).

Il est donc clair qu'elle a été marquée par la littérature et la critique française ou plus largement européenne. C'est un héritage auquel elle ne renonce pas. En effet, elle n'a jamais souhaité « tuer le père » pour reprendre l'expression de Mudimbe (1994). Elle a ainsi, toujours écrit et continue d'écrire en français sans que cela ne lui soit problématique.

Cependant, malgré cet héritage, Sow Fall n'a jamais cessé de questionner la littérature ni d'essayer d'en faire quelque chose d'original à l'écoute de la littérature orale. On peut d'ailleurs penser que si les auteurs africains sont restés si fidèles au réalisme, alors que ce genre est presque complètement délaissé en France, c'est par souci de continuité avec le réalisme de la littérature orale (Kane 1982: 61).

LES PERSONNAGES

Selon Watt (1982), la principale qualité du roman moderne (i.e. roman européen) est de placer l'homme dans son milieu physique. Les personnages mis en scène dans le roman moderne sont des individus qui ont des expériences particulières en des temps et des lieux particuliers. Ils ont des caractères psychologiques bien définis. Le tout dans un souci de réalisme. Ces individus ont des prénoms anodins. La banalité des prénoms serait un effet recherché par l'auteur européen. Aminata Sow Fall n'est pas aussi «moderne» (au sens européen) dans les personnages de ses romans. En effet, la plupart n'ont pas de caractères psychologiques bien définis. De plus, ils sont rarement très nuancés et sont plutôt extravagants, excessifs comme les protagonistes des récits oraux. De même, leurs prénoms sont rarement anodins et ont souvent une connotation morale très précise, connotation qui souligne leur destin. Sow Fall fait ici usage d'un réalisme symbolique. Par exemple, le personnage principal de *La grève des Bàttu* se nomme Mour ce qui signifie la chance. Or toute l'histoire est basée sur la superstition de Mour, sa croyance en la parole des marabouts, en sa chance. Toujours dans *La grève des Bàttu*, Lolli est l'épouse dévouée et soucieuse de l'avenir de son mari Mour. Or Lolli est le nom d'une saison vers décembre, ce nom évoque la femme qui a passé ses plus belles années. Sow Fall utilise donc un genre littéraire dit « moderne » mais y représente une société non individualiste.[17] Elle montre ainsi que les personnages des romans réalistes modernes ne sont pas forcément des individus au sens occidental du terme. Ici, Sow Fall se situe donc en continuité par rapport à la littérature orale par certaines caractéristiques de ses personnages, tout en étant dans la «modernité» de par le genre utilisé. Elle reproduit donc le genre romanesque tout en le renouvelant; le paradoxe du terme «roman moderne» apparaît encore.

HOMMAGE À LA TRADITION ORALE

Sow Fall rend souvent hommage à la tradition orale par la présence de griots, de contes ou d'épopées dans ses romans. Selon Kane, le réalisme de la tradition orale est souvent présent dans les romans africains sous la forme d'un «*discours traditionnel lent,*

répétitif, alourdi de références à l'histoire, à la légende et à la mythologie» (Kane 1982: 61). Cela est très clair dans *Le Jujubier du patriarche* où histoire des esclaves, des castes, légende et épopée sont très présentes.

Dans *Le Jujubier du patriarche*, Sow Fall fait largement appel à l'épopée. Le protagoniste du roman est une épopée qui est racontée et chantée par petits fragments tout au long du texte et à qui on accorde le dernier chapitre du livre. Cette épopée est une création de Sow Fall. Ainsi, l'auteur fait appel aux procédés narratifs de l'épopée pour en inventer une de toutes pièces ; elle emprunte la forme mais non le sujet. Elle présente cette épopée comme une épopée «authentique» (selon ses propres termes), et donc réaliste, comme faisant partie de la «tradition» collective. Elle a été ainsi fort satisfaite lorsque de nombreux critiques lui demandèrent s'il s'agissait d'une vraie épopée (Sow Fall 2004). Le procédé narratif qu'elle utilise lui permet de se situer dans la tradition tout en en renouvelant le sens par la place qu'elle attribue à l'auteur. Celui-ci est mis en avant sans pour autant nuire à la perpétuation et transmission collective de l'épopée. S'opère ici le passage du «nous» au «je». Sow Fall apporte dans cet exemple, expérience individuelle, originalité et nouveauté à la « tradition » orale, ce qui marque selon Watt (1982) l'entrée du romanesque dans l'ère moderne.

Le griot est un personnage très important de ce roman. C'est lui qui raconte l'épopée. Il y a ainsi deux voix dans ce texte : celle du narrateur et celle du griot. Sow Fall, qui fait réciter à un griot son épopée inventée, se place donc en continuité de la fonction du griot. Le romancier semble ainsi bien être le griot des temps modernes. Ce récit nous montre que les écrivains ont la même fonction que les griots mais que les modalités narratives sont différentes et doivent l'être car les contextes de production et de réception ont changé. Plus largement, Sow Fall situe ce roman en continuité avec le passé.

> Au cœur d'une écriture actuelle et d'une histoire contemporaine, elle réintègre les voix des griots transmettant les anciennes légendes, l'épopée de l'Almany Sarebibi et de Dioumana, qui se cacha dans le ventre de la baleine parce qu'elle n'était pas assez aimée. Ces voix traditionnelles prennent toute leur vigueur, transforment l'existence des personnages. Ce sont elles qui achèvent le roman, sans le conclure comme si l'avenir ne devait être qu'une continuation du passé héroïque (Borgomano 1994: 90).

Est ainsi figuré un temps national, continu et non brisé par la colonisation.

Ce roman, *Le Jujubier du patriarche*, a eu moins de succès au Sénégal que ses autres textes. Selon Kesteloot[18] (Sow Fall 2004), les Sénégalais ont boudé ce livre car il ne serait pas assez terre à terre, son réalisme mettrait en scène plus l'aspect symbolique de la société wolof que la vie quotidienne, matérielle. De même, Sow Dieye (Sow Fall 2004) voit dans le fait d'introduire une épopée dans un roman un moyen pour atteindre le public étranger: l'étranger pourrait trouver le conte, la fable, l'Afrique «ancestrale,» «primitive,» «exotique,» derrière cette fiction.[19] Au contraire, le public africain voudrait voir des histoires de son temps, d'aujourd'hui. La reproduction presque directe d'une épopée dans un roman ne satisferait donc pas le public local. On voit bien ici que l'écrit ne peut pas être la transcription directe de l'oral. Les contenus doivent différer mais non au dépens de la continuité.[20] Les autres romans de Sow Fall, plus ancrés dans le quotidien sénégalais, plus terre à terre, semblent avoir mieux répondu aux attentes du public sénégalais.[21]

Dans *L'Appel des arènes*, la tradition est également convoquée sous une forme directe : Aminata Sow Fall retranscrit les chants des lutteurs. De même, la lutte, considérée dans ce texte comme faisant partie de la «tradition,» est présente pendant les trois-quarts du texte sous forme orale : Nalla écoute des récits de lutte sur magnétophone et entend les tam-tams des combats de lutte et de vagues chants au loin.

CONTEUR POUR ADULTES : MORALITÉ ET TEMPORALITÉ.

Selon Watt (1982), le roman « moderne » assigne une très grande importance à la dimension du temps. Cela le différencie de la « tradition » littéraire antérieure qui « *consistait à se servir d'histoires intemporelles comme miroir d'immuables vérités morales* » (Watt 1982 : 28). Les contes, dans la «tradition» orale africaine, sont souvent didactiques. Là encore Sow Fall reprend cette « tradition » moraliste mais elle la resitue dans des histoires temporelles. Nous avons là encore adaptation et transformation.

L'Appel des arènes est particulièrement moralisateur : la mère de Nalla, Diattou est critiquée, condamnée par le texte pour avoir été totalement aliénée par l'occident. Le roman s'acharne véritablement contre Diattou qui est allée trop loin dans l'aliénation. Elle est ainsi rejetée de manière symbolique de la façon la plus irrémédiable de cette société : la sorcellerie. On accuse Diattou de sorcellerie, ce qui l'isole définitivement de la société. De plus, ce blâme est la condamnation la plus dure, la plus définitive puisque la sorcellerie se transmet de génération en génération par la mère. Diattou est donc punie pour avoir rejeté violemment toutes formes de «traditions,» de coutumes locales.

Le Revenant comporte également une dimension didactique: Sow Fall y dénonce l'importance qu'a l'argent aux yeux des Sénégalais urbains. Ces derniers croient que l'argent procure intelligence, gloire et grandeur. Yama, la sœur du protagoniste (Bakar), profite de chaque cérémonie pour montrer sa prospérité. Bakar se retrouve en prison après avoir volé de l'argent à son travail afin de satisfaire les besoins de sa femme. Yama renie alors son frère. Ce dernier lui donne ensuite une bonne leçon de morale: après avoir donné la fausse nouvelle de sa mort, Bakar assiste incognito à son enterrement. Sa famille qui l'a renié jusqu'à sa mort organise quand même de grandes funérailles pour récolter l'argent et les biens matériels donnés comme à l'accoutumée. La nuit, lorsque la famille réunie l'argent récolté, Bakar frappe à la porte et entre à la surprise de tous. Il leur dit que c'est dieu qui l'envoie chercher son « sarax » (tout cet argent). Il prend l'argent et s'échappe. Yama sort en criant que Bakar est revenu.

La morale de ce roman est d'autant plus claire que le roman oppose le comportement de Yama et Bakar à celui de Sada, le meilleur et seul véritable ami de Bakar dont la conduite est irréprochable, loyale, dévouée, honnête. Il est en quelque sorte, pour reprendre les mots de Guèye (2002), la « conscience morale » du roman. L'opposition entre Yama (et Bakar) et Sada donne à ce récit une structure dualiste (2002). Ce type de structure caractérise en général le conte (ibid.). On voit donc ici les romans de Sow Fall se rapprocher encore du conte, de l'oralité.

Toujours dans cette fiction, trois proverbes, présents à différents endroits du récits, indiquent l'orientation morale du texte : « *Ban gàcce nangu dee* », pas la honte, plutôt la mort (31) ; « *Addina neexul* », la vie réserve des surprises (32) ; et « *Nit nit ay garaba* », l'homme est le remède de l'homme (109). Tout le roman de Sow Fall est une dramatisation de ces proverbes (Gueye 2002). Le premier proverbe joue le rôle de la finale initiale du récit.[22] Par ce procédé, Sow Fall se rapproche encore des techniques du conte et du réalisme symbolique.

L'emploi de proverbes fait partie du réalisme de l'oralité au quotidien. Or ce sont les proverbes qui véhiculent la moralité de ses romans. Ainsi la moralité pour exister aurait besoin de l'oralité. Nous pourrions peut-être parler de (m)oralité.

L'aspect moralisateur, et donc didactique, de ses romans vaut à Sow Fall le qualificatif de «conteur pour adulte.» Sow Fall essaye par la morale non seulement de révéler aux lecteurs la situation sociale, mais également de réformer, d'orienter les mœurs en mettant en scène des contre-exemples.

Cet aspect moraliste est introduit à travers des récits clairement situés dans le temps. Le cadre spatio-temporel de chacun des romans de Sow Fall est bien défini. Les personnages évoluent tous dans le « cours du temps.» Il n'y a pas de restriction du temps de l'action (comme dans la tragédie) ou d'élasticité du temps (comme dans l'épopée). Le temps du récit est réaliste, il nous ramène à notre vie quotidienne. Le contexte socio-historique est toujours clairement déterminé : situation postcoloniale, d'indépendance, circonstances de l'immigration, problèmes des charters, etc.

En faisant coexister moralité et temporalité réaliste, Sow Fall opère donc encore une synthèse entre techniques du conte et roman «moderne.»

DE LA COMMUNAUTÉ À LA NATION

Tout comme dans les récits oraux, le réalisme de Sow Fall semble être un moyen pour assurer l'unité et la continuité du groupe social. Mais là encore Sow Fall réalise un déplacement. En effet, le contexte de la tradition orale a changé, il faut donc adapter le contenu de la littérature au nouveau paysage socio-politique. Ainsi, si le contexte de lecture et les circonstances socio-politiques de l'épopée étaient en premier lieu la communauté (une épopée raconte l'histoire d'une famille, d'une communauté), le contexte du roman moderne est celui de la nation. Si l'épopée avait pour objectif de rassembler, d'unir tous les « éléments » d'une communauté, les romans, faisant appel à la tradition orale, semblent avoir pour but d'unir tous les sujets de la nation. Par exemple, dans *L'Appel des arènes*, la lutte est un élément fédérateur, rassembleur. Tout le monde va à la lutte. De même, le libraire « par terre » attire tout public dans *Le Jujubier du patriarche*: « *d'honorables messieurs, des dames pimpantes et de nombreux toubabs* » (50) mais aussi « *des bandes de jeunes adolescents venus des quartiers populaires* » (51), Sow Fall fait ainsi l'apologie du décloisonnement des classes par le moyen de l'instruction, de la lecture. Le livre, et donc l'écrivain, est ici fédérateur.

ÉGALITÉ DE TOUS DANS « LA DIGNITÉ »

On trouve ce changement d'échelle à un autre niveau : la conscience de caste présente dans les récits oraux est remplacée dans les romans de Sow Fall par la conscience de classe.

Dans *Le Jujubier du patriarche* conscience de caste et conscience de classe sont superposées. Les classes, qui remplacent les castes sans pour autant leur correspondre, sont à l'origine de l'histoire : des « *aristocrates des temps anciens dont les conceptions n'ont pas épousé à temps les réalités de la société moderne vivent l'épreuve de la pauvreté due au sens communautaire et à toutes les conduites liées à la fierté des origines* » (*Le Jujubier du patriarche*, 1993, quatrième de couverture).

La conscience de classe est aussi présente dans *La grève des Bàttu* où n'importe quelle «catégorie» opprimée peut se reconnaître dans les mendiants. Plus largement on peut comparer les mendiants aux femmes, aux colonisés.

Sow Fall représente donc dans ses textes tous les « éléments » de la nation. Le « il » au détour d'une phrase devient un «nous.» Les personnages de ses romans sont des citoyens de « classes » économiques et sociales différentes et les lieux sont souvent des espaces publics. En effet, Sow Fall a cherché à étendre son champ de narration au domaine public. *L'Appel des arènes* par exemple, ne se borne pas à la sphère familiale, son centre se trouve être le lieu public des arènes. Dans ce sens, nous pouvons peut-être qualifier les romans de Sow Fall de romans nationaux. Si le paysage de ses romans est plus urbain, elle élargit cet espace local, l'urbain, au national par une sorte de métonymie.

Nous venons donc d'illustrer à travers six exemples comment Sow Fall adapte diverses techniques de la littérature orale au roman moderne et vice et versa. D'autres exemples auraient pu être choisis, nous en évoquerons rapidement encore deux qui sont particulièrement évocateurs.

Tout d'abord, Sow Fall, dans *Un grain de vie et d'espérance*, tout comme de nombreux récits oraux, chante les louanges de la communauté. Ce texte est un véritable hymne à la nourriture sénégalaise. Nous pourrions même parler de nationalisme culinaire. Elle montre dans ce livre que rien n'est meilleur pour les Sénégalais que leur cuisine. Elle aurait pu faire une critique de la cuisine sénégalaise (qui est particulièrement anti-diététique par exemple), se moquer des Sénégalais et d'elle-même qui refuse de manger de la lotte « car a mauvaise figure, » mais au lieu de cela elle reproduit exactement le discours élogieux des Sénégalais sur leur nourriture. Elle louange dans ce texte les talents culinaires des Sénégalais ainsi que tout ce qui entoure l'acte de manger.

Et enfin, les romans de Sow Fall sont des divertissements. Loin de penser que, comme l'Afrique va mal, les histoires ne devraient plus avoir pour but de divertir mais de déranger de manière austère, Sow Fall continue d'amuser, de faire rire son public. Elle reste en cela fidèle à la prestation des griots. C'est d'ailleurs une des raisons de son succès.

CONCLUSION

Nous avons donc vu comment Sow Fall, loin de s'impliquer politiquement, s'engage par le moyen du réalisme, par ce que j'ai nommé « l'exemple. » Cet engagement nécessite qu'elle n'écrive pas sur la base de souvenirs, mais en étant bien ancrée dans son milieu, en étant « située. » Ainsi Sow Fall, à la différence de nombreux écrivains africains qui ont commencé à écrire en situation d'exil, s'est mise à écrire au retour au pays. Il est certain qu'à la différence d'un grand nombre d'auteurs africains, elle avait la chance d'habiter Dakar, havre africain de la liberté d'écriture. Écrire au retour est tout de même significatif : certes l'exil lui a donné la distance sans doute nécessaire à l'écrivain, qui lui permet d'être ensuite et pour toujours « sur les marges, » sur les « frontières; » cependant Sow Fall a besoin du Sénégal, de sa quotidienneté pour écrire. Elle est donc, sans doute, dans son écriture, plus locale que des écrivains exilés ou émigrés, qui, même s'ils écrivent sur le Sénégal, ne peuvent que décrire un milieu lointain. De plus, leur lieu quotidien les influence certainement[23] (c'est d'ailleurs pour cela que l'on parle parfois d'une littérature de l'exil). Sow Fall reste en tout cas fidèle à son lieu d'écriture.[24]

Nous avons également analysé comment les romans de Sow Fall se situent à la jonction du roman « moderne » et de la littérature orale.

Ainsi, dans les romans de Sow Fall, oralité et écriture, roman et récits oraux cessent de se penser en opposition. L'oralité y est présente de deux manières: présence de la littérature orale et oralité du quotidien. Le style dépouillé, la narration multiforme, l'absence de profondeur psychologique des personnages sont un héritage de la « tradition » orale. Ainsi, ces « défauts » considérés comme des faiblesses constituent souvent un choix à partir duquel le roman africain se différencie du roman occidental. (Minh-ha 1982: 780). Par la présence de l'oralité du quotidien nous pouvons dire que les romans de Sow Fall se situent entre les romans de l'élite et la littérature populaire. Sow Fall réussit ainsi à allier roman de mœurs, roman populaire et qualité littéraire.

Outre ce mélange à l'intérieur même du genre romanesque, nous avons vu comment Sow Fall fait fusionner roman, conte, proverbe, etc. Le réalisme des romans de Sow Fall n'est pas strictement naturaliste, il est également symbolique et parfois spirituel et se nourrit du réalisme de la littérature orale.

Si la tradition littéraire européenne a imposé une nette distinction et séparation des genres et des modes, la littérature africaine en fait une synthèse hybride où l'écrivain se situe dans l'entre deux: aux frontières des genres, des modes, des cultures.

Concluons sur ces quelques mots de Sow Fall qui témoignent bien de sa conscience des liens entre réalisme et engagement:

«Il faut faire la distinction entre s'engager, une littérature engagée et l'engagement politique parce que quand un auteur s'engage par exemple contre la production, ce n'est pas forcément une prise de position politique mais forcément ça s'adresse à des politiques mais c'est votre conscience humaine qui n'accepte pas ce qui vous révolte.»

«Si vous voyez des faits d'injustices, des choses comme ça forcément vous les dites mais vous n'êtes pas dans un parti politique, vous avez votre conscience humaine qui se révolte parce qu'écrire c'est en quelque sorte être une conscience.»

«Alors l'engagement il est réel, si c'est ça l'engagement de ne pas être sourd ni aveugle devant tout ce qui peut nous interpeller. Si le fait d'entendre les échos du monde qui nous entoure, et d'être obligé de les prendre en charge, d'en parler, de les voir, de les sortir, de dire sa propre vision par rapport à ça, si c'est ça l'engagement, je dis oui engagement mais pas engagement politique. Moi j'entends par engagement politique quelqu'un qui oeuvre dans le sens d'un projet politique. Moi, je ne suis pas dans un projet politique, mon projet c'est la dignité humaine, c'est l'âme qui jouit de sa liberté, qui soit reconnue dans son intégrité, le fait qu'il puisse s'exprimer librement, et qu'il oeuvre à ça aussi, ce n'est pas dans un attentisme béat, qui attend qu'on oeuvre à tout, qu'il participe justement à ce qu'il doit devenir, qu'il puisse participer lui-même à ce qui détermine son destin. Pour moi l'engagement c'est ça» (Sow Fall 2004)

NOTES

1. Dans un sens historique; ses prédécesseurs étaient portés vers l'extérieur : le public visé était d'abord européen.

2. Dans le sens, tout ce qui vient du chez soi.

3. E.P: entretien personnel non publié

4. Sow Fall aime d'ailleurs préciser qu'elle écrit plus en tant que «citoyenne» qu'en tant que femme, car la citoyenne inclut la femme (Sow Fall, E.P, 2004). Ce statut de «citoyenne» lui permet de s'occuper, dans ses romans, non seulement des problèmes des femmes mais également de ceux de la société sénégalaise dans son ensemble.

5. Elle-même est d'ailleurs un exemple de femmes fortes positives.

6. Sow Dieye est professeure de lettres à Dakar.

7. La plupart des écrivains de romans écrits avant la deuxième guerre mondiale (romanciers de la première génération) annonçaient en préface : « voilà ce qu'est l'Afrique », ils s'adressaient ainsi d'abord à un public occidental qui accueillait leurs oeuvres comme des témoignages « authentiques » du vécu africain. De même, les romans d'après-guerre (romanciers de la deuxième génération), généralement anti-coloniaux, dans un objectif de réhabilitation s'adressaient davantage à l'Occident et aux élites intellectuelles qui, selon Sow Fall, « s'étaient un peu acculturées » (Sow Fall, E.P, 2004). Voir Ndiaye (2004).

8. Pour Sow Fall cette absence d'ethnotexte ne signifie en aucun cas qu'elle ne sera pas lue par les Occidentaux. En effet, elle pense que tout le monde, que « l'humanité » peut se retrouver dans ses romans. Elle croit ainsi en une espèce d'universalité culturelle de/ dans la littérature. Selon son propre expérience, toutes les littératures, française, italienne ou autres ont d'ailleurs toujours fonctionné de la sorte et cela ne leur a pas empêché d'être traduites et comprises par un lectorat étranger (Sow Fall, E.P, 2004).

9. Battu

10. Bassirou Dieng est professeur de Lettres à Dakar, co-auteur avec Lylian Kesteloot de, 1997, *Les épopées d'Afrique noire,* Paris : Karthala-Unesco

11. Il est important de rappeler la distinction entre le genre (roman, conte, théâtre) et le mode (réaliste, fantastique) d'un texte. Le genre n'est en général pas culturel mais il peut exister une « relation transculturelle par la convocation des motifs figés propres à une aire culturelle (légende/roman ou oralité/écriture) » (Semujanga, 2001 : 148)

12. Ce texte constitue le premier chapitre de son livre : 1957, *The Rise of the Novel,* Londres : Chatto and Windus.

13. Si l'histoire n'est pas en soi entièrement réaliste, ne pourrait pas arriver dans la réalité (une grève de mendiants (*La grève des Bàttu*) est par exemple très fortement improbable), elle permet de dénoncer des faits, valeurs, sentiments présents dans la société sénégalaise.

14. « De prime abord, l'intertextualité est limitée aux seules relations qu'un texte donné établit avec d'autres textes connus, tandis que la transculturalité et la transgénéricité visent la relation transversale de toutes les productions symboliques dans le champ sémiotique international» (Semujanga, 2001 : 143)

15. Nous ne remettrons pas en question le concept de modernité, nous souhaitons simplement souligner qu'il pose problème. De même, tout au long de cette étude, nous utiliserons les termes «modernité» et «tradition» mais les mettrons entre guillemets pour souligner qu'ils posent problème, mais que pour le moment nous n'en avons pas de meilleurs.

16. En effet, comment un roman qui a pour origine le roman dit

moderne (soit européen) pourrait-il ne pas être moderne ?

17. L'individualisme caractérise en général la société dite «moderne».

18. Lylian Kesteloot, spécialiste de l'histoire littéraire de l'Afrique francophone, est auteure, entre autres, de, 1963, *Les écrivains noirs de langue française : naissance d'une littérature,* Bruxelles : Éditions de l'université de Bruxelles.

19. Ce livre est sans doute un des plus étudiés au niveau académique mais un des plus ardus surtout pour un public occidental. Nous ne sommes donc pas sûrs qu'il ait réellement été mieux reçu en Occident comparativement avec ses autres livres.

20. « Selon Mohamadou Kane, l'efficacité du discours africain se mesure par sa référence à l'expérience des anciens, au passé du groupe social, à un ensemble de valeurs morales dont les proverbes constituent l'expression la plus belle, la plus profonde » (Guèye, 2002 : 72).

21. Cela n'est qu'une supposition fondée sur mes quelques entretiens avec divers professeurs de Lettres à Dakar. Il serait très intéressant de faire une étude de la réception des romans de Sow Fall.

22. «La finale initiale ou dialectique du conte est un procédé largement répandu en Afrique Noire qui consiste à énoncer, dans la partie initiale ou plus souvent à titre de conclusion, des remarques qui, sous une forme abrégée et d'allure proverbiale, disent ce dont le récit a été (ou sera) la forme développée, l'explication» (Guèye, 2002 : 72).

23. Certains, comme Seydou Lamine (1983), dirait que l'érotisme des romans de Calixthe Beyala par exemple, écrivaine camerounaise exilée en France, est un thème totalement occidental.

24. De même, loin de vouloir être d'abord lue par les Occidentaux, Sow Fall a le souci de distribuer ses romans au Sénégal, dans ce but elle a elle-même ouvert une maison d'édition à Dakar : Les Éditions Khoudia.

ŒUVRES CITÉES

Abèles, M. *L'échec en politique.* Paris: Circé, 2005.

Bâ, Mariama. *Une si longue lettre.* Paris: Le Serpent à plumes, 2001 (premières publications en 1979 aux Nouvelles Éditions Africaines du Sénégal).

Borgomano, M. « Les femmes et l'écriture-parole.» In: *Notre Librairie* 117 (avril-juin), 1994: 87-94.

Bugul, Ken. *Le Baobab fou*. Dakar: Les Nouvelles Éditions Africaines, 1982.

Chevrier, J. *Littérature nègre*. Paris: Armand Collin, 1974.

D'Almeida, I. A. «Femme? Féministe? Misovire?» In: *Notre Librairie* 117 (avril-juin): 1994: 48-51.

Dieng, B. Entretien réalisé par Léa Kalaora (juin), non publié, 2004.

Dieng, B. et Kesteloot Lillian. *Les épopées d'Afrique noire*. Paris: Karthala-UNESCO, 1997.

Guèye, M. «Écriture, développement et féminisme: Entretien avec Aminata Sow Fall.» In: *The Literary Griot* 12.2: 2000: 44-58

_____. «Tradition orale et philosophie wolof chez Aminata Sow Fall: une esthétique transgénérique et transculturelle dans *Le Revenant*.» In: *Langues & Littératures* 6 (janvier), 2002: 59-79. Disponible également sur http://www.critaoi.org

Hawkins, P. «An Interview with Senegalese Novelist Aminata Sow Fall.» In: *French Studies Bulletin* Spring, 1987: 19-21.

Kane, M. *Roman africain et traditions*. Dakar: Les Nouvelles Éditions Africaines, 1982.

Kesteloot, Lillian. *Les écrivains noirs de langue française: naissance d'une littérature*. Bruxelles: Éditions de l'université de Bruxelles, 1963.

_____. Entretien réalisé par Léa Kalaora (juin), non publié, 2004.

Koné, A. «Figures d'hier et d'aujourd'hui: vers une nouvelle perception du roman africain.» In: C. Ndiaye et Semujanga J. Eds. *De paroles en figures, essais sur les littératures africaines et antillaises*. Montréal : Harmattan, 1996: 23-39

Kuoh-Maukoury, T. «Noires». In: *Le magazine littéraire* 195 (mai), 1983: 26-28

Lamine, S. «Les héros sont fatigués». In: *Le magazine littéraire* 195 (mai), 1983: 23-26.

Laye, Camara. *L'Enfant noir*. Paris: Press Pocket, 1973.

Layoun, M. *Travels of a Genre, the Modern Novel and Ideology*, Princeton, New Jersey: Princeton University Press, 1990.

Melville, Bartelby. *Tristan et Iseult*, Paris: Nouveau commerce, 1976.

Mudimbe V.Y. *The Idea of Africa*, Bloomington: Indiana University Press, 1994.

Ndiaye, C. «De l'écrit à l'oral: la transformation des classiques du roman africain,» In: *Études françaises*, 2001, 37.2: 45-63

_____. Ed. *Introduction aux littératures francophones*. Montréal: Les Presses de l'Université de Montréal, 2004.

Okpewho, Isidore. *African Oral Literature: Backgrounds, Character, and Continuity*, Bloomington: Indiana University Press, 1992.

Pfaff, Françoise. «Aminata Sow Fall: l'écriture au féminin.» In: *Notre Librairie* 81 (oct-déc), 1985: 35-138.

Semujanga, J. «De l'africanité à la transculturalité: éléments d'une critique littéraire dépolitisée du roman». In: *Études françaises* 3, 2001, 7.2: 133-159.

Sow Dieye, A. Entretiens réalisé par Léa Kalaora (juin), non publié, 2004.

Sow Fall, Aminata. *Le Revenant*. Dakar : Nouvelles Éditions Africaines, 1976.

_____. *La grève des Bàttu*. Dakar: Nouvelles Éditions Africaines, 1979.

_____. *L'Appel des arènes*. Dakar: Nouvelles Éditions Africaines, 1982.

_____. *L'Ex-père de la nation*. Dakar: C.A.E.C. Khoudia Éditions, 1993.

_____. *Le Jujubier du patriarche*. Dakar: C.A.E.C. Khoudia Éditions, 1993.

_____. *Douceurs du bercail*. Abidjan: Nouvelles Éditions Ivoiriennes, 1998.

_____. *Un grain de vie et d'espérance*. Paris: Françoise Truffaut éditions, 2002.

_____. Entretiens réalisés par Léa Kalaora (juin), non publiés, 2004.

Trinh T. Minh-ha. "Aminata Sow Fall et l'espace du don." In: *The French Review*, 1982, 55.6: 780-789.

Watt, I. *The Rise of the Novel*, London: Chatto and Windus, 1957. [Voir aussi «Réalisme et forme romanesque.» In: Barthes R., Bersani L., Hamon PH., 1957].

Watt, I et M. Riffaterre. *Littérature et réalité*. Paris: Éditions du Seuil, 1982. 11-47

Ada Uzoamaka Azodo

Portrait of Aminata Sow Fall

1

Aminata Sow Fall and Ada Azodo, the editor of volume

Aminata Sow Fall at the UNESCO Celebration

Aminata Sow Fall and Cheikh Hamidou Kane

Aminata Sow Fall and former Senegalese President, Abdoul Diouf

Aminata Sow Fall and Idris Makward at the UNESCO Celebration

Aminata Sow Fall and Alioune Badara Bèye, President Union des Écrivants Sénégalais,

Photographs

Aminata Sow Fall and Bosom Friend Marième Diouri at UNESCO
Celebration

Samba Sow and two of the children

Aminata Sow Fall and Aly Meroueh, Founder of 4 Vents Bookstore on Rue Félix-Faure, Dakar

Friends and Family after the Marriage Ceremony

1963 Marriage of Aminata Fall and Samba Sow in Paris

BOOK TWO

The Imaginary in the Novels of Aminata Sow Fall

THE IMAGINARY IN THE NOVELS OF AMINATA SOW FALL

ADA UZOAMAKA AZODO

❄ ❄ ❄

INTRODUCTION

In the first section of this book, the focus was on the study of social realism in Aminata Sow Fall's work, due to the inability of new African leaders to alleviate the ills imposed on African societies by alien colonizing powers from the outside, as well as on those from the inside that Africans have put on themselves, due to corruption, greed, and cruelty. These ills caused the traditional system in place to fragment and break up, leaving nothing in place to replace what was gone, for what came from the outside was not valid enough to take the place of what it displaced. At the other end of the spectrum, however, is the authorial struggle to reclaim what was lost, through revolutionary thinking and action from the people. At those instances, the authorial tone also takes on epic dimensions as she and her protagonists fight and resist fate and destiny. It is this authorial double vision on African modern society and African traditions, which places the critic in a unique position to explore the African soul.

Ada Uzoamaka Azodo, Ph.D., is associate faculty in African and African Diaspora Studies in the Department of Minority Studies and Women's Studies at Indiana University Northwest at Gary.

Hence, in this second section on the imaginary, we examine how Sow Fall's texts have other longer lasting lessons on African worldview for Africans and the entire humanity beyond the authorial social vision. Certain critics have noted and commented on some of these symbolic, visionary, and ritual aspects of her writings, but have failed to profoundly study them. Our objective, then, is to study them in a sustained and profound manner. We shall employ psychocriticism in the study of individual characters, in order to understand their actions or reactions to their time period and the fate they suffer. On the other hand, we shall apply mythocriticism for the study of Wolof culture in particular, and in general, African cultures, which are embedded in the folktales, legends, epics, songs, allegories, not to mention food, clothing, arts and crafts, and language. Throughout the study, the African ancestral foundations or worldviews that privilege the supernatural will be in focus. Sow Fall resurrects them, refusing the notion of art for art's sake, but rather embracing art as a means of reintegrating, regenerating, and restoring African epistemologies and ways of knowing.

This study is on all of the author's eight writings from the angle of the imaginary. "Saga" as a term denotes a story of epic dimensions in prose form. "Song" employed as a term in this study means an interpretation achieved with African oral tradition in mind to either praise or satirize, in order to make the community or society better. Hence, the title and the sub-title of each chapter reflect the particular aspect(s) of African tradition highlighted.

Thus, the first chapter entitled "The Saga of Bakar Diop, the Ghost of Gueule Tapée" denotes, first, the epic adventure of Bakar Diop, representative of Everyman, and second, his experience as a ghost whose travails also deal with the collective issues of life and death, reincarnation and the hereafter in the African worldview.

The second chapter, 'The Saga of the Boroom Bàttu, the Dregs of Society," recalls the Islamic third pillar of *zakat* (almsgiving or helping the needy); the Haves are enjoined to give up a tithe of 2.5% of their earnings for the purpose of taking care of the Have-nots. The other four pillars in numerical order are the *shahada* (testifying); *salat* (praying); *saum* (reflecting and fasting), and *hajj* (making the pilgrimage to Mecca). It is worthy of note that in Wolof culture, the Islamic tradition is reputedly in perfect symbiosis with African traditions, and as such both traditions almost perfectly merge in this study.

The third chapter, "The Saga of Nalla, the Pupil of Teacher Niang" is the somewhat mythical adventure of a neophyte in search of self and his culture under the tutelage, first of his tutor, Mr. Niang, who, after having traced the pioneering path, cedes his place for more thorough reintegration of the child to two traditional guides, wrestlers André and Malaw who take up the relay. The outcome is a recall of African ways of knowing that the child needs for a rebirth into his culture.

The fourth chapter, "The Saga of Yellimané Badar, the Hero of Natangué" traces the heroic and pseudo-shamanic initiation of a culture hero at two levels, in the past and in the present. We are privileged to see the authorial modern myth invention for the restoration, regeneration and reintegration of the past and present of Africa. In this study, the hero kills the mother, so that he may the more gloriously flourish.

The fifth chapter, "The Saga of Madiama, a Failed Father of the Nation" is an exploration of the archetypal "Father" in African modern times. The image of the father is put to death, so that Africa can forge ahead with its development and progress.

The sixth chapter, "The Saga of Asta Diop, the Bosom Friend of Anne Lemaire" is a hymn, a praisesong to human friendship and human understanding across boundaries of race, culture, and color. The deep and human understanding between the two women, one African and the other French, portrays an imaginary understanding between peoples, nations, and races of the world that bodes well for the future of humanity.

The seventh chapter, "Song of Hope 1: About Life and Joy" is an invitation to look again at the good qualities of African culture, through its culinary art. It is a joyful song of hope and love.

The eighth and last chapter, "Song of Hope 11: About Afritude" continues the same invitation as the first song of hope on a grander scale, and calls on human beings to eschew materialism, but rather embrace spiritualism, in order to create an important basis for validating our common humanity.

As much as possible, we have stayed away from following the chronology of the writings in particular, and of history, in general, although we have not hesitated to follow the plot of the story, and cite historical events, when necessary, for indeed, many times myths and products of the unconscious permeate the social realistic scene before reaching the reader or critic. Some of the writings are definitely protestations of the times, while others are more or less initiatory in nature. Nonetheless, both categories demonstrate the need to reintegrate the African cyclical past into the present for human regeneration and renaissance.

CONCLUSION

In this second section on the imaginary in the novels of Aminata Sow Fall, I have attempted an oblique reading of all of Aminata Sow Fall's novels to the present. The anthropological methodology of the imaginary, as explained in the main introduction to this volume, has allowed us to fathom the African soul embedded in her literary works, enabling us to explore the deeper meanings of the symbols and images in these works, not to mention the lessons in such African genres as tales, legends, epics, allegories, and myths. I have discovered the author's obsession about the African past and the lessons they bear for the present, not only for Africans, but also for peoples of other cultures. It means that the dignity of a people resides in their ability to discover themselves, who they are as a people, and take pride in their heritage.

"THE SAGA OF BAKAR DIOP, THE GHOST OF GUEULE TAPÉE"

❀ ❀ ❀

This reading of Aminata Sow Fall's *Le Revenant*, employs the African trickster archetypal motif as method of study. The trickster in African mythology represents untamed basal human consciousness, and explores the physical, animal nature of the very inventive and creative character that plays it, an individual with a moral purpose that transcends his apparent amorality. The trickster can be a sort of Messiah or savior come to the rescue, for the trickster can articulate divine justice, fate, and destiny, just like Legba, another popular trickster and archetypal motif of the Fon mythology in present-day Benin Republic, West Africa (Leeming 1990: 171-172).

More specifically, this study will elucidate the meanings and implications of the ghost symbolism and the schema of images and symbols around it in *Le Revenant*, and explore the African soul inherent in the complexities of life in post-independent Africa. According to Roger Chemain, authorial language often hides radical, primordially rooted, values that go far beyond the usual concepts planted by colonization, protests, contestations, and decolonization in Africa (1986; Introduction, 13-26). *Le Revenant*, therefore, might have some eternal truths about human beings lurking behind the apparent castigation of the ghost's fellow citizens for their shortcomings.

The story line runs like this. Bakar returns as a ghost, *in cognito*, to his village community of Gueule Tapée as members of his extended family gather to share his *sarax*, that is money collected at his funeral, but reversals of fate and destiny cohabit with clashed illusions and hopes, and Bakar, who was taken advantage of, returns and swipes them of the booty they gathered to share.

Roger Chemain has also noted in his eminent work on the imaginary of contemporary African novels (1986) that human anthropological situation ephemerally echo the permanent human condition. In other words, the overt social ills and abuses that emphasize the human condition on the existential level also reflect the spiritual condition on the primordial level. All human societies are inherently similar in these ideas about the human condition and life, death, and human nature in general. It is only the local color that is different. Human beings get the destiny and fate they carve for themselves during their sojourn on earth (Chemain 1986: 11). The saga of Bakar mirrors on his individual level and on the collective level of his community human need for spirituality, in order to combat human anguish.

Thus, *Le Revenant* is a reflection on African spirituality. It mirrors true reality through the elements that transport messages from the dead ancestors to the living. It is a reality in which mysterious and dreadful beings in the parallel universes of invisible forces cohabit in a mysterious symbiosis with the elements, gods, spirits, and the supernatural.

It is in the style of the story that can be found the belief in the supernatural, which has given birth to the ghost symbolism in *Le Revenant*. Suffice it to say that a stylistic feature of traditional African tales is a fantastical, even phantasmagorical, narrative structure, which is neither chronological nor linear, but diachronic and synchronic. A number of the Wolof expressions, explained in the glossary at the end of this chapter, carry some of the wisdom of this oral tradition in written form.[1]

Bakar's fate seems wound up with the supernatural. Why, for example, does he fail in everything he does: career, job, marriage, friendships, and family? What does the ghost symbolism portend beyond the individual unconscious? Clearly, there is a certain coherence about this symbol, which unearths underlying African myths that elucidate human need to minimize, if not, escape the vicissitudes of history, and by extension, death.[2]

Bakar's comprehension of the African worldview on the mysteries of life and death help him to cope with his mental and psychological problems. In Wolof belief system as such, life is the road to death, and death the road to life, real life. Death's door opens only after the road of life is closed. The dead are held to continue to live with the living in a long line of ancestry that defies virtual boundaries of life and death. The real truth about death seems to be that human beings live forever, for death is only the other door, which human beings escape through when they have fulfilled their life's mission on the earthly plane. The communal system of relationship one with another also indicates an enduring solidarity between human beings and the dead. *Le Revenant* decries the sacrifice of traditional myths at the altar of modernity and materialism in post-independence Senegal. It demystifies society, exposing the lack of brotherhood between segments of society, and the hypocrisy and perfidy of those who purport to love without honestly doing so. More specifically, Bakar portrays the anguish of a people estranged from their culture, and from one another, due to class, elitism, work, and education.

Bakar embezzles money from his work to pay for an outlandish naming ceremony for his new born daughter organized by his perfidious sister, Yama, who had impressed on him the necessity to do things in a big way, in order to take the family out of a lower class to a higher one. Having married up herself to a rich trader, Amar Ndiaye, Yama becomes obsessed about money. She now sees herself as a *diriyanké*, a beloved and spoilt upper class wife, with her own retinue of sycophants and griots. Bakar is able to marry a rich girl, Mame Aïssa Guèye, the daughter of wealthy Adja Dado Sarr and d'El Hadji Wellé Guèye, thanks to Yama's machinations. Bakar's parents, Ngoné and Ossèye, counsel prudence at work in vain. Bakar's is soon arrested for embezzlement of funds and imprisoned for five years, despite the efforts of attorney Yoro, his brother-in-law, to keep him from being incarcerated.

During this period of seclusion in the prison, Bakar's eyes open to the hypocrisy of his community. He finds himself not only without a job, but his wife deserts him, then divorces him, and finally marries another man. Yama, completely forgetting her brother in prison, throws a party and plays hostess to her women friends, thus revealing to Bakar her false love and false devotion to him. Only his mother and younger sister, Bigué, and friends like Sada, and a new girl friend Helen that he acquired after his marriage crumbled, remain loyal to him. Both Sada and Helen fit the archetypal image of a friend in need, a friend who endures through thick and thin. Indeed, Helen will remain Bakar's spiritual guide to the end. It is to Helen that Bakar would confide his plot to trick his family and society by faking his death or suicide by drowning, which strategy would allow him to participate in his own funeral and from that vantage point study society. On coming out of prison, with no job, family or friends, Bakar loses control of his being, takes to alcoholism, and finally plays tricks against society. He hatches a plot with Helen to fool the people, by feigning his own death, to be followed by his return as a ghost. He makes use of bleaching cream, *xeesal*, to lighten his complexion, so that he would look most ghostly. He wants to avenge himself against all those who rejected him and held him in disdain (109). Bakar is fed up with everyone seeing him as a never-do-well, reserving for him no decent role with which to affirm his humanity after his disgrace and imprisonment. His intention, after observing human folly, lies and hypocrisy, is also to punish those who have betrayed his love for them (ibid.). His plot succeeds.

At the elaborate funeral thrown by Yama (118), he learns who among his friends and family really care about him. Several of the women at the funeral who praise him to the skies hardly ever heard about him when alive. Some even go as far as to think that since he died in the sea, his soul would bypass Purgatory and go straight to Heaven (117). Moreover, he learns that human beings are so selfish that they only really think about their own approaching death and their fear of dying when they attend funerals, if they are not crying merely because it is the convention and the right thing to do at funerals. Bakar's ghost notes:

> Parmi tous ceux qui sont là et qui me pleurent, il n'y en a pas un qui pense à moi, qui soit boulversé parce que Bakar Diop est mort. Les uns pleurent pour la parade, parce qu'il est de bon ton de pleurer à des funérailles, d'autres parce qu'ils pensent à eux, à leur proper mort et ils ont peur. Toute disparation leur rappelle la réalité, proche ou lointaine, de leur mort. C'est la seule raison pour laquelle ils pleurent; ils sont d'ailleurs les plus sincères (117-118).

> [Among those there crying for me, none is thinking of me, none is really troubled because Bakar is dead. Some are crying for show, because it is a good thing to cry at funerals, the others because they are thinking of themselves, of their own death and they are afraid. Every time someone disappears they are reminded about the reality of things, now or later, of their own death. That is the only reason why they are crying; nonetheless they are the more sincere ones; *my translation*].

Furthermore, says Bakar, people are afraid of ghosts, because they awaken their conscience to things they would rather not remember, for the return of a dead relative is troubling to them: "*Les gens n'aiment pas les revenants. Disparaître une bonne fois, foutre la paix à tous. Revenir, c'est troubler la conscience des gens, ce qui est impardonnable...* » (118).

[*People do not like ghosts, prefer a one-time disappearance, giving peace to everyone. To return is to trouble people's conscience, and that is unpardonable...*]. Feasts, conventions, and fashion parades at funerals, he adds, demystify death and the passing of a loved one. Do people really remember the one who is dead? Bakar thinks not: "*Ku dee yaa ñakk sa bakkan!*" The rich Amar Ndiaye, Yama's husband, presents a formidable cow along with 100,000 francs CFA to the bereaved in-laws (119) on the third day of the funeral, the very day when in Islamic tradition the dead body is said to swell to its fullest, filling the cavity of the casket. Why then the enormous feast on the third day of death? Does the cow, a sacrificial animal, represent the dead and the departed? If so, why would the living be happy to kill and eat meat abundantly on the very day that the dead is deemed to begin a long process of disintegration after physical death? Such are some of the pertinent questions that arise from the death and funeral of Bakar Diop.

Bakar's extended family is only too happy to take collections from sympathizers; they almost all seem to have forgotten about him. Bakar thinks the collection is a harvest, for the funeral goers give very generously: "*Je ferai une bonne moisson*" (118). [I will reap a good harvest]. His only regret is that he cannot take away the animals presented as well, but promises himself not to fail to grab his *sarax*, hand it to Helen as recompense for her friendship and loyalty, and then disappear for good. He is convinced that his real funeral when he dies properly will not be nearly as great as the faked one : «*Les vraies funérailles, quand je partirai pour le bon, quand tout le monde — sûrement une toute petite poignée d'hommes — saura que je suis enfin mort, ne seraient pas si grandioses*» (118). [The true funeral, when I will pass for good, when people — certainly a handfull — will know that I am finally dead, will not be so grandiose]. So, it appears that the family members are aware that Bakar faked his death. Still, they go along with the funeral. They share and enrich themselves at the expense of the dead.

Therefore, their emotions at the ghost's entry are those of fear (*la frayeur*), shouting (*la criarde*), fainting (*l'évanouissement*), trembling (*tremblant*), hiding, sweating, gazing (*grands yeux de chatte [biche]*). Indeed, long after the funeral is over and everyone is gone, no one in the family cares to ask the stranger from the North, still seated there on a bench in the compound [Bakar in his ghostly camouflage], who he is, what he needs, where he comes from nor where he is going. Eventually, the ghost bursts into the room where the family is gathered to share the *sarax*, and reveals himself. But, all disappear in all directions in fear, taking him to be a ghost.

But, why this unexpected welcome from family members gathered at a funeral in the name of a departed member? Indeed, what happens to the souls of the departed after death? John S. Mbiti explains African belief in the hereafter:

> When the living dead appear, it is to those within his household or family, and rarely if ever, to people not immediately related to him. But, however real the living-dead may seem to those who see him, there is no affectionate warmth such as one witnesses when relatives or friends meet in this life. There is no exchange of greetings, which in African societies is an extremely important social means of contact; and when the living-dead disappears, human beings do not give greetings to other living-dead. Socially, therefore, something has happened, something has cooled off, and a real distance between the living-dead and human beings has begun to grow (1990; 158).

Clearly, there is a social distance already between Bakar and his family. Bakar's family quickly forgets him, the funeral over, in order to fight over his property. When one thinks that in African belief system Bakar could still be in purgatory awaiting his fate in the land of the dead, it becomes even more objectionable that his family should so quickly forget the relationships he had with them. After all, it was in the struggle to give them a better social status that he succumbed to temptation and fell from the social ladder.

For punishment, Bakar's spirit subsequently possesses Yama, and makes her dance a ritual dance, proclaiming the return and resuscitation of Bakar. This scenario raises the issue of earthbound spirits that attach themselves to vulnerable human beings during funerals or other death spaces when an individual's vulnerability is highest. It also raises the issues of reincarnation, death, and the hereafter. Does the dead come back? Does he or she return happy or unhappy? Is there such a thing as reincarnation? Does the soul survive apart from the body that decays after death? First, it is not clear how Bakar died, if even he did die. Traditional Africans believe there is no such thing as a natural death, but that there is always someone or something that is responsible for every death. Textual evidence is ambiguous on the end of Bakar, for although his clothes are found at the beach where he left them before going away to bleach himself and appear during his funeral, there is nobody to affirm that he died, or that death happened by drowning. Bakar becomes, therefore, an unquiet dead, that is, an earthbound spirit, which still has a business to finish before departing.

Yama is subsequently possessed by Bakar's earth-bound spirit, demonstrating African belief in partial or total reincarnation. Yama repeatedly chants Bakar's return: "*Il est revenu — Wüoy il est revenu! Bakar dipo dekki na!*" She throws amulets at the ghost, and dances on bare feet, out in the street, in the dark, with torn clothes. Yama, being very close to him in life, externalizes her awareness of him by her delusion. She believes that Bakar has returned to her, for it has not been long since his death, and apparently it is his ghost she sees at the midnight (a ghostly hour in all world cultures) following the funeral. This humiliation of Yama also signifies that the dead do return to manifest their dissatisfaction with the living. There is no warmth in such a meeting at a personal level between the dead and living. What is more, Bakar would return, because, after all, he had been married and had had a child, a baby girl. With marriage and birth of a child his personal immortality is assured, according to the African belief system.

Is Bakar's reincarnation a temporary or lasting one? It is hard to say how long Yama is going to continue in her delusion. It is also not clear whether, in fact, the dead in Wolof culture reincarnate temporarily beyond days and weeks, after death occurs, for a long period, into collective immortality as an ordinary spirit of the clan or community. Perhaps, the fact that Bakar eventually disappears for good, shows that death is death. In African belief, there is no reversal of a process that begins the individual's ontological maturation and evolution into a spirit. The dead nonetheless continues to live in death through their progeny. Character or biological characteristics of the dead recur in the younger generations. From that point of view, Yama's proclamation that Bakar has come back holds ground.

Clearly, African trickster tales often problematize the binary of evil and good, in order to teach human beings a lesson on the moral nature of our world. (Levin 1977: 117). African belief in the irrationality of human life and destiny is seen in Bakar's return as a ghost to seek revenge on his family and society for their failings, when in fact it is Bakar who should continue to be punished for dishonesty and theft. That Yama is punished, rather than Bakar, mirrors "the irrationality and anarchy that rules Man's universe" (ibid.).

CONCLUSION

This study of an African trickster tale demonstrates how the ghost symbolism represents the irrational, mystical, and mysterious nature of African supernatural worldview. Yet the individual is a participant in this society with all its vanities and short-comings, relating to all facets of society in various forms, as brother, husband, worker, friend, but also as ghost, the symbol of all the ills of the past and the present, and a catalyst for a future of positive change. The ghost's shifting physical and multiple forms are symptomatic of traditional Africa, modern Africa, and Africa of the future. It is a clear statement that African traditions will continue to endure. The belief is that there is an immaterial element of the human ontological structure that persists after death, which is often called the soul, which can reactivate the body and visit the living at will and fancy. It is therein that can be found the mystery of life and death in African mythology. On the issues of fate and destiny, it appears that life is a continuum from pre-existence to post-existence, an irruption in time for a short while, followed by a disappearance into oblivion. This knowledge should help human beings to curtail greed and ostentation, to be more sincere in their relationships and dealings with one another. Indeed, the ghost symbolism holds a tremendous amount of African beliefs about human life, fate, and destiny. It is evident, however, that emphasis is on the here and now, rather than on life after death, the possibility of which is not evident.

NOTES

1.   Selected Wolof words and their translation:

A *diriyanké* is an upper class woman (usually a mulatto).

Ku dee yaa òakk sa bakkan (119): They already forgot the dead man.

Sarax (124): Collection taken at the funeral.

La illah ha ila là! Lii lan la? (123): God is great, is great?

Xeesal (120): bleaching cream/dorot/Ambi/Satina).

Maalikum Salaam (112): Peace be unto you too!

Eycat, cat a ko dugg! (111): (May the Good God deliver him safe and sound).

Nit nit ay garabam (109): Human being is medicine to another human being/Man needs Man.

Lu jongoman dêgg yal nay jamm (104): What a woman wants God wants).

2.   According to Gilbert Durand, the grand function of myths is to help human beings to escape from the vicissitudes of time:

« Mais qui ne voit que cet inventaire de l'imaginaire, du grand mythe sacré à l'émotion esthétique laïque, est axé tout entier par sa fondamentale inspiration qui est d'échapper à la mort et aux vicissitudes du temps » (16).

[But, whosoever sees only this inventory of the imaginary, from the sacred myths to the purely profane esthetical emotions, is altogether firm in his fundamental inspiration, which is to escape death and the vicissitudes of history].

WORKS CITED

Atwater, P. M. H. *We Live Forever: The Real Truth About Death*. Virginia Beach: A. R. E. Press, 2004.

Behrend, Heike & Ute Luig. *Spirit Possession: Modernity & Power in Africa*. Oxford. James Currrey, 1999.

Fiore, Edith. *The Unquiet Dead: A Psychologist Treats Spirit Possession*. New York: Ballantine Books, 1987.

Gadigo, Samba. "Social Vision in Aminata Sow Fall's Literary Work." *Du Pleissis*. Vol. 8, No. 3, Summer 1989: 411-415.

Grant, Robert J. *Universe of Worlds: Exploring the Frontiers of the Afterlife*. Virginia Beach: A. R. E. Press, 2005.

Madu, Raphael. *African Symbols, Proverbs, and Myths*. New York: Peter Lang Press, 1992.

Mbiti, John S. *African Religions and Philosophy*. (Second Edition) Oxford: Heinemann, 1990.

McGill, Graham. *No Death: God's Other Door*. Virginia Beach: A. R. E. Press, 1998.

Okafor, Ndidi. "Aminata Sow Fall: Cas du Revenant." *Neohelicon*. Vol. 8, No. 1, 1991: 89-97.

Sow Fall, Aminata. *Le Revenant*. Dakar: Nouvelles Éditions Africaines, 1976.

"THE SAGA OF THE BOROOM BÀTTU, THE DREGS OF SOCIETY"

❄ ❄ ❄

*L*a grève des Bàttu is an imaginary story of a mythical event, a beggars' strike. It is a fantastic story that makes one reflect, consider, or ponder the idea of beggars ever becoming masters or winners, and the givers becoming beggars. *La grève des Bàttu* thus conveys a reality, which is neither historical nor ahistorical. It is the myth of the beggars' strike imbibed from the surrounding Wolof culture and society, where individual relations to the supernatural world, the elements, and other human beings and events in their lives are not altogether far from mythical dimensions. Clearly, it is about the beaten [*battus*, a French participle adjective]; notice that the substantive *bàttu* refers to the gourd with which the beggars demand and collect alms], but also on a more symbolic, even allegorical plane, the story of human beings, the human condition, the supernatural beings, and their earthly agents like the griots and the marabouts.

Important, therefore, is the truth value of the myth of a beggars' strike, especially given its non-historical origin, and its fancy or fable nature. Following the inner workings of the universe and human life, strange things can happen, if society as individuals and as a group does not honor the age-old code of conduct of human beings being their neighbor's keeper, of giving and receiving. Nobody comes to life with anything, and nobody will leave it with something. Therefore, if goods and material things are acquired, they necessarily have to be

173

shared for the comfort of all. It is, therefore, not the historical details of myth that matter to the reader or listener, but the deeper meaning of the story. Aminata Sow Fall pulls the story from the social reality of the Wolof culture and merely adds to it supernatural elements.

La grève des Bàttu, although a tale about an imaginary strike of beggars, also has epic proportions, partly due to the radical change it brings about in the relationship between classes of people, and partly due to the complete reversal of roles, where the beggars become the leaders.

Then again, the authorial strategy of picking a topic that has a constant presence, due to the daily menace of beggars in Dakar, Senegal, also gives this story its epic proportions. Besides the numerous characters in this novel, such as the ministers, presidents and vice-presidents, beggars, clerks, secretaries, wives, mothers, marabouts, prostitutes, etc., the collective character that represents the people is the *Bàttu*, human waste, or dregs of society. There are also street scenes, which help to anchor the story in one cultural space—streets, fights with beggars, municipal roads, etc. The beggars' strike, therefore, has its epic proportions. The narrative structure goes from the very beginning of events, where the beggars are harassed, to the lofty apogee of the master, Minister Mour Ndiaye, becoming the beggar. The focus in this study is on the beggars as the heroes of the novel, and not on the minister.

PROFILE OF THE HEROES

As opposed to the town or city and the people who live in it, which are social and civilized, the human wastes, the beggars, are seen as obstacles, barriers that people have to constantly fend off before they can get to social centers, like school, church, mosque, office, bank, market, etc. Indeed, the people think they are impossible to get rid of. Yet, those who are more fortunate not to beg forget to think of what pushes the beggars to beg, how much healthier their life could be, if they give to, share with, the beggars (7). The Minister of Culture, Mour Ndiaye, calls them an oozing wound that must be hidden away from the city, so as not to hurt the booming tourist industry.

The marabout, Seringue Birama Sidibé, functions as a spiritual guide to neophyte Mour Ndiaye, both men having met earlier and fortuitously, when Mour had given him cool potable water to quench his thirst after a long walk in the sun from his village to the city of

Dakar. In recompense, the marabout offered to help him whenever he was in need.

Next are the fifty beggars congregated after their forceful removal from the city centre around their own spiritual guide and nurturer Salla Niang, mother of twins, who was first a maid, before turning to begging (16). Among them are people of all ages, men, women, children, the infirm, the healthy, the lame, and the poor, who like Salla Niang, were once respectable human beings, until they were forced by unfortunate life circumstances to turn to begging.

Nguirane Sarr is one such beggar, a blind music composer, distinguished, and always properly dressed. He became blind after he was already quite grown up. When his father died, he was given to a marabout for care taking. When they went to live in the city, there was no money for his education, and so he had to resort to begging for subsistence. When he places himself strategically at the round-about of the Presidential Palace, to harvest huge alms from those going to seek favor from the President, he is guided by the principle that *"La charité ouvre les portes"* [Charity opens up doors] (15). It appears that his blindness to the material world has opened up and extended his spiritual world. Indeed, Sarr will reveal himself in his own right as the spiritual leader of the pack of beggars.

The lame beggar Madiabel, a black smith in his natal village (17), is the first to be attacked by the brigade charged to rid the city of beggars. Misfortune struck and he no longer was able to compete with modern technology in the production of kitchen wares. Then again, a treacherous customer made away with the fruits of his whole year's labor. To support two wives and eight children he went to the city, becoming a beggar. He is chased by the brigade, which reins blows and blows upon his back. Precipitously, he runs into the street into the way of a speeding vehicle that knocks him down unconscious (18). He later dies from his wounds; he did not receive timely attention, for he could not pay.

After Madiabel, Nguirane Sarr is second to be attacked. Sarr wonders aloud why society has refused to honor age-old social contract of giving and receiving (30). He then sends out a call for war with the "mad men," as he calls the members of the brigade charged with ridding the city of beggars:

> We are not dogs, are we dogs? We are not dogs. You know we are not dogs. We need to persuade them as well that we are not dogs. We

need to mobilize, essentially because they need us as we need them. Giving alms is what they need for making wishes for long life, prosperity, pilgrimage, etc. It is the instinct of self preservation that makes them give, not a kind heart (32).

The dog in African tradition is a domestic animal that is scorned, for it eats up human waste and rotting material, like baby's excreta as it comes out, so that the baby's mother does not have to clean up the waste matter. So, to be called a dog is to be seen as a "nobody," to say the least. It is understandable, therefore, why Nguirane Sarr is very annoyed at the apparent perception of beggars as the dogs of human society. Sarr's call for arms literally repeats Mour's earlier indignation at the European master, who had treated him inhumanely in his work, forcing him to lose his job. Mour slapped him back, exclaiming: "*Ah non (...) Je suis un homme moi!*" (10-11) [Allah (...) I am also a human being!]

Indignant, the beggars affirm their humanity in turn, exclaiming that the members of the brigade are themselves mad dogs. Dogs here recall the hyenas, wild dogs, prototypes of ogres, Kronos the Greek archetype of historic time, which devours its children, the Western double of the devil (Durand 1984: 94).[1] Nguirane Sarr says repeatedly that they are mad dogs for hitting them like that: "*Ils sont fous, ils frappent comme des fous*" (18). A little later, the beggar cannot understand why their fellow citizens think they are dogs, just because they are beggars: "*Parce qu'on est des mendiants, ils croient qu'on n'est pas des hommes faits comme eux (...) Est-ce qu'on traite ainsi un être humain? (...) Ils sont pires que des chiens enragés?*" (29).

Master of verb Nguirane Sarr's call to arms reaches Salla Niang's ears. She picks up the call, transmits it to the group of beggars, and takes a stand, saying, "*Jüg jogna! Jüg jog na kat!*" (33), it is time to wake up and do something about the insults, pointing the right index finger in the direction of her audience of beggars. Nguirane Sarr lends support to Salla's call for action, by improvising a spontaneous song; he recently taught himself to play the guitar. As epics are normally graced with song, Nguirane's song elevates Salla Niang to the level of the archetypal Mother. He likens Salla Niang to Mother Earth, who nurtures and feeds her people with the products of her cuisine:

Salla, fais cuire le couscous
[Salla, cook the couscous]
Du bon baasi salté

[Good baasi salté]
Manioc, ñebbé et courge
[Cassava, ñebbé, and squash]
Baasi salté kajor
[Kajor bassi salté]
Bassi salté jolof
[Jolof bassi salté]
Gras de diwu ñor
[Fat with diwu ñor
Rouge de tomate
[Red with tomatoes]
Baasi salté buur (85).
Buur baasi salté]

Gorgui Diop is another distinguished beggar and an old man whose sense of comedy serves him well. He stages two theatres a month one at the bank from the 25th of the month to the 10th of the following month, and the other at the market, from the 11th of the month to the 24th of the following month. In these one-man plays, Gorgui Diop re-enacts family scenes, lovers' tiffs, and slap sticks about other kinds of betrayals in love, jealousy, and envy. Through Gorgui Diop, the reader laughs at human folly.

Companions of the Heroic Beggars

These are characters who, in carrying out their duties, unconsciously promote the cause of the heroic beggars, teaching humanity once again to be their neighbor's keeper. First is Kéba Dabo, efficient and honest civil servant, and for six years running assistant to the Minister of Health, Mour Ndiaye. His actions in clearing the streets of beggars with the help of twenty men, and carting them away three kilometers to Mbada, where they would not find mechanical means to return to the city, inadvertently advances them from individuals without much strength to a mobilized collectivity (20). Kéba Dabo would not hear of failure in this task, despite what he sees as the impossibility of keeping the beggars away for good. After all, they are human beings too. Nonetheless, getting rid of the beggars has become his obsession. He thinks the menace of the beggars has reached proportions of nausea: "*Je suis persuadé qu'avec les rafles quotidiennes, l'appel à la raison et à la dignité (…) nous arriverons à les faire disparaître. Ces gens-là ne sont quand même pas des butes, ils sont des hommes tout de même!* (21) With almost morbid apprehension, he polices the city to ensure that not one beggar is left in sight, the advice of his faithful secretary, Sagar Diouf, notwithstanding. It is misery and hunger that push the beggars to beg, Sagar later explains, in order to remind the more fortunate citizens that they the beggars also exist and are part of the people: "*Il (Kéba) oubliait que c'est la faim et la misère qui poussaient certains d'entre eux à mendier pour rappeler aux nantis qu'eux aussi ils existent*" (7).

According to Trinh T. Minh-ha, in an excellent article in the *The French Review*, "Aminata Sow Fall et l'espace du don," the beggars manifest a total degeneration of humanity, which is somewhat disturbing in the least, and at the most degrading, because by subjecting themselves solely to material existence they lose their choice of life or death.[2] Kéba Diop, a little selfishly, presents the same kind of argument about poverty that his own mother had while he was growing up.

It is insightful that many traditional African cultures took care of community aberrations simply by excising them out of the community, through exile, assassination, or delivery to the beasts and dangers of the evil forest.[3] In Chinua Achebe's *Things Fall Apart*, we have this story of indolent Unoka, the father of the hero Okonkwo, who was thrown into the evil forest. [4] In reference to citations like this above, some critics have made mention of cruelty in certain African cultures, but when seen from the point of view of human dignity, perhaps it is not such a bad thing; it is most probably conferring on the individual his or her human dignity by hastening death, rather than delaying it. That was just the point that Mahatma Gandhi had tried to make when he stated that he preferred to see his wretched Indian flock die, rather than watch them live an existence of misery and despair, due to poverty, when an end to such human suffering was not in sight. It is a lofty way of thinking that is not possible with the common man, says Trinh T. Minh-ha.

With Sidibé, the issue is not what to do when the situation is hopeless, to the point that alms giving cannot redress the dignity of Man, but rather to give to bring balance in the sharing of society's goods. Thus, Sidibé chastises the attempt to get rid of the beggars, disappointed that the same Minister, Mour Ndiaye, who gives him so abundantly very often, should be against the beggars. He calls his attention to the words of God that the poor should not be maltreated in any way by anyone. He fears that the city is about to dehumanize people. Mour has all but forgotten the sick, the handicapped, and the hungry when he requires everyone to work, in keeping with the modern times, and to assume responsibility for themselves and the nation. Sidibé asks him to sacrifice a big white bull, cut it up into seven places, and distribute to the beggars himself, as a way of praying God to help him get the post of vice-president that he hopes for at the national elections. The bull is a symbol of wealth and affluence in African mythology, and by asking Mour to immolate an ox, the marabout wants the dead to drink blood and be appeased, and the living to eat meat and be friendly disposed towards the giver.

Sacrifice for Sidibé is a way of redistributing God's blessings to the Have-nots, with thanks and humility. Fortune is given by no rational reasoning, and can go any time. So, one must make use of it while it is in one's hands (88). For the first time, Mour realizes the reversal of fortune, where he is now in the hands of the beggars (89), and sees first hand the psychological torture of the poor, dispossessed citizenry, who lose control of their being and destiny to the rich (91-92). He suffers pain, insomnia, and distress for injuring Sidibé's feelings, not to mention his inability to find a solution to giving alms to beggars in all the corners of the city as the marabout stipulates (93). In a half-dream, he sees beggars holding out their gourds to him for alms. He wakes up to his responsibility, and makes up his mind not to fail in that regard.

THE WOMEN

SAGAR DIOUF

It is Sagar Diouf who explains that beggars have existed since pre-historic times, and will remain forever. Since there is nothing that anyone can do about it, she continues, why waste valuable time trying to get rid of them? (22) It is better to give them when and what one has, according to one of the five pillars of Islam. Lucidly, she also asks: Who would the alms giver ingratiate, if there are no beggars? (23) When Kéba Diop despairs upon Mour asking him to go back and return the beggars to the city, just after he finally was able to cart them away to the outskirts of the city, it is again Sagar Diouf who intones the age-old wisdom of doing like the Romans when in Rome: "*Il faut bien même suivre le même rythme et ce n'est pas pour rien qu'on dit que dans une sociéte lorsque les gens dansent d'un pied, il faut danser d'un pied..."* (100).

SALLA NIANG

Salla Niang, as seen above, gains the beggars' confidence, due to her profound experiences of life. She is a woman who has seen the world. Orphaned at a very young age, she has had to fend for herself. As a house maid, she got to know people well, and to decipher their most intimate secrets. She was able to measure the antics of the rich, and the aspirations of the poor. She has been through the school of life, having lived in palaces and hovels. She has had the husband of her mistress flirt with her. When the mistress caught her husband red-handed, *she* was booted out of the house (34-36). At the moment of decision for the beggars, it is Salla, then, who adds prescriptions to her wake up call to the beggars — *"Jüg jot na! Jüg jot na kat!."* For a start, no beggar should receive small alms from the people, as a way of affirming their humanity. Then, the beggars should accord alms givers blessings, even if they do not receive big chunks of alms.

Salla Niang affirms that it is a question of realizing that human beings have departed from their humanity and must return to it for the good of all. She notes that people give for different reasons, adding that the rich people need the beggars as much as the beggars need them, although people in general would always pretend to have nothing but scorn for those who are vital to their survival: *"Chacun donne pour une raison ou une autre, nous leur sommes utiles comme l'air qu'ils respirent"* (53-54).

LOLLI NDIAYE

Several times, Lolli goes on behalf of her husband, Mour Ndiaye, to visit marabout Sidibé for thanksgiving and prayers for the success of her husband in politics. Lolli is already dreaming of being the wife of the Vice-president and towering above all other wives (37). Traditional education had prepared Lolli very well to be a submissive and doting wife, who gets blessed with wealth and children through her husband. If a good woman lives up to these expectations, woe betide any husband who would maltreat her, according to a Wolof proverb. Such a man brings God's punishment unto himself — *"Aqu jigéen baaxul"*

(42) Lolli, however, turns into a wounded lion, when Mour wakes her up in the middle of the night to inform her that he has been double timing her, seeing a beautiful seventeen-year old secretary in the office of tourism, whom he intends to make his second wife. The young one speaks correct English, and has given him an ultimatum to marry her or leave her alone to find herself another man (43). Lolli's gaze on Mour transforms into that of sparking flame (43-44), so much so that Mour no longer recognizes her. So wounded is Lolli, who would never forget how Mour picked her out from the group of young girls who just finished their puberty right of tattooing. The joy and festivity of the occasion was tremendous. A big cow had been killed for the marriage festivities. Mour at the time was swept off his feet by her gazelle-like beauty and her freshness like the sea breeze.

Mour's masculine aggression is inseparable from bestiality, and Lolli finally cowers to it. Like a good woman, though, she takes everything into account, and decides to stay, in order not to disturb the equilibrium of the family. Even though she does not give up, she decides to visit marabouts to attempt to keep her husband for herself; she doubles her energy, in order to keep the man who oppresses her.

THE STRIKE

Finally, the beggars' strike, the ultimate emblem that leads to the disintegration of the world as constituted, and to its reconstruction under a new light, happens. The death of the lame, Gorgui Diop, is the immediate cause of the strike, and becomes the rallying point for the beggars, who seek to avenge his death. Silence falls on the beggars' compound, worsened by the fierce sun that keeps beating mercilessly down (50). Shivers go through the beggars, and revolt shakes up their bodies. Fear and melancholy also bring terror and anguish on their faces. They transform into bats, when, to avoid the brigade, they must go to the city at night, and return to their base at the break of dawn. Bats are odious night animals with repugnant odor and habit of hanging upside down on eves of buildings. Finally, following orations from the blind Nguirane Sarr and Salla Niang, the beggars' troop decide to boycott the city.

Meanwhile, Mour Ndiaye receives a National Merit Award and is promoted to the Order of the Chevalier de l'Ordre des Méritants, the second to be so named after the Minister of Finance, Lt. Colonel

Massaer Sarr, who had cracked the league of contraband and fraud. Mour is touted for a position of vice-president. He is no longer playing a role by thinking himself as a providential help to his nation; he believes it. Then a nightmare brings him back to reality, through recalling past memories (69). The marabout, this time, prescribes seven kola nuts to be given to a woman who does not beg. It takes Mour's maid, after his son fails, a whole day to get to the City of Beggars, to deposit her load. The beggars no longer beg, but people continue to come from all corners to them.

Eventually, Mour changes marabouts, in order to better decipher God's intentions, from Sidibé to Kifi Boukoul that he thinks is a man that is not a man. According to legend, Kifi Boukoul had an unnatural birth. He was conceived after a sacred serpent danced with his mother who had been plagued by infertility until she fell into a trance. Boukoul's father had sacrificed a horse, a big cow, and gold at dawn to the gods at the foot of the Tree of Life of the village, in order to exorcise seventeen years of suffering (75). Everything about this personage Kifi Boukoul is outlandish and takes on epic proportions. He has an unusual birth, is an unusual marabout, and gives unusual prescriptions about life.

For seven days and seven nights, Kifi Boukoul is locked up in Lolli's room, when no one must set eyes on him. At the end of his seclusion, he gives his verdict. Mour must sacrifice again a tawny bull, a unique color. The beast will be killed in the yard and its blood must be allowed to flow. Notice that immolation is representative of the neophyte's surrender to higher forces and beings. The meat, which will be cut into seventy-seven parts, must be distributed to all the beggars, who are the real poor. Seven hundred kolas, three hundred of which should be red and four hundred white should also be given away. Notice that the numbers three, four, and seven in world mythologies are symbolic as signs of totality and plenitude. Hence Boukoul adds that if Mour is able to carry out his prescriptions, then he will become president in a week. If he fails to do it, he will also fail politically (78-79).

PEREGRINATION IN THE CITY

Pointing at the four corners of the city the magical horn that the marabout gave him, Mour Ndiaye leaves for a run around town, a veritable wandering in a labyrinth, to find the beggars. The beggars must accept his sacrifice, or without success his efforts to win the vice-presidency would be completely in vain (97-98). Paradoxically, the master now goes in search of the beggars, in a complete reversal of roles (105). Mour feels that he and his driver, Koulé, are going into an unending desert, stripped of landscape, lifeless, beaten by the wind with a rare violence whose wails mix with the clouds, sand dunes, and ferocious roaring of the foaming and angry sea (ibid.).

When they finally find the beggars in their new home at the out-skirts of the city, the beggars completely humiliate Mour Ndiaye, for they pretend not to notice him, having gotten accustomed to big people coming to visit them. Even when they eventually agree to return tem-porarily, after taking the money he throws to them, they do not follow through on their promise. What is more, the sun falling on him feels like a fire brand placed on his forehead as he and driver Koulé set out again a second time in their search for the beggars (127). Fate, he thinks, has dealt him a bad blow, making him a laughing stock for the beg-gars: "*Être devenu le jouet des mendiants, quel coup du sort!*" (130) Need-less to say that not having done the sacrifice as stipulated by marabout Kifi Boukoul, he loses the election to the former Minister of Interior, Mr. Toumané Sané. The decree of June 6 revises the Constitution.

The beggars win, along with their collaborators, men and women. The beggars' strike gives the reader the privilege to put in place a new world, by destroying the present world that has departed from the tradition of giving and receiving selflessly. The beggars' strike affords the opportunity to beggars to combat the monstrous social serpent and crush its head, and deliver the people, by recalling them to the beginning of their culture, tradition, and customs.

CONCLUSION

Indeed, it is the epic dimensions of *La grève des Bàttu* that gives this novel its more profound value. The mythic and legendary con-tents are imaginary, the song improvisation sustains the epic propor-tions of the synchronic story, and oratorical speeches flavor the saga of the dispossessed of the earth. The multiplication of characters who collaborate with the heroes, the multitude of speakers, from young to old, rich to poor, firm to infirm, who reject the oppression of the beg-gars, also foster African traditional views of humanity one to another.

The fact that people get progressively better, some like Mour changing their mind about their initial stance and manifesting compassion and understanding towards the beggars, shows that the teachings of the Dogon, the ancestors of the Wolof, are alive and well. They understand the value of giving and receiving in all honesty of purpose, making *La grève des Bàttu* an epic of no mean proportion. Perhaps, Mour Ndiaye will become a civilizing hero of his people, given his late, but humane, attitude towards his first wife, Lolli, and his second wife, Sine. Clearly, he will become a good family man, albeit a polygynist, living according to the words of the Islamic scriptures. The various collective and individual lessons from the beggars' revolt put *La grève des Bàttu* in the domain of the epic imaginary and African tradition.

NOTES

1. In Durand 1984, page 94, the text cites Carl Gustav Jung as having called Kronos *Deus Leontecephalus* in his *Libido*.

2. *The French Review*. Vol. LV, No. 6, May 1982.

3. Trinh T. Minh-ha states that the beggars and Kéba form respectively the non-violent and violent couple. She compares Kéba's lofty ideas about the inhumanity of the idea of begging to Ghandi's preference to see wretched Indians die, rather than see them reduce themselves to begging merely to exist, although he would always encourage the Haves to give to the Have-nots. See J. Herbert. *Ce que Ghandi a vraiment dit*. Verviers: Marabout, 1974," cited by Trinh T. Minh-ha).

4. Chinua Achebe. *Things Fall Apart*. New York: Fawcett Crest, 1959. 20-21.

   Unoka was an ill-fated man. He had a bad chi or personal god, and evil fortune followed him to the grave, or rather to his death, for he had no grave. He died of the swelling which was an abomination to the earth goddess. When a man was afflicted with swelling in the stomach and the limbs he was not allowed to die in the house. He was carried to the Evil Forest and left there to die. There was the story of a very stubborn man who staggered back to his house and had to be carried again to the forest and tied to a tree. The sickness was an abomination to the earth, and so the victim could not be buried in her bowels. He died and rotted away above the earth, and was not given the first or the second burial. Such was Unoka's fate. When they carried him away, he took with him his flute.

WORKS CITED

Ajala, John D. "*The Beggars' Strike*: Aminata Sow Fall as a Spokesperson for the Underprivileged." *CLA Journal*. Vol. XXXIV, No. 2, December 1990: 137-152.

Bobia, Rosa, et al. "Aminata Sow Fall: ses livres et son nouveau role." *Présence Francophone*. Vol. 36, 1990: 133-136.

Boni-Sirere, J. "Littérature et Société: Études critique de *La grève des Bàttu* d'Aminata Sow Fall." *Revue de Littératue et d'esthétique négro-africaines*. Vol. 5, 1984: 59-80.

Durand, Gilbert. *Les Structures anthropologiques de l'imaginaire*. Paris: Bordas, 1984

(1969). Livre Premier *Le Régime Diurne de l'Image*, 67-70 ; Première Partie : «Les visages du temps, » Chapitre premier « Les symboles thériomorphes». 71-96.

Egonu, I. T. K. "Aminata Sow Fall: A New Generation Female Writer from Senegal." *Neophilogus*. Vol. 75, January 1991: 66-75.

Jaccard, Anny-claire. "Le Visage de l'Islam chez Mariama Bâ et Aminata Sow Fall. Nouvelles du Sud. Vol. 7, 1986-1987: 171-182.

Miller, Elinor S. "Contemporary satire in Senegal: Aminata Sow Fall's *La grève des Bàttu*." *French Literature Series*. Vol. XIV, 1987: 143-155.

Mokwenye, Cyril. "Aminata Sow Fall as Social Critic: An Interpretation of *Le Revenant* and *La grève des Bàttu*. Neohelicon. Vol. XIX, No. 2, 1992: 211-221.

Okeke-Ezigbo, Emeka. "Begging the Beggars: Restoration of the Dignity of Man in The Beggars' Strike." *Neohelicon*. Vol. XIX, No. 1, 1992: 307-322.

Pfaff, Françoise. "Enchantment and Magic in Two Novels by Aminata Sow Fall." *CLA Journal*. Vol. 31, No. 3, March 1988: 339-359.

Sow Fall, Aminata. *La grève des Bàttu*. Dakar, Nouvelles Éditions Africaines, 1979.

Trinh T. Minh-ha. "Aminata Sow Fall et l'espace du don." *The French Review*. Vol. LV, No. 6, May 1982: 780-789.

"THE SAGA OF NALLA,
THE PUPIL OF TEACHER NIANG"

❄ ❄ ❄

The people's struggle for a return to African epistemologies, already seen in Sow Fall's first two novels, *Le Revenant* and *La grève des Bàttu*, is here accentuated. The boy hero, Nalla in *L'Appel des arènes*, leads the way as he struggles to make a return to African ways of knowing, taking with him his whole people. He can no longer tolerate his parents, father Ndiogou Bari and mother Diattou Bari, who keep him away from his traditional roots, including the wrestling sport and socialization into the young adult group in the community through the initiation of puberty rite. It takes the attentive observation of his conscientious teacher, Mr. Niang, to see that Nalla's studies are disturbed by not being allowed to follow the traditional ways of socialization for a young man in Wolof culture (15). This study will employ three symbols of circular structure, namely, cycle, circle, and arena, to fathom a call, by extension, for a return to the origin of things, which are very important for the future of the Africa continent. It is one way that African youth can grow properly, for human beings need a foundation, one's own piece of the earth, from which to take off to meet other people and their understanding of human existence.

Ultimately, it is the author's call for a return to African awareness and way of life as a means of anchoring the child in society. By the same token, it is the author's condemnation of the dark and false notions of modernity, which seek to denigrate African ways of knowing. Such hostile ideologies are in themselves those of isolation, and death. No wonder those who come into Diattou, Nalla's Mother's path are dead or maligned in the long run, because she is perceived as an agent of death.[1]

Eventually, Nalla makes a confession to his teacher regarding his troubles: *"c'est le tam-tam aux arènes. Quand il commence à battre, je l'entends ici et ça me donne envie d'aller aux arènes..."* (26) ["It is the tam-tam in the arenas," he says. "When it begins to beat, I hear it here, and I feel like going to the arenas..."]. Nalla's guides in his quest for a return to his roots are two wrestlers, André, and Malaw also known as the Lion, Tiger, that is to say, the best. Both men severally would become the young neophyte's idols, taking the relay from his teacher, Mr. Niang. The tam-tam symbolizes the drum at the dawn of creation calling the indigenes to be reborn.

André and Nalla met and became friends when Nalla's ball fell over the fence and André retrieved it and brought it back to him. André would tell the young man stories about the countryside every time he came up from the village to the city to sell palm wine, *"conkom,"* for subsistence. Palm wine is a symbol of their bonding, for invariably every morning on his way to the market, André would stop to see the pupil waiting agog for the master. André would give him palm wine, sweets, mangoes, guavas, and roasted peanuts, and they would drink and eat together. Nalla would listen to stories about nature, big trees like the tamarind, palms, oranges, mandarin, and flowing rivers with fishes in them for food (33). Nalla marveled at all these stories, and André was unreal to him, what with his simplicity and goodness (ibid.). Their daily meeting would become something of an obsession for both of them, a kind of ritual. André was carried away with the dream of conveying aspects of their culture to a child, and Nalla in turn was mystified by André's stories about the solidarity engendered by working together on the farm. Notice that Guinean Camara Laye had also written about the mysterious effect of rice harvesting on the workers singing and working as a group, in his seminal novel, *The Dark Child.*[2]

Returning from the movie theatre one day, after having seen the film *Zorro*, a gift from his mother, Nalla sees a group of young people dancing in half circles with colorful handkerchiefs from their girlfriends attached to their belts. People were trooping after them. They were wrestlers, and André was among them. They had not seen each other for quite some time, because Nalla attended school and was not yet twelve years old, and so could not be expected to join the wrestling group. Nalla was full of delirium and admiration of André (37). Then Nalla discovered the wrestling arena, a big and vast men's house made up of huts with thatched roofs. It seemed to beckon visitors from the four corners of the globe. He was intrigued to see so many people under the silk cotton tree in the middle of the yard, a symbol of the Tree of Life, talking boisterously, playing cards, or watching pee-wee wrestlers already learning the art of wrestling (38). It is in this arena that André teaches Nalla to learn to face his fear as a man and not be afraid of snakes or anything at all, adding that a man should not be afraid, or else he would open himself up to ridicule." *Tu es un homme,"* he tells him, adding that as a man he should not be afraid. André continues: *"Non, Nalla, ne tressaille pas...Tu ne dois pas tressailler. Un garçon ne doit avoir peur de rien, je te l'ai déjà dit. La peur déshonore...Tu comprends cela, Nalla?* (43) (...). Then, he advises him to respect their totem, the snake, which they are not to kill, because it symbolizes their ancestors under the earth and watching over them on earth: «*Nous ne tuons jamais le serpent. Il existe un pacte entre nous et le serpent depuis nos très lointains ancêtres. Nous ne le tuons pas, et il nous protège des maléfices. C'est notre totem"* (44). The snake does not bite its totem owner, because they are one and the same, André explains, to Nalla's extreme marvel. It is, therefore, André who shows him the joy of simple life, without artifice, constraints, nor servility.

Next, André introduces Nalla to Malaw Lô, who would become his other idol to teach him the values of communal solidarity through the wrestling sport. Malaw is the nephew of Mahanta Bally, son of Karaman Bally, nicknamed the hawk, because he never missed a match, "a prey," and also likened to a thunder, because he erupts, as it were, into the wrestling arena whenever he comes there. His adversaries think that he is supernatural and has secret knowledge of things, and mysterious and talks to presences. When he begins to tell a story, it never ends, but rather flows like an ocean.

When Mahanta Bally, Malaw Lô's uncle, became blind, he stopped wrestling. Right from their ancestral origins Malaw had a special bond of friendship with André, which deepened over time in the city. It is at his house that André lodges whenever he comes to town to sell his palm wine:

Une longue amitié, datant de nos ancêtres respectifs, s'est consolidée de génération en génération. Malaw est pour moi plus qu'un frère. C'est pourquoi, chaque année, je viens passer quelques mois chez lui pour vendre mon "conkom." Sa maison est ma maison...Sa maison est la maison de tous... (49).

[A long friendship, dating as far back as our respective ancestors, has become consolidated from generation to generation. Malaw is for me more than a brother. That is why, every year, I come to spend a few months in his house, in order to sell my "conkom." His house is mine. His house is everyone's house ..."].

Once Malaw took over the relay from André as Nalla's spiritual guide, André's work was finished, and like one who has accomplished his work, he vanished. He died. News of his death devastates Nalla (54), who recalls a particular story of his courage, fighting off a band of pirates who attacked at sea to take away their wares (55). However, Malaw counsels Nalla to take the death of his former guide bravely, because the brave never die.

Ne pleure pas, petit! Ne pleure pas! André n'a jamais aimé les hommes, au coeur faible. Ce qui importe aujourd'hui, ce n'est pas sa mort, mais son honneur. S'il avait souillé son sang et son nom, tout le monde aurait pleuré, non en versant des larmes, amis dans la chair et dans le coeur. Sois fier d'André si tu l'as aimé (…) André n'est pas mort,… il a simplement disparu. Les braves ne meurent jamais. Lève-toi et pense à cela. Penses-y toujours, petit…. (56).

[Do not cry my dear one. Do not cry. André never liked men with weak hearts. What is important today is not his death, but his honor. If he had soiled his blood and his name, everyone, friends in flesh and heart, would have wept, not by shedding tears. Be proud of André if you loved him (…). André is not dead… he simply disappeared. The brave never die. Get up and think about that. Think about it always, my dear one….; *my translation*].

Mame Fari, Nalla's grandmother, imparts traditional lessons to Nalla. She compares closely to André as guide, for she allows Nalla to be the person he wants to be and to eat what he wants to eat, not what he is given. Both André and Nalla are connected to Mame Fari through the drinking cup, which André serves Nalla palm wine with and with which he also takes water from Mame Fari's water jug to quench his thirst: *"Le pot en fer-blanc dans lequel André lui versait le "conkom" était pareil à celui qu'il plongeait dans le canari de Mame Fari pour se désaltérer"*

(62). Mame Fari's stories about tradition and African epistemology fill Nalla with mystery. The complexity and intricacies of the puberty rites and rituals of initiation, circumcision and socialization of the young into responsible and contributing members of the community make a lot of sense to him, in contrast to the kind of education to which his parents had exposed him, which was devoid of depth and functionality. Through the rite of initiation, the neophyte transcends his individual condition, and achieves a rebirth in the community as a new being.[3] Nalla hears the story of Banji Koto, and particularly of the orphan Coumba, who travels to the Dayanne Sea, which is inaccessible to all mortals. She descends into the hell created by her inhuman step mother. By divine intervention, however, Coumba is saved and furnished with tremendous riches (33). Nalla also learns about Mame Fari's grief in losing her beloved husband and child to small pox within two days of each other. He is taught that God imposes forgetfulness on human beings, in order to alleviate the weight of existence, for without this ability to forget, one would not be able to live. Forgetfulness helps human beings to deal with the vicissitudes of life. He says:

> L'homme doit avant tout remercier le créateur de lui avoir donné l'oubli, car sans l'oubli, personne ne pourrait vivre la vie (…) Lorsque tu découvriras les sommes de douleurs et de souffrances que la vie nous reserve, tu verras que l'oubli est un cataplasme pour le coeur et le meilleur ami de l'homme (61).

> [Man should first and firemost thank the creator for the ability to forget, without which nobody would be able to live life (…). When you discover the sum of life's pains and sufferings in stock for us, you will see that forgetfulness is a cataplasm for the heart, and Man's best friend].

Mame Fari's memory recalls are a sort of pilgrimage and a bath at the fountain of youth for herself, for Nalla thinks of her as a youthful girl in the Garden of Eden (ibid.). Therefore, it is not just Mame Fari's recalls of African rituals and rites that endure in the memory of impressionable Nalla; it is also her stories through legends, tales, and myths about her life and the life of wrestlers as custodians of African traditions, customs, and values.

Unfortunately, after a sojourn of thirteen years abroad in Europe, Diattou condemns this traditional education. Mame Fari responds before she dies by cursing her daughter, and avowing her belief that Nalla would never be kept forever from his roots of origin: "*La vie est devant toi, ma fille. Sache seulement qu'un séjour séculaire dans le fleuve ne fera jamais d'un baton un crocodile"* (64). [You have your life ahead of you my daughter. But know that a day spent in the river will never make of a stick a crocodile]. J. S. Mbiti explains this potency in the words of the aged, which all sensitive young people should be careful not to provoke:

> There is a mystical power in words, especially those of a senior person to a junior one, in terms of age, social status or office position. The words of parents, for example, carry "power" when spoken to children: they "cause" good fortune, curse, success, peace, sorrows or blessings, especially when spoken in moments of crisis (1990: 192).

Nalla's inner conflict begins when his mother takes over his education, to erase all traces of the grandmother, and implant in their stead her modern ideas. In the eyes of her community, her ideas are not laudable, because they are not well assimilated (65). She, Diattou Bari, and her husband Ndiogou, are therefore false Europeans, *"Toubabs Njallxaar"* and sorcerers, *"démm"* (68). Following the death of Birama, the son of Kani Sadio, in the hospital where Diattou works, the latter is condemned in the community as a witch. How does a whole community agree that the midwife Diattou caused the death of sick Birama? Diattou, principal midwife, also loses a still-born infant in the maternity while delivering it. The child's mother and all the nurses think she has again eaten the child's soul (96). Eventually, the family is forced to move out of the neighborhood. Ndiogou cannot understand how such an irrational accusation managed to be embraced by the whole community. Mbiti however explains that in African mythology death is not natural and unpreventable, but is caused by some evil person using mystical and magical powers to cause the death of people they do not like (151-161). Nalla's teacher, Mr. Niang, sees alienation from one's roots as the worst mutilation anyone could ever suffer, for collective alienation could cause mass disorder, with everyone refusing to be his- or herself, getting lost in the illusion that he or she can craft his or her own fantasy. People cease to have an ideal, and run towards darkness. An individual without roots is like a tree that has lost its roots (72-73). Whereas Nalla's parents are in the process of losing their physical, spiritual, and mental equilibrium, on the other hand, Malaw, Nalla, and André make contact with the spirit of the ancestors under the baobab tree when they are gathered under it.

The story has it that brave warrior Nar Lô of Malaw founded

their village of Diammar at a crossroad, where the sun never sets, where humans live in perfect accord with the animal and plant worlds, where trees dance at the beat of the tam-tam. Everyone has the same name Lô. The village is known as *"la jeune fille inviolable aux sept ceintures,"* because the new village is like a virgin secured by seven layers of impenetrable trees — *darkassous* (141). Nalla is circumcised at the hospital, and his prepuce buried in the earth. His teacher sees this as reaching out to the ancestor grandmother buried in the earth. Better that than nothing at all; it is a gesture of hope for Africa:

> Le cordon omblical coupé avec la mère, mais renoué avec la grand-mère. Un des signes de notre temps. Signe encourageant, d'ailleurs, meilleur que le vide. Peut-être même le salut... La grand-mère, c'est encore la terre. Le lien avec la terre (93).

> [The umbilical cord cut from the mother, but reunited with the grand-mother. One of the signs of our time. An encouraging sign, by the way, better than emptiness. Perhaps even salvation... The grandmother is still the earth. The link with the earth; *my translation*].

Grandfather Nar Lô at age seventy-one becomes the village "flag," due to his bravery in fighting off a female lion. The lioness' blood penetrating his blood turns him into a man-lion. The lion's tail and head, hang as his trophy on the three baobab trees at the center of the city, to the admiration of the villagers of Diammar. The baobab tree, it must be explained, is a symbol of endurance in the harsh savannah climate of the Sahel region of which Senegal is part. As animals die, it sheds its leaves to conserve its store of water, and waits patiently for the rains to quickly put out new leaves (Knappert 1990: 36-37).

After the founding of Diammar, according to legend, a feast takes place, accompanied with copious food consumed together, dancing, and recounting of the genealogical tree of the descendants of Lô (100). It is a moment of "at-one-ment" for the community. The griot, the spokesperson for the community, voices the communal belief that a descendant of Nar Lô cannot but be great; there is no room to plant shame in this family (101).

Indeed, Grandfather Nar Lô exhorts Malaw to go to the village of Louga and found a wrestling arena, as a central rallying point to traditional ways for the youth. This decision took place after Malaw's sister, eighteen-year old Anta Lô, had gone to the city, become promiscuous, had a bastard child that she killed, and was arrested by the

police. She died in police custody. What a shame for her and the extended family. The old grandfather goes into seclusion in this city of
beggars, dislocated people, and all sorts of social misfits (136-138). Her
mother renders apology on her daughter's behalf, knowing that she,
her daughter, would have regretted her conduct had she had the opportunity to explain herself before her death:

> Yaayoo booyoo si je savais
> [People of the fishing village if I had known]
> Le prix des chastetés bradées
> [The price of the chastities on clearance sale]
> Aïe Aïe mes reins écartelés
> [Aïe Aïe my loins torn apart]
> De la chair molle de ma chair
> [From the soft flesh of my flesh]
> Raide dans ma main muertrière (149).
> Stiff in my murderous hand]

The call of the arena, on the other hand, is the call of tradition. In the
words of the septuagenarian, Nar Lô, everything must be done to save
the people in these modern times by returning them to traditional ways.
He says to Malaw:

> Il faudra les sauver avant qu'ils ne s'y engouffrent… Sauve-les, mon
> fils. Va à Louga. Ouvre des arènes et remue-les. Fais-y bouillonner le
> tam-tam comme une mer en furie (…). Tu as saisit mille fois le vertige
> des gémissements hypnotiques du coeur de Diaminar. Malaw, mon
> fils, il faut que le tam-tam aux arènes ait cette même rèsonance. Qu'il
> gronde, et qu'il gronde! Ils l'entendront, et ceux qui ne sont pas les
> damnés éternels finiront par venir parce qu'ils ne pourront pas résiter
> à l'appel de la terre. Il y a toujours un coin pour la terre dans le coeur
> de ceux qui ont encore toute leur âme (13).

> [It is important to save them before it is too late. Save them, my son. Go
> to Louga. Open the arenas and move them around. Make the tam-tam
> resonate there like a sea in fury (…) You have seized a thousand times
> the vertige of the hypnotique moanings of Diaminar's heart. Malaw,
> my son, the tam-tam in the arenas must have this resonance. Let it
> resound, and resound. They will hear it, and those who are not per-
> petually damned will come because they will not resist the call of the
> earth. There is always a corner for the earth in the heart of those who
> still possess all of their soul; *my translation*].

So, before the grand wrestling match against Tonnerre, Malaw seeks to intimidate his opponent by proclaiming his bàkk, a form of oral praise poetry in which he vaunts his advantages as a seasoned wrestler from a long line of accomplished wrestlers, as against his opponent's paltry achievements:

Malaw Lô fils de Ndianga Lô
[Malaw Lô, son of Ndiaga Lô]
Qui me bravera moi Malaw Lô
[Who will challenge me Malaw Lô]
Lion du Kajoor fils de Ndiaga Lô
[Lion of Kajoor, son of Ndiaga Lô]
Malaw Lô "kor" Madjiguène Lô
[Malaw Lô, loved by Madjiguène Lô]
Maître des arènes du Walo
[Master of the Walo arenas]

Invincible aimé fort et beau
[Invincible, loved, strong and handsome]
Du Njambur qui vit naître Ndiaga Lô
[From Njambur that gave birth to Ndiaga Lô]
A Ndar Géej drapé dans son pagne d'eau
[To Ndar draped in her water cloth]
Tous chantent l'épopée de Malaw Lô (14-15).

Moi Malaw Lô Kor Madjiguène Lô
[I am Malaw Lô Kor Madjiguène Lô]
Dans Diaminar où l'on ne dit que Lô
[In Diaminar where one speaks only of Lô]
Le plus fort le plus brave le plus beau
[The strongest, bravest, most handsome]
Moi Malaw Le fils de Ndiaga Lô
[I am Malaw the son of Ndiaga Lô]
Qui de tous les braves fut le héros… (78).
[Who of all the brave is the hero…].

Malaw wins the match and is happy. Nonetheless, he does not hold Tonnerre as an adversary, whether before or after the match, but rather as one with him in communal solidarity, since they both adhere to African traditional forms of education, which requires that the youth be integrated into the community. He states: « Le combat que je livre contre Tonnerre n'est pas seulement un combat physique…je ne me bats pas contre Tonnerre. Au contraire, Tonnerre est de mon côté, il m'aidera à gagner… " (135). The important thing is that the whole community takes part in the match, that the individual bends to the collectivity, becoming one with it. The people must make a spiritual return to the past of African values of harmony, solidarity, and compassion in the body politic, states Malaw.

CONCLUSION

The grand lesson of myths is to represent the community with honor in the superior interest of the human condition, as Ndiogou tells Diattou, after he is reconverted to traditional ways. He confesses that as parents they have messed up their son's education, by filling him with abstract, vague, and wavering ideas, and separating him from his environment (143). Ndiogou adds that the struggles of modern professionals in the modern Africa are worth the while — nurses (Sogui), physicians (Saer), attorneys (Anthiou), state inspectors (Fara), and teacher (Gartinet) (137-142). However, their efforts should not be at the expense of African communal traditions and epistemologies.

Eventually, Ndiogou reunites with Nalla, promising to live by communal African structures and ways of knowing, symbolized by the arena, and the notion of circle for totality and of cycle for return to the origins. These are ways of knowing that anchor the individual in the world, affording him or her the opportunity to understand his environment and become part of it without conflict in his innermost being. This is the lesson that Nalla learned. But, Diattou, on the other hand, remains on the outside, still blinded by European myths of progress and civilization, and estranged from her family and her roots. In the end, Diattou stands alone as the agent of a foreign ideology on African soil, moved by the foreign myths of Petit Poucet, Merlin the enchanter and Blanche Neige [Snow White]. The negative force that moves her seems to destroy her and everything for which she stands. The call of the arenas is a call for a return to African mythology and ways of knowing. Nalla returns to the circular form of African epistemology, which moves towards the future, by recycling the present and the past before it. It is a circular movement that is different from the linearity of modern vision of things. In the words of Crosta, *L'Appel des arènes*, by its insistence on the image of the circle, the cycle and the arena calls back attention to the values of African traditions and customs, to the need to find one's identity through a return to the past:

La forme circulaire évoquée par les arènes, les danses, le regroupement des voisines suggère l'intégration de l'individu à un ensemble. Au début du texte, on signale les demi-cercles que font les lutteurs (33); le cercle des voisines qui entourent Diattou, Ndiogou et Nalla (63); l'encerclement du village, Diaminar (73); le rythme circulaire d'accueil aux lutteurs qui font trois fois le tour des arènes et qui appellent les spectateurs à participer à leur combat (140-141), dépassent leur fonction de lutteur pour célébrer symboliquement le rassemblement de la communauté (61).

[The form of the circle evoked by the arena, the dances, and the congregation of neighbors suggests the integration of the individual in a group. At the beginning of the text, there is the half circle made by the wrestlers (33); the circle by the neighbors who encircle Diattou, Ndiogou and Nalla (63); the encircling of the village of Diaminar (73); the welcoming circular rhythm of the wrestlers who go round the arena three times, inviting the spectators to become part of their match (140-141), all these go beyond the simple act of wrestling, becoming, symbolically speaking, a celebration of a communal gathering; *my translation*]

NOTES

1. In an excellent work on "Les Structures spatiales dans *L'Appel des arènes* d'Aminata Sow Fall," Suzanne Crosta notes the authorial use of light or absence of it to distinguish between agents of African tradition and modernity respectively. André, Malaw, Mame Fari and Mr. Niang are agents of light, whereas Diattou is an agent of death:

"Ce qui distingue nettement l'univers de cette communauté, c'est la présence de la lumière que ce soit le soleil, les étoiles ou les lampes. André, Malaw, et Mama Fari sont plus souvent évoqués le matin (32, 39, 58, 78, 111, 123, 137) et l'auteure fait souvent reference à la présence du soleil — ardent, de plomb (27, 49, 51, 83). S'il est question de la nuit on fait mention de la lune (32), des étoiles (38), ou de la lueur de la lampe à pétrole (59). Il est tout aussi essential de noter qu'André prévient Nalla des dangers d'être dehors à l'approche du crépuscule (45). Cet avertissement devient significatif lorsque nous apprenons qu'André est mort sous un ciel sans étoile. Ce détail est d'ailleurs répété trois fois dans l'espace de deux pages (52-53). Quant à M. Niang, il est ancré dans un cadre temporal bien spécifique — l'après-midi (9, 11). Cette indication temporelle semble indiquer l'appartenance de ce personage dans l'univers clos de Diattou et de Ndiogou et dans l'univers expansif des lutteurs (60).

2. Here illustrated is the deep psychological and spiritual impact that André has on Nalla:

Et le lendemain, André avait retrouvé Nalla devant sa maison. Et chaque matin, à la même heure, Nalla attendait impatiemment André; et André arrivait, et le match reprenait et finissait, et la conversation recommençait, transportant Nalla là-bas, dans le Saalum, parmi les cultivateurs paisibles qui le soir, au clair de lune, se régalent de couscous et de lait frais; le fleuve aux mille reflets réapparaissait, serpentant autour de Noojoor, Jonwar et de nombreuses autres îles où la sérénité procure une vie toute heureuse. Nalla se retrouvait au coeur des fôrets mystérieuses où les lianes entrelacés servent d'abri aux fétiches ancestraux" (35-36).

3. According to J. S. Mbiti, on initiation and puberty rites in *African Religions and Philosophy*:

Initiation rites have many symbolic meanings, in addition to the physical drama and impact. We can mention some of the religious meanings before we come to concrete examples. The youth are ritually introduced to the art of communal living. This happens when they withdraw from other people to live alone in the forest or in specifically prepared huts away from the villages. They go through a period of withdrawal from society, absence from home, during which time they receive secret instruction before they are allowed to rejoin their relatives at home. This is a symbolic experience of the process of dying, living in the spirit world and being reborn (resurrected). The rebirth, that is the act of rejoining their families, emphasizes and dramatizes that the young people are now new, they have new personalities, they have lost their childhood, and in some societies they even receive completely new names.

Another great significance of the rites is to introduce the candidates to adult life: they are now allowed to share in the full privileges and duties of the community. They enter into the state of responsibility: they inherit new rights, and new obligations are expected of them by society. This incorporation into adult life also introduces them to the life of the living-dead as well as the life of those yet to be born. The initiation rites prepare young people in matters of sexual life, marriage, procreation, and family responsibilities. They are henceforth allowed to shed their blood for their country, and to plant their biological seeds so that the new generation can begin to arrive.

Initiation rites have a great educational purpose (118-119).

WORKS CITED

Borgomano, Madeleine. *L'Appel des arènes d'Aminata Sow Fall*. Dakar: Nouvelles Éditions Africaines, 1984.

Brown, Ella. "Reactions to Western Values as Reflected in African Novels." *Phylon*. Vol. XLVIII, No. 3, 1987: 216-228.

Cazenave, Odile. "Gender, Age, and Reeducation: A Changing Emphasis in Recent African Novels in French, as Exemplified in *L'Appel des arènes* by Aminata Sow Fall." *Africa Today*, 3rd Quarter, 1991: 54-62.

Crosta, Suzanne. "Les Structures spatiales dans *L'Appel des arènes* d'Aminata Sow Fall." *Revue Francophone de Louisiane*. Vol. 111, No. 1, Spring 1988: 58-65.

Knappert, Ian. *African Mythology: An Encyclopedia of Myth and Legend*. London: Diamond Books, 1990.

Mbiti, John S. *African Religions and Philosophy*. Oxford/London: Heinemann, 1990.

Niang, Sada. "Modes de Contextualisation dans *Une si longue lettre* et *L'Appel des arènes*. *The Literary Griot*. Vol. 4, Nos. 1 & 2, Spring/Fall 1992: 111-125.

Sow Fall, Aminata. "Du pilon à la machine à écrire." *Notre Librairie*. Vol. 68, No. 1, 1983: 73-77.

_____. *L'Appel des arènes*. Dakar: Nouvelles Éditions Africaines, 1993.

"THE SAGA OF YELLIMANÉ BADAR, THE HERO OF NATANGUÉ"

❄ ❄ ❄

This study of Aminata Sow Fall's *Le Jujubier du patriarche* explores the caste system, a political and social order reflective of Wolof cosmology and worldview, focusing on an epic tradition, the Epic of Foudjallon, and a culture-hero, Yellimané Badar, whose heroic accomplishments and those of his family denote fundamental aspects of Wolof culture. Like all heroes in world mythologies, he is the representative of human beings in the dream world. He mirrors their greatest existential preoccupations, namely, the essentials of love, brotherhood, solidarity, and compassion one for the other. According to Joseph Campbell in *The Hero with a Thousand Faces*, the universal pattern of myth, what he calls "monomyth," is that process whereby the hero departs from the ordinary day world of the living to enter the dark world of the supernatural, where he must combat monsters, intent on destroying him, before making a return to his people, armed with the fruit of his quest, that is, new and profound knowledge of the universe (Leeming 1990: 30).

THE LEGEND OR MYTH OF THE CULTURE HERO

The Epic of Foudjallon is a fictive invention of Aminata Sow Fall's imagination meant to explore a system of inequality and/or domination in the Wolof society, the caste system. The griot Naani recounts the story of the hero Yellimané Badar's shamanic journey to the spirit world to recoup a lost member of his father's family. Daughter Tarou had run away from her mother Assata, and entered into the belly of the whale where she remained lodged, causing untold wars and anguish during twenty years of attempts to retrieve her. The hero's trial is a chance to prove himself worthy to don the mantle of war, in order to stop a long standing feud between the royal family and the hunter's clan.

The hero goes forth as a Wolof culture hero, a metaphor for the darker human side, where in the unconscious realm horror dreams or nightmares become reality, where the monsters of the wilderness or the underworld come alive in real forms, where human profound wishes sometimes take on real forms and fulfillment. The myth of the culture hero is human search for knowledge, what Teilhard Chardin has called the path to complete consciousness. It is also for Joseph Campbell a "wonderful song of the soul's high adventure," and for Carl Gustav Jung an attempt by an individual to achieve individuation. In following the hero in his journey quest, we get lost with him and find ourselves going along with him (Leeming 1990: 217).

THE LITERARY BACKGROUND OF THE EPIC

Le Jujubier du patriarche has multifunctional dimensions. One is a model for a fight against the traditional Wolof caste system that divides the people, introducing difference and marginalization among them. We have said this before. The author describes Wolof society, not as it actually is, but rather as it should be. That is Aminata Sow Fall's attempt to change an oppressive culture and to acculturate a whole people anew. The novel is therefore a ritual, a rite of passage, which teaches present-day Wolof people, and by extension all Africans and peoples of the world, the need to return models and guides for human existence through rituals.

The strategy or structure of the epic is that the griot Naani goes first, recounting the past, with a mid-course relay by another griot Lambi, and ending with a modern sequel several years later by griot woman Naarou. The role of the three narrators of the epic—griots Naani and Lambi, and griotte Naarou—is to transmit history and legend, entertain, and preserve social values and customs. They also mediate as seers, diviners, intercessors, and spokespersons of Wolof people.

The epic proportions of *Le Jujubier du patriarche* lie, first, in its structural characteristics—the narrative style, the heroic content, the great length—[it covers a major part of the full length of the novel], the poetic language, and several other generic qualities. Second, there are such contextual traits as the fact that the Wolof believe in epics and legends as systems of knowledge, as well as in their cultural and traditional transmission. Third, the Epic of Foudjallon as recounted in the novel manifests all three modes of epics: the narrative mode that recounts the people's story, the song mode employed spontaneously to celebrate significant events in the course of the narrative, and the praise proverb mode, which moves along the plot from one scene to another. The epic, then, is a recall of the community to the mythical beginning of times for a rebirth, in which master and slave, rich and poor, noble and plebeian, lived with their honors and integrity intact in total dependence one on the other.

An initiatory structure is evident, seen the plot of the narrative, which divides the novel into three cardinal stages of the hero's adventure: chaos, symbolic death, and renaissance. The ritual begins with a catalyst as the hero responds to the right questions, and ends with the hero learning his lessons after the rite of passage, followed by his return. But, before we explore the initiatory structure of the saga of Yellimané Badar, it is important to explain the history of the Wolof caste system of inequality and domination, which remains an important issue in Wolof society today.

THE HISTORICAL BACKGROUND OF THE EPIC

In *La Société Wolof, Tradition et Changement: Les systèmes d'inégalité et de domination* (1981), Abdoulaye-Bara Diop, a Senegalese sociologist and researcher at the Institut fondamental d'Afrique noire (IFAN, part of Cheick Anta Diop University in Dakar), provides a theoretical study of the past and present of the Wolof caste system in Senegal, which is useful for our present study on the historical background of the Epic of Foudjallon. Diop states that the Wolof "*homo socius*" manifests solidarity towards others based on a system of reciprocity and mutual help in a well stratified system, the caste system. There is a hierarchy, which is not always biological, because it includes such things as the professions, ideologies, politics, religion, etc. These are all aspects of the subdivision of the Wolof into a caste system, a system which makes the Wolof, to quote Diop, *"homo hierarchicus"* as well. Individuals and groups are stratified according to their access to things and according to dominant values, professions, behavior, beliefs, etc. The social stratifications are truly multidimensional (8).

The Wolof caste system has two groups characterized by heredity, profession, endogamy, and are hierarchically ordered in a relationship of mutual dependence. The first group in the caste system has to do with social division of work, and the other, the system of order, has to do with political power. Both systems are categories that really do not meet although they influence each other (Diop, 33). The Wolof caste system has a binary of social categories, the superior caste *géér* and the inferior group *ñeeño*. The géér are not artisans, but generally peasants who engage in agriculture, animal husbandry, fishing, etc. The ñeeño are further subdivided into three professional categories: *jëf-lekk* (those who live by their job, such as blacksmiths, leather workers, and weavers), *sab-lekk* or *géwël* (griots who live by their music and songs, such as artists, oral historians, and praise singers), and *ñoole* (those who function as courtesans, buffoons, and servants). Hence the two cardinal caste systems, the *géér* and the *ñeeño*, further divided into three others, for a total of four castes in Wolof society, are marked by distinctive features, such as profession, heredity, endogamy, and hierarchy. This does not yet include the slaves, often badly defined and sometimes seen perhaps as a sub caste, or a separate, third, caste group, which includes the categories of peasants and artisans. The order of slaves can be separate, but also integrated into the order of political power as a pseudo-caste.

Observe that as time went on and a political state was created with centralized power, the order of slaves was constituted following internal and external wars that their masters had to fight. All depends, then, on how one looks at things. It is important to note that the slaves were foreign elements integrated into the monarchical ruling order with political power as Wolof society evolved into a political state. This was necessary to enable the slaves to participate fully and loyally in the system. This resulted in incorporating the slaves into the two principal Wolof social caste systems, the *géér* and the *ñeeño* (Diop 1981: 34-36).

Finally, the repulsion that people of the caste caused to those out of it may have all died out, like their unsociability, except the issue of biology and endogamy. In Wolof society today, it is somewhat like racism, which connotes a myth of superiority of the *géér* and of inferiority of the *ñeeño*. It is only a logical deduction, and by no mean historical, although historically and traditionally slaves were not always regarded as inferior, explains Diop (45). Only artisan members were seen as inferior beings. Now, once the criterion for cultural stratification became biological, it at once became racial, and consequently, mythical, and no longer real, even if it ever was at the time it depended on the kind of work you did — the lower the occupation the worse the disdain (ibid.). The role of the ideology of race and biology, then, is to assure the reproduction and continuity of the caste system.

The reproduction of the caste system in Senegal is just what Aminata Sow Fall seems to write against in *Le Jujubier du patriarche*, whose thesis seems to be that the Wolof culture caste system divides its own people with a mythical resource that casts a group as superior and the rest as inferior.

THE EPIC OF FOUDJALLON

According to the textual narrative, Tacko is a secretary by profession, a peaceful woman and wife, guided by the traditional principles of pride, submission, marriage for life, and no insult to adoptive family, and living in harmony with the community. She marries her cousin, polygynist Yelli. Whereas Tacko struggles to save the family plunged into debt, due to Yelli's squander mania, Yelli is complacent, merely pays water and electricity bills. He feels let down by the wrong turn of the wheel of fortune for himself and his family, erstwhile members of the superior caste. All his good time wives leave him when he loses his money, leaving Tacko to pick up the family pieces, including children that are not her own. Even the griots, ordinarily faithful, are also gone, except one, Naani (14-15; 18-19).

Griot Naani is a griot not like others, for he knows what fidelity means *à outrance*. He is faithful even to the point of being an anachronism. He is proud of his descent from the line of Lambi, who knew very well Almany Sarebibi, son of mother Thioro. Naani inherited 110,000 verses, which make up the Epic of Foudjallon, constituted by 700 years of history of the Almamy Sarebibi's lineage and that of the hunters of the Foudjallon. One day only in the course of every year, griot Naani, as the voice of the ancestors visits Yelli and Tacko in the city to recount the Epic of Foudjallon to the living, who must model themselves against the hero Yellimané for a return to tradition and morality (20-21).

According to the griot Naani, Almamy Sarebibi falls in love with Dioumana, the daughter of the hunter/magician Gueladio. This anisogamy, crossing of class boundaries between a noble and a caste member in marriage, is rare, but sometimes happens when the caste woman is very beautiful. The unusual nuptial union engenders enmity between the two clans, the royal family and the hunter's clan, quite in opposition to the former neighborly, reciprocal, and peaceful co-existence they had had. After long bloody battles caused by Dioumana's flight back to Gueladio her father, who wanted her returned to him, and the Almamy, who challenged Gueladio's authority to have his daughter back, the two clans finally settle their quarrel (20). That is the synopsis of the epic of Foudjallon, a creation of Aminata Sow Fall. It portends an initiatory structure.

INITIATORY STRUCTURE OF THE EPIC OF FOUDJALLON

THE CATALYST

Naarou becomes a catalyst for the impending initiation of a whole people, which will culminate in their ritual of rebirth at the foot of the jujube tree. Naarou comes to visit her mother Penda to complain that Tacko treats her as a slave (87). Indignant, Naarou affirms her descent from a line of slaves, but without shame, for she recognizes that the royal family could not have done well without her people as servants. Implicitly, Naarou is protesting the injustice of being treated as a slave, instead of being recognized as one of those who "collaborated" with another family to get things done, albeit in a long distant past and in a subordinate position. It is a reminder of the need to treat one another fairly, not to trample on individual human dignities. Naarou now affirms her identity in the face of her oppression at the hands of she whom she regards as her mother. She affirms her descendance from Warèle and Biti, both key players in the epic, according to the griot, Naani, who told her the story when she was young (89). Naarou recounts the twenty-one doors of the long poem, constitutive of the whole history of her people, to the point that her mother Penda believes that any attempt to exclude her from the epic of the people would be tantamount to killing her: *"L'exclure de l'épopée: autant lui couper une veine"* (92).

CHAOS

Naarou, daughter of Yelli's older sister Penda, has become somewhat a griot (34-36). She grew up in the household of Yelli and Tacko, and later married a young school teacher, Amsata Gaye, known for his ideas and sense of organization (71). Once every year, when the griot Naani recounts the Epic of Foudjallon, Naarou would visit the couple, Tacko and Yelli, whom she now regards as her parents, to learn about her legendary people. She is particularly interested in the epic songs with long titles, "Thioro la Linguère" and "Biti la petite fille de Warèle de chez Thioro la Linguère" (37), which seem to help to internalize the marvel and fortune of being connected with such lofty personalities as the Almamy and the members of his family.

Naarou, according to legend, is descended from Warèle whose hereditary line were the slaves of Almamy Sarebibi's mother, Thioro (22). Warèle passed down the same status of slavery to her grand daughter, Biti. The children of Almamy Sarebibi were raised by the Damels. However, despite the passage of time, even centuries, things have not changed, for the complex mentality of master/servant, domination/submission persist in Wolof culture.

SYMBOLIC DEATH

The griot Naani enters the Epic of Foudjallon by the Twelfth Door, the predominant aspect of the hero's myth, which is the hero's quest. The quest begins with a call to action, which the hero accepts by going through an initiation rite at the age of twenty years, followed by trials, confrontations with his inner monster, surmounting all the obstacles, thanks to the talisman from his spiritual guides, and eventually directly confronting death itself, or the ultimate nemesis. According to Leeming:

> Through the descent, the hero takes us to the very depths of the unconscious world where individual destiny and human destiny lie. In the death motif we confront the essence of what we are. In facing our death-defined nature, we rob death of "dominion" and emerge in rebirth from the womb of the earth into a new individuated existence,

a new wisdom or wholeness. It remains only for the hero to return to the Supreme Being in an act of apotheosis or ascension signifying that wholeness. In many of the myths the hero, like the dying god, descends into death and in returning brings great boons to his or her culture (219-220).

Griot Naani begins the evening, first, with praise song for hero Gueladio, the Man-Lion, bidding farewell to hunting, after his daughter Dioumana, the wife of the Almamy, a veritable scapegoat, enters into the belly of the whale, Tarou (123-125). The story of Dioumana affords the generality of human beings the opportunity, just as the stories of dying goddesses and gods do, to die to the old self, in order to be reborn into a new being, into a new path, individually and collectively. Dioumana's destiny is to facilitate her people's rediscovery of normality in a new nation where the rich and the poor cohabit in peace and harmony.

Next, Gueladio, a caste member, enters into the baobab tree to arm himself with occult medicine for the impending war against the royal family, and to bring back his daughter. Notice that caste members, such as griots, were refused burial in the earth, because they were seen as repulsive and able to contaminate mother earth's nurturing of the people. They were therefore always buried in the hollow trunk of the baobab tree. Today, in Wolof culture, they are still referred to as *guy-géwël*, baobab griots (Diop 1981: 38-39). Griot Naani sings the entry of the hunter Gueladio into the baobab tree to arm himself for the extraordinary and supernatural fight for his daughter (126). Notice that the baobab tree in Wolof mythology is sometimes held to be the abode of spirits of the clan, so they may not be cut down without adequate notice to the spirits to migrate to other trees. Even when cut down or during long periods of drought, baobab trees are known to spontaneously sprout leaves, so long as even the minutest roots still remain unbroken and attached to the soil. Members of the hunter's guild see red, and want nothing but a just war to return Dioumana to her father.

The griots Sangré and Lambi support the war against the Almamy, seeing Almamy's rapt of Dioumana as a collective affront to the hunters' guild. Sangré and Lambi and others in the inferior caste resent the privileged caste. Yellimané therefore is born in a period that turns out to be a dark one in the cultural history of his country. There is no miraculous conception and birth under unusual circumstances, such as Jesus brought into the world by virgin birth, Buddha that conceived himself in her mother's dream, nor Adonis born of a tree. However, Warèle, a slave woman in the Almamy's household, who took care of his son Yellimané, is scandalized by the effrontery of the hunter's clan. She turns into an agent of the hero, a veritable *femme fatale*, and tricks three of the hunters going to the Almamy's palace into her "web," by feigning she had been bitten by a snake. The hunters, Sangré, Lambi, and another, run to her aid to rescue her, believing she had been genuinely bitten by a snake. With a pen-knife they extract what they take to be a snake's venom from her foot. She rewards them by hosting them and feeding them. While they are asleep, Warèle steals the talisman that Gueladio had given them. Then, because she is already about hundred years old and expecting her death any time, she confides it to her grand daughter, Biti, who must pass it on to Yellimané during his initiation rite at puberty (128-130).

The Hero's Quest

The hero's quest, then, is an opportunity for the people to relive their destiny individually and collectively, and prepare themselves psychologically and spiritually for a new beginning. Eventually war breaks out between the two factions, and is waged in several stages, each stage bringing the two parties closer to the futility of their quest. This is perhaps the longest part of the initiation, for it recounts in detail the various battles fought over Dioumana. War is seen here as immolation, and is a cardinal aspect of symbolic death in any initiatory structure.

Yellimané, at fifteen years of age, intervenes between the two opposing groups, requesting to talk over things, in order to avoid a war. For five years he succeeds, for Gueladio holds off on the war. On the contrary, however, the Almamy Sarebibi remains stubborn, even becoming more powerful, thanks to his military exploits in subjugating neighboring countries (131). Almamy Sarebibi would become a military and a spiritual idea to be feared, especially as he no longer appears in public, and so no one can say he is like this or like that. He is the invisible saint incarnate, and an ascetic, who gives birth at once to a legend of fear, veneration, hatred, terror, and mystery about himself. He has succeeded in subjugating all communities, except that of the hunters. He is also seen as secretly and surreptitiously guiding the path of his son, Yellimané, for whom he has become a mentor (131).

THE HERO'S CALL TO ADVENTURE

At age twenty, Yellimané undergoes a rite of initiation by circumcision in his own right as part of his age group. This initiation socializes him as a responsible active adult in the community. It is during this ceremony that Biti, daughter of Bannê, grand daughter of Warèle the slave woman in the Almamy's household, who raised Yellimané, infiltrates the group of the uncircumcised as they dance. Wearing proper clothing like all male neophytes, she is able to evade detection as she dances with all the candidates of initiation. Then, surreptitiously, she goes to Yellimané and passes to him the talisman, *bille de cuivre*, which her grandmother had confided to her before she passed away. Biti could feel the dead woman's spirit infiltrate her being as she makes her way to Yellimané. Yellimané had always heard about the existence of the talisman, but really was not sure of its existence. Yellimané, therefore, welcomes this sign as his call to adventure, without arguments or doubts. He does not refuse his summons, as some heroes have been known to do—a Moses and a Jonah—fearing that they are inadequate, psychologically or physically for the job at hand.

THE TRIALS OF THE HERO

Yellimané now takes center stage, thanks to the leverage that Biti and the slave woman Warèle have given him. He dances, turns, and somersaults like every other boy in the group of the uncircumcised. Then comes his turn to symbolically forgo childhood and embrace adulthood, by throwing into the devouring fire his personal effects. He does so, and instantaneously a thunder-like power infiltrates his being. He feels himself swept into the air, becoming immaterial in a world seemingly mysterious. The atmosphere is exhilarating. Yellimané perceives with his right eye a signet ring, when eventually he comes back to reality. Is it from Warèle? Is it Warèle, who had promised to be there when it came the time for Yellimané's initiation?

The newly initiated young men attest to their rebirth by taking hold of any member within reach and challenging him to a fight. A youngster challenges Biti, by giving her a stud, thinking he is a boy like all of them. Biti does not fall, but enters into a fight with the challenger. Eventually, Biti throws him. Upon falling down he realizes that his opponent is a woman, because he inadvertently brushes against her breasts. He lets out a tremendous cry: *"C'est une femme! C'est une femme!"* [She is a woman! She is a woman!].

For having contravened convention and tradition, Biti has to be put to death. She is killed with a poisoned arrow. It is already too late for Biti when Yellimané realizes what is going on. Besides, everything has gone according to tradition: *"On n'a que ce que l'on mérite"* (35) [You get what you ask for]. Yellimané could not save her, but when everyone has gone home, he returns in the dead of the night to the initiation site between two hills to cover up her corpse with a shroud, put some perfume on it, and offer prayers for the repose of her soul. Yellimané sees Biti as a general fallen in the field of battle, and further feels no obligation to explain to anybody what really happened except to her family, that is to say, her husband and three children. What has happened at the esoteric level is the disappearance of the Mistress of Fire, so that the student may flower and flourish. Warèle's prophesy has been fulfilled, and it is time for Biti, and Warèle as well, to depart, so that Yellimané may grow.

THE HERO'S CONFRONTATIONS WITH HIS INNER MONSTERS

Several people are tired of the war, and happy to hear rumors that Gueladio's oracle has prophesied that the problem cannot be solved by war, but by negotiation. The oracle suggests a compromise, whereby Dioumana's son will go to the ancestor Tarou and give him a ring, which belongs to him in reality, and in exchange he will give back Dioumana. In that way, peace will reign where armies have failed. As he says to him:

> Fils de Dioumana, maintenant et maintenant seulement tu pourras réaliser ce que ni l'armée de ton père ni aucune armée ne réussira jamais. Va sur le chemin qui te mènera chez Tarou l'ancêtre. Tu lui rendras cette bague qui, en réalité, lui appartient, et elle te rendra Dioumana (136).

> [Son of Dioumana, now and only now can you accomplish what neither your father's army nor any other will ever accomplish. Take the path that will lead you to the ancestor Tarou. You will give her

this ring, which really belongs to her, and she will return Dioumana
to you].

Members of the Almamy's fighting league feel disappointed, and one
of them, Fara Maram, who goes as afar as to voice his objection by
saying that the Empire is plunging into dishonor, is instantaneously
killed by Yellimané with his sword (137). Meanwhile, the Almamy
orders Yellimané to go and fulfill the words of the oracle of Gueladio,
supported by his griot Lambi, master of the word.

The hero Yellimané goes through innumerable obstacles on the
way: a thousand and one fantastic adventures, strange barriers, swarms
of bees, hordes of elephants rampaging and destroying all in their path,
suddenly an enormous depression inside the ground, even as the surface remains deceptively firm, thousands of writhing snakes hissing
and turning as if they are doing a nauseating ballet, incandescent arrows flying from everywhere at once and burying themselves in the
warrior's bodies, and the list continues. Undaunted, Yellimané pur-
sues his course, holding the ring between his incisors, according to the
stipulations of the oracle, who also added that Yellimané's tongue must
not touch it (138-139).

THE HERO'S JOURNEY QUEST:
FIRST ENCOUNTER WITH TAROU, THE WHALE

Eventually, Yellimané has crossed the last obstacle, and is in front
of the River Natangué covered by a fog. The time is before noon, between nine o'clock and eleven. When the mist clears up, there is Tarou,
the Whale, seated on his majestic couch on the sea. Biting hard on his
signet ring, Yellimané advances into the waters. The crocodiles, ordinarily a menace, disappear at his approach. Is his totem the crocodile?
Notice that when the hero is on his right path all obstacles vanish.

Nonetheless, Tarou tricks Yellimané by offering the tip of her tail,
which the latter takes for a finger. As Yellimané tries to put the ring on
it, he discovers the deception. He nonetheless pulls his sword and
plunges it into the belly of the whale, unflinching and determined to
triumph against adversity. Alas, the beast double-crossed him, ex-
pertly, and like a boomerang the metal cut Yellimané flesh at the thigh.

Curiously, when Yellimané comes back to consciousness, his signet ring is miraculously on his finger. It takes him two months to recover from his wound. More than ever, he is determined not to return

to Babyselli without the Golden Fleece, Dioumana. Indeed, it has become an obsession, which occupies his waking and sleeping moments, namely, to make a triumphal return to his people with Dioumana as trophy: *"Sans Dioumana, je n'entrerai pas dans Babyselli"* (140) [Without Dioumana, I shall not retur to Babyselli]. Many times, his obsession is supported with a *bàkk*, a song about his noble lineage and expected bravery.

> Yellimané fils de Sarebibi
> [Yellimané, son of Sarebibi]
> Flamme chaude dans le coeur des jeunes filles
> [Hot fire in young girls' hearts]
> Elles chantent tes exploits
> [They sing your exploits]
> Quand la brise de mer caresse les dunes… (141).
> [When the sea breeze caresses the dunes]

The young man, Yellimané, is already dreaming of his upcoming wedding to Diakher, following his triumphal return with Dioumana. Right from his youthful days, he always knew that she was a very beautiful woman, full of courage, not fear.

Yellimané was also brought up to put duty first and emotions last. He had listened to Assata, one of the wives of his father's slaves, tell the story of her monstrous daughter, Dioumana, a daughter so monstrous that she threw herself into the mouth of the whale. It is primarily because her sacrifice did not yield any treasures for the aggrieved mother that Assata has never seen eye to eye with Gueladio and his ambition to fight the Almamy over Dioumana. Gueladio even forgot her existence until circumstances forced him one day to remember her spirit, through sacrifices of respect and devotion on her tomb.

The Hero's Journey Quest:
Second Encounter with Tarou, the Whale

After a period of two months of convalescence, Yellimané now healed and reinvigorated, reassembles his troops and sets out again to conquer the whale and bring back Dioumana. This second campaign lasts some forty days, a mythical number that spells totality in most world mythologies. Through thick and thin, Yellimané continues the fight. He is all bones and sinew at the end of his ordeal, for the whale would tantalize him, and tease him, with imminent success of his mission, only to dash his hopes to pieces at the end in a scenario reminiscent of the mythical ordeal of Sisyphus, that representative of Everyman:

> Même retraite sur un coin de terre, non loin des rives du Natangué. La découverte de la bague au bout d'un sommeil plutôt assommant. Et la détermination à recommencer tout de suite. Sisyphe sur les terres du Natangué. Le calvaire dura quarante jours (143).

> [The same retreat in a corner of the earth, not far from the banks of the Natangué. The discovery of the ring at the end of a somewhat tedious sleep. And the determination to begin all over again immediately. Sisyphus on the lands of the Natangué. The Calvary lasted forty days; *my translation*].

The mythical words "calvaire" and "Sisyphe," further place the hero's experience in the mythological domain, where the hero goes through grueling trials in search of the Philosopher's Stone. Calvary is a word often used to denote the trials and tribulations of such a hero as Jesus Christ in the wilderness for forty days and forty nights while he was tempted by the devil. Sisyphus in Greek mythology is condemned to eternally roll a great rock to the summit of a hill, which would without fail roll back, constraining Sisyphus to again roll it back up the hill. It is a metaphorical and mythical rendering of the human condition. And Yellimané as representative of all Wolof people, and by extension, all humanity, continues to struggle against all odds. At this point the hero's mettle still needs to be proven, before he is deemed worthy of his calling.

Thus, as with the first encounter with Tarou, the whale, there are again a million obstacles on the hero's path, except that this second time it is worse, for as soon as he puts his ring into the water the whale disappears. Is this a tender gesture on the part of Tarou to avoid an encounter that is sure to prove fatal for the young man Yellimané? *"Un geste de tendresse, peut-être, pour éviter au fougueux rejeton la tentation d'une croisade sanguinaire qui lui aurait coûter cher"* (143). Yellimané could not give an answer to his own question. However it seems that, mythically speaking, Tarou's strength is matched with the strength of Yellimané's fairy god mother, Warèle, who is in charge. Ordinarily, in a patriarchal culture such as the Wolof culture, one would expect the hero's life to be severely threatened by a *femme fatale*. That this does not happen at this point, I suppose, is due to the influence of the Mistress of Fire, Warèle (Leeming, 219). The next step in the hero's journey quest at this point is the confrontation with death itself.

THE HERO'S JOURNEY QUEST:
FINAL ENCOUNTER WITH TAROU, THE WHALE

Yellimané must now journey to the Land of the Dead to confront his ultimate nemesis. This is the domain of individual and human destinies. The hero confronts his essence while at the same time confronting human essence. It is the forty-first day of this final confrontation with Tarou. The Almamy even has the drums normally reserved for the coronation or death of the Almamy sound. Each citizen is summoned to the palace. Some rumor mongers say the Almamy himself is leading this prodigious match. To punctuate this ultimate march of a whole people, an ocean of men, women and children, dressed in white as far as the eye can go, to the palace, *"un ocean d'hommes, de femmes, d'enfants, tout de blanc vêtus, à perte de vue"* (144). The griot Lambi interjects a song:

> Le jour et la nuit pour faire un jour
> [Day and night for a day]
> La lumière et l'ombre pour toute vie
> [Light and darkness for every life]
> Au nom du turban je jure
> [I swear in the name of the turban]
> Pas de vie si l'étincelle ne jaillit (ibid.).
> [There is no life, if there is no spark].

Evidently, song interjection, as griot Lambi does above, is a cardinal aspect of an epic tradition. The opposing Gueladio camp, to which the griot belongs, is amused to hear that the Almamy has decided to go to Tarou himself. After a derisive and mocking laughter, Gueladio summons the hunters' guild and they all proceed to the other side of the bank of the River Natangué. It is a beautiful sight to see, adds the griot, the two opposing camps that were once living in solidarity, then separated by the love of a woman, now coming together again at the same place, thanks to the beauty of the woman (145).

Then, the hero, Yellimané, arrives mysteriously under a thick cloud covering the earth. In the name of the Supreme Being, Yellimané moves deftly to put an end to the state of war between two factions of his people. He feels like a warrior of the good against the forces of evil.

Before the people could tell what is happening, he places the ring on Tarou's tail, and Dioumana comes out of the water, naked. Several servants of the Almamy move quickly to cover her up from the gaze of the commoners, even as she herself attempts to cover herself up (147).

Then, the Almamy, manifesting an uncommon gesture of humanity summons his griot Lambi who has received lessons of compassion from his father, Koumane, while he was still alive, to reach out to the Gueladio camp that is feeling humiliated by their defeat. The ancestor Koumane had impressed on the apprentice Lambi, that equilibrium in all human activities is the responsibility of three citizens: woman, marabout, and griot. As he put it: *"L'équilibre de notre monde repose sur les épaules de la femme, du marabout et du griot"* (148-149). At another time, the old man re-phrased his words of wisdom, saying that secrecy is the inexhaustible gold mine shared with women and all marabouts conscious of their dignity: *"Lambi, écoute bien et retiens: le secret est la mine d'or inépuisable que nous partageons avec les femmes et les marabouts conscients de leur dignité..."* (149). Above as he tells Lambi in figurative language, the Almamy on his honor must return Dioumana to her father. That is the view of the Almamy's personal griot, who says that: *"...l'amour a ses limites. Au delà, c'est la perdition"* (151); *"Ce serait de l'orgueil... Veux-tu oublier que tu n'es qu'un homme... ?»* (ibid.). [...love has its limits. Beyond that, it is perdition (...); It would become pride...Do you want to forget that you are only a human being...?]: Lambi, understanding the humanity of the Almamy's predicament, in not wanting to easily give up Dioumana, adds philosophy to his father's wise sayings, stating that even saints cannot but be human, for it is by their occasional manifestations of human weakness that they avoid thinking of themselves as God. If this is not done, they place themselves on the side of Satan in opposition to God: *"S'ils ne péchaient pas, ils se prendraient pour Dieu et se mettraient pour de bon du côté de Satan..."* (152).

Suddenly, the thick cloud that had come over the earth lifts as the two giants face each other, Almamy Sarebibi and Gueladio, their griots, Lambi and Sangré, respectively are behind them. Stillness overwhelms the universe, not a single creature, animate or inanimate, moves. A blinding sun is out sending its arrows into the waters. Clearly, the two men share Yellimané, simply because Yellimané is the son of Sarebibi, and the only son of Dioumana, the daughter of Gueladio. How amazingly human beings link with each other in society. Then, why fight one another?

A tragedy occurs, nonetheless; Yellimané kills his mother Dioumana with his sword before his father Sarebibi, who had ordered her returned to Gueladio, or the griot Naani, could stop him. Dioumana is subsequently buried at the bank of the river Natangué by the whole people. Dioumana has become a sacrificial lamb for the unity of her people. According to the griot's song, she refused shame and embraced death:

> *Subbaanama* Dioumana
> L'antilope du Foudjallon.
> *Bañ gacce nangu dee*... (162).

Why does a dutiful son who has just rescued his mother from the belly of the whale turn around and murder her? Does she constitute a threat to the hero's life and/or mission? Does the heroic side of the hero, and his society that desires a new dawn, prevail against his ordinary side of a child human born by an ordinary woman? It seems that Yellimané of a patriarchal Wolof culture is ready for the process of individuation, a shamanic journey into the world to accomplish his father the Almamy Sarebibi's business, namely, discover the true essence of things, and discover his and his society's relationship with the Supreme Being. So, the mother, who symbolizes the human family, must disappear (Leeming, 218-219).

When the griot Naani has finished his tale, starting from the twelfth door of the Epic of Foudjallon, the people are divided as to the appropriateness of his narrative for the modern times in which they live. Some think the griot should have known that the times have changed, and they punctuate their reservation with a proverb: "*Est-ce que les chats faméliques avaient miaulé comme ils avaient l'habitude de le faire à pareille heure?*" [Have the female cats meowed in the way and manner they are wont to do at such an hour?] (163). In other words, how does the epic apply to the present condition of the people? It is Naarou, the third narrator, who will respond to this question, by applying the lessons of the Epic of Foudjallon to their present situation in life, namely, the division of Wolof culture by the caste system into superior and inferior beings.

RENAISSANCE

When Naarou takes up the relay a couple of years later from

Naani, dead, long replaced by his son Khourédia, it is to mourn Bouri, killed by a drunk driver as she crossed the street at a red light.

The rain after the drought in Babyselli, is hope and light at the end of the tunnel, for the jujube tree, symbol of the Tree of Life for the community, long taken for dead, suddenly comes back to life: "*Mais cette pluie, quelle aubaine! La souche du jujubier de la tombe du patriarche s'est mise à bourgeonner. Le jujubier va-t-il reverdir?*" (109). The jujube tree in the cemetery, which has now sprang back into life, thanks to the deluge of rain, is a symbol of the people's renaissance, and the rain an agent of the cleansing birth. Again the press headlines broadcast the miracle of the long-dead jujube tree that has come back to life: "*Le jujubier de la tombe du patriarche a bourgeonné...*" (116).

The people have learned the lesson they are supposed to learn, namely, that the divided house of one Wolof people must be reconciled. Two generations of the rich and the poor separated by the caste system must be reunited. A press communiqué in the newspaper, given by the descendants of the Almamy Sarebibi, summons together everyone without regard to sex, gender, ethnic group, or religion for a pilgrimage to Babyselli, in order to do honor to the memory of the saintly man ... (117).

The Return

The pilgrims are all dressed in white, the color of purity (118). Leading the pilgrims is Salimata, almost hundred years in age, just like Warèle in legendary times. They arrive in more than twenty tourist vehicles to Babyselli, at dawn, on a Friday, by a path full of rocks that a car has never been through as far as anybody knows (119). Rock here denotes a symbol with archetypal and connotative qualities, a specimen of mythological motif that recalls the tomb of Jesus or the cave, the birth place of Mithras.

In this way, the knowledge that this pilgrimage is a return home in every sense of the word, a "*rentré au bercail*" (128), suddenly strikes them, for the group going in a single file to the place of initiation looks like human representatives making an ontological entry into the primordial hole of the beginning of times for rebirth. Moreover, the drum beats and the tam-tam that accompany them in their journey are, in mythical terms, the voice of the mythical ancestors of the beginning sounding for creation. Food and feasting are not absent either, for the neophytes commune with one another and with the ancestors, through the act of eating. The feast starts about noon, which in mythology is the middle point of the day, when the earth and the sky meet. It is a propitious moment loaded with mythical connotations. Salimata's voice is the voice of the ancestors; it salutes the gathering at the tomb of the patriarch. Then following Salimata, men, women, children, in that order, file into the cemetery to salute the great ancestor in calm and slow rhythm at the tomb of the patriarch (121).

At first, Yelli, Tacko, and Naarou stand around the tree. Then, Tacko, repentant, kneels down on the ground, smells the leaves, and plucks some off a twig, saying *"Je veux vivre"* [I want to live] (122). At night, by the full moonlight, [the time of day and the astral details are connotative and significant] the ceremony of rebirth and cleansing takes place, with the party watching and waiting all night, like the disciples of Jesus Christ (122).

In the end, it is a full reconciliation of all, the *géér*, the *ñeeño*, and the slaves. It is the dawn of a new era in Babyselli, and by extension, the land of the Wolof.

WORKS CITED

Diop, Abdoulaye-Bara. *La Société wolof, tradition et changement: Les systémes d'inéagalité et de domination.* Paris : Éditions Karthala, 1981.

Knappert, Jan. *African Mythology: An Encyclopedia of Myth and Legend.* London: Diamond Books, 1990.

Leeming, David Adams. *The World of Myth: An Anthology.* New York, Oxford: Oxford University Press, 1990.

Rosenberg, Donna. *World Mythology: An Anthology of the Great Myths and Epics.* Lincolnwood, IL: NTC Publishing Group, 1994.

Sow Fall, Aminata. *Le Jujubier du patriarche.* Paris: Le Serpent à Plumes, 1993.

"THE SAGA OF MADIAMA, A
FAILED FATHER OF THE NATION"

❄ ❄ ❄

This confession of a failed hero is unique in the body of literature by Aminata Sow Fall, because the destiny of a whole people is traced and implicated in the enigmatic destiny of the ambivalent leader. Madiama, the former president, or Father of the nation, loves his nation enough to want to guide its destiny as its ultimate ruler. Yet he is too weak to control the ministers and other agents who work for him. Owing to a fatal flaw, he is out of touch, for his background does not allow him to be part of his people's aspirations. In the end, a coup d'état topples him. Madiama fails and resigns from office after five years of rule, not having achieved his objectives.

Immediately, we see a sort of picaresque epic around the story of an enigmatic figure with an archetypal name "Ex-Father" of the Nation. The appellation can fit just about any ruler that sees himself to be such. The city, from which he rules, is full of intrigues, revolts, demonstrations, drought, and lies by the mass media. The corruption is symptomatic of tragedy in the city, which mythically ought to be a representation of protection, nourishment, and shelter for all that live within, a feminine construct reminiscent of Jerusalem, Troy, or Thebes. Madiama's rememory of the past mirrors closely that of the region soon after independence from the colonial masters, in the sense that machinations of ministers, veritable sycophants, who praise the ruler for doing nothing, who hide the true reality of things from him until things are too late, are rife, and so is the cynicism of the people, who are moved by selfish interests all the time.

As the ex-father puts down his memoirs, his historical recollections colored with subjective thoughts of what happened, he uses elements of water, wind, earth, and fire to paint the fullness of the city after the drought. He also dwells on the sun symbolism, which had eluded him. Unlike the natural sun, which wanes and disappears only to return the following day at the appointed time, Madiama's sun disappears never to return. He resigns from his mission as his people's guide, forgetting that he is called to serve, due to his people's need of him.

Madiama fails the nation by recoiling from his call halfway through his mission.[1] His election to replace the departing colonial governor had been a unanimous decision. He would govern for fourteen months as Interim president, and a general election would then be held. All the arms of government were already in place: finance, army, defense, administration, etc. He was fortunate to have Andru as aid, for Andru knew their country thoroughly, having been an advocate for dialogue rather than revolutions. As President of the council, Andru always advocated peace, negotiation (10). He thought Madiama was *"souverainement choisi"* [sovereignly chosen] by the people (11-12).

MADIAMA'S ENTHRONEMENT

This takes place during the year of the drought. The sun is implacable, the vegetation dry, and the harvest poor. Andru assures the president that the cycle will pass as usual, and that the harvest is intact in the south. Bambi, the Minister of Agriculture concurs. Madiama resists Bambi's advice, namely, that farmers pay tax, asking rather for their exoneration in the name of humanity, justice, and truth. Bambi acquiesces, calling him a true guide of his people.[2]

Madiama finds his residence, his castle as he calls it, suffocating, and his new name, "Excellency," which has replaced his youth nickname Runk Tunk (K leg), abominable (49). Gone are his days as a union leader, as athlete, goalkeeper for the national soccer team, and successes with the basket ball team. How isolating power is, he laments (50). He no longer can visit friends nor attend worship in the mosque like everybody else (51). Andru tells him that as the representative of the thirty million people of the land, he must be mystified, so that the people identify him as a myth of power and glory (51). He must think of himself as the wind that infiltrates everywhere through his agents, for the state requires this (52). Madiama regrets nonetheless the widening gulf between him and his brother, Bara, whom he can no longer visit when he wants. He suffers doubly the reality he lives, and the knowledge that his human rights have been stripped by being the Father of the nation (53).

THE WOMEN

COURA CISSÉ, MADIAMA'S SENIOR WIFE

Coura Cissé married Madiama as a hard virgin at fifteen years of age, becoming his first wife. She was indignant when Madiama took a second wife, Yandé. Their daughter was then only fifteen months old. Coura tells him that despite her hurt feelings she is going to remain married to him, in order to honor the words of the departed Madiama's own mother, Coumba Dado Sadio, who had asked them to remain married throughout their lives, and had brought up Coura with a certain amount of heroism in her character. Coura reincarnates the old woman, Coumba, but the said reincarnation would also end their life as husband and wife. In anger over Madiama's betrayal, Coura crushes to pieces the gold trinkets Madiama spent fifteen months of salary to purchase for her. She and Madiama make a pact that would keep them together, although they will no longer sleep together as husband and wife. But, Madiama must not share the secret with anyone else. Coura, for her part, will thenceforth become Madiama's mother reincarnate. To seal the pact, in a purely African way, then, Coura, who is nursing a three-month old baby, squirts breast milk in the direction of Madiama, and it enters his mouth (59). That is their bond to keep the terms of their relationship thenceforth secret between both of them. Coura has dealt with her personal problem of a devoted wife whose husband has taken another wife her own way. She begins to see herself as her husband's mother, forgetting him as a sexual partner. There is certain heroism in her gesture.

223

COUMBA DADO SADIO, MADIAMA'S MOTHER

When Madiama's mother, Coumba Dado Sadio, died, it was believed that she simply walked away into oblivion in the form of her well-beloved Lélo, the goat, which she cherished like a fetish. Lélo was the sole descendant of a goat that her mother had offered her as a wedding gift (57). Her fisherman father was the son of Mangoné the wood-cutter and executioner for the colonial government (60). Sadio was raised by the famous philosopher Kothie Barma Fall, who was full of sobriety, discretion, and hard work. Fall's father helped him to work his piece of earth, and his grand father sold the proceeds from the farming and with it took care of his family. Sadio's father also took care of the grandfather, his wife and her children, the oldest of who was Coumba Dado Sadio, Madiama's mother (60).

Madiama's father met his mother Coumba Dado Sadio at Saly, where she sold the products of their farm to sailors. The man was old enough to be her father, but they got married nonetheless. Coumba was raised as brother and sister with his son Bara from his dead first wife. It was the old woman Coumba Dado Sadio's wish that Coura, whom she adopted, stay in the household and not marry out. When another daughter upon getting married wants to take Coura to live with her, she refuses (62).

Coumba Dabo Sadio, who grew up in the fields, braving the elements, wind, lightning, sun, rain, brought up Coura under her wings. She taught her that the will of the Creator and the courage of the farmer who braves the elements make the grain germinate, flourish, and flower, in order to give forth a thousand fold what is put in the earth. Fear, on the other hand, vilifies human beings, turning them into traitors and cowards (62). Personal merit is the highest of honors. It is honorable to earn one's living, in order to be free and escape greed and rancor that turns human beings into wicked persons.

Coumba Dabo Sadio and Coura developed a close relationship and worked out a ritual with which they communicated with each other. To ask a question, Coumba Dabo Sadio would clap her hands twice and then spread them out before Coura, as if asking for an offering (62-63). Coura, for her part, and for each response, would take a step, turn like a top, and stop point dead at the point when she finished giving the response with a genuflection before Coumba Dabo Sadio. Coumba always wore a simple everyday pagne knotted in her belt. Field work done, both women would walk back home in a single file, Coura in front and Coumba bringing up the rear (63).

DROUGHT AS CATALYST

The drought is the catalyst that triggers the sycophants to work on His Excellency, the president, convincing him to stop worrying about his people, who must be made to work hard like the ancestors. They must labor to take care of themselves, and not look up to the government for help (65-66). The state calls for international aid, and the North sends them cereals in exchange for financial aid in the amount of $220 million for management. Meanwhile the ministers tell the people that the nation's guide, His Excellency, is the source of the nation's prosperity. Evidently, the sycophants are guided by self-interest and self-gratification.[3]

Despite the sycophants and Yandé his second and greedy wife, Madiama feels that things are not all right with the nation and the people. Dicko, his arch rival writes in his privately owned newspaper, pointing accusing fingers at the overfed leaders at the expense of the people: "*Profiteurs, assassins! Halte à la boulimie*" (68). Mythically, words such as "ficelle" [Cord] and "Bouée de sauvetage"[safety mud] translate the anguish of the well-meaning president, who is losing hold of the ship of state, through something quite beyond himself. He thinks that appointing a Prime Minister will help him get back a hold on the reins of power (69). He will call for a constitutional review that will allow him to delegate some of his powers. He thinks that Latsouk, the Minister of Communication has the same principles as himself (69-70). But, soon detractors go to work against Latsouk (72-73), making use of the mass media. Andru, the president's assistant, goes to a great length to convince him that it is wrong and unrealistic of the Prime Minister to redistribute wealth and revenue to everybody. What is better, he says, is to have a few privileged persons control the rest of the populace, becoming their voice, and canalizing their wants and opinions.[4]

In his newspaper, *Dolé* (Big Fish), Dicko accuses the Father of the nation of gross incompetence, of standing by as the nation totters at the brink of collapse. He says: "*La marmite du pouvoir en grande ebullition. Bientôt elle explosera. Le Président assiste, impuissant, à la disintegration de son gouvernement*" (75) [The power pot is dangerously boiling and soon will explode, yet the president looks on powerlessly as his governement disintegrates]. And Madiama thinks of himself as a voyager lost in a desert, alone, hence his extreme lassitude and nervousness. He says:

> La sensation douloureuse d'être un voyageur déboussolé, perdu dans le desert, accroché désespérément à l'instinct de vivre et obéissant à tous les réflexes pour tenir bon. Le malheur qui en découlait lorsque j'y pensais, j'étais seul à le vivre. Une lassitude extrême m'envahissait, la nervroisté me gagnait (75).

> [The painful sensation of being a disoriented traveler, lost in the desert, hanging desperately on his survival instinct, and obeying all his reflexes to stay afloat. When I thought of this, I alone bore the pain which came out of it. An extreme lassitude overwhelmed me, and a nervousness overtook me]

Then, Bara, Madiama's older and wise brother, whom he had not talked to for a long time, sends for him through Gana, a relative, in order to warn him about the people's disappointment.[5] In response, Madiama tells his brother about his plans of government, which accord with traditional African way of governance, namely, working for what is possible with passion (78-79).

Madiama'a return to his brother's house brings back memories of their dead father Diobaye and his moral values. In a fit of introspection, he finds out that people in his office serve their personal and material interest first, and that nepotism has tarnished his image.[6] Madiama cannot believe how much he has ceded to corruption (81). He becomes afraid of seeing his vulnerability before a complex system where materialism silences all moral values (ibid). His brother's words keep ringing in his ears to remember the moral teachings of their father and govern in peace and cleanliness: *"Voie de paix et de propreté... Gouverne dans la propreté. Père y tenait"* (82).

Mangoné, Madiama's grandfather, according to Coumba Dado Sadio, was the father of Diobaye, Madiama, Bara, and Lansana. He was an extraordinary person. Mystery surrounds Mangoné's life, says Coumba Dado Sadio, for he lived in the forest, where a snake bite soon killed his first wife. He had the strength of Heraclites with which he was able to pull tree trunks for his boat building. His head disappeared into his throat at such occasions. He took mysterious voyages to town, bringing back no treats for children as custom demanded. No one knew the secret of his life. People then concluded that he was not just a man (83), but a supernatural being that lived in the forest with spirits. He wore the same khaki outfit to town as he worked in. People fled at his approach for rumor had it that he killed people.[7]

When Madiama announces his decision to step down, it has been already twenty-two years that he has not slept with his first wife Coura. He feels, he says, like someone put him under the hammer and Bara was about to crush him to pieces. Andru, surely, is also waiting to drive his arrow into his side (92).

Epidemic, illness, death, and hospitalization are all part of Madiama's life. According to the story, four years after his father's death, Madiama had made his decision to become a nurse, in order to cleanse the earth of its stains (98). Madiama is a reincarnation of his father (99). From the day his mother miraculously cured his grand-mother of small pox, he decided to become a nurse, in order to pro-long his father's hope of curing humanity of its stains (ibid). Madiama recalls his doubt, deception, and disillusions and his Calvary as a cru-sader (109). The army he was up against was invisible, but omnipres-ent and subterranean, except for Dicko's front.[8] To his daughter, Borson, he stresses the importance of respect for human dignity, not the superficial glories of power and influence.[9] In regret, he looks forward to returning to his job as a nurse, in order to set an example for his fellow country men and women (116).

Madiama met Yandé in the hospital, for hospital work and sav-ing lives brought Madiama together with Yandé who was a patient in the hospital, having been hurt by her brother, Yatma (126-127). Madiama takes care of her wounds. Yandé was a prostitute, a child with many problems, and according to her mother a bad child intro-duced into their family to spoil it. Yandé's father, Silèye, was a driver, who also thought that sorcerers had introduced Yandé into his family as a third eye. A third eye or evil eye, we must recall, is the harmful use that evil magicians, sorcerers, witches, and medicine-men make of magical objects to harm someone. They may send magical snakes, flies, ants, bats, animals, birds, and spirits to cause harm and death. Evi-dently, no one can feel safe, due to extreme fear of an evil eye (Mbiti 1990: 195-196). Yandé's father had used all within his means to bring Yandé back to normal human dimensions to no avail. After listening for a long time to Yandé recount her story, including her failed mar-riage to Fado, and proscription from public work, Madiama offers to marry her, rather than leave her to go back into the world with her handicap (127).

Meanwhile, the Ship of State is in jeopardy, reflected in the repetition of mythemes like *"le navire* [ship]," *le brouillard* [blizzard]," *la mer* [the Sea]," *les requins* [sharks]," and *le Rubicon* [the Rubicon]." The people revolt (130-143), and congregate at the Presidential Palace. The state intervenes, and drives them away. Worse, the president's daughter, Nafi, is killed during the demonstration, probably trampled to death by the massive crowd. The president is yet unable to resign, and more commotion follows with more repression of the people.

The people's aspiration for freedom and liberty is compared to the seven-headed hydra; you cut off one head, others grow up to continue the struggle. In African mythology, the hydra is a water monster, which could stop the flow of the river, if annoyed by his worshippers. So, people bring him regular offerings and food to pacify him (Knappert 1995: 112-113). Eventually, it is the coup d'état staged by Masari that topples the president out of office. His entire household is imprisoned for various terms. He has no choice, but to resign.

What are the factors that lead to the hero's downfall? What is his Achilles' heel? As he confesses in this memory recall, fear is Madiama's Achilles heel (12). Like a novice abandoned by his captain in a small boat at high tide, he is dead with fear. The weight of the office of president is too colossal for him. Despite his height and physical build, he feels like a child confided the ancestral vase that he must not allow to break. To break it would be tantamount to breaking the hopes of a whole people (thirty million of them); it would be like a malediction (ibid,). However, at the beginning, he surmounts the shame, which he sees as a poisonous beast, promising himself to succeed, in order not to shame or disappoint his people. A second problem for him is his political rival, Dicko, who cannot understand how Madiama could love his country and still cooperate with the imperialists. A third obstacle is vanity, which also tracks him right from the beginning, despite his feelings of euphoria and beatitude, for he believes that after God it is him, just as the people say everywhere, in the media, and in their songs. Nonetheless, his second wife, Yandé, sees the scenario as an Apotheosis at the end of a long road in which she has been her husband's guide and shining star (14). Fourth, the opposition party, the Renovation Party, seeks to discredit Madiama, whom it sees as a simple nurse catapulted to presidency. They make prices rise, causing inflation (25). There is corruption through bribery, lack of modern medicines in the dispensaries, stolen when available, patients milked to see the doctor for an x-ray, etc., etc. (26-28). The people cry their

disappointment up to God in heaven, wondering where they are going. Even when the whites were in the country, they say, things were
not as bad (28). Meanwhile the colonial government waits in the corner to see how the drama would play itself out, if possible to return
and take over. Fifth, Maas, a discredited minister, along with his hench-
men, hatches a revolt to torch the Presidential Place. They are caught
by the police. Madiama refers to the incident as a hidden ghost in the
northwest, which is open to the ocean and the Big River, a chameleon
hand that is hard to get, hidden in the oriental desert and in the forest.
The mythemes ghost, ocean, river, chameleon, desert, forest, spell danger and disaster for the presidency. Maas, his second wife Ada, along
with his followers are caught and imprisoned. Their newspaper, *Dolé*
stops publishing.

Madiama takes the opportunity of the foiled coup d'état to re-
press the opposition, in spite of himself. He even later publicly par-
dons Maas, who, having finished his prison sentence, writes him an
apologetic letter, calling him a savior and a marvel (32-36). Little does
Madiama know that Maas is a big joke playing a game. Madiama
slaps his second wife Yandé, who seizes the opportunity to remind
him how she labored clandestinely to ensure that his enemies were
put away (45).

CONCLUSION

In exploring the symbolism of father, and/or ex-father in this
study, the objective has been to present Madiama as an anti-hero,
whose saga teaches present-day Wolof people, and by extension, all
Africans and beyond, that power should be appropriately and respon-
sibly used by he or she on whom it is bestowed or it will be taken
away. The image of father or ex-father of the nation recalls mythical
understanding of the Supreme Being or God. It is a metaphor for patriarchal, authoritarian, or elitist approach to the governance of one's
own people. The father fails, because he is not able to control his agents.

NOTES

1. Andru, one of the faithful ministers, a confidant, and a catalyst
    reassures him at the beginning:

    Votre pays, Excellence, vient tout juste d'accéder à l'indépendance.

Vous avez acquis un pouvoir tout neuf. C'est comme si vous étiez debout sur la cime d'un arbre sans racines. Si l'arbre bascule, votre vie est en danger. Nous sommes ici, Excellence, pour consolider votre règne (8).

[Your Excellency, your country has just gained its independence. And you have acquired a new power. It is as if you are standing at the summit of a tree without roots. If the tree sways, your life is in danger. We are here, Your Excellency, to assure your tenure; *my translation*].

2.   Madiama reminisces over his fall from grace:

Et je buvais à la coupe du bonheur remplie par le peuple enchanté. Un enfant du pays pour le destin du people, cela manquait depuis si longtemps! J'étais le fils prodigue. J'étais le miracle. J'étais le don de Dieu, l'homme de la Providence, l'élu, le héros, le phare. Après Dieu, j'étais tout. C'est le peuple qui le disait, qui le répétait, qui le chantait et qui l'écrivait (13-14).

[And I was drinking from the fountain of happiness of a mesmerized people. A son of the soil for the destiny of the people, something that has been missing for a long time ! I was the prodigal son ! I was the miracle ! I was God's gift, the man of Providence, the elected, the heros, the guiding light. After God, I was everything. The people said it, repeated it, sang it, and wrote it ; *my translation*].

3.   The sycophants, Minister of finance Mapaté, Dolé, and the rest sing up to the president in like manner:

Inch Allah, tu dureras, car tu sais qu'il est de ton devoir d'aider. Il faut aider autant que tu pourras. C'est une pratique que nous avons trouvée sur terre et que nous y laisserons. Au revoir, notre fils, que dieu te protégé (66).

[Inch Allah, you will endure, for you know your duty is to serve. You need to help out as much as you can. That is a practice we have found on earth and which we shall leave behind. Good bye, my son, may God protect you; *my translation*].

4.   Andru counsels him on the affairs of state as being not about morality, but rather about paying attention to the sycophants who make things work for the president:

L'État n'est pas une affaire de morale (...). Ce sont ces hommes qui font que le peuple vous acclame et vous applaudit à chacune de vos sorties, malgré les difficultés de toutes sortes dans lesquelles il se débat (74-75).

[Statehood is not about morality (…). It is these men who ensure that the people acclaim and applaud you everytime you come out into the public, despite all their difficulties; *my translation*].

5. His brother Bara, on the other hand advices him to pay attention to the people who put him in power, saying:

L'espoir du people, c'est tout le poids du monde sur tes épaules. Tu avais dit: "Oui, je le porterias. Maintenant le people est en train de lorgner au-dessus de ta tête pour chercher l'espoir…avec le hantise d'une cassure… Ce n'est pas très bon signe… C'est ça que je voulais te dire (78).

[The people's hope is the weight of the world upon your shoulders. You had said : « Yes, I will bear it ». Now the people are looking over your head for that hope…at the risk of breaking their necks…. That is not a good sign. That is what I wanted to talk to you about; *my translation*].

6. Madiama regrets falling into the temptation of nepotism:

J'avais pensé que ce n'était pas un péché que d'aider ma soeur. Et le ministre de la Fonction Publique à qui j'avais confié le problème leur avait trouvé des postes de conseillers et et d'attachés de direction dans des enterprises de la place (81).

[I had thought that it was not a sin to help my sister. And the minister of Public Affairs to whom I had assigned the problem had found them managerial positions of counsellor and attaché in businesses in the city].

7. A young child asks whether Diobaye's father actually killed people as they say:

C'est vrai, ce qu'on dit? Que votre père Mangoné le bûcheur, quand il est en tenue de fête, c'est pour tuer des gens! (85)

[Is it true what people say, that when your woodcutter of a father Mangoné wears the head gear it is to kill people? *my translation*]

8. Madiama confesses his lassitude of power:

Je ne me croyais plus capable d'exercer le pouvoir dans un contexte où des hommes s'en servent pour intriguer, se déchirer, se jeter l'oppbrobre comme dans une galerie infernale où les plus forts en manoeuvres inavouables écrasent les autres et où l'hypocrisie est érigée en règle de vie (109).

[I no longer felt capable of weilding power in a context where people use power to plot, tear, and throw opprobrium on one another as in a fiery galery in which the strongest crush the others in untold manouvers, and in which hypocrisy is the rule of life].

9. Madiama tells Dughet Borson that he will always have a conscience to do the right thing:

Il ne faut pas que les aspects superficiels du pouvoir te cachent l'essentiel, qui est le respect de notre dignité et celle des autres. Tu ne peux pas t'imaginer les pièges que c'était le pouvoir (…) pièges matériels (..) pièges moraux. Je veux toujours haïr la laideur (111).

[The artifical aspects of power should not hide the essential, which is respect of our dignity and that of others. You cannot imagine the material and moral traps that power is. I will always hate ugliness in all its shapes and colors].

WORKS CITED

Knappert, Jan. *African Mythology: An Encyclopedia of Myth and Legend.* London: Diamond Books, 1990.

Mbiti, John. *African Religions and Philosophy.* Oxford: Heinemann, 1990.

Sow Fall, Aminata. *L'Ex-père de la nation.* Paris: L'Harmattan, 1987.

"THE SAGA OF ASTA DIOP, THE BOSOM FRIEND OF ANNE LEMAIRE"

❄ ❄ ❄

In *Douceurs du bercail,* a modern myth of a return home responds to the ordeal of African peoples in contemporary times vis-à-vis the world. What started as a rite of passage for Asta Diop, called to go for a professional mission to France from her native Senegal, soon becomes a whole people's struggle for human dignity, and love for one's own motherland, in order to earn prestige and recognition for hard work from other peoples and cultures of the world. Two cardinal symbols "douceurs"/sweetness, and "bercail"/home," spell hope and joy of return home, with the right attitude. The idea of home is that of knowledge that accrues from virtual self-sufficiency, if only one would take time to discover one's abundant resources. Aminata Sow Fall creates a new, contemporary myth, inspired by real world events.

The adventures of Asta Diop become an archetype of the African immigrants' Odyssey in Europe. More importantly, it is about the absurdity of their suicidal adventure to Europe, which seems to ignore all reasonable limits and dictates of common sense. Albert Camus' *Le mythe de Sisyphe*, describes this absurdity of the youth hell bent on suicide, against all odds. It is a veritable philosophical problem, an absurdity inherent in the sheer conflict between the youth's yearnings and the deafness of the Western world that ignores their human dignity and needs (1942). African youth flock there daily by air, sea, and land in search of work and knowledge, yet at the end of the day, lose their jobs when they are not maltreated at the airports and deported. The airplane cabin, airports, and custom passport control are spaces where the monster of modernity devours African youth, never allowing their restitution. Even customs agents are empowered to violate them in the "forbidden places," to employ Aminata Sow Fall's own expression. Africans fleeing from presumed hunger, joblessness, and ill-heath at home are constantly hailed, interrogated, insulted, detained, and imprisoned in Europe. Individual and collective hope for decent life and survival is gone. The worst distress is that hope is gone too: *"l'espoir s'en va (...) c'est le plus dur."*

THE CATALYST

Colonialism, the colonialists' coming to Africa that exposed Africans to the lure of the First world, is perhaps the remote catalyst that engendered Asta Diop's ordeal. Monsieur François Lebeau, ex-colonial administrator, and Lise Lebeau his wife, brought up their child, Anne Lemaire, Asta Diop's friend, to see the value of travel in opening up the spirit. As M. Lebeau says: *"les voyages forment la jeunesse (...) Faut voir les gens et leur diversité pour comprendre le monde (...) Mais tu trouveras bien partout le même soleil"* (31-32). Despite this advice, namely to travel, in order to see the world and grow, adding that indeed there is intrinsically no difference between one's own corner of the world and other places, the colonized never fails to admire the colonialists: their ease of living, buildings, guards, authority, order, uniform, tax, and festivities (32-33). Lise establishes a modest library full of books, and sees no sense in the Africans going abroad at all odds to study. When she is on vacation, she is happy to go into the hinterland to meet Africans in the market, artisan quarters, bush, and feast days (36).The immediate cause of Asta's ordeal is an award to attend a conference on the World Economic Order in France. She gets into trouble at the airport control in France. Because she is from Africa, all the standards change for her, until feeling humiliated she attacks the female customs agent, who tries to force her hands into her vagina to search for contraband goods. The symbols of bestiality that describe this violation and the attack in reaction are evidence of the chaos and degradation of humanity on both sides, due to the objectification of a section of humanity by another that believes in its superiority and the other's inferiority.

Anne Lemaire's search for her friend Asta, whom she thinks apparently did not arrive at Paris airport, approaches the dimensions of a labyrinth, as she runs from one end to the other in the underground airport "cave" reserved for "illegal" immigrants, in vain (40; 44). She calls Dakar by telephone to enquire about her friend, thereby opening up a window on the ills of a continent. There is a lot of despair and exasperation about the laxity of workers, poverty, and lack of productivity.

Who are responsible for this situation of things? Africans are, due to their lack of love for their own corner of the world. Europeans as well are part of the problem, because they concoct development plans for Africa on a draw board far away from Africa, without taking into account the real human beings on the ground and the realities of things (59; 60-61). Four telephone calls, back and forth from Paris to Dakar, show that Asta did travel, had all her travel documents correct, was going to attend an international meeting widely covered in the news all over the world, yet was not seen in Paris. Evidently, she was detained at the border by the French police (62). Rumor mongers in Dakar go to work spreading the worst about what happened, thanks to their mental conditioning by the Western propaganda after colonization; they see always the best in the West and the worst in Africa. What is more, they surely do not have much work to do, due to lack of jobs, worsened by the World Bank's Structural Adjustment Program and devaluation of the local currency (64-65). Shanty towns, overpopulated barracks, chic villas see their doses of rumors. The fat, green flies that fall into people's noses and eyes are only symbols of the city's degeneration and decadence. It is unbelievable that the people immediately and cynically take the side of Europe against their own people (65).

CHAOS

Yet despite the ill-treatments they receive in the French airport underground Depot — the term evidently objectifies the Africans sequestered in this underground "prison" for "illegal" immigrants — the Africans continue to flock abroad nonetheless, with correct papers or without. Many times, in these horrible bunkers, the detainees are all

Third World people, blacks, hybrids, mulattos and Arabs, awaiting deportation to their countries of origin (39). They are forbidden to lie down, and harsh lights that seem like search lights are positioned on them at all hours of the day and night to ensure that they get neither rest nor sleep (40). It is an image of hell, if ever there was one. The Africans are seen as slaves of yesteryears still, prompting Yakham, one of the detainees to interject that even his ancestors in the Middle Passage, in their *"cale des négriers,"* [negro cages], probably faired better than present-day Africans in Europe, treated like dirty, repulsive beasts. Zoological allusions, like *"pestiférés,"* and the spraying of these detained immigrants with insect spray, translate the horrors of the situation for those who are held like infectious animals (42).

Since the beginning of times, human beings have visited untold and wanton hardships on other human beings. Sow Fall recalls the horrors of the Spanish Inquisition, The Italian Gladiators, the Atlantic Slavery and the Middle Passage, and the Jewish pogrom: *"La bête immonde, depuis l'aube des temps, bouge dans nos entrailles: l'inquisition, la traite des nègres, l'holocauste juif ..."* (47). In the contemporary world, this inhumanity includes wars or shedding of human blood in the name of Fatherland or Motherland ideologies (48), hunger, poverty, inter ethnic cleansing, joblessness, bad health management, and hopelessness for the future (48). Detained abroad, Africans are subjected to various techniques of oppression and torture, including suspension in a state of timelessness, for they cannot tell the time of day, nor the day itself. Harsh lights, like those of hell, are kept twenty-four hours focused on the detainees to ensure they neither rest nor sleep (40, 44). We have said this before. Then again, they are kept disoriented, for they are not told what day it is, or time, or anything (83-84). Questioning follows questioning, followed by violation of one's body through rape, and belongings that are searched endlessly, demand of valid papers of travel and refusal to accept their genuineness, and use of the multimedia to give wrong reports about the goings on. You almost become bestial in your attitude, due to the inhuman treatment to which you are subjected (84). Asta could not have guessed she would ever descend so low in her life (86). You almost feel like you are drowning (ibid.). There is a conscious effort on the part of the oppressors, Asta further states, to so deal with you that you would never think of coming back to their borders. Yet the oppressors escape public outcry, due to their power to deny the public knowledge of what goes on in those bunkers under the airports. They claim they are doing their jobs, arguing that if indeed they were oppressive the Africans would have stopped coming. It is in the insistence of immigrants to keep going to the light and good life that the West promises like insects to the light that burns them up, despite their travails, that the novel *Douceurs du bercail* constructs the entire initiatory structure of Asta Diop's psychological itinerary into awareness.

Symbolic Death

Waiting becomes a presence, and is perhaps the worst part of the ordeal of the sequestered Africans, for the voyagers do not know when they can go home. Like Samuel Beckett's two existential wretches, Vladimir and Estragon, in *En attendant Godot/Waiting for Godot*, they do not know when nor if they will have salvation, and from who, God, time, or human beings. They wait and wait, and that constitutes their existence, Everyman's existence. Vladimir says to his companion Estragon as they wait at the foot of a tree at the corner, and they have been waiting from time immemorial, apparently:

All I know is that the hours are long, under these conditions, and constrains us to beguile with proceedings which — how shall I say — which may at first sight seem reasonable, until they become a habit. You may say it is to prevent our reason from floundering. No doubt. But has it not long been straying in the night without end of the abyssal depths? That's what I sometimes wonder. You follow my reasoning?
And Estragon responds: ".... We are all born mad. Some remain so" (*Waiting for Godot* 46).

Certainly, the Africans belong to the group that stay blind, in the sense that they refuse to put on their clothes of self dignity, and also in the sense that they appear to enjoy martyrdom, as if there are no other choices left for them. Yakham, for example, asks:

Jusqu'à quand? Ça fait trois jours que j'attends et je n'ai même pas le droit de savoir jusqu'à quand. On m'a expulsé, d'accord. Mais qu'on me ramène chez moi! (50).

[Until when? It is already three days that I am waiting and I do not even have the right to know when. I have been thrown out, sure. But, let somebody get me back to my home!].

And Dianor, musician and composer, clapping his hands to a blues rhythm intones, invents a rhythmic song repartee out of Beckett's proverbial illustration of human existential anguish (ibid).

Dianor's second concert, in which all present, even the police, find amusement and gaiety, performs the Beckettian tramps that represent human beings waiting, and waiting for God that never comes, and constitutes a short break in the monotony of waiting to go home. Observe that the blues is significant as a musical mode of protest. Here, in conjunction with Samuel Beckett's exploration of the philosophical implications of human existence and condition in his play, we get a glimpse into Aminata Sow Fall's imagination on the primacy of power in human existence, the endless tussle to see whose power is greater. It is a world of might is right, a world in which the bigger animal eats up the smaller one.

Later, some of the detainees are called away to take the next flight home, and the rest remain, including Asta Diop. The irony of the situation is that Asta was always one of those patriots who urged her people to have pride in their country and stay home. Yet there she is in the hole and unable to get out. One thing Asta is sure of is that on getting out, if she ever does, she would be able to tell her people of all walks of life and age that the so-called Eldorado is certainly not in Europe, but there is a possibility of finding it on African soil (87). The use of the mythical Eldorado here to reflect human search for happiness, including wealth and health, is poignant.

PEREGRINATION IN THE BUNKER

Anne's peregrination in the airport depot, cave, or bunker, as it is variously called, in search of her friend is like a wandering in the belly of the earth. It is a true labyrinth, a true Calvary. She goes from terminal to terminal, then underground, into corridors that wind their way in spiral, only to return to her point of departure: *"un marathon épouvantable entre terminaux, sous-sols, couloirs en spirale et retours au point de départ"* (67). Anne turns and turns as she goes around looking for her friend Asta Diop. At the end of a long underground corridor, she sees writing on a door that says *"interdit"*/No Entry, in a severe kind of tone, more severe than others. She passes this same door to the cage several times. Then, more out of curiosity than anything else, due to the sign on it, she pushes it open. A police officer appears and with gestures reminds her that she is not allowed into that room. Anne is at her wits end. She makes a decision to contact the Senegalese ambassador in Paris. Her visit yields no immediate fruit, for the Senegalese ambassador and the embassy officials are not on seat. Then, when the embassy gets to know the situation of Asta, they want to do nothing about it, because, they explain, you cannot go against the laws of a host country and get away with it. When the news filters down to Africans abroad in Senegal, they also blame Asta for allowing herself to be exposed like a fish to be dried up at the fishing village of Guet Ndar in Saint-Louis (72). The cynicism of the people is so biting that you quail at the depths to which a people have fallen about their own human dignity as a collectivity. Observe the complicity of the local media in the denigration of their people, through the radio that brought the news from abroad (65-66). In this, they are no better than the Paris airport video that presents a one-sided version of what really happened at the airport between Asta and the female custom's officer that was about to violate her body, causing her to lash out at her (215).

Anne is convinced as she leaves the ambassador's office with her husband Didier that might is indeed right, that there is no morality when interest and ambition get in the way, that words have no meaning, if they do not win the oppressed their deliverance (79). She is nonetheless elated to see that she, a white woman, is exerting herself so in search of a black woman. By the same token, she thinks all will be well with the hundred-year old plane-tree whose leaves are turning yellow and falling off. Seeing the flame tree in full autumn season, but still keeping its usefulness, gives her strength to continue her search, for she sees herself in the image of this beautiful, majestic and resilient tree, whose sap never dries up in its trunk: *"Il est beau, il est majestueux. La sève, dans son tronc, ne tarira pas."* (82).

News about Asta is distorted by media report, which completely misses the cause of the altercation. As it states, a Senegalese woman almost strangled a female custom's officer to death: *"Une sénégalasie ...a falli étrangler une douanière au cours d'un simple contrôle"* (53). Anne is horrified to see on the front page the picture of her friend Asta trying to snuff life out of the custom woman (56). Anne is overcome with fear, trembling and fainting. She is appalled by the picture of Asta's bestiality in the newspaper article. It is not until she talks to the Senegalese ambassador, a friend of Asta's director in Senegal, that she learns the lesson that will help her deal with the situation and prepare her for a "rebirth" in Senegal.

Keur Ndongo, Lesson in Human Survival

Mabaye Sèye, the Ambassador of Senegal in France, is a friend of Asta's Director General, Birane Ndour. Mabaye would send Birane delicacies from Senegal as he moved from place to place in his ambassadorial work. Mabaye tells Anne a story about his people, the Keur Ndongo, a hard-working people, who live by the sweat of their palms.

In the village of Keur Ndongo, he says, every man harvests thirteen times the amount of food required by his family. Those who fail to do so at the annual *Journée de la Revue des Greniers*, when accounts are taken yearly three days after the harvest, are banished by the villagers, and allowed to leave without their wives or children (73-74). Many of the about-to-be-exiled always choose to immolate themselves at the foot of the village hill, rather than depart. Still, their families live in shame perpetually for their lack of productivity. Therefore, most people work hard to produce more than enough for one season's survival, thanks to the instinct of self preservation (74). What remains of the custom is the mystique of hard work. In Keur Ndongo, the festival thus celebrates for one month life's abundance, and all kinds of excesses are permitted.

In African traditional society, recalls Asta, everything happens in cycle, including time, seasons, drought, famine, epidemics, and all, such that material poverty is not so important. Hence her present torture will pass, she believes, and she will prevail in the end, with hope and certitude in God the great, just like her grandfather. When she gets out, she says, she will be able to tell fellow Africans that Europe is no Eldorado, and that their fate lies rather in the bowels of their own piece of earth, Africa. They simply have to have faith, hope, and love (88)

Lesson for the Youth

Through conversation that Asta holds with a young man detainee in the bunker, Yakham comes out with a lesson for the youth. Yakham represents the typical Senegalese youth today, ambitious, but held back by corruption and nepotism in the national fabric. Yakham is a brilliant child, born at Fagarou Diamaloye, City of Peace, and the third son of Cora Cissé and Daba Sangharé. A short one-year stint at the faculty of medicine at the Université de Dakar had not worked out for

him. He enters France with false papers, and after months of joblessness is able to find one at the Market Place as a load carrier. For his
father the West is a lost paradise. Yakham later chooses wisely to go
back home. It is *"un acte de sagesse,"* a wise decision (103; 108).

A corrupt bureaucracy at home had blighted Yakham's future,
for his name was erased from the list of twelve children chosen to
receive a scholarship to go abroad to study. His scholarship was given
to another child from a rich and influential family who was on the
waiting list (110-111). He was to attend a military academy. The corrupt officers in the ministry of education alleged that the Post Office
was at fault for not delivering his mail to him. Yakham bore his ordeal
well, recalling that his mother would have urged him to be brave like
a man, for a child who cries will never become a man: *"Un enfant qui
pleure ne sera pas un homme"* (112). His mother had comforted him,
counseling him more than ever before to arm himself with dignity (jom)
and force of character (*fayda*) (113):

> Quant aux corrompus qui saignent les pauvres gens sans soutien ni
> defense, laisse-le avec le Bon Dieu. La sentence viendra un jour (113).

> [As for the corrupt who bleed the frail and defenseless poor, leave
> them with the Good Lord. Their sentence will come one day].

Still, Yakham could not understand his ordeal and that of his mother
who lost four fingers in the car rapide when the door slammed on his
fingers (115-116). Is this the hand of fate and destiny? He sees why
human beings should be their neighbor's keeper. It is a fundamental
Wolof philosophy of resistance and confidence, which says: "

> Nit nit ay garabam. [L'homme est le remède de l'homme: il n'y a de
> salut que dans l'Humain] (117).

> [Man is Man's remedy : salvation comes only through human be-
> ings].

The immigrant quarters Yakham knew in Paris was first a hotel. Owing to noise from the railway nearby, it was sold (124). Then it became
another hotel, which was too expensive. After several years, it was
sold again and transferred into a quarter for immigrant workers with
a population five times the original design for it (125). Soon "decent"
Parisians left the area, cursing the immigrants from all the four cor-

ners of Africa for whom it turned into a mythical Haven (126-127). In the end, the district was bulldozed down by the state.

Meanwhile the rest of the detained immigrants in the depot continue to wait to be sent home, Asta among them. A totally chaotic situation ensues when two immigrants get involved in a brawl. The harsh lights are turned off and two women are raped. Only then do the airport oppressors see fit to send home some two hundred and twenty-seven detainees (134). The image is that of a modern world gone mad, where there is no longer love or compassion for one's fellow human being. Progress and leaping advances in technology seem to dehumanize human beings. What is needed, however, is a return to the beginning, the paradise of the past, which is in the Wolof Teranga philosophy:

> Quand on perd son chemin, il faut retourner là d'où on est parti (139).

> [When you lose your path, you need to return to where you began].

Teranga is the Senegalese art of conviviality elevated to the dimension of worship. It means hospitality, the duty to take care of the stranger, to share, help one another, with solidarity. This philosophy is a national phenomenon today, and dictates love, tolerance between peoples, and beyond racial and belief considerations. With this philosophy, one could hope that human nightmares stand to be abolished with love, reason and respect, and in spite of wars, hatred, blood shedding, massacres, and genocides (148-149).

THE HEROINE'S RETURN

Asta's obsession is to return home to the land, which she has named Bakhna. For six months, she has been looking for a piece of land in the country to plant her garden, and it had become a dream and an obsession: *"C'était un rêve, une obsession"* (187). Metaphorically, it is a return to life, tradition, and self. The road to the new earth is full of rocks, rocks of the ontological beginning. And the party — Asta, Anne, Labba, Paapi, Yakham, Dianor — going into the bush in search of the land, in absolute silence, after they had gone round several bends to a depression, seems like human beings at the beginning of creation taking part in the work of creation with the gods:

Le spectacle est impressionnant. Grandiose et severe (…). Les yeux

sont fixés sur la vaste étendue de terre déployée comme un tapis
multicolore avec des teintes noires, ocres, grisâtres ou dorées. Le fleuve
y court (154).

[The spectacle is impressive. Grandiose and severe (…) Eyes are fixed
on the vast stretch of the earth laid out like a multicolor rug with
black, ochre, grayish or golden colors. The river is flowing there].

Human beings have a duty to share and the right to partake of
what is available, for the sake of human dignity (155). Compared to
the modern city where people beg, in the villages the story is different
for everybody works and does not beg. Those who have help those
who do not have. People drop off what they have *in cognito*, so that
those unfortunate ones who pick them up are saved from feeling
shame. Those who deny themselves through sacrifices have a feeling
of inner pride in them for what they do (155-156). A word of caution;
there must be measure, otherwise the equilibrium is broken and the
society broken and the individual lost (157). You cannot give more
than you have, nor should you cheat yourself in giving to others. The
best things of this earth are the elements of the sublime: warmth, feeling for others, respect, solidarity, honesty, mirth that save one from
distress and desolation, anguish, and misery (198). The mystery of the
earth resides in the happiness that one has of feeling the earth, of being in communion with it as it nourishes human beings with food, life,
and sustenance (200).

Back home to Senegal, Asta wants to found her own earth, which
she calls Naatangué (Land of Happiness, abundance and Peace), a
sort of Nirvana, where she will practice all the ideals of tolerance,
love, friendship, devotion, etc. She sees her piece of the earth as a
chance to create like the demiurgic god on the first day of creation:
"comme le jour de la Création" (195). She believes that the spirit of the
ancestors is there, as well as those of the djins of the river Natangué.

The culmination of Asta's saga is conquest of her piece of the
earth. She posits that it is by knowing how to feel and respect the soul
of others and things that the future will become a road to life and not
to poverty and death (157). Dianor, the blind sage, will write the hymn
for the celebration of her exploits. Asta will send her son Paapi to
France later, after his Bachelor's degree at home, to learn how better
to give of his sweat and his knowledge to the earth project (202). When
Anne visits her friend Asta in Africa, again she feels chills and faints
as she turns and turns trying to reach Asta's piece of earth (159). Her

view is that Africa must resist the attempt by others to define it, map its life. Africa must learn to invent things, not merely consume others' inventions (160).

Waa Reewu Takli, the people of the Barbed-Wire Town, as the Asta's group is nicknamed, have their first harvest in the village of Naatangué. At first, they are products that yield money. But, the long-term plan is to add other things, like pottery, tie dye, etc. Doro, the shepherd, after years of wandering in the town, and serving a term of imprisonment, etc., has also found peace on the land (207-209). An old woman tells them that the earth does not lie: "*La terre ne ment pas!*" (214; 215); that is, they might be sitting on a gold mine (213). Later, they find a treasure in the plant (215). For these people who had been detained in the depot and who had been repatriated by charter plane loads as undesirables, but who later found themselves and discovered their earth, the term "Douceurs du bercail" (217) becomes their shout of joy at finding the Golden Fleece or the Philosopher's Stone, their eureka. They discover that this earth is so generous that it yields more than you put into it. It is a noble way of finding their equilibrium and human dignity. Happiness is always just there at arm's length; you only need to know how to find it. "Douceurs du bercail" is a label of reconciliation with one's self, a trademark, and a living style.

Dianor, blinded by snake poison years ago, is a metaphor for the ancestors. He sees into the future as the spiritual guide of the new group of patriots. Later, it is Doro who takes up the relay. Then Babou takes over from Doro, so that the latter can pay more attention to the village of Naatangué, the new village founded by the patriots. They all finish by organizing a harvest feast in honor of Anne and her husband Didier visiting from France. When later Anne dies, she continues to live on in Naatangué in the trees that she had sent to her bosom friend Asta for planting.

CONCLUSION

The saga of Asta Diop takes her through the gamut of an itinerary in self-awareness from chaos, symbolic death, rebirth, and return to her people, and privileges a lesson learned on two levels: a realization that happiness is possible on one's corner of the earth, and the value of human dignity. But, first, you must know what you are looking for.

WORKS CITED

Aas-Rouxparis, Nicole. "'Ecrire, c'est un banquet où tout le monde apporte': Entrevue avec Aminata Sow Fall." *Women in French Studies* 8 (2000): 203-13.

Camus, Albert. *Le Mythe de Sisyphe: Essai sur l'Absurde*. Paris: Édition Gallimard, 1942.

Gordon, Lois. *Reading Godot*. New Haven and London: Yale University Press, 2002.

————. "*Waiting for Godot*: The Existential Dimension." Chapter 2, 55-69. In: *Reading Godot*. New Haven and London: Yale University Press, 2002.

Lebon, Cécile. "L'écriture, une parcelle de rencontre: Entretien avec Aminata Sow Fall." *Notre Librairie: Revue des littératures du Sud* 136 (1999): 65-68.

Pfaff, Françoise. "Aminata Sow Fall, l'écriture au Féminin." *Notre Librairie: Revue des littératures du Sud* 81 (1985): 135-138.

Sow Fall, Aminata. *Douceurs du bercail*. Dakar/Côte d'Ivoire: Nouvelles Edition Ivoriennes/Edition Khoudia, 1998.

Stringer, Susan. *The Senegalese Novel by Women: Through Their Own Eyes*. New York: Peter Lang, 1996.

"SONG OF HOPE 1: ABOUT LIFE AND JOY"

❄ ❄ ❄

À mes petits-enfants
Écoutez le chant qui monte
Du coeur de la graine.
Chant de vie, chant de joie.

[To my grandchildren
Listen to the song rising
From the heart of the grain.
Song of life, song of joy ; *Azodo's translation*].

Aminata Sow Fall "Dedication," *Un **grain** de vie et d'espérance*

❄ ❄ ❄

In her seventh novel, *Un grain de vie et d'espérance*, Aminata Sow Fall manifests, "sings" a song of life and joy in hope of the restoration, regeneration, and reintegration of the African soul, through the act of cooking and the act of eating food, in community, as an extension of the individual self into collective culture in all its facets — philosophical, religious, and moral. *Un grain de vie et d'espérance* presents an ontological chaos, which must be rectified before a rebirth can take place. The first part of the text is composed of thirty-three questions and responses, explanations, illustrations, and examples, followed in the second part by a book of recipes by Margo Harley, a Senegalese woman chef based in Paris.

Before exploring the structure of this text, an explanation of the term "song" is in order, taken as it is out of African oral literature to encapsulate the textual question and answer strategy. There is no clear boundary between prose and poetry, for even though there is no apparent accompaniment by music, still the rhythm of the question and response form of presentation gives a certain musical quality to the text.

First, the author manifests consciousness of her audience or literary public, as if engaging them in a dialogue. She begins the text thus:

> Par ou commencer? Peut-être en cherchant le sens, le sens de ce fait commun, tellement commun que la question peut paraître risible, une question que personne ne se pose. L'acte de manger, c'est quoi?" (9).

> [How do I begin? Perhaps with searching for the meaning, the meaning of this common fact, a fact so common that the sheer question can appear laughable, a question that nobody asks himself or herself. The act of eating, what does it mean? *my translation*]

Second, no sooner does the author begin the exploration of the act of eating, along with its attendant repetition for stylistic effect, than a page further on she digresses into the story of the pretty diriyanké Nogaye.

> La voici, Nogaye, la jolie drianké du quartier des pêcheurs, une femme imposante par son embonpoint, ses toilettes, ses manières. Toute en rondeurs. Elle est assise sur une natte multicolore, gracieusement adossée au tronc d'un manguier géant, au beau milieu de la cour..." (10).

> [See Nogaye, the pretty diriyanké of the fishing community, an imposing woman, thanks to her plumpness, her toilet, and her manners. She is all decked out. She is seated on a multicolor mat, with her back graciously against the trunk of a giant mango tree, right in the middle of the yard...; *my translation*].

This digression is also a stylistic effect often evident in songs and music, and has the added effect of creating some tension in the narrative. The author seems to make the reader wait to hear more about what the act of eating is exactly.

Third, almost like a refrain, the author takes up again and again repetition as a motif in the unfurling story: "l'acte de manger...l'acte de manger" (21, 26, 27; and later, "l'art culinaire... 28, l'art culinaire ... 29...etc., etc.), confering on the narrative some musical quality. The repetition and the variation between "act" and "art" turn the statements into a performance of sorts with an internal balance all its own. According to Isidore Okpewho: "It is on these grounds that the American scholar Dennis Tedlock has argued that oral narratives should be treated not as the sort of 'prose' we find in written fiction, but as some sort of 'dramatic' poetry" (1992, 131). Indeed, the antiphonal form of dramatic poetry approaches the dimension of a traditional African song. At this instance, it is no longer merely a question of whether the text is poetry or prose, but rather the degree of musicality. The text is of such a high degree of musicality that the reader envisages the presence of a virtual audience, where the author is the solo performer, who utilizes the highest level of vocal manipulation of speech to achieve rhythm and an affective melody, the kind that is possible in chants, as Okpewho has noted (1992: 253-272).

Suffice it to say that African oral literature records important instances of life, reflects activities and occasions of rejoicing and merry-making, such as baptism, marriage, puberty rites, etc., and even mourning, such as war, death, etc., through songs and chants, where chants as such are recitations of poetry. It is for these reasons that the term "song" interprets *Un grain de vie et d'espérance* as a song of life, joy, love, and hope. Focus is however on the themes of life and joy implied by the title of the written text, because those two themes encompass most of the other themes in the text in celebration of life in the community.

More particularly, Aminata Sow Fall seems to praise the Wolof tradition of *Teranga* or hospitality, which enjoins the African to take care of the stranger as if she or he were herself or himself. Second, she also seems to be critical of certain etiquettes and practices in modernity that do not go well with the African traditions in culinary act and the act of eating. Third, she explores the theme of universal love and hope that all human beings can someday eat on an all encompassing round table of brotherhood, sisterhood, and love. Four, it is a testimony against war, but rather for friendship. Fifth, employing an initiatory strategy the author summons humankind to manifest a ritual against death, by prolonging human communication, through the act of eating.

CHAOS: TAMKHARIT NIGHT

This first stage of the initiatory structure is the stage of mythical, primordial chaos, the night before the Tamkharit, the Islamic New Year. The extended family has held the usual annual extended family reunion, when the family dedicates itself anew to every member of the clan and to the ancestors and the living dead. The whole clan has congregated round a table of *bassé salté*, a ceremonial couscous or rice dish for the special occasion, followed by prayers and supplications to the ancestors. Thereafter, community members are let loose to do whatever they want, and everything is permitted between boys and girls until dawn when order returns once again to the land (65-67). It is like a return to the mother's womb, a *regressus ad uterum*, to the night and darkness of the primordial beginning to be reborn. The female protagonist Nogaye Sène, the once-upon-a-time milk girl, who became the wife of defunct Arma Sène, has just polished off the rest of the leftovers of the *bassé salté* from the last evening's ritualistic event. Nogaye thus affords author Aminata Sow Fall the opportunity to discuss for posterity the Senegalese culinary act traditionally, esoterically, vulgarly, sensually, and sexually, and in conflict with modern times.

The act of eating is seen here as symbolic. First, the family sitting around a bowl of food or around a table to eat together, mirrors humanity in communion one with another. There is a sense of solidarity, belonging, and sharing, which consolidates the social model of family, community, and nation (77). Members of the family or community learn a lot from the single act of accomplishing a task together, just like peasants working the fields learn cooperation, tolerance, decorum, decency, discipline, among so may other ethical values. The act of eating together teaches the meaning of measure, know-how, living, and respect (ibid.).

Moreover, communal eating is only the outward sign of an inner and more fundamental gathering high above on the spiritual plane. The eating ambiance is the reflection of another landscape behind it, namely, the desolation and distress of all those unable to find food to eat. It is for this reason that Africans are eternally grateful to have food to eat and do not fail to pray God thankfully for providing it. Then again, stories about famine are a calamity without name, for they spell death of the mind and soul. The eating landscape, exhorts Aminata Sow Fall, is the presence of a sweet song of love or a hymn to the glory of the conquerors of battles, and by extension, all sorts of battles that individuals and groups wage daily in their lives (52). Indeed, it is a hierogamy, the coming together of Heaven and Earth, given that those who are seated together to eat bond with one another in love, which passeth all human understanding. Aminata Sow Fall states:

> Notre destin est d'être soudés autour du manger qui est un acte de vie et d'aspiration à l'éternité tant il est vrai que tout ce que nous mangeons est le fruit de la relation sublime que Dieu a instaurée entre le Ciel et la Terre (76).

> [Our destiny is to bond together around the act of eating, which is an act of life and aspiration to eternity, seen that all that we eat is the product of the sublime relationship that God has instituted between Heaven and Earth; *my translation*].

As Sow Fall explains hereunder, in Saint-Louis it is the emotion behind the act of eating that gives it all its esoteric meaning, otherwise eating comes down to filling the stomach to keep the machine going: "*À Saint-Louis (...) l'acte de manger n'a de sens qu'en son rendez-vous sublime avec l'émotion*" (27). In Saint-Louis, eating has no meaning unless it is emotional. So, even a stranger who drops by gets invited to join in. If the food is already gone, more is prepared (26). Nobody is ever allowed to go hungry. To be miserly about food is always very badly seen: "*Faire grise mine pendant le repas est considéré comme un manquement très grave qui suscite le mépris*" (94).What is more, the plate is never left completely empty, for some must be left for the ancestors, the poor, "*la part du pauvre,*" the unknown visitor, "*la part du visiteur inconnu,*" the cat, "*la part du chat,*" or simply to honor the plate, "*l'honneur de l'assiette*" (14). Traditionally, you do not speak when eating, in order to do honor to the food and the person who prepared it, although today people generally speak, except for children who are still forbidden to speak lest they choke on their food (ibid.).

The Wolof prefer foods with colors and condiments from nature, not prepared foods with additives. An example of Wolof favorite food is "*Soupa Kandia*" — palm-nut sauce soup, common in the whole of West Africa. It is always a dish composed of a variety of meats, vegetables, and other condiments that give off a million odors, and a unique taste (88; 114). Palm-oil on white rice, adds Sow Fall, is like a red stain on a white lake in a calabash full of golden corn. This image compares to the full moon on a radiant sky. The red, white, and gold are colors of love and light on a slice of life and a grain of hope (53).

African foods ought to guard their authenticity jealously, adds Sow Fall: "*À chaque genre de tambour, sa baguette,*" a wise saying that insists that local condiments must not be mixed up with foreign ones in a dish, for each culture's food is a gift from God. Thus she states: "*Le mariage contre nature est une abomination. Il faut respecter les aliments et les plats: un don de Dieu*" (92). [Unnatural marriage is an abomination. You must respect the aliments and the dishes: God's gift ; *my translation*].

Because human beings take their nourishment from nature in the form of the air, sun, earth, water, elemental involvement in the act of eating is hardly unexpected. Humans owe their existence to nature, for humans plant and grow food for sustenance. Humans, thanks to their eating preferences and habits, are the sum of minerals and elements. The food on the table or in the bowl mirrors traditional and essential cultural beliefs and aspirations about who a people are. Therefore, any attempt to redefine foods, making them unrecognizable to the indigenes is unacceptable, for that would break the ritual involved in the choice of what to eat (91-92). In other words, the food that one eats mirrors the people's history, worldview, dreams, fantasies, and the anguish that people wish to banish by making food offers to the poor: "*Notre cuisine est le pur produit de notre histoire, de notre vision du monde, de nos rêves, de nos fantaisies et aussi des angoisses que nous voulons chasser en offrant à manger au pauvre...*" (96). Particular foods are appropriate to particular places, due to the history and cultural patrimony of the people. Out of this "natural" environment, the dishes lose their flavor, their meaning, with the loss of their history.

The culinary art, says Sow Fall, is an act that reaches toward beauty, contemplation, and enjoyment: "*La cuisine est un art; elle est donc une aventure qui tend vers le Beau, la Contemplation, la Jouissance*" (28). Culinary art is implicated in the human condition and the development of a people's values according to their life principles and innate aspirations for happiness, and each cook, male or female, begins with a lot of imagination about the food's color, savor, nature, etc., before putting together a perfectly unique composition.

Take for example the "*tiébou dienne,*" rice dish with fish, red tomato, and red pepper sauces, purple of the egg plant, white of the cassava, green of the cabbage, bright yellow of the squash, and sometimes snail. It is Senegal's national dish and the third national emblem after the baobab and the lion (30-34; 134-135; 140). It is always a colorful, rich dish, distinguished by its unique flavor, for according to a Wolof proverb, the dish announces itself by its sheer odor: *"Quand la marmite bouillonne, l'odeur annonce la succulence du mets"* (30).

FROM CULINARY ACT INTO SOCIETY

Having explained the culinary act, author Sow Fall moves onto the Senegalese society in general. We learn that the premise of any given thing announces its end: *"Les premices en toute chose annoncent le résultat final"* (ibid.). Even enmities and quarrels inside the family between co-wives, with mothers-in-law, sisters-in-law, etc., wait for the meal to be served to manifest themselves, these feelings of dislike or hatred towards a wife of their male relative. For that reason, wives are very careful when they cook, and families ensure the prospective wife can cook well before she is brought into the family (30-33). There is the story of a new wife, Dianka, who failed the test and was killed along with her extended family by her in-laws (32-34).

The art of cooking, says Sow Fall, is neither a dream nor a fantasy, but rather a strong aspiration towards the ideal of happiness. The ideal of happiness is equivalent to human beings' ultimate desires and mental and affective representations. It is harmony, which cannot be achieved or realized in mediocrity, dislocation, or cacophony (62). Nonetheless, the art of cooking requires imagination, talent, and dream. To celebrate all instances of happiness, big or small, human beings cook and then eat the food they have cooked around a table. Insightfully, the author adds that couples who eat together are more likely to develop a stronger bond of love and companionship (64).

Foods are not always solid, for foods can be in liquid form. yet giving life, through irrigating the system (53). For this reason, drought can be fatal to human life when the system is starved of fluid. Hence, drinking fluids preserves human life, the spirit and the heart (54). Water is the cardinal drink that comes from nature. Other drinks have been invented by human beings to assuage their fantasies and desires, and escape the realities of the world sometimes. The *"bissap,"* a brew from the red hibiscus flower, enjoys a particular position in Wolof culture as a relaxing and colorful drink excellent for fatigue, flu, and pains (55).

The consideration of solid and liquid foods as sources of life, *"un grain de vie,"* as social model of communion, solidarity, and harmony, leads to seeing the act of eating in community as hope for the future, *"un grain d'espérance"* (54)

The leaders of the nation should learn to share the national cake with the people they are supposed to serve, as stated here: *"À condition que les maîtres voleurs qui pillent nos pays leur laissent [au peuple] des miettes! Ils bouffant tout, réduisent les gens à la misère et au chômage..."* (22). Then, Sow Fall recites a tale in a tale, of a shocking follow-up to an attempt to consecrate the corner stone of the building of a Mosque. Politicians are invited to make speeches; they speak, but the people do not listen. The marabouts pray to dedicate the stone. The people do not listen either, tired as they are of being taken advantage of by their leaders. They pounce on the marabout and the politicians and smash the stones to pieces, and eat them up, as if they were food. Then the people go further; they carry away to their homes all the assembled blocks for the building of the mosque. There is no more radical way of protesting the abuse and impoverishment of the populace by the elite, including religious clerics (46).

Any wonder then that Senegalese culinary language mirrors the people's disgust at the lack of services from their government? At a time of political crisis, they say the peanut is calcified: *"Les cacahuètes sont calcinés/ ("tiaf kheum na")*. They also talk of sand falling into the couscous: *"Il y a du sable dans le couscous/ ("tiere dji khaiam na")* (84). The people dream of good, resourceful leaders, who can accomplish the national business with stones, if need be, even when what they need are snow flakes from the North Pole. All the people ask for is that which is possible, for with faith and belief in their leaders rocks can turn to milk in their empty stomachs (50).

AGAPE:
CONVOCATION OF HUMANITY AROUND THE WOLOF FEAST TABLE

The convocation to eat the Senegalese way could be seen as an Agape, in the sense that humanity is called upon to imagine, dream, and commune with one another, instead of making wars against one another. There is such a convergence of culinary art, sensuality, and sex in Dakar, giving rise to a neologism: *"mokk pothie,"* where *"mokk"* means assimilated, and *"pothie"* means the lap. Together both terms translate the feminine art of totally "pocketing" a man by charm, seduction, submission, sensuality, availability, gait, grace, dress, make-up, smile, culinary art, etc. Just like Ngoaye who is reputed to lure her husband any time to bed, due to her charms, in the kitchen and in the bedroom, human beings must rekindle the art of fraternal love in place of making war against one another (80).

CONCLUSION

Un grain de vie et d'espérance remains a touch of life and joy, and a flicker of hope for humanity, which could happen by emulating the art of cooking and eating food so fundamental to human life in all cultural spaces of the world; Senegal provides a model. The play on the words "grain/slice" and "graine/grain" is eloquent, for a slice of life begins with the germination of the grain. In the dedication of the book, the author enjoins the youth and future generations, along with her grand children, to listen to the song that the grain of seed sings, which is a song of birth, rebirth, and joy of giving life and hope. The Senegalese example manifests an invitation to savor little life's secrets and variants with imagination. This can be accomplished by revisiting the classics of African cuisine in one cultural space, the Wolof country, and from there make a leap to humanity for human restoration, regeneration, and reintegration.

WORKS CITED

Sow Fall, Aminata. *Un grain de vie et d'espérance*. Paris: François Truffaut Éditions, 2004.

Okpewho, Isidore. *African Oral Literature: Backgrounds, Character, and Continuity*. Bloomington and Indianapolis: Indiana University Press, 1992.

"SONG OF HOPE 2: ABOUT AFRITUDE"

❄ ❄ ❄

Ces gens qui se nourissent de la détresse des autres que viennent-ils faire ici! Et le comble, c'est que personne n'est mort ici! (23; *my emphasis*)

[What are these people who feed on the misfortune of others doing here?
And the worst part is that nobody is dead here! (*Azodo's translation*)]

— Aminata Sow Fall. *Festins de la détresse*

❄ ❄ ❄

This chapter will seek to explore the ideology of Afritude—a loan translation from Negritude—as a new twenty-first century humanism espoused in *Festins de la détresse* by Aminata Sow Fall. It is an African system, which is also universal, because it cuts across borders, races and cultures, and valorizes a local set of values that evolves and expands into a global system. This study, therefore, privileges African ways of knowing and knowledge from visionary characters, through dreams, legends and legendary heroes, ancestors and philosophical musings, and symbols and images. Clearly, author/narrator Sow Fall is conscious of the meaning of her work at two levels, namely, the social and material level, and the spiritual and mystical level. From this angle of vision, *Festins de la détresse*, Aminata Sow Fall's eighth full-length writing is not merely a chapter in the fictional chain of her socio-realistic satire of present-day Senegalese society, what some critics have seen as her brand of *La Comédie Humaine* (Honoré de Balzac). That would be a simple, almost simplistic, way of interpreting the meaning of *Festins de la détresse* in which the rich get richer and the poor poorer, in which the poor are constantly treated like fools incapable of apprehending reality, a world of corruption, wickedness, religious impiety, drug trafficking, with their attendant disastrous consequences for all human beings (91). *Festins de la détresse* is much more than a socio-realistic novel, for a focus on the mystical, spiritual, and moral aspects of the novel provides a different set of meanings.

In the epigraph above, Aminata Sow Fall explicates the title of her eighth novel, through the voice of retired and intelligent principal character Maar Diagne, obsessed with human dignity, moral uprightness and honesty, and deeply resentful of funeral hoppers, who feed off of the moral, physical, and spiritual distress, misfortune, and misery of others. Throughout the text, the author affirms the dignity of all human beings, through hard work, honesty, and nobility of soul. Imam Fara, aptly described as the soul of his community, sees that the victims of social ills, shamelessly abused by the powerful and privileged, are the same upright human beings busy working for a world of common good, free of suffering, for all (124).[1] The textual discourse decries the death of the sacred in our profane world. Even the university, once held to be sacred, like a temple, now harbors academics devoid of humility, which humility is the watch word of the great (43). Furthermore, university intellectuals, who should be beacons of light and symbols of the best for society, have turned into fakes, further regrets Maar Diagne (ibid).[2]

❋ ❋ ❋

Quand l'homme meurt en l'homme, plus besoin de creuser des tombes, le chaos et déjà là (19)

[When human beings die in other human beings, there is no longer need for grave diggers, for chaos has already arrived] (*my translation*).

Afritude is a peculiar humanism, for despite its focus on human beings it is not devoid of spiritualism. It is an ideology of hope of rebirth for human beings endowed with innate intelligence, conscience, and moral turpitude of the Golden Rule, which enjoins one to do unto others as one wouldst that others do unto her or him. Human history over the ages is replete with stories of cruelty and the need to relearn to place human beings at the center of human values, in order to teach time-honored and noble values of honesty, moral uprightness, and dignity to all (65). It is a positive-looking and expansive system that manifests hope in human beings without shunning the otherworldly contributions of the mystical and the supernatural. Obviously, since this is not a perfect world, sometimes human beings may falter in their march forward towards spirituality, yet one must not despair, but rather should be eternally prepared to help one another along the way, providing succor and hope whenever possible (69). Ultimately, it is a song of hope for human resilience before the destructive power of death to the soul, which forms part of the teachings of Islam.

❊ ❊ ❊

The "song" motif pushes for a return to African epistemologies. It is at once a satirical and laudatory song, which follows the Odyssey of the Diagne family as an exemplar of the life struggles of Everyman, reopening critical philosophical questions of human existence, namely, what life on earth is all about, how to survive the ordeal of everyday living, how to adequately take care of life and health, for oneself and dependents, in order to escape the discourtesy of death. Sometimes, human beings need rituals of rites of passage, such as those of marriage, birth, and funeral to temporarily ward off death.

Therefore, the song motif opens up the spiritual and moral dimensions of the textual narrative. Critical imagination perceives subject themes of love, praise, and satire in the narrative events. Although the characters do not use some form of instrumental music or another form of rhythm as accompaniment to their speeches, yet there are some innate rhythms present in their speeches, which approximate to the effect of musical instruments used as accompaniment in speech acts (Okpewho 1992: 131).

Evidently, highly visionary and spiritual leaders, Maar Diagne, Imam Fara, or a blind but "seeing" Larry, alias Nouvelle Brève [News in Brief], "la non-voyante qui chaque jour étonne par sa clairvoyance" (113), create tension with their words, at the beginning, during, or after their speech, because their words disturb the status quo. The contents of their various speeches are not tautological, but rather intermittently create a repetition effect that is musical and rhythmic, because they are reflective of African oral traditions (ibid).

Furthermore, as readers, we are accomplices in the act of deciphering the humanism inherent in the textual narrative. And Sow Fall seems to be conscious of the author and reader's engagement in a work of creation and dialogue, asking questions and making comments in time, although separated by space. Given this proximity of author and reader, the reader personally and effortlessly follows the textual discourse and the evolving itinerary of a stereotypical and modern-day family struggling with problems of existence. The tenacity of the human spirit in daily struggle is ennobling, and the hope it promises for humanity is exhilarating.

Thus, the author Sow Fall presents as a griotte, that intelligent, insightful, and skilled artist of impressive language, a praise singer of sorts, engaged in laudatory poetry in celebration of the African past. Through counseling the characters as the need arises, and recording within the context of the narrative text human events and milestones of marriage, childbirth, divorce, and death, the artist demonstrates her ability to educate with grace and subtlety. As the critical imagination, analysis, and interpretation move from the social to the spiritual, the resultant lesson is on how human beings evolve and change over time their views of life, living, and the world, from the material to the moral principles of existence.

❊ ❊ ❊

Despite the local color, recognizable in the sights and sounds of modern-day Senegal and its shortcomings, the ordeal of the members of the Diagne family is set in a ritual context of spirituality and mysticism.

First, it is a world in which Kiné Saar, that traditional, but very dignified wife of Maar Diagne, commands respect from the men in her life, namely, her husband and her sons, and also others in the entire community. She sees in everything that is living and beautiful, a song of life and happiness. She advises her two sons, Biram and Gora, to eschew all that is dirty and dishonest in their lives. Gora, the younger, would find out in a hard way the consequences of not keeping to those moral admonitions when he is imprisoned for fifteen years for embezzlement of funds. But, did he really commit the crime? Textual discourse seems to state he did not do it. Yet what is important is that he did not pay attention to the moral principle not to associate with people of shady and dubious character.

Second, Larry, another neighborhood visionary, mystical, and imperial woman, lost her sight at eighteen years of age to river blindness. Paradoxically, the physiological shutting down of her vision results in the spiritual opening of her inner powers. She functions as a sort of shepherd of the flock of the lost sheep in the community, "*les brebis galeuses*" (130). Larry sings songs, especially of the legendary heroine Penda Dièye Rombe Dayo, half human and half genii, who lived in the North from whence she came down to dictate laws for human beings to follow. Penda Dièye Rombe Dayo would surround herself with two columns of crocodiles whenever the urge to spend some time in the depths of the river hits her. Human beings offer prayers to this legendary heroine in their hard fight for survival, when thick clouds of pain rear their ugly heads in the horizon (10). Larry's vision is unquenchable, for she is endowed with inner light and whiteness (55). At one time, she sings to straighten out Kiné Saar, who chooses to sleep in the morning of her wedding to Maar when she should be up and doing at dawn:

> *Kiné bul di bidenti* – Kiné ne te lève plus si tard
> *Kor Maar Diagne yeewoul* – Toi l'amour de Maar Diagne, réveille-toi
> *Yaayou Biram ak Gora* – Toi la mère de Biram et Gora
> *Bul di nélaw ba diant bi takhaw* – Ne dors plus quand le soleil est debout
> *Sounou Kharit sounou sope* – Toi notre amie, toi que nous admirons
> *Bul di didanti* – Ne te lève plus tard (112).

> [You, Maar Diagne's love, awake
> You mother of Biram and Gora
> Stop sleeping when the sun is up
> You, our friend, you whom we admire
> Stop waking up late].

Suffice it to say that the two symbols that move Kiné Saar are her grand mother Penda Dièye Rombe Dayo, who feeds her dreams of the past, and the great River Senegal, which nourishes her reflections on the mysteries of life (108). Through memory recall of the past, Kiné Saar calls on her fellow human beings to embrace uprightness in their dealings with the other.

Third, Imam Fara, another visionary with demonstrated ability to perceive the suffering of souls, rather than the outward appearances of beings, pierces through Weurseuk's spiritual and existential vacuity and calls him to order, by offering him a job for an honest living as children's Koran teacher, rather than leaving him to persist in his old ways of funeral hopping for material gains. Imam Fara also persuades his bosom friend and former classmate Maar Diagne to forgive Weurseuk, who has become an obsessive image in his psyche. Maar must, in spite of himself, cease to see Weurseuk as an obsessive incarnation of supreme abjection (113), but accept his penitence and confession influenced by Imam Fara. Following Imam Fara's intervention, for the first time, Maar sees the commonality of his fate with his adversary's; they are two human beings suffering existential anguish, marooned in the same boat of the human condition. Maar then sees that it is violence and social harshness that push individuals to live by dishonest means, like tics sucking life and blood out of their victims, or like *"rats des funérailles"* [funeral hoppers], living off the grief of others.[3]

It is important, therefore, to work hard for one's living, and also help people trying to work hard to make an honest living. Biram, the first son of Maar Diagne and Kiné Saar, is a jobless medical doctor. Implicitly, he is excluded from public service, thanks to nepotism and corruption in the fabric of society. Finally, he decides to found his own private practice in his village community, rather than wait endlessly for manna from heaven that is the government. The plan works. The fact that he makes it is a lesson that hard work still pays and should be emulated by all honest people. As a result, Biram is able to get married, although in his thirties, to nurse Sarat, who also had been a victim of society until she met Biram, and they have a child, Kiné Touti, named after her grandmother Kiné Saar. Second, we learn that devotion to one's duties and ability to let go are virtues to be inculcated and emulated. For another example, Kahl's devotion to his work as an agent of the governmental tourist organization, Celeste, is highly commendable, although he works with employers who cheated his family of their beach-front expensive ancestral lands. The by-lesson in this is that human beings should always judge when it no longer makes sense to continue to pursue a cause, that is, know when it would do more harm than good to stay in a particular direction. One must learn to forgive and forget when necessary. Maar and Kiné persuade their two sons Biram and Gora to forget their grandmother's ocean front property and their dreams of selling it for initial capital to set themselves up in business. On the other hand, the parents change strategy. They find funds, which they advance to their sons to help them get on their feet in an honest and dignified way, through setting up their own shops.

This search for a dignified way of living could come from rememory of the past. Maar Diagne is engaged in just that type of search through his memoir, *L'Extase du Petit Matin* [Ecstasy of Dawn), a reaching back to the past for explanation of the present and a projection for the future. Each time Maar sits down at his small writing table in their small bedroom, he feels like a neophyte at the altar of worship. He undertakes his writing task with fervor and humility (7), when he does not feel like a traveler going towards his soul, into a garden of his dreams. He would allow himself to be enveloped and carried away, with hope of a rebirth and a return later to harsh reality of history, what he calls *"les monstruosités du siècle"* (ibid).[4]

We learn that there is dignity in sharing what one has, since all is lost when death comes. Kiné Saar, a descendant of the legendary Penda Dièye Rombe Dayo, sings the song "Domm Yaay," which she always sang with her mother-in-law Maam Yaay, a courageous and morally upright woman, who embraced the philosophy of sharing with the needy what one has and helping one another in life: [5]

> *Boo améé, doom yaay* – Si tu as les moyens
> *Fadial gatié, doom yaay* – Chasse le déshonneur
> *Ndakh bou dé dioté* – Car lorsque sonnera l'heure de la mort
> *Alal menou fa dara* – L'argent ni les richesses n'y pourront rien (51).

> [If you have the means
> Get rid of dishonor
> For when death knocks at the door
> Neither money nor riches can stop him; *my translation*].

Furthermore, money and other material things are not important to human existence vis-à-vis the benefits of spirituality. Indeed, nothing is worth sacrificing for the name, honor, and dignity that the ancestors leave for the younger generations, as seen in the example of Keuri Diamm (90). [6]

In this regard, life is like being in a battlefield and one must be constant and defensive of one's integrity. Human beings are like actors on the stage, and they must adorn noble arms for a dignified and honest fight for life, says Kiné. In what Maar would see as a song-statement proffered the way it should be, Kiné addresses Gora, who has come back to the family fold after his tragic escapade with corrupt Dr. Kanitoli, Executive Secretary in charge of the AIDS agency, about the importance of guarding his self dignity and integrity:

> N'oublie pas que le désastre serait de te laisser pomper la sève précieuse de ta dignité. Celle-ci ne se porte pas en bandoulière; elle palpate quelque part avec le coeur; le chemin qui y mène est ardu; tout devient facile et agréable quand on a bien assimilé sa musique… (130).

> [Do not forget that it will be disastrous to allow yourself to be drained of the milk of your human dignity. It is not something you wear on your sleeve. On the other hand, it beats somewhere with your heart. And the road to it is arduous. Everything falls into place, easily and comfortably, only when one has well assimilated its music; *my translation*].

As noted earlier, Kiné readily collects her due from the cooperative she belongs to, hands it over to his two sons to build themselves each a store to set themselves up in their own businesses. It works for them; they employ themselves, and some others, and so are able to keep their dignity intact.

❀ ❀ ❀

CONCLUSION

This study set out to posit Afritude as humanism for the twenty-first century, a system of values that affirms the dignity in the African as a human being without fear or shame. Afritude offers the world view on uprightness, honesty, hard work, and human dignity as an ontological view on law, morality and inexorable beauty, implicit in social justice, tolerance, sense of co-existence, peace, and harmony. Afritude eschews the static and stale white/black, North/South dualism, but rather distinguishes between body and soul, matter and spirit, conflict and analysis, separation and opposition, and the list continues. Animate and inanimate objects act in complementary capacities one to the other, since there is a connective force between the smallest creatures and the highest beings, the ancestors. It is a criticism of hollow religiosity and exhibitionism. A new brand of humanism *à l'Africaine*, Afritude can contribute to universal humanism, because it respects the individual as part and parcel of the community, and does not seek to crush it. Implicitly, it is a call for peace and harmony in the community. At the larger global, international, and intercultural human relations level, there is need for more dialoguing and working in groups, not conflicts and wars. It is an attempt to recreate the world, bringing it closer to what traditionally and idealistically African civilization is all about. There is need to research the past, in order to understand the present and guide the future. Creative writing as an art form tames nature, such that the real and the imaginary sit harmoniously together. Vis-à vis literary criticism, it is an aesthetic that mixes the satirical and the laudatory calls to unite in harmony, in a similar way forces of the cosmos intermingle with one another in their chaotic relations, resulting in the convergence of opposition and repetition, the symmetrical and the asymmetrical, and the union of opposites. While focusing on the centrality of the human being, Afritude mingles also the sacred, mystical, and spiritual and the supernatural. It is a humanism that does not eschew God and his divine teachings, and so embraces African cultural and spiritual ethos in its historical perspective.

NOTES

1. Maar states: "Tandis que ceux-ci travaillent dans l'humilité pour l'idéal d'un monde débarrassé de ses souffrances, les autres pullelent aux quatre coins de la planète et sucent sans vergogne le sang des malades, des victimes, des arbitraires, des guerres, et des fléaux de toutes sortes"

    [While some are working with humility for the ideal of a world rid of its sufferings, others are all over the four corners of the earth sucking blood without shame from the sick, victims, arbitraries, wars, and all sorts of plagues; *my translation*].

2. The author says about Biram: "L'Université! Il l'avait toujours considérée comme un temple. Y officiaient des éminences parées de leur charge sacerdotale dans la grandeur et l'humilité. 'L'humilité est la force des grands,' disait Maar.

    [He has always considered the university as a temple. In it eminent personalities adorned with their priestly duties worked in grandeur and humility. 'Humility is the strength of the great,' Maar used to say; *my translation*].

3. Maar's regret: "Ces hommes respectables étaient des symboles. Tout est fait pour consacrer la mort des symbols. Lorsque des gens comme le Secrétaire executif et sa bande organisent ces mascarades mauvais goût sur un terrain aussi noble que la médicine, on n'y comprend plus rien, vraiment plus rien.

   [These respectable men were symbols. Everything is done to consecrate the death of symbols. When people like the Executive Secretary and his clique organize these masquerades of bad taste on a terrain as noble as medicine, all is lost, completely lost; *my translation*].

4. In the words of Imam Fara: "Des cruautés, l'histoire humaine en est pleine. Chaque siècle avec ses défies tant que durera le temps du monde. Le combat essential est de réapprendre à placer l'homme sur le piedestal de nos valeurs afin que nos appétits énormes, nos ambitions et nos instincts contre nature n'étouffent plus la part noble de nous-mêmes. Nous ne devons pas nous lasser d'entretenir la flamme délicieuse de notre dignité. De la rallumer dans le coeur de ceux qui l'ont perdue."

   [Human history is full of cruelties. Each century has its own challenges. The essential struggle is to relearn to place Man on a pedestal of our values, in order that our enormous appetites, our ambitions and our unnatural instincts no longer stamp out the noblest part of us. We must not tire of keeping alive the delightful flame of our dignity. We must not give up rekindling it in the hearts of those who have lost it; *my translation*].

5. According to the Imam: "L'homme n'est pas toujours ce qu'il paraît. Il ne faut jamais se décourager d'aller le chercher là où il se trouve si jamais il s'est égaré la nuit de sa propre conscience (...). Il peut arriver que l'animal est débordé. C'est un risque perpétuel. Nous devons alors nous entraider à rétablir l'humain à sa juste place."

   [Man is not always what he seems to be. It is never a waste of time to go in search of him wherever he may be, if he ever gets lost in the night of his own conscience (...). It could be that the animal is overwhelmed. That is a perpetual risk. That is why we must help one another to reestablish the human being in her or his place; *my translation*].

6   Maar and Kiné advise their sons to let go, hinting that the oppressors may not always be as happy inwardly as they seem to the public: "Elle nous habitera pour toujours. Ceux qui l'ait volé, qui sait s'ils n'ont pas déjà perdu le bonheur fugace d'une jouissance usurpée..."

[They will live in us for ever. Those who have stolen it, who knows if they have not already lost the transient happiness gained from a usurped joy...;" *my translation*].

WORKS CITED

Azodo, Ada Uzoamaka. *L'Imaginaire dans les romans de Camara Laye*. New York, Bern, Berlin, Paris: Peter Lang Publishers, 1993.

Edwige H. "Interview avec Aminata Sow Fall." *Africultures* (www.africultures.com), September 26, 2005.

Guèye, Médoune. "Tradition orale et philosophie wolof chez Aminata Sow Fall: une esthétique transgénétique et transculturelle dans *Le Revenant*." *Langues & Littératures*, Université G. B. de Saint-Louis, Sénégal, no. 6, janvier 2002. (www.critaoi.org)

Julien, Eileen. *African Novels and the Question of Orality*. Bloomington: Indiana University Press, 1992.

Okpewho, Isidore. *African Oral Literature: Backgrounds, Character, and Continuity*. Bloomington and Indianapolis: Indiana University Press, 1992.127-162.

Sow Fall, Aminata. *Festins de la détresse*. Lausanne: Éditions d'en bas, 2005.

Xalimac. "*Festins de la détresse* d'Aminata Sow Fall: un cri de coeur pour le retour...," 23 July, 2005.

BOOK THREE

INTERVIEW WITH AMINATA SOW FALL

TOWARDS A SEARCH FOR THE AFRICAN SOUL

WRITING AND IMAGINATION IN THE NOVELS OF AMINATA SOW FALL

ADA UZOAMAKA AZODO

❆ ❆ ❆

Azodo: Bonjour, Madame Sow Fall.

Sow Fall: Bonjour, Madame.

Azodo: Obviously, you write socio-realistic novels on postcolonial, post-independent, and modern Africa. However, collectively, your novels do also appear to be a "Note-Book of a Return" to African traditions. In fact, a mythocritical reader like me can see an authorial obsession, perhaps unbeknownst to you, to restore and reintegrate the values of African mysteries, legends, myths, and visions.

Cursorily, let me recount your literary and cultural activities, and please correct me when and where I go wrong. You often give lectures on solidarity and peace issues in the world. The Centre of Excellence, *Centre International d'Études, de Recherches et de sur la Littérature, les Arts et la*

Culture (C.I.R.L.A.C.), which you have founded in Saint-Louis, seeks to create with the University of Saint-Louis "a pole of exchanges, research and creativity." It is also projected to house a theatre, a library, a guest house, and a socio-educational center for creativity and works "on all issues related to human balance in harmony with dynamic values, while still remaining open to the world."

Then, there is the *Bureau Africain pour la Défense des Libertés de l'Écrivain* (B.A.D.L.E.), an arm of the *Centre d'Animation et d'Échanges Culturels* (C.A.E.C), which you also founded in Dakar in 1989. The *Institut d'Études et de Découvertes* (Institute of Research and Discovery), an integral part of C.I.R.L.A.C., attracts young people, academics, researchers, women and men from Africa as well as the whole world for six weeks, in May/June yearly, for a program on the historical, social, geographical, and cultural realities of the ethnic groups in Senegal and its sub regions. This Institute also seeks to develop the human being, while allowing the collaborators to cultivate their mind. Normally, the themes of study are policy, democracy, poverty and the future of Africa, creativity (production, artistic expression, museums, art workshops, and craft industries), women's issues, and so on.

The goal of the three-session introductory courses of three-hour duration each is to facilitate the comprehension of change and the situation of African countries in the modern era. Then, the field visits to symbolic places in particular villages and important towns, not to mention the cultural excursions, have the objective to restore the original intentions of African traditional festivals, such as wrestling, songs, naming ceremonies, and initiation rites of marriage, puberty, and circumcision, among so many others.

The above introduction applied to our conversation today, Madam, will allow us to focus on the contributions of recurrent and archetypal symbols and images in your literary works, which are also found in abundance in African traditional festivals and rites. Accordingly, our conversation will dwell on the search and delimitation of the implications and meanings of the African soul, that is to say, the imaginary of the African world....

❀ ❀ ❀

Le Revenant

Let me begin with your first novel, *Le Revenant* (NEA, Dakar, 1976), translated into German and Russian. In Africa, we say that the dead are really never dead but, easily can and without fail, do get involved in the daily business of the living. Could you explain to me your strategy of using Bakar's ghost as one of the principal characters of this seminal novel? Why did he steal the *sarax*, for example, which was supposed to link him with his people after death?

Sow Fall: Thank you, Madam. But, I would like to take a step back to your introduction for a short while. You speak about my obsession about African traditions, the imaginary, etc. You have enumerated many things on which I focus, which interest me, through the organizations that I have created. Your observations, I believe, signal that there are issues to be clarified. First and foremost among them is culture. You have addressed that issue in your introduction. Truly, I speak about the dynamic prospects of culture, because our tradition is our culture. But, in all that I do, and in all my vision, which speaks of the past, I think that what is important is that the past should direct the future. If one wants to summarize into two or three words the greatest benefit of my literary and organizational activities, it is the importance of being oneself. It is necessary to be oneself and while at it, inevitably, put down one's foot in some place. Where there are roots there is tradition. But tradition in itself does not explain everything. It cannot solve our problems. Then again, I believe that it is fatal to severe oneself from tradition. It is like human beings, Africans, Americans, Europeans, whosoever that may be, each has a history. In Africa, I do not know why this is so--perhaps because it was not written, and not transmitted through books — but, we do not speak about history, but rather about traditions. Yet history or tradition, it affects the modern times. That means that it makes projections for the future. It is always dangerous to think that modernity is from the West, and that tradition is in opposition to modernity, where tradition is seen as our oral culture, etc., etc.

But, the great European Renaissance in the 15th century was also modern. Its flag-bearer, Erasmus, lived in the 1400s. He was educated by monks in Holland, for he was Dutch and spoke Latin. The monks, who brought him up, who cultivated his mind, said that it was necessary to be modern, and in the transmission of the religion of the Old Testament and all that they saw an abundance of obsolete materials that needed to be dropped, in order to be able to move towards modernity. Already, at that time, the priests who educated him were talking about modernity. In my own thinking, I have never talked about any ideology. I have never advocated the opposition of modernity to tradition. No, I have never done so. But, I always was aware that one needed to have a piece of luggage to move towards modernity. But, this luggage should not be static, one that never changes. I never even think of it, because as soon as you start thinking about it, it turns into an ideology. Those who study ideology, it is their stock-in-trade, not mine.

I grew up in a home, where there was tradition and where I learned how to be modern, without talking about it, because one needs to belong to one's historical epoch. The future should be sought, but through tradition. Thanks to time and context, certain things pull human beings back, but it is always necessary that they work towards human dignity. My obsession is human balance and dignity, while holding on to the best, which can contribute to human balance. Yes, I agree that it is necessary to move forward. Therefore, for me, culture is the way towards advancement. Tradition moves, in order to lead us towards the future, because if one wanted to live as people did in the 14th century, one would not exist. It is one sure way of making tradition die, of killing our history, stultifying it, locking it up in a ghetto, and that blocks our all-important creativity. If we do not advance, we die culturally. It is necessary for us to move towards modernity.

Now, Africa is late to things, and because of that we are not advancing politically. What is happening is that we are right in the middle of all our hopes and all our searches and dreams, and we cannot disavow who we are. We need to be able to assimilate what we borrow from the modern times. Never forget this admonition: "Know thyself." That is how each people reconstitute themselves. For me, it is so obvious and simple. I was lucky to grow up in a family and an environment where one knew what it meant to understand oneself and to be oneself, how to respect oneself while opening up to others. But, that also implied perspicacity, and the idea of tolerance, of accepting others, not only physically, but mentally as well.

When I read texts available to me in French from France, Europe, and all over the world, I never felt lost or uprooted, because I was aware of the existence of other cultures. Culture is important, essential even, for if we lose our culture, then we are nothing. When one has one's own culture, and receives those of other places, then one can become enlightened in making a synthesis. It is important to remain yourself all the time while moving forward. Remaining yourself does not mean turning your back on reality, the future, etc. That is how I see these issues. But, then, critics and thinkers ponder my writings and see things that *I* do not see....

In Africa, we were never taught tradition as such. No one ever said to us, this is your tradition. Curiously, however, we knew how to live according to our traditions. For example, in our family, we knew that we were not slaves. Just because one was a girl did not mean that one was inferior. That was an exception allowed in a setting where my parents knew what modernity was and pro-

ceeded to do things from that point of view, without dis-
avowing what we were. So, that was how we saw things.
And I think that the world can function like that, but
from a dynamic point of view. That is not being ideological; it is not being militant either, but existing and going
straight ahead, broadening one's horizon.

Now, let me turn specifically to Bakar. You have seen in
Le Revenant that there is nothing mysterious about the
character of Bakar, nothing supernatural about him, yet
Bakar is hiding. There is, however, something mysterious
in the imaginary of the people there; they exploit the traditional belief, according to which the dead can return to
the living. There is no boundary between death and life,
between reality and dream. Bakar took advantage of this
belief. Everyone started from that belief and everyone
knew that Bakar was hiding himself. There is nothing
mysterious about it. He hid himself in life. He said something like this to himself: All right, I will hide. I will return, and they will believe that I have reincarnated. So, it
is a problem of belief. But, it is necessary also to see the
context of Bakar's death. There is the emotional aspect of
it, the mystery of death, and, it is so apparent in this context. Everyone believes that he is dead, but there he still is
and that creates a disturbance. But, that shows the impact of our beliefs in mysteries on a given situation. Now,
that also is part of tradition.

Even today, there are intellectuals who cannot function
on these two levels. That is the human being for you. What
interests me is the complexity of the human being. Today, in the West, there are doctors, thinkers, people who
always use their brains, their intelligence, who one fine
day deliver themselves body and soul to a guru. Therein
exactly lies the problem. They abide by these beliefs, which
have nothing, nothing, nothing rational about them. But,
there again, that is human, that is the human being for
you. When these people block all their intelligence, their
reason, and believe in a man who has become a guru,
believing that they must deliver themselves bound, body

and soul, feet and head, to the guru, well, that reproduces a fragile effect, literally, before this need they have
to hang on to something that is impalpable. That, nonetheless, is human.

Azodo: Bakar seeks happiness, like everyone, and believes that
he can get it with the birth and baptism of his daughter.
However, he fails, due to his dishonesty; he had embezzled
money from his office to pay for the baptism. What do
you think of such a conceptual construct as human search
for happiness?

Sow Fall: I think that it is normal that human beings search for
happiness. In the revealed religions, for example, Christianity and Islam, there is this belief that God brought
down human beings on earth, and provided them all that
was necessary for their happiness. That is the essence of
life. The human being had all that was necessary for him
to be happy, but he partook of the forbidden fruit. It was
at that point that he was told: You, because you have
blown your chance for happiness, you now will earn your
happiness with the sweat of your forehead. Therefore,
according to *Genesis*, according to the history of religions,
human beings will always seek happiness. But, anyhow,
that is not happiness at all cost, at any price. Human beings must also control themselves, must know which happiness they are after, because there is happiness that can
destroy one. There is happiness that can destroy completely, physically, such as when one is hooked on drugs,
etc. You believe you are searching for happiness, but then
you go ahead and destroy yourself and the family fabric.
You believe you are searching for happiness through
power, but you can even destroy the world, due to extreme ambition. One can easily say: Well, I have a weapon,
my happiness is to achieve power, and I will decimate
others. The human being should be aware of his responsibilities as he searches for happiness. When I write, exert
myself, suffer, to produce a text, it is so that when finally
I read it I will be happy, and have a measure of pleasure
also in having produced it.

Azodo: When one looks more closely at Bakar and his ghost, *Le Revenant* can become an allegorical account of the conflict between Truth and Illusion. Why did you absolve Bakar and punish Yama?

Sow Fall: Again, that as well is a whole set of issues having to do with literary creation. I did not seek to exonerate Bakar and to punish his sister. That arises from the unfurling of the plot of the novel. You know, very often, when one is not in the business of creative writing, it is rather difficult to believe this. But, I have seen authors who say that they control completely their characters. It is all intellectual, cerebral, and from the beginning to the end they have total control of them. Well, I write differently. I cannot put my intellect forward, as if it were a mathematical formula, which I calculate. I prefer to write emotively and emotionally. And, when I do so, I am not responsible for what a character does. I cannot reconstitute a text of fiction. If I lose a page of fiction, I could never reconstitute it, because I am in a different dimension when I write. On the other hand, when I give a lecture, I can lose even all the lecture, but that will not pose a problem for me, because the lecture is a work of criticism. But, for me to lose a page of novel will be catastrophic. I could never reconstitute such a work.

           So, characterization follows the logic of the text, and it is not a rational logic. All right, you may take issue with me on the subject of coherence, but in terms of moral choice only, I believe that Bakar is not at all dishonest, no, not at all.

Azodo: But, he did steal, didn't he?

Sow Fall: He embezzled money, yes, but who pushed him to do it? It is his sister and his family. It is his sister Yama who wanted him at all costs to work towards the revalorization of the family. It is she who told him that he needed to marry this girl from an influential family. It is she, along with all the family, her friends and all, who told him that it is necessary for him to do things in a big way.

Obviously, Bakar is a weak man, because if someone says to me, as the proverb goes, "put your hand in the fire," will I put my hand in the fire? It is important to acknowledge the strong social pressures present. One must have a strong personality, really, to escape from these social pressures. Therefore, it is Yama, who seems to be at fault. Everything that happens to Bakar is his sister Yama's fault. I wanted to show at one and the same time the force of these social pressures. One cannot exonerate Bakar completely, because rationally one can always say to him: "you're a big boy, you shouldn't have succumbed." But, it is Yama who is at fault. Logically, I accept that Yama reaped what she sowed.

Obviously, feminists will say to me, as always, you have again sacrificed the woman. No, I did not mean to sacrifice the woman. Paradoxically, Yama is a character that I admire very much, for everything is not always the black/white binary. What I admire about Yama is her strong personality. She knows where she wants to go and she goes there. But, she is also a human being. One cannot say that all women are good and that all men are bad. Everyone has his or her good or bad qualities.

The issue with Bakar should be seen for what it is, pure and simple. There is no need to look at the women, for I find that women, especially African women, Yama aside, are very strong. But, they should direct their actions to useful ends. I did not punish Bakar, and I did not punish Yama. Everything flows from the textual logic.

❁ ❁ ❁

La grève des Bàttu

Azodo: Your second novel, *La grève des Bàttu* (*The Beggars' Strike*, NEA, Dakar, 1979), adapted to cinema by Cheick Oumar Cissoko under the title *Bàttu*, pre-selected in 1979 for the Prix Goncourt and crowned with the Grand Prix Littéraire de l'Afrique Noire in 1980, is translated into English, Rus-

279

sian, German, Chinese, Danish, Swedish, Italian, Dutch, Finnish, Swahili, and Spanish. You produced a completely imaginary work, where the trickster is tricked, thanks to the gourd (bàttu), this emblem of gift exchange between the endowed and the wretched. What is your thinking on the theoretical concepts of fate and destiny?

Sow Fall: Well, as a believer — I am a Moslem and a practicing one — I believe that God controls human destiny. But I do also believe that God gives human beings free will. If I do evil as a Moslem woman, saying that my destiny dictated it, logically therefore God should not punish me, because I would argue that God made me do what I did. Now, I do not believe in that at all, because human beings can control their destiny. Religion and tradition recognize the human will. In Wolof tradition, there is a proverb that says: "*Yalla Yalla bey sa toll,*" [You beseech God in vain; you need to cultivate your own garden.] If I remain idle, while always requesting God to give me wealth, etc, if I do not work, I cannot have these riches. Therefore, a human being can act on his or her destiny, because God has left him or her necessary leeway for control. It comes down to what we said at the beginning: God said to human beings, you can have happiness, but, it is also necessary to work for this happiness. Therefore, I believe in destiny, because I am a Moslem, but I also believe in the strong responsibility that human beings have to control their destiny.

Azodo: Begging is a motif that recurs rather redundantly in the *La grève des Bàttu*. Does begging have a spiritual function in the novel?

Sow Fall: No, begging does not have a spiritual function as far as I am concerned. What has a spiritual function is solidarity, the act of giving. In my opinion, the giver who gives with all generosity, for the love of his or her neighbor, to save the dignity of the neighbor, that has a touch of spirituality. But, precisely, what I wanted to denounce in *La grève des Bàttu* is the devaluation of the meaning of gift-giving. When giving to the beggars, people no longer think of the beggar's misery, rather they are full of their own selfish thoughts. That is what I condemn. When one gives, it is necessary to give out of pure generosity. That is not only in Islamic religion, it is also in the Christian religion. It is necessary to give for the love of giving the other. You see that the other is suffering. He or she does not have anything. The duty of solidarity must be exerted. One does not even need to reach the beggar in the street. That is what Islam explains. One of the pillars of the Islamic religion is to give a percentage of one's wealth to the poor. If one gives them, then, they will not need to go to soil themselves in the streets begging. That is the double function, spiritual and social, of begging.

Azodo: Blindness is also a recurrent symbol among some principal characters in your novels — Nguirane Sarr (*La grève des Bàttu*); Grand-père (*Le Jujubier du patriarche*); Dianor (*Douceurs du bercail*), and Mahanta Bally (*L'Appel des arènes*). Why did you make Nguirane blind, he who is such an accomplished artist — musician, composer, and orator?

Sow Fall: There, again, I wanted to confer a lot of importance on what is physical. That does not have anything at all to do with the spiritual dimension, intelligence, and all that. See, all the blind men you have mentioned are very brilliant human beings. I said so in *Douceurs du bercail*, specifically with regard to Dianor. He is a being of light, light which is the more important aspect of this man, his spiritual dimension, his intelligent side. I wanted to pay homage to the blind. I wanted to say that they are people who see deeply. My reference to light in *Douceurs du bercail* is explicitly, specifically, made with regard to Dianor.

In my forthcoming novel [*Festins de la détresse*], there is also Larry, a blind woman who is a singer and a soothsayer. Thus, physical handicap is nothing. What is important to human beings is light, which they can project without regard to their physical state. The blind should not be scorned, because the blind can be sources of light. Inner strength in an individual is very important to me.

Speaking about women, for me it boils down to the same preoccupation; women have enormous inner strength, which they need to use. It is necessary that they seek to make it come out.

❄ ❄ ❄

L'Appel des arènes:

Azodo: I will return to this light motif when we discuss your sixth novel, *Douceurs du bercail*. For now, let's talk about your third novel, *L'Appel des arènes* (NEA, Dakar, 1982), pre-selected by the jury for the Prix Goncourt in 1982 and later for the Prix Alioune Diop, crowned by the I.C.A with the Prix International pour les Lettres Africaines, adapted to film, and translated into Russian and German, and forthcoming in Japanese and English. In this novel, the arena seems to be a closed place and an imaginary space, the prototype of a nest, which calls the neophyte to partial immolation in the cradle for rebirth into a new being under the supervision of the guides or idols, through wrestling. For you, is it also a call to lost Africans in the modern era to return to African ways of knowing, African epistemologies?

Sow Fall: The return is symbolic, because everything in the *L'Appel des arènes* is symbolic. It means you should remember where you come from; you must draw from your own source. Simply put, that is what it is.

I did not live in the village, and so I have no nostalgic feelings about the village. But I did have a lot of poetic feelings when I spoke to people who returned from the village. I was born in Saint-Louis. And, I never knew the village until quite recently. Presently, even in my secondary home near the University of Saint-Louis, which is indeed in a village, I have met many, many people who came from the villages. These people worked on our premises during the dry season and would go away when they were done. I made contact with the village in that manner, which was very fascinating to me. I was always fascinated by nature. In Saint-Louis where I was born and grew up, there were only rocks and water. There were not many trees. I therefore took to everything that grew in the soil. I have always liked things that come from the soil. For this reason, I eat a lot of fruits.

Therefore, I will never catch myself today saying that I would like to live like my grandmother or our grandparents. Neither in my ideas nor in my practices will I ever say that we ought to live like in the last century. I want to take control of time. It is necessary to seek to be the master of events and things. As a militant in the feminist movement, I used to ponder why we should tell lies about women to researchers and men. Woman needs to be given the necessary weapon to help her get up on her feet, to be herself, and to advance in the world. That is for me the small difference between the militant and the Moslem. Many people did not understand my position then. I repeat that it is necessary for the woman to be educated. It is necessary that she be free like a human being. It is necessary that she be respected, that she be made aware that she has an inner strength. Like that, she will not even need to ask, beg, or share. No, the woman has tremendous strength, not only intellectually, but spiritually. She has something mysterious, which she can use to free herself. She will get up and she will go for her dignity.

So, I think that right now we are not going anywhere, because we are carrying within us a baggage. At every moment, with each step of our life, we work on this baggage, in relation to the debt we owe, the advances we have made, our vision of things, which changes, adapts, etc., etc., but never sacrificing who we are. This is what I have said in *L'Appel des arènes*.

Azodo: A considerable number of critics have observed the use of oral tradition aesthetics in *L'Appel des arènes*. What is the meaning of *mbaar* from the point of view of the initiation and socialization of the young boys?

283

Sow Fall: The *mbaar* [men's hut] has two different functions, a real function and a laudatory function, in the acquisition of the essential values of society, namely, courage, solidarity, and identity. Mbaar teaches the morality of the group to the community. But, it also has a dream function, for every human being needs a dream. All our artistic activities, the science of wrestling, along with all that accompany it—poetry, dance, music, song—are occasions for dreaming. All those who engage in these artistic activities are all great athletes. The *mbaar* plays, to a certain extent, the same role that professional athletes play. When men are in the mbaar they are not cloistered. It is always an occasion for festivities, and for the youth to admire great champions.

              In Saint-Louis, some of my brothers had get-togethers. Each night, there was the tam-tam. Yet, my father was a very modern man. There were these wood fires, there was this drumming, there were these things that dazzled and nourished the soul. It was a spectacle, which had the same function as the music or the big concerts you talk about. The *mbaar* did not sequester young men, but rather it was an occasion for creativity and praise, for human beings need these.

Azodo: If one can say, therefore, with a measure of accuracy, that the grand lesson of *L'Appel des arènes* is that human beings can stave off death through the constant re-actualization of rites of passage, how would you explain the back-cover synopsis of the book, according to which "all the gods are not dead, for born in their midst is one of these demigods that each generation creates to satisfy its need for transcendence"?

Sow Fall: Yes, I believe that. It is true. It is even written like that in the book. I said so somewhere in the book, *L'Appel des arènes*. The quotation on the back cover is the publisher's synthesis. When Diogou discusses with Diattou the need to bring Nalla closer, in order to explain to the child his identity, his idea of revival, it is because everyone needs that. We all need myths. We need role models. This is

284

why, today, things are not working out, and there is not much anybody can do about it. Things are in disarray. Clearly, today, human beings need these demigods. They have need of models and demigods. I said so somewhere in *L'Appel des arènes*. And, it is normal to have these needs. All the people who defend Michael Jackson and the big athletes do so because they regard them as demigods. Each generation needs these myths. Human beings cannot live without myths. All generations, all cultures, all religions, need to have these myths. That is part of our inexplicable, inner need, the need to soar towards some unspecified ideal. We all need idealism.

Sometime in the past, I wrote an article in the French newspaper, *Libération*. In that article, I said that sports have become the only space for ideals to flourish in contemporary times. There are no more huts. There are no more rituals. Sports have become the new myth in full modernity. We are fully in a modern mythological era. When people hustle in the stadia, push against one another, because their idol is playing, it is because human beings need myths. It is part of the inner needs of human beings. Therefore, if a sport, for example football, provokes this kind of passion, it is because sports have become the only terrain from which one can soar to a new dimension. However, people want athletes to be demigods. And, if they fail to fulfill their demigod roles, they are massacred. When a big sportsman gets beaten in a game, people never think of the pleasures that he had provided in the past. He is lacerated, torn to shreds....

❄ ❄ ❄

L'Ex-père de la nation:

Azodo: Elsewhere, regarding *L'Ex-père de la nation* (*The Ex-Father of the Nation*, L'Harmattan, 1987), translated into German, you distinguished between the the meaning of L'ex-père with small letter "e" and L'Ex-père with big letter

"E." I still do not understand the distinction between the two. What, exactly, did you want to say?

Sow Fall: The distinction is not between those two. That distinction is, perhaps, the publisher's. Right from the very beginning, my book was neither *L'ex-père*... nor *L'Ex-père*.... The title of my book is *Ex-père de la nation*. It was the publisher who put his title *L'Ex-père*...when the book was published. That changed everything, all my intention. In my title, I put *Ex-père* to mean any former father no matter who that may be. The former father is unspecified. It is like that in the French version, on the first page. But, the publisher, I believe—he has even reprinted the book several times, but has not corrected the mistake, although I had talked to him about it--had the intention of making people think that I wrote about Senghor, because Senghor had just left power. Well, he did not succeed, because I told a nephew of Senghor's whom I know and who believed that I criticized Senghor that that was wrong, and that I did not write about Senghor. Therefore, as far as I am concerned, I did not write about Senghor. I only wanted to talk about somebody who fell into the trap of power, someone who saw himself as the ex-father of the nation. I only wanted to show that it is applicable to all former African Heads of State who thought of themselves as fathers of the nation. Senghor never was mixed up in the Fathers of the nation business.

Azodo: I believe that you have already answered my next question, on the use of the common noun "father" to indicate the deposed guide of the people. For me, the word father is an innate, paramount, and collective image.

Sow Fall: Yes, for me also, it is a general term. For me, that means that it is not a localized word. *Ex-father* of the nation is a vague term. It is as if I said "man" and you said "woman." It is not the same as *the* man. It is not the same as *the* woman. It is *all* the men and *all* the women who could recognize themselves in this novel.

Azodo: Why could not President Madiama escape the machinations of his advisers who attacked him from all sides and this in spite of his goodwill? Can human beings control their destiny?

Sow Fall: I believe that the political system is always strong, too strong even. The question is whether a person can change a system, especially a system of machinations like that, when the person is not a professional politician. I did not want to write a novel on politics, but on the hypocrisy of people who surround the man in power. And, that can be political power, money power, even spiritual power, because big religious leaders, be they Muslim, Christian, or other are surrounded by people. They do not always have a good sense of reality; they do not know what is going on. Their advisers tell them things. They are not in direct relationship with what they judiciously should control. That is what I mean.

This question has always bugged me: do men in power realize that they are hostages of the people who surround them? The opportunists can be family members, friends, forces, etc., who tell them what to do. And, I have checked into this in reality. I have had a personal experience of it. When I had already corrected the proofs of my novel, there was a poll in *Le Point* on whether men in power get told the truth. I kept this issue of *Le Point* in my luggage, because I wanted to ensure that, if one day somebody really wanted to know, such a person would come to see that I was not influenced by this newspaper. There is only a similarity between what is in my novel and what is in the poll. They interviewed French politicians, asking them whether people told them the truth. All of them, one by one, said that people told them what they thought that they wanted to hear. And, one of them particularly — I do not remember whether it was Chirac or Raymond Bâ — said that when one is a political head, when one is powerful in politics, it is only the wife that undertakes to be his cleaning lady. Nobody wants to argue with you, everyone tells you what they think you want to hear. It is only your wife who protests. She is the only one who truly says her mind. That's that.

❀ ❀ ❀

Le Jujubier du patriarche:

Azodo: In *Le Jujubier du patriarche* (C.A.E.C. - Khoudia, 1993), republished by L'Édition Poche, Serpent à Plume in 1997, and translated into Italian, songs celebrate the great warriors and the old heroes. Please tell me more about this memory of the African Soul, which inhabits traditional songs.

Sow Fall: Yes, and rightly so, we reproach oral history, traditional songs, for singing only about famous heroes and chiefs. Traditional songs, genealogies, etc., sang about chiefs in grandiose acts, in the family, and in associations. But, that is all about tradition, which was in essence our history. Traditional songs, epics, and genealogies were our history books. At the same time, there were oral history, dances, and creative activities, songs that spoke about everyday life, songs that made jests, and songs that condemned. Folktales and songs did everything that literature does in general. At the same time, songs educate, satirize, and castigate behaviors. That is as much as to say that there is need for solidarity in the community; that is the essence of the songs. The songs were very critical when they were satirical, but they also talked about beauty, love, and patriotism. So, songs did not only sing about chiefs, but also about Mr. and Mrs. Everyone who can see themselves, recognize themselves in them, all those who are able to think of integrating themselves into societal norms.

Azodo: Nalla's tutor in *L'Appel des arènes* refers to the tree as a source of life when he says: "When a man loses his roots he shrivels up and dies" Can one see the jujube tree here as The Tree of Life, an archetype of ascension, facilitating the transformation of the community?

Sow Fall: Yes, in a way, for it is so said, or suggested, at the end of the book. The jujube tree had died. Everyone brawled, bickered, and only wanted riches and money, but not to preserve the symbols. It is when they thought that the leaves of the jujube tree gave wealth, health, and riches that people pounced on them, fought to take them and sell, in order to become rich. It is then that the jujube tree lost its sap and died. The arguments continued until there was this miraculous rain, which caused brawls also, but the jujube tree was determined to blossom. Those who were brawling, and those who were not feeling well, like Tacko, left to become reconciled one to another. That is what I wanted to say; it means that a return towards the past is a movement towards the future. It is not a mere turn of the head. The past implies beckoning the future, hope and happiness in the future.

Azodo: Tell me more fully, if you will, about the communal rebirth at the foot of the patriarch's jujube tree. Would one be right to think that you envision the rebirth, the return, of Africans, some day, to authentic African traditions?

Sow Fall: Yes, that is, indeed, the meaning of rebirth. The word for rebirth in Wolof, my language, is the same word which says that the tree is budding, has come back to life: "*doundat.*" When a baby comes into the world, we say it has come to life: "*djoudou.*" When someone says to you that somebody is born again, "*djoudou att bess,*" the expression means to become new again. When a plant germinates, say in the spring season, we say, "*djebi or jebi.*" The term rebirth means that one gets a *second* chance, another orientation, to one's life. That is essentially the meaning of rebirth. Therefore, I think that the tree completely symbolizes human life. A human being with roots planted in the ground rising towards the future, without branches scattered everywhere, ought to be harmonious in his or her movements. Once the branch is cut, the tree loses its sap. It is disposed of and will need to be replanted into the soil.

❋ ❋ ❋

Douceurs du bercail:

Azodo: In *Douceurs du bercail* (NEA, Abidjan, 1998), forthcoming
          in English translation, you say this: "Let us love our earth;
          we will sprinkle it with our sweat and will plough it with
          all our strength with courage." For a reader, like me, who
          pays attention to symbolic and mythical aspects of the
          word, the mythemes "sweat," "dig," "forces," and "cour-
          age," give the impression that you are speaking on two
          levels, the African continental level and the planetary level
          in which the earth is seen as a cradle, where human la-
          bor (*laborare*), in this instance writing, becomes a prayer
          (*orare*), for human survival. Would you please explain the
          moral, mystical, and philosophical juxtapositions in this
          beautiful novel, your sixth, *Douceurs du bercail*?

Sow Fall: Exactly, I cannot say it better than you have done. You
           have said it very well. When you speak about the planet
           earth and all that, you speak about what is important for
           Africans. The African situation is explained by our colo-
           nial past. Colonization is not only about the black per-
           son, etc. It is about all that has made us all suffer men-
           tally. Many among us Africans believed in our inability
           to change our fate. The mind was colonized. We came to
           believe that we cannot of our own be free from coloniza-
           tion. The reference to the earth is therefore symbolical.
           But, there are African intellectuals who have said to me
           that they believe I am telling them to come back to Africa
           to help the peasants. Would you believe that some big
           professors have said this to me? I tell them that I did not
           say so. The earth symbolizes that place from which we
           sprouted. It is the symbol of what has nourished the pri-
           mordial being. I do not even say primitive, but rather
           philosophical being, completely in that symbolic sense of
           the term.

           Therefore, right from birth, the human being is nourished
           by the earth, our mother. Therefore, we must ask the earth
           to nourish us, not only physically but also spiritually. We

must also lean on the strength of this earth that we dig and integrate it like the field, for we garner strength simply from digging. And then, afterwards, when we have enough strength to approach others, even with callous hands that means we have worked for our dignity. When your hands are callous, you should not be scorned, rather you should be respected, because human dignity is the most important thing in the world, and you have earned your dignity. One can never take human dignity from a person who has earned it. When you move towards your dignity, you are sharing. Clearly, it is a question of shared bonds. And I have noticed that almost everywhere.

The Japanese felt humiliated, Japan being a small parcel of the world where there is no natural resources. In the 1950s, I believe, I read an article in the newspaper, *Le Monde*. I must have cut it out, but lost it in heaps of papers. It came in two installments. The article was signed by one Mrs. Butterfly, perhaps that was a pen name. I was really allured by these papers in the years between 1970 and 1980, which explained the Japanese miracle. The long and short of the story is that Japan became the miracle it is known to be today. The Japanese became aware of the necessity to work for their dignity, by sheer amour-propre. They told themselves that they had to get out of their quagmire, and they bent down to work to make it happen.

I remember when I was small the earrings and jewels, all products of Japanese imagination, with the inscription "Made in Occupied Japan." People were wont to say, Oh, the Japanese, nothing but so many imitators! The West said the Japanese were merely imitating them. Even in some developing countries, people saw Japanese articles as inferior goods. Africans scorned Japanese goods, because Africans were conditioned to do so. But, through hard work the Japanese were able to pull themselves up with help from their culture. They drew from their earth, their culture, the means of gaining their freedom, earning their strength, their power. Obviously, one might tell me that the revolution was not perfect, because they won their gamble on a development plan. Fortunately, they have their culture, although now they also are suffering the harmful effects of modernity.

One day, a Japanese woman came here and told me that the problem I highlighted in *L'Appel des arènes* is exactly what Japanese teenagers are going through today; they no longer recognize their culture in these modern times. The Japanese have everything, but are nonetheless worried on the issue of culture. Therein is the modernity-culture conflict, how to find in the past one's identity. A Japanese woman whose husband is an ambassador in Senegal told me all this.

Azodo: Now, I would like to take up again the "light" mytheme you mentioned earlier. In *Douceurs du bercail*, you speak about the "light of hope" that will guide humanity, and the hope that human beings will harvest and build. And, you repeat this line of thinking in your next novel, *Un grain de vie et d'espérance*. Does the term "light of hope" convey life's most important ideals for you?

Sow Fall: Yes, in my opinion, it is the best expression that describes the happiness that we all seek, which every human being wants to attain. As far as I am concerned, money is not happiness. Notoriety, celebrity, is not happiness. Possessing the power to control human beings, make them go by the rod, is not happiness. Happiness is in the beauty of art, in its light. Light, in my understanding, is when intelligence, when emotion clarifies our vision, so much so that if we tread in the path of happiness and hope, we would, symbolically speaking, dominate the world. We can enjoy all that can contribute to our pleasure, our happiness, without destroying ourselves. When we destroy ourselves that means there is no light; we sink into obscurity. In a world where globalization talks are in vogue, where we denounce its misdeeds, if despite all the wealth that humankind has accumulated, not only on the material level, but even on the scientific level, on the level of our discoveries, the great conquests that humanity has realized, if one can still say that we are in the worst stage of the history of humankind, because despite everything that we have human beings do not feel happy, it is because everything is oriented towards the economy, politics, and money. If everything is directed towards the economy and towards money, the human being gets forgotten, and that means sidetracked human value, beauty, the light that ought to guide our way. The path of dream is forgotten, for the ideal is forgotten. Then, when that is forgotten, whatever the human being may have is lost, and the human being cannot afford to lose his sense of measure. The biggest problem for any human being is to lose his sense of balance.

Azodo: For you, the subject theme of *Douceurs du bercail* is neither immigration nor globalization, contrary to what a good number of critics believe. Then, why the reference to "voyageurs sans baggage/travelers without luggage," an expression which points to human existential anguish, and which tends to imply complaint about the fate of Africans maltreated as outcasts in Europe and elsewhere in the world?

Sow Fall: If you read the interview I gave to Francoise Pfaff, published in *Notre Librairie* between 1981 and 1982, at the end of that interview, she asked me what the subject of my next novel would be. I told her that it would be on immigration. There was nothing said about globalization or any such thing, simply because at that time in 1981 I had observed that in Africa people, especially the teenagers here, were beginning to think that nothing was possible any more, that one could do nothing any more, that one could not create wealth here. I had said that it was necessary to do something to sensitize the young people to want to try initially to do something at home. I also know that travel develops young people. I know that it is good to go to see other places. When I traveled to France, I chose to return to my country. Nobody told me to come back. Nobody asked me when I was departing if I thought of returning. And, almost all of us have been abroad. I tell you that that did not even cross my mind, if I would remain in France or not, because I knew we had everything here in the country. However, travel to other places is a gesture of solidarity. It opens the eyes and the mind. It is a reaching out to others. That is how it should be. It helps you gain experience. It sensitizes you to tolerance, although tolerance here in Senegal is at its lowest ebb now.

So, I told the Minister of Culture of the importance of orienting the young people towards the thinking that they can make it here. It is necessary, if they do not have a scholarship to go to France that they try to attend university here up to the Master's level, which program was just starting then. That was when I began to think of the book, *Douceurs du bercail*. I had not thought of the title yet, and that is as much as to tell you that I did not know about the immigration or race problems. But, I saw that it was necessary that people think of digging our earth and creating their happiness and wealth here before going elsewhere.

What I describe in *Douceurs du bercail*, I say to you, on my honor, I did not even know existed in reality. On my honor, it is my imagination. I did not even know that there are places where people are barreled up. All I had wrought is fiction, and I had made it up at the time. But, then, one day, the former director of the Nouvelles Editions Africaines told me that I really digested very well the book I described so well in *Douceurs du bercail*, for nobody is allowed to enter those places.... I told him that I did not know the book he was talking about. And, he informed me that situations like the one in my book do exist in reality. Now, he was an ambassador with UNESCO and he had had a female relative detained over there. As ambassador, he must have had to go there to intercede for the woman. That was how I became aware of the problem. And, later, I also learned of it on Radio France Inter. The week before, police officers were saying among themselves on the radio how hard things were. A journalist with an NGO was working with the people being pursued, and has lately published everything on that in a book. So, I think that human beings must work for their dignity. They should not always make excuses. It is important to believe in yourself. One should not allow oneself to be pushed around. One should always believe in oneself.

❈ ❈ ❈

Un grain de vie et d'espérance:

Azodo: Your seventh novel, *Un grain de vie et d'espérance* (Edition Françoise Truffaut, 2002), which can be translated into English as *Food for Thought and Tomorrow's Life*, is crowned with the Prix Best Food Literature Book in French, by Gourmand World Cookbook Awards. For me, it is a novel with a postmodernist touch: 33 questions about Senegalese eating followed by some twenty recipes by Margo Harley, a Senegalese chef living in Paris, on Senegalese culinary art. Are you surreptitiously sending an invitation to everyone to embrace African ways of eating for the restoration, regeneration, and reintegration of the human community?

Sow Fall: Yes, that is true, in a way. But, honestly, I must say that the initiative for the book was not mine. The journalist, who created the collection, which I was not acquainted with before, telephoned me from Paris one day. She says to me: I have a project and many people tell me that Africa has really something to contribute and that you will have something to say too. She tells me what it is all about, explaining the subject: I am doing a series on how human beings eat. What does the act of eating mean? I mean, that is a question one can evade if need be by saying that a chef wrote the recipe. The journalist hoped to entitle my text "Manger sous le ciel sénégalais/Eating the Senegalese Way." But, I was not enchanted by the title. And, she explained that she was there to tell me that if she chose me for the project, it was because all the other contributors for the series were also creative writers. Therefore, it was going to be a text by authors, adding that I would have total freedom to create, to write fiction, to say what I thought. It was then that I dove into the writing. And, when I started to write, I brought out things, which I had always had in my head, as if I had lived them. That is how the book on the social importance of eating in our country was born.

Therefore, I tell you that it was not about militancy nor was it ideological, but rather narrating a lived experience in an atmosphere where eating was something of essence, where many people who came at meal times came to a feast. Eating, for us, is a feast. Therefore, I lived in this atmosphere and I created my text around that. I was seeing then, but did not explain what I saw. When there is a big ceremonial marriage, it goes beyond merely, simply, putting food in the belly. It exceeds the supernatural; it is connecting to the cosmic forces. It is normal to offer food to the genii of the sea. When there is a marriage, life expectancy, prayers for the fertility of the bride, it is this hope that makes it possible for the grain of life to come down in torrents. What germinates and nourishes is a great referential life.

I am not talking about a worldwide table, because food ought to be spiritual as well. The idea is also that of a banquet. A banquet means an exchange of intelligence, because around the banquet table, one discusses, makes bets, sees the other, and discovers what the other thinks. It is also tolerance and sharing. Isn't global sharing very important? How genial it would be, if that were possible.

Azodo: Is the tale about the man who ate *bassé salté* on page 13 of *Un grain de vie et d'espérance* true or fictional?

Sow Fall: No, it is fiction. Hundred percent fiction! When I was a very small girl, *bassé salté* was a ceremonial dish. The composition was so good! Really, *bassé salté* is a ceremonial dish. Then, I added *salté* with the meaning dirty, which comes from the French [la saleté: dirtiness or filthiness]. When I was small, I asked the meaning of *bassé salté*, but nobody ever explained it to me. To explain it, I started with an interjection. In Saint-Louis, when something is really beautiful and tantalizing, we say, "it is dirty." By saying the opposite we mean that it is "perfect." So, I framed my meaning of the term from that understanding. I invented the story of a very mischievous small girl, who says to the gentleman, "But, it is salté." She created what could have been an incident, by saying the opposite of what she meant, in order to bring shame on the gentleman. But, her statement provoked laughter, and that saved the situation.

Azodo: So, it is a play on words ...

Sow Fall: Yes, indeed, it is a word play.

Azodo: On page 79 of *Un grain de vie et d'espérance* you say this: "My feeling is that eating time — given all the symbols with which it is imbued — is incompatible with television time." Do you disapprove of watching television while eating? If so, is this because you believe that the images on television sets are disadvantageous to the ethical values and traditional beliefs of our ancestors?

Sow Fall: Well, in a way. It is not for that reason, however, that I would say that television should not be watched while eating. There is the fact that television brings many negative values, but also it gives many positive values. All is never, never, never black. Television contributes many things, which render service to us. But, when one eats, I think that one should share. It is a time to eat; you have put a fork in the hand of every eater. Therefore, there is no longer communion when you eat and watch television at the same time. Eating is a time to commune with one another. I know that one can eat while listening to the news. But, eating time is not the best time for that, or for reading, for that matter. I do not think that it is a question, even with those who invented television. I think that it is not a question of ancestral values either, because even Westerners deplore the effects of the television that they invented. Eating time for me is human time. It is time to commune on the human level, at the level of sharing.

Eating time for me is time for relaxation. It is time for joy. It is time for friendliness. I do not think it should be a time for arguing.

❄ ❄ ❄

General Questions:

Azodo: Are you a moralist? Why do the principal characters of your novels fail?

Sow Fall: Well, I do not think that the principal characters of my novels fail. It is the rule of life that when people refuse to learn they fail. But, a novel, literature in general, creates subversion, malaise, social ideal, or conflict. It is not for no reason. When one speaks about fiction, one speaks about plot. Therefore, these are things that affect one another. And, when, some times, I say that literature is inevitably committed in itself, it is because there are people who do not believe it. I, myself, also would like to write love stories. But, have you ever seen a completely dull love story? When love is the subject of literature, it is not only for the first page. Something always contributes to the plot. Well, then, my characters fall into that domain. And, if it is fiction, that means that all is not dull. One can already see that some are able to escape and succeed.

Let us take them one by one, the principal characters of my novels. Yes, in *Le Revenant*, Bakar fails. In *La grève des Bàttu*, Mour fails, because he is bad. But, Kéba wins, nevertheless. In *L'Appel des arènes*, Nalla wins and Mr. Niang too. It is Diattou who fails from the logical development of her own actions. I am not the one that ruins the characters that fail. In *L'Ex-père de la nation*, Madiama fails, because he is bound to fail. But, in my opinion, he loses, so that he will learn the lessons of history. After that, in *Le Jujubier du patriarche* all the principal characters succeed, because they are successful in recreating harmony, which is important. They achieve success in everything around harmony. What I like is the tolerance between

Gueladio and Sarebibi. Can we act, write, pray together? They prayed together, and they found each other. In *Douceurs du bercail* also, it is total success for everyone. It is victory for Astar. It is victory for all those who left that cave. It is victory for the project, given that everyone gives before leaving for the parcel of land. That comes simply from the earth; there is zeal, which is a rich resource for the project. I say that when one digs, when one tries, success comes. I do not believe in fruitless effort. I believe, in an almost mystical way, in the ability of the human being to achieve. I think that when the human being wants to have his or her dignity, will, and intelligence, he or she can achieve salvation.

Azodo: I take up again here a question that you have been asked before by some other interviewer. Is there a big idea behind your literary creativity? Are you in the process of constructing your own "Comédie Humaine"?

Sow Fall: It is your place as critics to judge. But, the organizing idea behind my work is human dignity. It is the link between all that I write, simply because I do not write for personal reasons. And, it is a question, undoubtedly, of temperament, because I have not personally experienced any of the sufferings evident in my characters. And, perhaps, it is even for that reason that I create them. I was brought up to respect others, even when they have nothing. I do not seek to control the other because of his social position. I was raised to be respectful. That is perhaps why, on my return from France, when I saw that people gave more importance to money than to intrinsic human values, I was shocked. And, therefore, I acclaimed human dignity. That's just that.

Azodo: Let us return now to the beginning, to your career as cultural coordinator and Senegalese writer. What was the problem between your organization and the Senegalese Writers' Union? Was there a conflict?

Sow Fall: No, there was no conflict of a personal nature with the Association of Senegalese Writers. *I* quit the Association.

They all thought that I should stay, but I had not asked to be part of the Association. They had invited me to join them. I do not have the penchant for associations. And, for many years, they asked me to join them, but I did not want to. And, some writers also came to my house and, in front of my husband, pleaded with me not to do things like that. Later, when I went over to the National Assembly, they welcomed me. Two people must have voted against me, but that was not important. It was even better that way. I was president from 1980 to 1984.

I myself asked to be relieved of my position, so that I could write. After two years of tenure, I told them that I had created the C.A.E.C., and had even organized myself the lectures, adding that I wanted to leave. As writers, it is not worth the while to be selfish I say to them. We need to work hard. It is necessary that each one works for survival. In the general Assembly, they refused to let me go. So, I said, I will give you some more time. So, I remained president of the Association till1984.

But, really, there were people who were not in my camp for various reasons. Because I wanted to do things appropriately, I was somewhat strict. These same persons said to me that we needed to be face to face with the State, and that the State should be forthright about its relationship with us. And, in effect, I had said the same thing to the president of the Association of Senegalese Writers, when I told him that we were free people, and that we did not need to lose our freedom to power. I said that as Senegalese citizens we ought to be like a child vis-à-vis the parents. At one time, the child is helped, adding that we hoped to have funds that would help us to become autonomous. And, I had in mind the kind of things I do here at C.A.E.C. I have never asked for money to run C.A.E.C. So, I told the president to give us a subsidy, for there are conventions and associations to attend. I asked him for three airplane tickets to be placed at the disposal of the Association, each year, so that one would have them available, if and when needed. I told him that, personally, I would never touch the tickets. I had never traveled with a ticket of the Association. Then we got along well like that.

But, later, there was a new election and someone else was elected. At that point, I could not continue with the Association. I had my own work to do. I was not interested in militancy. What is more, there were writers on the Association who did not agree with me. But, I must say that the majority, even the current president and the one who is still the secretary-general, had always supported me and even to this day remain loyal to me. They come here and we talk and all that. Really, they like me.

Then, a group of writers, at a point in time, thought that I was not part of them. Some believed that I did not support them. It was indeed a misunderstanding. Those ones on their own have called on me. Now, they know the truth. Therefore, their coming here made me happy. They said to me: All right, we shall create another association in which you will take part. I told them that it was not reasonable to expect me to drop the organizations that I created and from which I have earned my living. How can I earn wages and put people outside at the same time? I told them that I did not advocate that they drop the writers' association to create another either, because we did not have time for that. They said that we would create another association. I tried to dissuade them from doing that, but the others did not know that I did dissuade them. They nevertheless went ahead with it and created the association. They elected Cheikh Aliou Ndao president. I became the vice-president. And, there was Boubacar Boris Diop, the Secretary General, and all that. But, there was no time to make the association function. The president who was supposed to obtain administrative papers for the legalization of the Association did not do it, and I had no idea why. That was where the conflict was.

But, afterwards, they said, really, we do not need to bicker. We need unity between Senegalese writers. Naturally, they came here, to C.A.E.C. We held meetings and cleared up the misunderstandings. The two associations have remained close. There is no problem. There is no brawl at all. There is nothing. We get along. They are active. They do things. We do not have time. I do not have time. I tell you that's the supposed conflict, which is not even a conflict.

When they had a session, which happened not too long ago, they invited me and paid me tribute. And, in February, they had a conference on the literature of Saint-Louis and made me the guest of honor. Really, there is no problem. There is no conflict.

Azodo: Is there really a novel in the offing?

Sow Fall: Yes, there is a novel on the way, to be published in Switzerland in April. I have even here the proofs for the final corrections, as you can see.

Azodo: What is its title?

Sow Fall: It is entitled *Festins de la détresse.*

Azodo: What is it about?

Sow Fall: I have repeated myself, namely, that there are people who prey on human misfortune.

Azodo: Thank you very much, Madam.

Sow Fall: Don't mention it.

Azodo: Really, you responded to all my questions.

Sow Fall: It is my pleasure.

SELECTED BIBLIOGRAPHY

❄ ❄ ❄

Aas-Rouxparis, Nicole. "'Écrire, c'est un banquet où tout le monde apporte': entretiens avec Aminata Sow Fall." *Women in French Studies* 8 (200): 203-13.

Ajala, John D. "*The Beggars' Strike*: Aminata Sow Fall as a Spokesperson for the Underprivileged." *CLA Journal* Vol. XXXIV, No. 2, December 1990: 137-52.

Azodo, Ada Uzoamaka. *L'Imaginaire dans les romans de Camara Laye.* New York: Peter Lang Publishers, 1993.

_____. "Interview with Aminata Sow Fall: Towards a Search for the African Soul: Writing and Imagination in the Novels of Aminata Sow Fall." In: *Emerging Perspectives on Aminata Sow Fall: The Real and the Imaginary in her Novels.* Trenton, N.J.: Africa World Press, 2007.

_____. "Entretien avec Aminata Sow Fall: Écriture et Imagination chez Aminata Sow Fall." http://www.iun.edu/~minaua/

Balibar, Etienne. "Racism and Nationalism." *Race Nation, Class: Ambiguous Identities* 1991: 37-67.

Bobia, Rosa and Cheryl Wall Staunton. "Aminata Sow Fall; ses livres et son nouveau role." *Présence Francophone* Vol. 36, 1990: 133-136.

Boni-Sirere, J. "Littérature et Société: etude de *La grève des Bàttu* d'Aminata Sow Fall." *Revue de Littérature et d'esthétique négro-africaines* Vol. 5, 1984: 59-80.

Brown, Ella. "Reactions to Western Values as Reflected in African Novels." *Phylon* Vol. XLVIII, No. 3, Fall 1987: 216-228.

Cabakulu, Nwamba and Boubakar Camara. Comprendre et faire comprendre *La grève des Bàttu* d'Aminata Sow Fall. Paris: L'Harmattan, 2002.

Cham, Mbye B. "Islam in Senegalese Literature and film." *Faces of Islam in African Literature.* Ed. Kenneth Harrow. Portsmouth, NH: Heinemann, 1991. 163-186.

D'Almeida, Irène Assiba. *Francophone African Women Writers: Destroying the Emptiness of Silence.* Gainesville: University Press of Florida, 1994.

_____. "Femme? Féministe? Misovire? *Notre Librairie* 117 (avril-juin), 1994: 48-51.

Dieng B. et Kesteloot L. *Les Épopées d'Afrique noire.* Paris: Karthala-UNESCO, 1997.

Diop, Abdoulaye-Bara. *La Société wolof, tradition et changement: les systèmes d'inégalité et de domination.* Paris: Éditions Karthala, 1981.

Durand, Gilbert. *L'imagination symbolique.* Paris: Presses Universitaires de France, 1984 (1964).

_____. *Les Structures anthropologique de l'imaginaire: introduction à l'archétypologie générale.* Paris: Bordas, 1984.

Flowers, Betty Sue. ed. *Moyers, Bill: A World of Ideas.* New York and London: Doubleday, 1989.

Gadjigo, Samba. "Social Vision in Aminata Sow Fall's Literary Work." *World Literature Today* Summer 1989: 411-415.

Guèye, Médoune. "La Question du féminisme chez Mariama Bâ et Aminata Sow Fall... L'examen de la typologie du personage féminine chez Mariama Bâ et Aminata Sow Fall." *The French Review* Vol. 72, No. 2 (1998): 308.

_____. "Écriture, développement et féminisme: entretiens avec Aminata Sow Fall." *The Literary Griot* Vol. 12, No. 2, 2000: 44-58.

_____. "Tradition orale et philosophie wolof chez Aminata Sow

Fall: une esthétique transgénérique et transculturelle dans Le revenant." *Langues et Littératures* Vol. 6 (janvier): 59-79.

Hale, Thomas A. *The Epic of Askia Mohammed.* Bloomington and Indianapolis: Indiana University Press, 1996.

Hawkins, Peter. "Marxist Intertext, Islamic Reinscription? Common Themes in the Novels of Sembène Ousmane and Aminata Sow Fall." *African Francophone Writing: A Critical Introduction.* Ed. Laila Ibnlfassi and Nicki Hitchott. Oxford: Berg, 1996. 163-169.

Hemminger, William. "The Former Father of the Nation" (translation). *Southern Humanities Review* Vol. 26 Fall 1992: 313-348.

Hitchott, Nicki. *Women Writers in Francophone Africa.* Oxford: Berg, 2000.

Jaccard, Amy-Claire. "Les visages de l'Islam chez Mariama Bâ et chez Aminata Sow Fall." *Nouvelles du Sud* Vol. 7, 1986/7: 171-182.

Johnson, John William. *The Epic of Son-Jara.* Bloomington and Indianapolis: Indiana University Press, 1992.

Kesteloot, Lillian. *Les Écrivains noirs de langue française: naissance d'une littérature.* Bruxelles: Éditions de l'université de Bruxelles, 1963.

Knappert, Jan. *African Mythology: An Encyclopedia of Myth and Legend.* London: Diamond Books, 1990 (1995).

Leeming, David Adams. *The World of Myth.* New York and Oxford: Oxford University Press, 1990.

Lemotieu, Martin. "Interférences de la religion musulmane sur les structures actuelles de la société négro-africaine: l'exemple de *La grève des Bàttu* d'Aminata Sow Fall." *Nouvelles du Sud* 6 (1986-1987): 49-60.

Madu, Raphael Okechukwu. *African Symbols and Myths: The Hermeneutics of Destiny.* New York, 1992.

Martin, Florence. "Echos et grains de voix dans *Le Jujubier du patriarche* d'Aminata Sow Fall," *The French Review* Vol. 74, No. 2 (2000): 296.

Mbiti, John S. *African Religions and Philosophy.* Second Edition. London: Heinemann, 1989.

Miller, Elinor. "Contemporary Satire in Senegal: Aminata Sow Fall's

La grève des Bàttu." French Literature Series Vol. XIV, 1987: 143-151.

Mokwenye, Cyril. "Aminata Sow Fall as Social Critic: An Interpretation of *Le Revenant* and *La grève des Bàttu.*" Neohelicon Vol. XIX, No. 2, 1991: 211-221.

Niang, Sada. "Modes de contextualization dans *Une si longue lettre* et *L'Appel des arènes.*" *The Literary Griot* Vol. 4, No 1-2, Spring/Fall 1991: 111-125.

Obinaju, Nwabueze Joe. "Human Rights Echoes in Aminata Sow Fall's Beggars' Strike." *Neohelicon* Vol. 22, No. 1 (1995): 295-310.

Okafor, Ndidi. "Aminata Sow Fall: Cas de *Revenant.*" *Neohelicon* Vol. 18, No. 1, 1991: 89-97.

Okeke-Ezigbo, Emeka. "Begging the Beggars: Restoration of the Dignity of Man in *The Beggars' Strike.*" *Neohelicon* XIX Vol. 19, No. 1, 1992: 307-322.

Onyemelukwe, Ifeoma M. "Drame conjugal et voix féministe dans *La grève des Bàttu* d'Aminata Sow Fall." *Neohelicon*, Vol. 26, No. 1 (1999): 111-124.

Ormerod, Beverly et Jean-Marie Volet. "Aminata Sow Fall." *Romancières africaines d'expression française: le Sud du Sahara.* Paris: L'Harmattan, 1994: 133-136.

Pffaf, Françoise. "Enchantment and Magic in Two Novels by Aminata Sow Fall." *CLA Journal* Vol. 31, No. 3, 1988: 339-359.

Rosenberg, Donna. *World Mythology: An Anthology of Great Myths and Epics.* Lincolnwood, IL: NTC Publishing Group, 1986 (1994).

Siga, Niang Fatou Niang. *Reflets de modes et traditions saint-louisiennes.* Dakar: C.A.E.C. Éditions Khoudia, 1990.

Sow Fall, Aminata. *Le Revenant.* Les Nouvelles Éditions Africaines (NEA), 1976.

_____. *La grève des Bàttu.* Dakar: Les Nouvelles Éditions Africaines (NEA), 1979.

_____. *L'Appel des arènes.* Dakar: Les Nouvelles Éditions Africaines (NEA), 1982 (1993).

_____. "Du pilon à la machine à écrire." *Notre Librairie* Vol. 68, 1983: 73-77.

————. *L'Ex-père de la nation*. Paris: L'Harmattan, 1987.

————. *Le Jujubier du patriarche*. Dakar: C.A.E.C. Éditions Khoudia, 1992 (Éditions Le Serpent à Plumes, 1998).

————. *Douceurs du bercail*. Abidjan: Les Nouvelles Éditions Ivoiriennes (NEI), 1998.

————. *Un grain de vie et d'espérance*. Paris: Françoise Truffaut Éditions, 2004.

————. *Festins de la détresse*. Lausanne : Éditons d'En-bas, 2005.

Stringer, Susan. "Cultural Conflict in the Novels of Two African Writers, Mariama Bâ and Aminata Sow Fall." *Sage. Supplement* (1988): 36-41.

————. *The Senegalese Novel by Women: Through Their Own Eyes*. New York: Peter Lang, 1996.

Trinh T. Minh-ha. "Aminata Sow Fall et l'espace du don." *The French Review* Vol. 55, No. 6, 1982: 780-789.

APPENDICES

DECLARATION DE DAKAR SUR LES DROITS ET LIBERTES DE L'ECRIVAIN EN AFRIQUE

-:-:-:-:-:-:-:-:-:-:-:

Les participants au Colloque International sur: L'ECRIVAIN ET LES DROITS DE L'HOMME. tenu A Dakar les 25, 26, 27 et 28 septembre 1989 sur l'heureuse initiative du CENTRE AFRICAIN D'ANIMATION ET D'ECHANGES CULTUREIS (C.A.E.C.), tenant compte de l'adhésion des Etats africains à la Déclaration Universelle des Droits de l'Homme ainsi qu'à la Charte africaine des Droits de l'Homme et des Peuples :

-constatant les nombreuses violations de ces instruments en Afrique et pire, la justification de ces violations basée sur le prétendu niveau de notre développement socio-économique :

Ainsi, les persécutions mentales, les arrestations arbitraires, les détentions illégales, les tortures physiques et morales, les exécutions sommaires sont légion en Afrique et singulièrement au Kenya, au Malawi, en Afrique du Sud entre autres pays.

Aussi, les participants au Colloque de Dakar condamnent sévèrement ces pratiques inhumaines étrangères et l'éthique,

-denoncent les régimes barbares et réclament en dernière analyse leur isolement,

-lancent un appel pressant aux Organisations et Associations Internationales, aux intellectuals, aux hommes de droits en Afrique et à travers le monde, pour une coopération en vue de renforcer et d'appuyer le combat pour la défense des droits de l'Homme et des Libertés de l'écrivain.

-affirment leur détermination inébranlable en vue de l'isolement diplomatique des régimes connus pour leurs violations délibérées et notoires des dits Droits et Libertés.

Félicitent les initiateurs du Colloque de Dakar sur Droits de l'Homme et des Libertés de l'écrivain.

-saluent la naissance du BUREAU AFRICAIN POUR LA DEFENSE DES DROITS ET LIBERTES DE l'ECRIVAIN qui s'est fixé comme objectif ultime : la défense des Droits de l'Homme, des Libertés d'expression, d'organisation et de circulation des idées, fondements du progrès social, éonomique et théorique.

Dakar, le 28 Septembre 1989

Le Colloque

STATUTS DU
BUREAU AFRICAIN POUR LA DÉFENSE DES LIBERTÉS DE L'ÉCRIVAIN

I. DÉNOMINATION – NATURE – SIÈGE

Article 1
Il est crée à Dakar un BUREAU AFRICAIN POUR LA DÉFENSE DES LIBERTÉS DE L'ÉCRIVAIN (B.A.D.L.E).

Article 2
Ce Bureau est un organisme rattaché au CENTRE AFRICAIN D'ANIMATION ET D'ÉCHANGES CULTURELS (C.A.E.C.); son rôle spécifique étant la promotion et la défense des Droits et Libertés de l'écrivain sur le continent.

Article 3
Le siège du B.A.D.L.E. est à Dakar au CENTRE AFRICAIN D'ANIMATION ET D'ÉCHANGES CULTURELS, H. L. M. Fass Paillote, BP 5332 Poste de FANN – DAKAR.

II BUTS

Article 4
Le B.A.D.L.E. complète les différents organes du C.A.E.C. qui est une structure d'animation, de promotion et de coordination d'activités culturelles, artistiques, littéraires et scientifiques diverses.

Le B. A. D. L. E. a pour but de:

1) réaliser ou renforcer l'unité transnationales des écrivains et, plus largement, des intellectuals évoluant en Afrique.
2) promouvoir, consolider et defender leurs droits.
3) d'engager des actions multiformes sur le terrain pour le respect des droits et libertés de l'écrivain (liberté d'expression, de circulation et d'organisation entre autres).
4) promouvoir et organizer diverses activités d'échanges et formes de coopéation entre écrivains regroupés ou non en association ou sous forme d'institutions) d'origines nationals, culturelle et confessionnelle diverses.
5) contribuer à la promotion et à la materialization des Droits de l'Homme au profit des individus et des peuples en Afrique, pour l'émergence de cultures et d'oeuvres fécondantes pour le développement et la Démocratie.
6) contribuer à l'avènenment de cultures de développement au service de l'Homme.
7) susciter la solidarité des écrivains d'Afrique avec toutes les actions de sauvegarde, de défense, ou de réhabilitation de la dignité humaine partout où elle est bafouée, car l'écrivain et l'homme de culture sont partout engagés dans le combat pour l'Homme.
8) contribuer, par des initiatives multiformes, au développement et au renforcement de la compréhension entre les peuples, facteur important d'une paix internationale durable.

III. STRUCTURE ET FONCTIONNEMENT

Article 5
Le B.A.D.L.E. est placé sous l'autorité de la Directrice Générale du C.A.E.C. qui en assure bénévolement le Secrétariat Général.

Article 6
Le fonctionnment du B.A.D.L.E. est assuré par un SECRÉTARIAT EXÉCUTIF composé de:
- un Secrétaire Général)
- un Secrétaire Permanent) = placé sous l'autorité du
- d'un Attaché de Presse)   Secrétaire Général.

Article 7
Dans la réalisation des objectifs du B.A.D.L.E., le Secrétariat

Exécutif s'attache la collaboration de :
- Correspondants Régionaux qui représentent le B.A.D.L.E. dans les diverses régions du Continent africain.
- Conseillers à travers le monde.

Article 8
Les Correspondants Régionaux et les Conseillers sont des membres associés du B.A.D. L. E.

L'ensemble des Correspondants Régionaux forme le COLLEGE RÉGIONAL.

L'ensemble des Conseillers constitue le COMITÉ CONSULTATIF.

Article 9
Les fonctions de Correspondant et de Conseiller sont bénévoles; mais les projets d'activités émanant des Correspondants, une fois retenus par le B.A.D.L.E., peuvent faire l'objet de recherche de finacement pour leur réalisation.

Article 10
Les membres du COMITÉ CONSULTATIF sont désignés pour une période de quatre années renouvelables, sur la base de leur expérience, leurs qualités et leur autorité reconnues dans l'un des domains de l'activité intellectuelle, culturelle, artistique, littéraire, ou des droits humanitaires, etc...

Article 11
Le Secrétariat Exécutif réunit, tous les deux ans, le COLLEGE RÉGIONAL et le COMITÉ CONSULTATIF pour dresser le bilan des activités et discuter les actions à mener dans les deux ans.

Cette rencontre sera élargie à une représentation la plus large possible des écrivains du Continent et d'observation extérieurs.

IV RESSOURCES

Article 12
Les moyens financiers du B.A.D.L.E. sont constitués de:
1) la contribution du C.A.E.C.
2) les cortisations de volontaires (écrivains et autres particuliers qui veulent soutenir l'action du B.A.D.L.E.

3)   les subventions ou les dons.

Article 13
Le budget du BUREAU AFRICAIN POUR LA DÉFENSE DES
LIBERTÉS DE L'ÉCRIVAIN est géré par le C.A.E.C. et le Secrétaire
Général du B.A.D.L.E. qui détient le pouvoir de signature et de
négociations au nom du B.A.D.L.E.

V   FORMES ET MOYENS D'ACTION
Article 14
Parmi les formes d'action du B.A.D.L.E. on peut citer:
1)   des enquêtes sur le terrain relatives à la situation des écrivains
et de leurs droits et libertés.
2)   des interventions sur les plans juridiques et humanitaires.
3)   la collecte, la centralization et la diffusion d'informations relatives à la situation des droits de l'écrivain en Afrique.

Article 15
Le B.A.D.L.E. procédera à l'information et la sensibilisation par
un organe de presse et tout autre moyen à sa disposition.

Dakar, le 28 septembre 1989

INDEX

ABOUT THE EDITOR
Editor's Bio-Bibliographical Sketch

Dr. Ada Uzoamaka Azodo obtained her Diplôme d'Études Supérieures de Français (DES) from the Université de Dakar, her B. A. (Honors) from the University of Ife, her M. A. and her Ph. D. from the University of Lagos in African Francophone Literature. Dr. Azodo has taught in various capacities at the University of Lagos, St John's Fisher College, Rochester, New York, State University of New York at Geneseo, Valparaiso University, and is currently affiliated with Indiana University Northwest at Gary. Dr. Azodo's research interests include African Literature, African/African Diaspora Studies, Women's Studies, Gender Studies, and Cultural Studies. Publications include books: *L'Imaginaire dans les romans de Camara Laye.* (New York, San Francisco, Berlin, Paris: Peter Lang, 1993); *Emerging Perspectives on Ama Ata Aidoo.* Co-ed. (Trenton: Africa World Press, 1999); *Emerging Perspectives on Mariama Bâ: Postcolonialism, Feminism and Postmodernism.* Ed. (Trenton: Africa World Press, 2003); *Gender and Sexuality in African Literature and Film,* Co-ed. (Trenton: Africa World Press, 2006); *Critical Essays on Aminata Sow Fall: The Real and the Imaginary in Her Novels.* Ed. (Trenton: Africa World Press, 2007). Scholarly articles are in refereed journals, several chapters in critical and scholarly anthologies, and book reviews in academic journals, *Research in African Literatures, and Palabres,* and two entries in international *Who's Who in Contemporary Women's Writing.* In progress is a co-edited volume, *Emerging Perspectives on Ken Bugul: From Alternative Voices to Oppositional Practices* (Trenton: Africa World Press).

Think Home

A Reentry Guide for Christian International Students

LISA ESPINELI CHINN

International Student Ministry
InterVarsity/USA
6400 Schroeder Rd.
Madison, Wisconsin 53711
www.intervarsity.org/ism

ISBN # 978-0-9835848-0-3

Acknowledgements

Thank you to my colleagues in international student ministry in the U.S. and around the world who share the vision of reentry preparation for international students.

To the thousands of international students who sat through my seminars on transition, played my reentry simulation game, Customs and Culture, and shared their stories with me these past 27 years, thank you!

Special thanks to Nate Mirza of the Navigators USA and Terry McGrath of ISM New Zealand who provided valuable feedback to this edition.

Thank you to Janet Atkins for painting the cover art and Laura Li for designing the layout.

Most of all, I am very grateful to my husband, best friend, co-laborer, and critic, Leiton E. Chinn, who encouraged and empowered me to keep my *Think Home* vision alive.

Table of Contents

Introduction

I am not very good with driving directions. Without a personal navigator, a detailed map, or my GPS, I will get lost. The same is true of life and its many transitions. We need good directions.

When I returned to the Philippines, the word *reentry* was mostly understood as a space shuttle's return to earth. In fact, there were no seminars or books on the subject of reentry and reverse culture shock. My own preparation was a day retreat to read God's Word, reflect on what God had done in my life while I was away from home, and pray for the appropriate reentry attitude. It was a necessary pre-departure commitment, but it did not address the larger questions and concerns of reentry.

The first *Think Home* edition was my attempt to capture, through over 200 questions, the issues a returning Christian international student may face. Since its first publication 27 years ago, it has been adapted for use in the U.K., New Zealand, Australia, Germany, Japan, and with Chinese students and scholars. This new version, though written for internationals who studied in the U.S., has applications for Canadian students as well.

This revised *Think Home* is your transition guide. It has a new format and includes additional materials. Treat it like a map to help you navigate your way back home. It provides you with the general landscape, but you will have to build your own roads. The questions in the book serve as markers to provoke you to look deeper. They are signs to point you to an unseen path, to alert you to a potential danger, or to invite you to stop, take in the scenery, and dream about your future. You will also read of heroes of the faith who reentered their countries and left you with helpful signposts. Advice from other fellow travelers are added in this edition.

I invite you to linger in this book. Do not rush answering the questions. Pause. Meditate. Invite God's Spirit to speak to you (and to others who may be working on this guide with you). Stop and notice what new paths you have created. Share your insight with others.

In the end, I hope your reentry preparation, through this guide, will encourage and inspire you to re-imagine your future back home and re-align your dreams with God's purpose in your life and in the world.

Lisa Espineli Chinn
Director, International Student Ministry
InterVarsity/USA
April 2011

How to Use *Think Home*

Suggested Approach	If you are...	Advantages	Comments
Personal Study	Self-motivated Able to work on it over a period of time	Privacy protected Freer expression and honest answers may be encouraged	Consider sharing with a friend your discoveries and any new reentry path you are creating
One-on-One (You and another returning Christian international or an American Christian friend)	A new or young believer Not fluent in English Motivated by structured style of learning Willing to meet several times	Built-in accountability Enhances your relationship with another person Areas of need are more easily recognized and considered because of the interaction	For best results, come prepared to share your answers Identify which chapters you want to work on alone or together
Group Study	Motivated to learn in a group Already part of a fellowship Used to group discussion and sharing	May be less intimidating than one-on-one Learn from others Group becomes a support community after your return Provides multi-cultural interaction and insight	Needs a good facilitator Do assigned chapters ahead of time Encourage commitment to complete the book
***Think Home* Getaway Weekend** (Building on the advantages of Group Study)	Eager for a returnee community Willing to invest time Need to get away to focus and reflect	Extended time for guided study, reflection, and prayer Strong community and prayer support Personalized attention and mentoring	Consider a winter break or an early spring date as a possible time Look for a place that allows for undisturbed personal reflection and group discussions

YOU
ARE
HERE

↓

A helpful map tells you where you are in order to find your location and direct you to your desired destination. Naturally, pondering the why question is a good place to start thinking about returning home.

1. Why Are You Returning Home?

Deciding to return home is not an easy task. Consider Grace's example. After finishing her graduate degree, she extended her student visa and interned with a non-profit organization. As the internship was about to finish, she asked her family if she should go home. They said no and told her she would be of better help to the family if she remained in America. However, she was also convinced that she could make a contribution to her country by serving with a Christian ministry. With her student visa about to expire, she had to make a decision.

What about you? What is your situation?

1. Consider the following reasons for returning home. Check the ones which apply to you:

   ☐ Visa has expired

   ☐ Finished your studies

   ☐ Family needs you

   ☐ Country/church needs you

   ☐ Job waiting for you

   ☐ Honor your commitment to company/government/church

   ☐ Other commitments to honor

   ☐ Ready to go home

   ☐ Want to go home

   ☐ Home is God's place for you

   ☐ Financial reasons

   ☐ Goal(s) for coming to the U.S. achieved

   ☐ Other

2. Have you seriously considered staying in the U.S. long-term or permanently?

   ☐ Yes   ☐ No

   Why?

3. What are your concerns or fears about returning home?

4. Are you confident that returning home is God's plan for you? If yes, how did God show this to you? If not, what do you need from God at this time?

5. How will the confidence or absence of assurance that God is leading you to return home affect your reentry experience?

2.   Your Life in the United States

Takuya was extremely sad at the thought of leaving the United States. He called it his "country." He became a Christian in America, made numerous friends, finished his degree, and loved the lifestyle of freedom and creativity. As he packed, he was grieving the loss of his community.

This exercise will help you remember and establish the significance of your overseas experience. You may feel sad along the way, but accepting your sadness is part of the grieving process.

USE A FEW WORDS TO DESCRIBE YOUR EXPERIENCE IN THE U.S.:

_____   _____
_____   _____

General Experience

1.   What factors (people and events) made your stay positive and pleasant?

2.   What experiences made your life unpleasant and difficult?

3.   What do you like or not like about living in the U.S. (e.g. beliefs, values, attitudes, practices, products)?

4.   From the list of things you like, which ones would you want to take home with you? Why?

LIKE DON'T LIKE

_____   _____
_____   _____
_____   _____

5.   What were your goals in coming to the U.S.? Were they accomplished?

6.   Who are the significant people in your U.S. experience?

7.   What friendship(s) influenced you the most? Why?

Church/Christian Experience

1.   What are your observations of Christianity in the U.S.?

     How is it different from Christianity back home?

2.   How did your relationship with American Christians affect your attitude towards Christianity?

3.   What factors helped or hindered your Christian growth while in the U.S.?

4.   What did you appreciate about your American church life and experience?

5.   What American church practices will not work or fit back home? Why?

6.   How do you distinguish between cultural and biblical values?

7. Mark "C" if you think the statement below is a cultural value and "B" if you think it is biblical:

For Example:

<u>C</u> To be on time at every meeting and appointment.

<u>B</u> To be prayerful.

____ To line up when waiting for a bus or paying for something.

____ To make sure you call before visiting a person's home.

____ To send thank you cards.

____ To express your feelings openly and directly ("tell it like it is").

____ To be honest.

____ To have wine, instead of grape juice, at communion.

____ To think of others before yourself.

____ To support your parents materially and in every way you can.

____ Everyone is entitled to freedom and the pursuit of happiness.

____ Save up money for your retirement.

____ Respect the elders among you.

____ God helps those who help themselves.

____ Greet each other with a kiss.

____ Have a church building.

____ Cleanliness is next to godliness.

____ Do things decently and in order.

____ Drums, pianos, guitars—any musical instrument can be used for worship.

____ Little children should have their own church service.

____ The democratic process.

____ Practice hospitality.

____ Give to those who are in need.

____ The capitalistic way of life.

____ Caring for the environment.

____ Tolerance towards a gay/lesbian lifestyle.

____ Pursuit of life, liberty, and justice for all.

____ Right to happiness, wealth, and health.

3.   Who is going home?

A returnee to Asia declared, "Coming home is like re-caging a freed bird." International students from other regions of the world may also experience that same feeling. The foreign sojourn invariably expands the "wings" of international students. But imagining "being re-caged" as a returnee helps with determining realistic expectations.

"I had to be well-dressed all the time and meet the expectations of being lady-like." For a returnee who may have enjoyed the casual American ways, the adjustment to socially conform and not offend people could be very challenging.

How Much Have You Changed?

1. PHYSICALLY:
    a.   What are noticeable differences about you now?
    b.   Are you more or less fashion-conscious? Who or what influences your choices now?
    c.   Have you developed a taste for other kinds of food? Give examples.
    d.   Other changes:

2. SOCIALLY:
    a.   What kinds of friendships have you developed and appreciated?
    b.   In what ways have your attitudes towards people of different race or ethnicity changed?
    c.   Have you become more or less outgoing?
    d.   Have you changed your manners or attitudes towards older people?
    e.   Are you more or less class/status-conscious?
    f.   Do you now prefer being or living by yourself?
    g.   Other changes:

3. ACADEMICALLY:
    a.   What new intellectual habits have you developed?
    b.   Do you feel more or less academically prepared in your professional field?
    c.   What academic pursuits motivate or interest you now?
    d.   Other changes:

4. EMOTIONALLY:
    a.   Are you more or less comfortable expressing your feelings with others?
    b.   How differently are you handling your emotions (happiness, anger, disappointment) now?
    c.   What surprised you about your emotional responses to life in the U.S.?
    d.   Other changes:

5. POLITICALLY:

    a. How much attention have you paid to the political situation at home?

    b. To what degree have your attitudes about politics been affected by the U.S. media, professors, fellow students, or other people?

    c. Have your views concerning the role of government back home or concerning U.S. foreign policies changed?

    d. How has your friendship with students from other parts of the world changed your interest and engagement with global issues?

    e. Other changes:

6. FINANCIALLY:

    a. In what ways have you changed your attitude towards material wealth?

    b. How have your buying habits changed?

    c. Are you more or less generous with your money and possessions?

    d. What have you learned about the use of credit cards?

    e. Other changes:

7. SPIRITUALLY:

    a. How has your attitude changed regarding the religious beliefs and practices of your family and/or friends back home?

    b. To what degree have your theological or doctrinal views changed?

    c. Is your relationship with God stronger or weaker?

    d. What new spiritual disciplines or habits are you practicing now?

    e. Other changes:

8. PURPOSE AND AMBITION:

    a. How have your purpose and goals in life changed?

    b. Would you consider your foreign experience life-changing? Why or why not?

    c. Are you more or less ambitious?

    d. Other changes:

4. Your Experience with Christ

1. Write your story. How did you first know about Jesus? When did you decide to follow him? Who and what did God use to attract you to him?

2. What is Jesus changing in your choices, attitudes, relationships, and decisions?

3. What area of life is hardest for you to surrender to God?

4. What have been some of the greatest needs and concerns in your life?

5. How have you experienced the grace of God in relation to these needs?

6. How are you integrating your faith with your profession and career?

7. What new things is God teaching you about how to love your parents and family?

8. What are your responsibilities towards God's creation?

9. How and where do you see the Kingdom of God expanding in your home country?

10. What have you learned and appreciated about:
    a. God the Father
    b. Jesus Christ the Son of God
    c. The Holy Spirit
    d. Bible/Word of God
    e. Prayer
    f. Fellowship
    g. Church
    h. Spiritual Gifts
    i. Christian Witness/Sharing the Gospel
    j. Christian Service/Ministry
    k. World Missions

↑ LOOK UP

You just finished looking at your reasons for returning home, your life in the U.S., the changes you have experienced, and your relationships with Jesus and his people. The following chapters will help you to look to God and his provisions for you.

5. Developing a Spiritual Support Group

One returned student advises: "Have a good fellowship in the U.S. They will pray for you and communicate with you." "Have a vision," says another returnee "and share it with an important person (friend or pastor) in North America for prayer and accountability."

God's family is worldwide. When you became God's child, you became a part of his global family. Perhaps your first taste of that family was in the United States, or maybe it was back home. Nonetheless, you have experienced in your host country and in varying degrees the fellowship of God's people and its value in your own growth as a Christian.

As you anticipate returning home, consider the following:

1. Recognize the importance of a community of supportive people and begin to make a list of friends you can invite to be a part of your prayer support group. Have a plan on how to communicate regularly with them.

FRIENDS TO INVITE:

_____   _____

_____   _____

_____   _____

2. Remember you are returning as Jesus' ambassador back to your home, workplace, and community. Which group(s) could send you off with a commissioning prayer? Your church, Bible study group, or your campus fellowship?

PEOPLE TO CONTACT:

_____   _____

_____   _____

_____   _____

3. As you are being sent off, you should also be making important connections back home. Who are your Christian contacts back home? If you do not already have Christian contacts back home, check with your staff member or campus pastor as well as with other Christians from your country who are on your campus or in your community.

In addition, you can check the following:

www.ifesworld.org – IFES (International Fellowship of Evangelical Students) is a Christian network and fellowship of high school and college campus groups around the world. InterVarsity/USA is a founding member of this organization.

www.acmi-net.net – ACMI (Association of Christians Ministering Among Internationals) is a North American network of ministries, churches, and individuals working among international students.

www. jcfn.org – JCFN (Japanese Christian Fellowship Network) focuses on helping Japanese Christian students transition back to Japan.

Facebook groups

Other groups

4. How do you maintain a healthy balance between maintaining your American Christian relationships and cultivating your local Christian community after returning home?

•

6. Reentry Bible Studies

These studies will encourage you to look up to God. Encounter him and see what wonders he can do!

You are not alone in your reentry. Meet Moses and find out how different life was for him after his reentry. Follow the chain of events after his return to Egypt and pick up precious lessons along the way. Or learn about Naomi, the widow, who took the difficult journey back home. Share her delight as she held her grandson, Obed, and imagine what could have happened if she did not decide to return to Judah.

Discover how Jesus expressed his humility and obedience in Philippians 2. Learn from Paul about loving and caring for others who have different views from you.

A. Naomi: A Returnee Surprised by God
Book of Ruth

CHAPTER 1

1. Why did Elimelich's family leave their home country (v. 1)?

2. Describe their foreign experience (vv. 2 5).

3. What major turn of events caused Naomi to return home (v. 6)?

4. What realistic options concerning moving to Bethlehem did Naomi present to her daughters in-law (vv. 7-14)?

5. How do you think Naomi felt as she and Ruth made the trip back to Bethlehem?

6. What kind of reception did Naomi receive? In what ways had she changed (vv. 19-21)?

CHAPTER 2

1. Describe Ruth's first job in a foreign country. What made her experience a pleasant one?

2. In what ways was God watching over Naomi and Ruth's welfare (vv. 3, 10 12, 19-21)?

Chapter 3

1. What did Naomi ask Ruth to do? What does that tell you about Naomi? After 10 years of being away from home, what did Naomi remember?

2. What stands out about Ruth (vv. 5, 13-14)?

3. How did Boaz respond to Ruth (vv. 9-15)?

Chapter 4

1. What is the happy ending (vv. 9-13)? What factors brought about this good finale?

2. In what ways was Naomi an effective returnee?

3. What rewards did she enjoy (vv. 14-16; see also Matthew 1:1, 5, 16)?

Application

1. What bitter experiences did you have, if any, while away from home? How did you respond to them? How are you dealing with them now?

2. How do you see God's hand in your life in the U.S.?

3. As you imagine yourself returning home, what role do you see yourself in? How is Naomi's life and example an encouragement to you?

4. Who are the foreigners in your country? How are they treated?

5. What groups are reaching the foreigners in your country (v. 2:10)? What are some ways you can help and partner with these groups? What individual steps can you take to welcome the strangers?

2. Paul: Love Supersedes Knowledge
1 Corinthians 8

1.   What issue or problem does Paul address in this chapter (vv. 1, 4)?

2.   What knowledge does Paul say is not possessed by every Corinthian believer (vv. 4-7)?

3.   How does this knowledge or lack of it affect a person's behavior (vv. 7, 10)?

4.   How does Paul resolve the issue of differing views on what is sinful and what is not (v. 13)? Who is more responsible? Why?

5.   Why is wounding the conscience of a weak brother a serious offense?

6.   What is more important, your freedom or your brother or sister's spiritual welfare? Why?

7.   In the end, what truly matters before God?

Application

1.   What practice(s) or behavior could potentially become a source of conflict between you and other Christians when you return home?

2.   What principle should guide your response and behavior?

3.   You have enjoyed much freedom while in the United States. Now surrender it to God and ask him to help you put people and their spiritual welfare first in your life. Personalize this by writing your own prayer of surrender.

3. Moses: The Reluctant Returnee
Exodus 3:1-4:17

1. In what setting did God choose to reveal himself to Moses? What does this show about God?

2. What did God want to impress upon Moses in verse 5? Why?

3. Why did God introduce himself in the way he did (v. 6)?

4. Look closely at verses 8 and 10. Are they contrary to each other? Why or why not? What do they reveal of God's way of achieving his purpose?

5. What are Moses' objections and excuses (vv. 3:11, 13; 4:1, 10, 13)? What was his basic problem? How did God answer each objection?

Application

1. Where and when has God appeared or spoken to you? How did you respond?

2. Who might be the "Pharaoh" that God wants to send you to confront?

3. What other tasks is God asking you to do back home? How do you feel about them? How will God's answers to Moses comfort and give you courage?

4. When and why do you find it difficult to trust God? What things about God should you remember when faced with the temptation of unbelief?

5. How may you be a part of God's plan to liberate your people?

4. Jesus Christ: The Returnee's Model
Philippians 2:1-11

1. What would make Paul's joy complete (v. 2)?

2. What is unity's enemy (vv. 3-4)? How can unity in the Body of Christ be maintained?

3. Who is Jesus Christ (v. 6)?

4. What was Jesus willing to give up? What was he willing to learn and become (vv. 7-8)?

5. What does it mean to have the "mind of Christ?"

6. After humiliation came exaltation. What honor and authority came with Christ's exaltation (vv. 9-11)?

Application

1. In what areas may you be tempted to be proud as a returnee?

2. How may you learn from your people back home? What do they offer you? What can they teach you?

3. Jesus Christ, who is God himself, was willing to be a servant. What do you need to give up in order to serve others?

4. Identify a few people who you can serve now. List ways you can put their interests first.

LOOK OUT!

In this reentry journey, you need warning signs. They point to difficult and dangerous places ahead. A wise person who sees danger will be careful, but the foolish keeps going and suffers (Proverbs 22:3). Remember you are not facing these challenges yet, but by knowing them ahead of time, you will know how to prepare and respond.

7. Potential Reentry Challenges

Returnees advise:

Expect difficulties. Deal with them with God's power.

Go slow, stay low. Don't blow it. Change does not come overnight.

Be prepared to make adjustments in all aspects.

Try to be a good observer and gradually readjust to the situation.

Every returnee will have his or her own set of reentry adjustments. Your success, however, will depend on how well you adjusted to your host culture, your emotional resilience, your unique situation, and your reentry preparation.

The following list is a compilation of challenges other returnees have faced. Identify which ones you think you may face.

Cultural Adjustment

☐ Identity confusion—who are you now?

☐ Unrealistic expectations

☐ Changes in lifestyle

☐ Changes in fashion

☐ Localized or "provincial" mentality of relatives and friends

☐ Different concept of time

☐ Different pace of life (faster or slower)

☐ Family or community pressure to conform

☐ Other

How are you going to handle the challenges you identified?

Who can help you face these issues because they have walked that road before?

Social Adjustment

- ☐ Loneliness and alienation
- ☐ Envy and distrust in interpersonal relations
- ☐ Tension between individual and family focus
- ☐ Feelings of superiority due to international experience and travel
- ☐ New and different interests from local peers
- ☐ Lack of modern conveniences
- ☐ Role or status changes
- ☐ Dissatisfaction with some patterns of social interaction like…
- ☐ Indifference of friends and relatives to your foreign experience
- ☐ Lack of serious, interested, and willing listeners to your stories
- ☐ Adjustment to noise, pollution, crowds, city congestion, unsanitary conditions, etc.
- ☐ Other

How are you going to handle the challenges you identified?

Who can help you face these issues because they have walked that road before?

Communication Barriers

- ☐ Adoption of verbal and non-verbal codes which are not familiar to your own people like…
- ☐ Speech mannerisms which may be misinterpreted
- ☐ Impatience with roundabout, indirect communication style
- ☐ Absence of colleagues who speak the same "language"
- ☐ Unfamiliarity with new forms of communication and modes of expression; current jargon and slang
- ☐ Difficulty in speaking your own language
- ☐ Other

How are you going to handle the challenges you identified?

Who can help you face these issues because they have walked that road before?

National and Political Problems

- ☐ Changes in country's conditions, national priorities, policies, or views
- ☐ Political climate not helpful for your professional activity and/or advancement
- ☐ Economic uncertainties and conditions
- ☐ Changes in leadership or ruling parties
- ☐ Bureaucracy
- ☐ Reluctance to live in a setting of political uncertainty
- ☐ Dissatisfaction with political situation
- ☐ Observed lack of national goals
- ☐ Other

How are you going to handle the challenges you identified?

Who can help you face these issues because they have walked that road before?

Educational Problems

- ☐ Relevance of U.S. education to home situation
- ☐ Lack of facilities and resources for research or application of skills
- ☐ Absence of professional education programs to keep up with new developments and knowledge in the field
- ☐ Little opportunity to improve skills
- ☐ Incomplete fulfillment of educational goals in the U.S. and its implications back home
- ☐ Lack of opportunities to apply U.S. education and expertise
- ☐ Other

How are you going to handle the challenges you identified?

Who can help you face these issues because they have walked that road before?

Professional/Work Problems

- [ ] Long work hours
- [ ] Gender bias
- [ ] Relationship with supervisor
- [ ] Expectation to participate in questionable or unethical behavior
- [ ] Inability to work in chosen specialty
- [ ] No job openings
- [ ] Feeling of superiority due to U.S. training
- [ ] Isolation from academic or scientific developments in the U.S. and in own field
- [ ] Non-recognition or appreciation of foreign degree
- [ ] Jealousy of colleagues
- [ ] Unrealistic expectations (job position, salary, what a U.S. degree "should" bring, etc...)
- [ ] Low compensation; few benefits
- [ ] Concern with quick material success
- [ ] Corruption issues
- [ ] Impatience with rate of promotion
- [ ] Perceived lack of enthusiasm and/or commitment among co-workers
- [ ] Other

How are you going to handle the challenges you identified?

Who can help you face these issues because they have walked that road before?

(The above list is a modified version of an inventory by participants in the University of Texas' Janus Program.)

Spiritual Problems

☐ Absence of fellowship, support, and security of Christians who love and care (especially for those who became Christians while in the U.S.)

☐ Difficulty in finding a good church, which leads to "church hopping"

☐ Not being welcomed in some churches

☐ Young people are expected to listen and accept what older people say

☐ Some churches want to check the returnees' commitment to Christ and to the church before accepting them

☐ Returnees may be viewed as threats to the pastor or church leadership

☐ Over eagerness to be a part of the church either the person ends up ignored or overloaded with work

☐ Judgmental attitude toward the church at home in comparison to the U.S. church

☐ Sharp contrast between the clergy and laity

☐ Returnee is often perceived as aggressive, pushy, arrogant, critical, and know-it-all

☐ Difficulty in distinguishing between what is Christian and what is "American"

☐ Some U.S. methods or models of promoting Christianity using mass media or one-on-one; forgetting the family approach

☐ Lack of appropriate small group fellowship or Bible study

☐ Difficulty in using or applying some ministry skills learned in the U.S.

☐ Impatience by the returnee: program, process, or "production" may be slower compared to the U.S. church experience

☐ Temptation to feel superior towards church leaders who did not have an experience abroad

☐ Other

How are you going to handle the challenges you identified?

Who can help you face these issues because they have walked that road before?

8.   Tough Questions

This part of the reentry map is where you find yourself before a "fork in the road." It means you are faced with a situation where you do not know what to do or which direction to go.

The following questions relate to the various ethical, moral, social, and religious dilemmas which you may face back home. This section **raises the questions but does not give you the answers, intentionally.** As you work through the questions that apply to you, ask more questions, like:

> *What does the Bible say about the subject?*
> *Who do I know faced this problem before? How did they handle it?*
> *Who should I ask to help me with this question?*
> *What is written about this subject?*
> *Does "Google" know?*

1.   Is **idol worship** part of your former religious life or culture? How should you behave when put in a situation where you are asked or expected to participate in idol worship?

2.   Is **ancestor worship** part of the religious setting to which you are returning? How should you relate to it as a Christian?

3.   Will you be the **only Christian** in your immediate family? When and how might you start sharing your testimony and/or the gospel with them?

4.   Will your **life be in danger** because of your commitment to Christ? How are you preparing for it? What do you think of "secret Christians?"

5.   Will you go home to **pre-arranged marriage** practices? How would you respond to a pre-arranged marriage to a non-Christian? What are your standards for a life partner? What does the Bible say about marriage and whom to marry?

5.   Are you seriously **dating someone in the U.S.**? How is that relationship going to affect your decision to return home? If the person is of another race, culture, or religion, how will your family respond?

6.   What attractive **job offers** or options do you have **in the U.S.**? What factors should affect your decision to accept or decline these offers? How will accepting the job affect your Christian walk, influence, and impact in the U.S. or at home?

7. Is **bribery** a widespread and accepted practice back home? How are you going to respond when you see it happen in your presence or you are directly confronted to participate in it? How will you answer if your boss asks you to tell a lie on his/her or the company's behalf?

8. What do you consider an **"honest day's work?"** Will you face pressure from society to put in less or more time for a day's work? How will you respond?

9. How will you respond to **crowded housing conditions** or relatives visiting and staying indefinitely?

10. What do you say to relatives or others who perceive you as rich and want to **borrow money from you?**

11. Are you part of a **minority group** in your country? How do you view the dominant group(s)? How will you respond when you are discriminated against (professionally, racially, etc...)?

12. If you are a **woman**, will your foreign education be recognized and accepted back home? Will you experience gender discrimination? How will you respond if you sense that you are unjustly treated in your profession or society? How might other women, who did not have your foreign experience, relate to you?

13. How involved will you be **politically** when you return home? How will your political involvement affect your Christian witness?

14. What involvement will you have in your country's **social issues**? How will you relate the gospel with issues like poverty, malnutrition, HIV-AIDS, human trafficking, and other forms of injustice and oppression?

15. If you wanted to **introduce change in your church** back home, what, how, and when would you do it?

16. **What additional tough situations might you face?**

TAKE A BREAK

On any journey, it is important to pace yourself and take appropriate breaks. You recall the stress of learning a new language and a new culture. When you return home, you will feel like the new outsider again. Someone described himself upon returning home as "a stranger in my own hometown. Out of touch in many conversations. I remind myself continually to keep my eyes open and my mouth shut. Not an easy task."

Consider a break while still in the United States

Dr. Richard Swenson, in his book, *A Minute of Margin*, describes our lives in the Unites States as non-stop. He writes, "We walk fast, talk fast, eat fast, and then excuse ourselves by saying, I must run." He also reminds us that overload and hurry are really enemies of faith.

You may have picked up that fast pace of life or feel it more as your time of departure nears. You may feel like going 100 miles an hour. Instead of stepping on the gas even more, take your foot off the accelerator. Schedule a time to slow down. Ask someone to help you find a place where you can catch your breath. Or find someone to go with you to a quiet place. Find out what feeds your soul and discover God's invitation to wait, be still, and rest.

Consider a break when you are back home

This may sound like an impossible idea, but it is necessary. God designed our bodies to take regular rests. That is why he commanded us to take the Sabbath—a day to rest from work. Taking your breaks back home may call for both determination and creativity. Here are some ideas: unplug yourself from all electronic connection and stimulation for a few hours or a whole day; sit still for 5 minutes; mark a place in your home where you meet God; sit in a church or sit in your car and breath slowly. Whatever it is you do, make sure that they re-connect you to God and recharge your spiritual, physical, social, and emotional batteries.

Consider what other returnees have said:

- ▶ *"Do not overrate yourself. Be more humble."*
- ▶ *"Set your focus on Jesus."*
- ▶ *"Be patient and humble and rely on God."*
- ▶ *"Trust in the Lord that he will do his best for you."*
- ▶ *"Be in fellowship with the Lord always."*
- ▶ *"Work slowly and prayefully."*
- ▶ *"Keep in mind that God is always with you regardless of where you are."*

When you take time to slow down, their advice will be easier to follow.

LOOK CLOSELY

→ ←

This is the part of the reentry map where you stop to look and listen closely.

Imagine a tour guide giving you a little historical background and additional information in this section of the reentry landscape. The information may sound theoretical and distant from your home situation, but trust me, you will be grateful you know about the reentry phenomenon before you return home!

9.   Resettling In

The reentry transition has similar components as the entry transition into a new culture. In 1955, Lysgaard (sociology professor from the University of Oslo, Norway) developed a tool to help describe the transition phenomenon. He called it the U-curve. It describes the different feelings that one experiences when entering a new environment from a definite high point, a clear low point, and another high point, signifying recovery and adjustment. Although life in another culture is not a clean series of ups and downs, the model nonetheless helps identify the feelings and when they occur. There are various names given to the phases in the U-curve, but I have named them Fun, Fight, Flight and Fit Stages. (See first half of the diagram.)

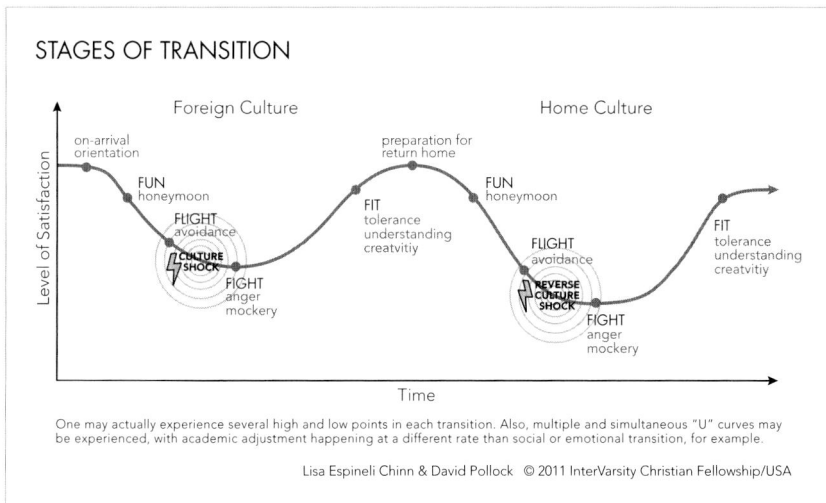

STAGES OF TRANSITION

Foreign Culture   Home Culture

Level of Satisfaction

on-arrival orientation

FUN honeymoon

FLIGHT avoidance

CULTURE SHOCK

FIGHT anger mockery

preparation for return home

FIT tolerance understanding creatvitiy

FUN honeymoon

FLIGHT avoidance

REVERSE CULTURE SHOCK

FIGHT anger mockery

FIT tolerance understanding creatvitiy

Time

One may actually experience several high and low points in each transition. Also, multiple and simultaneous "U" curves may be experienced, with academic adjustment happening at a different rate than social or emotional transition, for example.

Lisa Espineli Chinn & David Pollock   © 2011 InterVarsity Christian Fellowship/USA

In the early 1960s, Gullahorn and Gullahorn studied a similar pattern of feelings when returning home and they called that pattern the W-curve. The same up and down feelings in the U-curve are experienced in the W-curve.

FUN honeymoon

FLIGH

The FUN Stage: *When everything is working fine.*

This period is characterized by a brief or extended time of euphoria over being back home. You may be excited about certain features of the home environment. You may cherish the time spent with family and friends. The initial days and weeks may be spent visiting people, enjoying local food and sights, and sharing photos, videos, stories, and souvenirs.

The FLIGHT Stage: *When your "celebrity" status is over and you are faced with the daily demands of work and life back home. You begin wishing for your life back in the U.S.*

The Flight Stage may last for days and weeks, and the feelings of loneliness or "homesickness" for friends and experiences abroad may begin to dominate your world. You may be more aware of how different "home" is from the home you recall. You may feel "out of step" with the rest of your people and culture. You may have the sinking feeling of being the outsider in your own home.

You may begin to withdraw from people and be critical of how things are done. This is when you may begin to experience reverse culture shock – that emotional and social imbalance that results from a variety of changes in yourself, in others, and in your environment. It is your response to the magnitude of adjustments you have to make. At this stage you may want to "flee" abroad, or wish for your former life in the U.S.

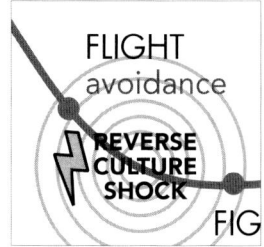

The FIGHT Stage: *When there's a lot of frustration and anger towards your home situation, and you criticize and distance yourself from others.*

This is the bottom of the W-curve. You slide into this stage as your reverse culture shock intensifies. At this phase you may begin to seriously question why you even returned home. You may hear yourself say, "I hate this place!" Others may experience acute loneliness and depression.

The late David Pollock of Interaction, Inc., in his reentry seminars for missionary kids, diplomats and business people, described anger and mockery towards home as a typical response at this stage of transition. You may be angry towards things which have changed and which now look bad to you and your new standards. Or you may mock or make fun of practices in your culture that now seem to you, "old fashioned," unnecessary, foolish, and even childish.

When you look at the U and W-curve diagram, you will notice that the bottom of the curve on reentry is lower than on the entry side. You may be surprised at how much harder it is to readjust back home. You expected to make adjustments when you entered another culture, but you did not expect or prepare to make adjustments when you were returning home. You thought you were "just" going home.

"Continuing reentry stress," says Dr. Clyde Austin, a Christian psychologist and editor of two reentry books, **"is normal for six to twelve months.** A significant minority may experience readjustment stress beyond that point."

FIT
tolerance
understanding
creatvitiy

The FIT Stage: *When you are able to resolve your inner conflicts, find your place back home, and feel confident you are making a positive contribution to others.*

Over a period of time, you may discover that the things that used to bother you have diminished. You may find yourself making your peace with what is different and what you cannot change back home. You may find that your internal disharmony and discontent are being replaced by acceptance. At this stage you may be more open to understanding your culture again. You may be energized to re-engage and participate in life back home. However, your merging with your culture does not mean uncritically embracing everything at home. You may now have a greater confidence in the "new you" and can therefore hold your own views and values and still relate with those who are different from you.

Transitions can be messy. Remember you are readjusting on many levels simultaneously. You may be in the Fit Stage in your job, but you are in the Flight Stage in your home. Relationships may be great, but you are disappointed with the political situation of your country.

Returning home is like being in two worlds.

You may discover that although you may feel comfortable at home and you are more accepting of the ways things are done, you *do not feel fully at home*. This is what Dr. Miriam Adeney, an anthropology professor, says is "the price we pay for the richness of having experienced more than one culture deeply." She further tells her students that they "will never be able to go home again...they will probably always leave part of themselves behind, and thereafter will be split...and home may be in more than one place."

So remember to:

- Be patient with yourself and others. Do not rush your readjustment.

- Let your reentry work for you. Use it to discover what it means to be a global person.

- Not take yourself too seriously. Learn to laugh at yourself.

- Not be surprised if some people, including family and friends, do not listen too long to your stories of being in America. Be sure to ask them about their lives too.

10. Your Coping Responses

Someone, long ago, observed that we are not distressed by things, but by the views which we take of them. Reentry transition can be stressful, but how you view this experience will affect your well-being and full participation back home. Therefore it would be helpful to consider the following responses.

1. **Imitation**—You may find yourself copying what others are doing or reverting to old routines and habits. Or you may quickly plunge into the pace and rhythm of life back home as if you never left. You may have a strong need to meet people's expectations and at the same time discover that the things you used to do are no longer appealing.

   Word of Advice: Some imitation is necessary to fit back into your home culture, but it should be done without compromise or loss of your values and integrity.

2. **Isolation**—It may seem strange to discover that you are feeling like a foreigner in your own culture. Your response may be to retreat or be in the company of expatriates or other fellow returnees. This is a normal response. Longing for your former lifestyle and friends in the U.S. may bring pain, intense loneliness, and isolation. Isolation is not all negative; in fact, you may welcome times to be alone as a "breather" from the stress and fatigue of reentry.

   Word of Advice: There is a place for appropriate isolation without loss of opportunities to grow, relate, and give to your people.

3. **Integration**—You are beginning to merge with your home culture with ease and you like being back home. Without abandoning your newly acquired values and perspectives from abroad, you feel that you are making significant strides in readjusting. You have a new appreciation for your home culture and an increased ability to relate on different levels. Congratulations!

   Word of Advice: Integrate in every way possible and be true to who you are becoming.

Summary

During your life back home you will find yourself moving from one response to another, but remember that:

- To relearn your home culture, a good amount of imitation is a must.

- To maintain some amount of cultural equilibrium and sanity, some isolation is necessary.

- To be effective back home, integration is required.

Like a dance, you will need to learn all three steps. Use them frequently and gracefully. **Imitate, isolate and integrate.**

↑ LOOK AHEAD*

You are not home yet. You are just focusing
on home. You are thinking home. As you
stop at this part of the reentry map, you will
have different feelings. Excited, sad or fearful,
perhaps. These are natural emotions. Pay
attention to them. You will also notice how
much you have changed as you respond to
the questions. Accept and recognize
those changes.

*If you are doing this study with others, this may be a good time to play Customs and
Culture, a reentry role-play, designed to be a fun and interactive learning experience.
See Reentry Resources, pg. 51-52.

11. Evaluating Your Ties Back Home

"While away, keep yourself informed of current events in your home country so that you'll be up-to-date and not be shocked by major changes when you return home."

1. Do you feel informed and close to people back home? Why or why not?

2. What are your sources of news and information about people and events in your own country?

3. Do you have friends in the U.S. from your country? How does your relationship with them affect your ties with your people?

4. Do you enjoy being with your own people while in the U.S.? Why or why not?

5. What major changes have occurred in your country while you were away? How will they affect your return home?

6. How many times have you traveled to your country while studying in the U.S.? How did those visits help you connect with your own people?

If you were a Christian before coming to the U.S.

1. How have you maintained and strengthened your relationship with your church back home and with other believers?

2. What can you do now to renew or strengthen those relationships? If you were not a Christian before coming to the U.S. (Should this be below the bar?)

If you were not a Christian before coming to the U.S.

1. Who, from home, knows that you have become a follower of Jesus?

2. What kind of help do you need as you relate with your family and friends back home?

3. What is your family's attitude towards Christianity or towards Christians? How are you praying for them?

12. Who Is Back home?

"I was changed a lot while I was away from my country. That made me really confused."

"My country is too competitive. I felt like everyone was pressed for time, money and so on. They don't smile a lot and never say "excuse me" when they passed or even touched me."

"Do not expect that you can share all your experiences and memories with your family and friends."

"Because I was away for so long, I had to visualize meeting my family at the airport and what that was like. I imagined what kind of greeting would welcome me."

If you have been in the U.S. for over 2 years and did not have the opportunity to visit your country:

1. Due to advanced technology, communication around the world is now possible at a fast speed. Faces of loved ones and live videos of them instantly appear on the screen of your computer or your smart phones. But do they mean that you understand the magnitude of the changes they have undergone? Do they comprehend the ways you have shifted in your tastes and values?

    Recall what you remember about your family. Write a sentence describing each person:

    Father:

    Mother:

    Brother(s):

    Sister(s):

    Grandfather:

    Grandmother:

    Aunties/Uncles:

    Cousins:

    Other:

2. What have been some major changes in your family since you left (marriage, births, deaths, new home or location, etc.)?

3. What aspects of family life do you expect to be the same?

4. What family practices and traditions have you come to appreciate more while in the U.S.? Which ones will it be difficult to re-engage in?

5. Who are your friends back home? What are they doing now?

6. How different do you think your relationship might be when you return?

7. What concerns you about your reunion with your friends?

8. Describe what you remember of the physical, social, economic, and spiritual conditions of your neighborhood and community.

9. What concerns do you have about finding a job or returning to a former job back home?

10. How are you preparing to interview for a job back in your own country? What office behavior do you need to remember and readjust to? Who can inform you about the differences between job interviews in your own country and the U.S.?

11. What major adjustments will you make as you join or re-join your church back home?

12. If you were not part of a church before you came to the U.S., what qualities would you be looking for in a church back home? Why?

13. Welcome Home!

Imagine your plane landing and you are about to meet your family and friends.

By anticipating what kind of reception you will receive, you will be better prepared to respond to people.

1.   What do you think will be the kind of reception you might receive from the following:

Who (be specific)	Kind of Reception	Why
Family		
Friends		
Colleagues/Work		
Neighbors		
Church		

2.   What will your family and friends first notice about you? What will they say?

14. Growing Spiritually Back Home

Like a plant, you will be transplanted again from foreign soil to home soil. How will you grow in loving God in the midst of change and a different spiritual environment? Here are a few words from those who returned:

- *"Seek Christian fellowship or a join a cell group and be close to God."*

- *"You need to reach out, to get to know, to encourage, to fellowship with other Christians."*

- *"It is hard when there is an absence of Christian fellowship."*

- *"Keep close to God. He is the only one who can help you in every problem you face."*

- *"Guard your personal devotional life."*

- *"Be patient in finding your place of service in the church."*

1. What spiritual habits and disciplines have you developed in the U.S. that will help you flourish back home?

2. What do you think are the basic essentials to your spiritual growth? Where and how will you find them?

3. What is spiritual warfare? What does it mean to be involved in spiritual battle?

4. What do you need to know and do to be victorious in Christ?

5. Can you recall some spiritual victories in the U.S.? Describe them.

6. What spiritual battles might you face back home?

7. Do you feel prepared to face spiritual battles back home? Why or why not? If not, how can you prepare and who can help you?

8. What are some other factors that could affect your spiritual flourishing after returning home?

15. Serving God Back Home

Gifts and Service

1. What gifts has God given to you?
    (See Romans 12; 1 Corinthians 12; Ephesians 4; 1 Peter 4.)

    - [ ] Prophesying
    - [ ] Serving/Helping
    - [ ] Teaching/Speaking
    - [ ] Encouraging
    - [ ] Giving
    - [ ] Leading
    - [ ] Mercy
    - [ ] Healing
    - [ ] Hospitality
    - [ ] Preaching
    - [ ] Evangelizing
    - [ ] Pastoring
    - [ ] Other

    To what degree were and are you able to discover and use your gifts while in the U.S.?
    Are you being encouraged to do so, and in what context?

2. In what area(s) of God's work at home do you see your gifts being used to his glory?

3. Who could be a potential mentor who can help you identify and use your gifts?

4. What does it mean to serve God in your profession? Check all that apply.
    - [ ] Having a Bible study in your office
    - [ ] Keeping a good, unblemished performance record
    - [ ] Being an honest worker that will lead to being trusted
    - [ ] Being committed to biblical standards in your values, relationships, and behavior
    - [ ] Seeking to excel in your profession
    - [ ] Sharing the gospel
    - [ ] Other

5. What training do you need while still in the U.S. to serve God more effectively back home? Where is the best place to get that training, and from whom? Why?

6. What do you think may be some possible problems or barriers in your service?

7. What dreams and visions do you have of what God may do in and through you back home?

Sharing the Gospel

1. Do you know the basic contents of the gospel, and do you feel confident sharing it with another person? Have you shared the Good News with people in the U.S. with those from your own country and/or others?

2. Who do you think is most spiritually prepared and hungry among your relatives and friends?

3. Which do you think is an appropriate approach in sharing the gospel back home? Why?

    - ☐ Have a party and share
    - ☐ Share one-on-one
    - ☐ Allow your relatives and friends to observe the change in you first, and then share later
    - ☐ Loan evangelistic books, CDs, videos
    - ☐ Invite people to a Bible study
    - ☐ Use every natural opportunity
    - ☐ Share your testimony in public
    - ☐ Use the *Jesus* video in different ways (host a showing, loan it, give it as a gift, etc.)
    - ☐ Other

4. What are some barriers for you in sharing the gospel?

5. What are some bridges for the gospel you can use?

6. What evangelistic resources should you take home with you?

7. In what other places can you serve God?

16. Closure and Packing

You are about to close the U.S. chapter of your life. How do you do it?

1. **By saying "thank you" and "goodbye."**

   List those to whom you should say thank you and goodbye (e.g. professors, roommates, host family, church and fellowship group, etc.):

2. **By leaving behind good relationships.**

   Is there anyone whom you should forgive or from whom you should seek forgiveness? When will you seek reconciliation?

   Are there bills to pay? Books or other borrowed items you need to return?

3. **By keeping tangible reminders of your foreign sojourn** (photos, souvenirs, music, etc.).

Checklist for Packing

ACADEMIC LUGGAGE

- ☐ Computer
- ☐ Hard copy of thesis/dissertation
- ☐ Books
- ☐ Diploma
- ☐ Class notes
- ☐ Other

SPIRITUAL GROWTH LUGGAGE

- ☐ Bible in your own language
- ☐ Bible in English
- ☐ Christian books (relevant to personal growth, ministry, missions, your country, etc.)
- ☐ Reference books: concordance, Bible dictionary, one-volume commentary, Bible handbook
- ☐ Journals
- ☐ Bible software, e.g. e-Sword
- ☐ Other

PHYSICAL LUGGAGE

- ☐ Identification tags; locks
- ☐ Clothes
- ☐ Camera
- ☐ Passport (current?)
- ☐ Gifts for family and friends
- ☐ Souvenirs
- ☐ Other

OTHER

- ☐
- ☐
- ☐
- ☐
- ☐
- ☐
- ☐
- ☐

FINAL
INSTRUCTIONS

When Joshua was very old, he assembled
the tribes of Israel and gave them God's
instructions. Find out two important transition
guidelines as Israel faced changes ahead.

17. God's Instructions through Joshua

Read Joshua 24 slowly. Read it a second time. Imagine what Joshua was feeling. Observe the action words used. Stop to meditate on a statement or a word.

This chapter can be divided into two main instructions. As Israel was about to transition to losing Joshua as their leader, God reminded them of their history and gave them a challenge.

1. **Remember** (vv. 2-13):

    a. What did God want Israel to remember? Why?

    b. List the different things God did for Israel.

    c. What does memory of God's work do to a nation? To you?

    d. List God's acts and interventions in your life while you were away from home.

2. **Recommit** (vv. 14-28):

    a. What did God, through Joshua, command Israel to do (v.14a)?

    b. What specific action did God want Israel to do to show their faithfulness to God (v.14b)?

    c. Joshua was clear about where he stood in relation to God. What choices did he give the Israelites?

    d. The Israelites were quick to recommit. Why did Joshua not believe their immediate response?

    e. What idols did your ancestors worship? What idols are you tempted to worship in the United States?

    f. If jealousy is the intolerance of any rival, what reasons may God have to be a jealous God with you?

    g. Why is it important to have a visible reminder of your commitment to God? What reminders do you have to help you in your walk with God?

Joshua used several words to indicate commitment to God: *fear the Lord and serve Him with all faithfulness* (v. 14), *serve the Lord* (v. 15), and *yield your hearts to the Lord* (v. 23).

Write a prayer of recommitment.

Remember and recommit: Take these words with you as your transition back home.

18. On the Plane Home

This page may be completed while you're flying home.

Leave with a GRATEFUL HEART.

As you reflect on your time in the U.S., what are you thankful for (Psalm 57:9-10)?

Leave with an EXPECTANT HEART.

What are you trusting God to do in, for, and through you back home (Psalm 37:3-5)?

Leave with a CONFIDENT HEART.

What promises can you claim from God (Psalm 11)?

Arrive with a SURRENDERED HEART.

Write out Romans 12:1-2; Philippians 1:20-21; Luke 9:23. Meditate on and apply these verses.

You are grateful because God has done great things for you; expectant because God promises to do great things through you; confident because he goes before you; surrendered because he is worthy of your complete devotion and undivided worship.

Reentry Resources

Books:

Austin, Clyde. *Cross-Cultural Reentry: An Annotated Bibliography.* Abilene, TX: Abilene Christian University Press, 1983.

Austin, Clyde, ed. *Cross-Cultural Reentry: A Book of Readings.* Abilene, TX: Abilene Christian University Press, 1986.

Chinn, Leiton. *International Student Reentry: A Select, Annotated Bibliography.* NAFSA: Association of International Educators Publications, 1992.

Chinn, Leiton. *NAFSA Working Paper #24; Reentry/Professional Integration: NAFSA A.I.D. Project Grants Summary Report 1974-1991.* NAFSA: Association of International Educators Publications, 1991.

Chinn, Lisa Espineli. *Back Home: Daily Reflections on Reentry. Madison, WI: InterVarsity/USA.*
store.intervarsity.org

Eaves, John. *Preparing Your International Friend for Life Back Home.* Colorado Springs, CO: International Students, Inc.
www.isionline.org

Hamrin, Carol Lee and Stacey Bieler, (eds). *Salt and Light: Lives of Faith that Shaped Modern China.* Eugene, OR: Pickwick Publications, 2009.
www.wipfandstock.com

ISI. *New Horizons.* Colorado Springs, CO: International Students, Inc., 2008.
www.isionline.org

Mirza, Nate. *Home Again: Preparing International Students to Serve Christ in Their Home Country.* Colorado Springs, CO: Navpress, 2005.
www.navpress.com/store

Returnee Handbook: On the Road of Homebound Journey. Torrance, California: Overseas Campus Ministries, 2008.
Email: info@cefocm.org; oc.org

Returning Home to China: An Equipping Guide for Chinese Christians Returning Home. Mechanicsburg, Pa: China Outreach Ministries
Email: ChinaOut@aol.com; www.chinaoutreach.org

Storti, Craig. *The Art of Coming Home.* Yarmouth, ME: Intercultural Press, 1997.
www.nicholasbrealey.com

Role-Play/Reentry Simulation Game:

Chinn, Lisa Espineli. **Customs & Culture.** Madison, WI: ISM Department,
    Intervarsity/USA, 2005.
    store.intervarsity.org

A reentry role-play designed to be a fun and interactive learning experience. Participants "pack" their luggage with the host culture's values, which they have ranked and chosen according to their perceived importance. Upon their arrival back home, they encounter a very strict customs officer who decides if they should be allowed to reenter their home country with this new baggage. The game centers on the lively and often revealing exchange between the returnee and the customs officer.